Ready-Made Democracy

Ready-Made Democracy

A History of Men's Dress in the American Republic, 1760–1860

Michael Zakim

The University of Chicago Press
Chicago and London

Michael Zakim teaches history at Tel Aviv University.

The University of Chicago Press, Chicago 60637
The University of Chicago Press, Ltd., London
© 2003 by The University of Chicago
All rights reserved. Published 2003
Printed in the United States of America

12 11 10 09 08 07 06 05 04 03   1 2 3 4 5

ISBN: 0-226-97793-5 (cloth)

Library of Congress Cataloging-in-Publication Data

Zakim, Michael.
    Ready-made democracy : a history of men's dress in the
American republic, 1760–1860 / Michael Zakim.
        p. cm.
    Originally presented as the author's doctoral dissertation,
Columbia University.
    Includes bibliographical references and index.
    ISBN 0-226-97793-5 (cloth : alk. paper)
        1. Men's clothing—United States—History.
    2. Costume—Symbolic aspects—United States.
    3. Costume—Psychological aspects—United States.
    4. Political culture—United States.   5. Capitalism—United
    States.   6. United States—Politics and government.
    7. United States—Social life and customs.   I. Title.
    GT203 .Z35 2003
    391'.1'0973—dc21

                                            2003010000

⊗The paper used in this publication meets the minimum
requirements of the American National Standard for
Information Sciences—Permanence of Paper for Printed
Library Materials, ANSI Z39.48-1992.

For Netanel and Itai

Contents

Acknowledgments

This book was first written as a doctoral dissertation in history at Columbia University. As such, it owes its existence to three remarkable historians of eighteenth- and nineteenth-century America: to Elizabeth Blackmar, who explained to me the social meanings of the commodity; to Richard Bushman, who taught that materialism is as much about stuff as about dialectics; and to Eric Foner, who guided a year of reading about American democracy and the market that became the conceptual foundation for a dissertation about clothing, which he then saw through to completion. The book also reflects the critical contributions of Adam Rothman, Charles Forcey, Michael Sappol, Daniel Purdy, and Igal Halfin, all of whom read parts of what I was writing and then helped me to write them better.

Thanks are due, in more general fashion, to the history department at Columbia University for having invited a thirty-year-old clarinet player from Haifa to come to New York and study history, and for then making a place for his sometimes rambunctious intellectual style. Several other institutions have also had a hand in this endeavor. Financial assistance was provided by a research grant from the Hagley Library of Business and Science, by a Rovensky fellowship in American business and economic history, by a Mrs. Giles Whiting fellowship in the humanities, and by a grant from the School of History at Tel Aviv University. Columbia University awarded *Ready-Made Democracy* its Bancroft dissertation prize, which brought with it a handsome subvention. Heartfelt acknowledgment is also due the probability seminar at Columbia, where I accrued a considerable debt over the years. I am also grateful to Robert Scott, director of the Electronic Texts Services at Columbia's Butler Library, who helped track down innumerable historical sources, in both digital and predigital form, and who also offered assistance in a variety of other technologically intensive tasks.

Robert Devens read the first chapter of an earlier draft of this manuscript, enthusiastically asked to read the rest, and then responded with a note about language, fashion, and irony, to which he appended a short reading list. I knew then that I wanted to include him in this project, and so I was gratified when he became this book's editor at the University of Chicago Press.

The postdissertation process of reading and rewriting (and then rewriting again, and then again) took place in my new home in the History Department at Tel Aviv University. Because the study of American history at Israeli universities enjoys a standing inversely proportionate to the amount of foreign aid the country receives from the United States, I have found myself in a scholarly milieu informed far less by prototypically American problems of liberal politics than by questions about the medieval family, Christian confession, Stalinist terror, and postcolonial feminism. My own historical practice is richer for it, and so I offer a collective thanks to my colleagues in Tel Aviv.

Portions of this book have been published elsewhere. Parts of chapters 1, 6, 7, and the conclusion appeared in "Sartorial Ideologies: From Homespun to Ready-Made," *American Historical Review* 106, no. 5 (December 2001). Parts of chapter 2 appeared in "A Ready-Made Business: The Birth of the Clothing Industry in America," *Business History Review* 73 (spring 1999). Parts of chapter 3 appeared in "Customizing the Industrial Revolution: The Reinvention of Tailoring in the Nineteenth Century," *Winterthur Portfolio* 33, no. 1 (spring 1998).

Introduction

Sartorial Politics

Ready-Made Democracy is a history of men's dress in America. It is also a social history of capitalism and of America's "great transformation" into a democracy. Such a broad view of the sartorial underlines the important place of clothing in the political imagination. We need only recall Gandhi's mobilization of the spinning wheel as a symbol of colonial resistance, almost two hundred years after the Americans first employed it against the same empire, to recognize how clothing has consistently served as both material and metaphor for the social question. When early modern sovereignty was located in the king's body, for example, courtiers' access to his toilette—to the appareling of that body—signaled their proximity to power. When such embodied monarchical authority began to wane, Goethe's romantic individual, Werther, appeared on the scene in an anticourtly ensemble of blue jacket, yellow vest, and leather breeches that soon became a popular style of bourgeois masculinity. Indeed, a historical inventory of sartorial politics yields an impressive list of classical togas, liberty caps, silk stockings, sans-culottes, bloomers, brown shirts, denim jeans, Mao jackets, and burning bras.[1]

The elevation of homespun to a political ideology in America on the eve of Independence was an especially striking expression of the wider social implications of dress. Breaking flax and shearing sheep, and then transforming the raw fibers into cloths through a chain of tasks mobilizing the entire family, rehearsed the republican credo of propertied independence. When yeomen then donned the coarse products of their home industry they embodied an equally republican frugality. In both instances, the homespun constituted a conscious opposition to British corruption and luxury. In so doing, it also bridged the dual meaning of "domestic manufactures," tying the productive efforts of the household to those of the nation, and thus also becoming a most tangible expression of the citizen's attachment to the public's happiness.

Such coarseness did not long remain in the wardrobe, particularly not among those political classes who talked most about it. Nevertheless, homespun exhortations of industry and simplicity became a fixture of American ideological discourse over the following century of industrial revolution. By then the mass-produced (and usually ready-made) suit had emerged as the badge of a uniquely virtuous American polity, the only place in the civilized world where citizens could not be classed by their appearance, as contemporaries never tired of insisting. Plain woolen coats, vests, and pantaloons—the products of hundreds of men's clothing firms based in all Northern cities, but most especially in New York, making up one of the country's most prevalent commodities—represented the same industriousness, modesty, resistance to fashion's corrupting influences, and common civic life that homespun had. The "simple dress of an American citizen," in fact, emerged as a political slogan in the 1850s, referring to Benjamin Franklin's countrified appearance as American representative to the court of Versailles in 1776 as a model of civic behavior for life in the industrial century as well.[2] Such continuity from the homespun era to the ready-made one demonstrated that, in spite of shifting partisan fashions and countless development schemes, the republic did indeed rest on a transcendent social order.

And yet, as the homespun evolved into the ready-made, the republican credo of industry and simplicity actually came to mean its opposite. Sartorial virtue changed from homemade to mass-produced. It moved from a Malthusian world of scarcity to a machine-driven cornucopia of plenty. It no longer signaled the self-sacrifice of elites but, rather, the propertied mobility of all. And instead of being a family project, it became a male prerogative. Thus, while the fundamental categories of civic experience seemed to remain intact, their contents were inverted. That inversion is the subject of this book: how capitalist revolution came to America under the guise of traditional notions of industry, modesty, economy, and independence, and how the new social arrangements of bourgeois life acquired an aura of inevitability, if not of manifest destiny.

Homespun acquired its symbolic power in the mid-eighteenth century, as America began to fill up with factory-made cloths imported from Britain. The growing material surfeit hastened the passing of a world of sumptuary controls in which social order rested on the containment of private initiative by the authorities. In a postsumptuary age, when "the supreme power cannot take away from any man part of his property without his own consent," responsibility for the "common wealth" increasingly lay with the citizen himself.[3] Homespun celebrations of independence and industry were a complicated response to this condition. On the one hand, they grounded civic virtue in the productive efforts of proprietary farmers and so realized the emerging association of politics and private property. On the other hand, homespun commemorated the indigent circumstances of colonial beginnings in the New World and emphasized the continued contrast to Europe. In that respect, American yeomen who stubbornly preferred their coarse domestic tow to fine British broadcloth pointed to a more corporate past, and to the social dangers inherent in material progress.

By the middle of the nineteenth century, of course, production had left the household. "Domestic manufactures" consequently lost the dual meaning that had famously wed household to nation during the Americans' republican revolution. Likewise, the mutuality of private industry and public happiness became far less obvious. That was not, however, because the relationship between politics and property was sundered. Nor was it because economy, industry, and even modesty lost their ideological resonance. But what kind of virtuous polity could issue from fly shuttles, boss sweaters, and a continental market driven by steam and free banking? Americans answered that question by adapting their republican inheritance to capitalist reality and calling it democracy.

By addressing these issues, *Ready-Made Democracy* becomes not just a social history but a political history as well, although it includes no discussion of elections, parties, or referendums. Instead, it traces the commodity's movement through society, first as business initiative, then production project, and ultimately as goods bought and worn. The narrative begins with the birth of a clothing industry and the nineteenth century's redefinition of the making of things, of "industry" itself. It continues with the development of an urban retail culture served by a "white-collar" class of clerks whose individual ambitiousness simultaneously realized the promise of industrial progress while no less personifying its dangers. But the clerk was not the only new source of anxiety. Hordes of seamstresses, whose depressed wages made the men's clothing trade so profitable to begin with, became the favorite subject of antebellum protest against the iniquities of the industrial system, a protest that actually naturalized capitalist power since it turned class conflict into a far more manageable sexual scandal. Finally, one encounters a sphere of male fashion mediating between the two emergent but not always consonant values of the age, individualism and universalism—a mediation that made fashion itself into no less than a paradigm of liberal governance.

The subjects of this history, then, are the wholesaler and retailer, employer and employee, urbanite and provincial, white-collared and smock-clad, Broadway dandy and Bowery b'hoy. The relations between them were not defined as essentially political ones. Quite the opposite, in fact. But in a market society increasingly dominated by free commercial exchange outside the reach of official state authority, such economic and cultural agents began to decisively shape the nature of social intercourse in general. The myriad relations essential to the suit's existence constitute an extensive catalogue of habits, systems, conflicts, and explanations that were born in the wake of the commodity's rise to social dominance. That is why getting dressed proves to be a central event in modern life. Making a profit in the expanding market, organizing a waged force in the city, shopping in new kinds of stores called Marble Palaces, buying at fixed prices for the first time, standardizing not only commodity exchange but a male business persona as well, and reconceiving fashion for an age of unprecedented material abundance—all were activities of acute political significance. Clothing was both commodity and sign, and in a commercially driven reality it united what the precapitalist world had carefully separated—a transcendent sphere of ideas and an ephemeral realm of things. The production of the suit thus became inseparable from the production of culture, and the frock coats featured each month in the *Mirror of Fashion*—those new styles especially "suitable for wear to the office"—were no less than a facsimile of the body politic itself.

And so a history of clothing belies its ostensibly narrow focus and becomes a vantage point for examining some of the central themes of the times. One of those themes is a perennial subject of American historical debate: the place of capitalism in the nation's democratic tradition. *Ready-Made Democracy* seeks to engage two distinct approaches to this question that have, together, dominated scholarship over the course of the American century. The first is known as the "consensus school," whose influence reached its zenith during the Cold War. Consensus historians were famous for equating democratic politics and capitalist economics. They, no less than I, were deeply impressed by the political power of the market and the centrality of property in American social thought. But these scholars were also haunted by the specter of communism, and apparently felt it incumbent upon them to prove that private property and commercial competition were inherently democratic practices, endemic to the English experience in America and brought to the New World by a protobourgeoisie of self-disciplined Calvinists already in the seventeenth century. "Even in earliest New England," a characteristic version of events went, "one can see the marks of that colonial situation which would decisively affect all American political thought through the era of the Revolution, and which helped shape the moderate, compromising, and traditionalist character of our institutions." The appreciation of capitalist ascendancy demonstrated by consensus historians consequently often lacked a historical dimension. Property was not considered to be a value that actually changed over time. And because they insisted on identifying free markets with free persons, and then depicted that equation as a transcendent reality of the American experience, consensus studies ultimately offer little insight into how the "logic of capital" actually became the social logic of its times. In fact, many seemed to deny the revolutionary nature of capitalism itself, if not the bourgeoisie's own industrial provenance.[4]

An interpretive corrective to the consensus school's blind spots, unabashedly inspired by the general challenge to cultural orthodoxy in the 1960s, has gained ascendancy over the last quarter century. Many of these "social" and "labor" historians have sought to show that the "market revolution" was not democratic at all and that the social equalities it did effect were so delimited and conditional as to make them entirely specious. Much of this scholarship has accordingly devoted itself to recovering a purported anticapitalist democratic tradition in the American past. The result has reemphasized the instability of industrial experience and its inherent social conflicts. Curiously, however, this "republican" interpretation shares the consensus school's predilection for stasis, albeit of the opposite variety, in its focus on the stubborn persistence of a precommercial ethos in American life. As a consequence, many of the more recent studies of industrial change in the United States are uninterested in examining, and sometimes even in acknowledging, capitalism's rise to greatness.[5]

This "greatness" is the present subject of inquiry. Like the consensus school, and in contrast to the republican school, *Ready-Made Democracy* identifies capitalism's emerging domination of American life as the central event of antebellum history. Like the republicans, however, and in contrast to consensus interpretations, this study presents that domination as a revolutionary event, one that overturned a previous cultural logic. Democracy, meanwhile, does not function here as a pristine tradition of ancient provenance or a manifestation of man's best instincts. It is, rather, a historical event: a collection of political practices and cultural styles that acquired a wholly new importance as a means for distributing power during the Industrial Revolution, when democracy and capitalism emerged as the two principal systems of social organization in the United States. In this respect, my study can also be read as a sign of its times, for the perspective presented here on the power of the market and the historical symbiosis between democracy and capitalism is deeply affected by the current omnipresence of commercial values in Western life, the commodification of all of contemporary culture, and liberalism's embrace of oxymoronic "market freedoms" as the logical culmination of the Enlightenment.[6]

- - - - -

The counterintuitive character of a work that presents the history of menswear as the story of our times, and that also seeks to rescue such categories as business, fashion, and the commodity from the dustbin of political history, makes it practical to include a brief glossary of the principal concepts that inform *Ready-Made Democracy*, concepts whose meanings are a matter of ongoing contention, both between historians and within modern civic discourse.

The first is democracy. Democracy entered the American lexiconic mainstream when the country began to industrialize, at about the time that Alexis de Tocqueville crossed the ocean and asked how Americans had uniquely succeeded in making democracy a practical form of government. Tocqueville famously published his answers in a two-volume work he entitled *Democracy in America*, the first part of which appeared in 1835 and was principally devoted to explicating the workings of government and the political system. A second volume appeared five years later, the result of further reflections by Tocqueville on what he had seen in America. It shifted the analysis of democracy from the function and apparatus of governance to the way of life in civic society. Tocqueville focused here on the existence of a permanent tension in American life between equality and freedom and on the ever-growing number of citizens vying for both. This was not just the subject of political philosophy but also a topic of general conversation, prevalent as much in the everyday encounters between citizens as in congressional debate. The chapter titles of Tocqueville's second volume are indicative of the nature of this democratic discourse: "How Equality Suggests to the Americans the Idea of the Indefinite Perfectibility of Man," "Why the Americans Are Often So Restless in the Midst of Their Prosperity," "How American Democracy Has Modified the English Language," and, perhaps most famously, "Of Individualism in Democracies." These suggested a new social definition of the political that led Tocqueville to his most important insights into the nature of modern democracy, including his profound observation that the same private impulse that had undermined corporate obligations now had to serve as the new basis of community. This understanding of politics is the starting place for a social history of American dress: a view of democracy as a novel set of cultural assumptions that bind the regime, define the subjects of government, and constitute common truths.[7]

What was the relationship of "ready-made" to democracy? How, in fact, did material culture become political culture? If Tocqueville considered democracy to be everyone's "eager desire to acquire comfort," then the ready-made presented an obvious avenue for realizing such ambitions. This was how Horace Greeley, one of nineteenth-century America's great champions of industrial progress, explained the signal importance of ready-made clothing in his *Great Industries of the United States* (1872). Greeley located the origins of mass-produced raiment in the working class "slops" and cast-off garments worn "by those who could not afford to employ a tailor or buy better articles." Such pitiful beginnings then allowed him to draw a linear ascension from shame to respectability, for by mid-century "there [were] thousands of men, even among those who are most fastidious in matters of dress, who never think of being measured for a suit of clothes, but who go to a clothier, and supply themselves from his stock." This narrative of a successful shopping trip paralleled Greeley's political program, which celebrated the progressive, democratic character of American industrialization.[8]

Significantly, however, Greeley got his facts wrong. Ready-made clothing was not a newly successful commodity. It had been in circulation at least since English tailors invoked traditional guild prerogatives in the sixteenth century to suppress the "trade of salesmen" who sold clothing made up at another time by someone else. Likewise, we find the merchant tailor John Shephard offering ready-made satin breeches and silk jackets to his genteel clientele in New York City in the 1780s. But for Greeley to have acknowledged this older provenance would have taken the shine off of industrial progress. The marriage of commercial advance and political equality in this most tangible and universal of material experiences—clothing—would have been ended. What's more, the ambiguous fact that not all "great industries" issued from dramatic leaps of the imagination, technological wonders, or visions of social progress would have been exposed. Clothiers, for instance, applied the well-worn material logic of cutting and sewing to the growing availability of labor, credit, and varieties of cloth. Their "great industry" was an amalgam of hybrid arrangements that gradually emptied traditional craft practices of their former meaning—a modest act with revolutionary results (see chapter 2). "Ready-made" consequently becomes less a sign of industrial novelty than a historical pun, one, moreover, revealing of how commodity society seeks to fetishize everything as new.

The citizens of a ready-made democracy increasingly met each other at market, which had become too extensive to be restricted any longer to a specific time or place. Markets, of course, were an ancient institution. However, they now underwent such a quantitative leap that a qualitative change in social life ensued. This was the "industrial revolution" that, as admittedly hackneyed as the phrase has become, is an essential chapter in any history of modernity. The emphasis in *Ready-Made Democracy* is on "revolution"— the sharply altered nature of persons' lives and relations with one another. "Industrial," meanwhile, refers here less to the era's remarkable technical breakthroughs in production than to the growing prevalence of commercial concerns in social intercourse. And so, for instance, the most important technology in this history of industrial revolution is the tape measure, an old tool now applied to the new aim of creating a universal system of measurement that would make bodies more profitable in the integrating market. Thus, custom tailoring became a system of mass production (see chapter 3). "Mass production" and "standardization," in fact—important terms in this study—are not defined by any specific technical criteria but by their social ramifications: as new ways of doing business, redividing labor, and systematizing difference, the latter being of equal importance to both fashion and liberalism (see chapter 7).[9]

The industrial revolution was led by a revolutionary class—the "bourgeoisie." *Bourgeoisie* is a foreign term, but an unavoidable one in this book, which, in many ways, is a history of how this new class reinvented American society in its own image. It was not an easy task. The "release of energy" and "creative destruction" that brought the bourgeoisie into existence was a source of worry and crisis for everyone, most especially for the bourgeoisie itself, which now strove to bring order to industrial society without sacrificing that society's revolutionary spirit, that is, its volatile material growth and extraordinary social fluidity.[10] In attempting to solve this conundrum and, more generally, to obscure the challenge to American values posed by industrial change, these adherents of progress assumed the mantle of the eighteenth century's "middling classes." Just as an older country ideology had identified the social middle as a virtuous compromise between aristocratic corruption and plebian wantonness, the new industrial middle, too, claimed to encompass the most reliable and moderate elements of society. It connoted a common ground, synonymous with the civic sphere, manifest in the ability of "every sober mechanic [with] his one or two suits of broadcloth" to "make as good a display, when he chooses, as what are called the upper classes" (Greeley again).[11]

Bourgeoisie is also a problematically facile category. The term's reference to the growing segment of the population that owned industrial property obscures the sexual, generational, geographical, cultural, religious, and material tensions that fractured relations within this same class. No one, for instance, provoked greater suspicion and worry among city clothing merchants than their clerks, those white-collared paragons of market "i-dollar-try" (see chapter 4). Nevertheless, *Ready-Made Democracy* ultimately emphasizes the common denominators of industrial experience and describes an insistent process of embourgeoisement as characteristic of life in the republic. New York City was at the center of this process, not because it was representative of all American experience (industrial revolution was hardly a uniform event, in spite of its standardizing ambitions), but because it was a site where so many of the new social and economic practices first cohered. True, there was no single, homogenized middle class in America. Nor did all men dress alike. However, the most important social problem of the times—and the most important question for the historian of American capitalism and democracy to ask—is how the better-dressed succeeded in making theirs the democratic "standard of living," in spite of its obvious exclusions and iniquities.

American democracy and capitalism both rose to power on the ruins of patriarchy, that social system by which wives, sons, daughters, servants, slaves, and sundry others lived and worked under the single authority of the father, who was also the freeholder. The decline of this homespun household as the common nexus of industry and citizenship opened the way to a far less hierarchical society of self-making men. This new society was a "plain system, void of pomp, protecting all and granting favors to none," as Andrew Jackson himself described what others less enthusiastically perceived to be "an anxious spirit of gain," in which the traditional checks on personal ambition were falling away in wholesale fashion. Such equalities, the new Whig journal, the *American Review*, continued in 1845, were "natural to the circumstances, but not natural to the human soul," for the result was a permanent restlessness that suited market relations but threatened the social order. This nineteenth-century anxiety echoed James Madison's warning in the *Federalist* that democracy would invariably devolve into "spectacles of turbulence and contention . . . incompatible with personal security or the rights of property."[12]

And so industrial society required a new Archimedean point upon which "peace and order and prosperity" could be reconstituted in the absence of traditional, that is, agrarian and patriarchal, structures of authority. The basis for such industrial peace was to be the difference between men and women, an old truth that now acquired a new importance. It could be said, in fact, that the death of agrarian patriarchy amplified the significance of gender. An axiomatic opposition between the sexes proved central to American democracy because it respected the emerging principles of mass (male) membership in the republic. At the same time it established new social boundaries (also between formally equal male citizens) that might appear to be apolitical (because they primarily governed relations between the sexes) but were particularly effective in restraining the "turbulence and contention" endemic to democratic life. [13]

This gendering of antebellum life found obvious expression in the growing contrast between male and female fashion, which reached a climax in the Bloomer scandals of the 1850s, when feminists demanded the right to wear pants. But the dichotomy between draped and pantalooned silhouettes was only symbolic of a more profound dynamic. This was most insistently manifest in the trope of the victimized seamstress, whose exploited condition (at the hands of the new clothing industry) became the era's favorite example of the ills of the new wage economy: the asymmetrical relationship between employer and employee that violated republican tenets of propertied independence (and democratic promises of "protecting all and granting favors to none"). Such asymmetries had to be resolved before the ready-made could become a viable successor to the homespun. They were resolved, in fact, by means of the very same protest over the seamstress's suffering. For while she may have highlighted the inequality of the "wage nexus," the seamstress, more importantly, turned this inequality between employer and employee into the far less controversial inequality between men and women. A political problem was thus transformed into a sexual one. The consequences were far-reaching. Virtue consequently became a private trait (rather than a political duty), industry became a competition (rather than the cooperative effort of citizens), and democracy became a polity tolerant of hierarchies of wealth and power (thus belying the republican fears of Madison) (see chapter 6). [14]

And so it was that political culture, commodity fetishism, industrial change, bourgeois standardization, and the end of agrarian patriarchy gave birth to a ready-made democracy explicitly devoted to the republican past and hungrily anticipating the capitalist future. That duality was a sign of the psychic strains inherent in such revolutionary times. Men's dress, being one of those "images in the collective consciousness in which the old and new interpenetrate," was deeply implicated in these events. Proper attire became a means by which the capitalist classes dressed up their ready-made revolution in the primal myth of a homespun past. The result, as we shall see, was a novel democracy that seemed as deeply rooted in the American experience as the "soil of freedom" itself. [15]

1

A Homespun Ideology

Homespun clothing became a means of revolutionary agitation in colonial America. A patriot donned these unrefined products of household labor to renounce imperial hubris and promote its antithesis, domestic manufactures. In 1765 Daniel Dulany declared that Tyranny would be resisted with the "Spirit, and Vigour, and Alacrity" manifest in such productive efforts. In 1767, after British passage of the Townshend duties, Boston's town meeting voted to resuscitate linen production throughout the colony. Bounties were proposed for each yard of Massachusetts homespun produced. Newspapers published instructions for raising flax, the raw material from which linen is made, and in Providence a prize was offered to whoever produced the most. The goal was to "prevent the unnecessary Importation of European Commodities, which threaten the Country with Poverty and Ruin." Mercantilist anxieties over the drain of specie and artisanal worries over competition from abroad were not the only concerns, however. Political principles no less informed the homespun campaign. As Benjamin Rush, president of the United Company of Philadelphia for Promoting American Manufactures, argued, "a people who are entirely dependent upon foreigners for food or clothes must always be subject to them."[1]

"Industry and Economy" were the antidote. They would ensure American independence, which meant that when "thirty-three respectable ladies . . . met about sunrise, with their wheels, to spend the day . . . in the laudable design of a spinning match," they became actors in the great revolutionary drama. "At an hour before sunset, the ladies then appearing neatly dressed, principally in homespun, a polite and generous repast of American production was set for their entertainment, after which . . . Mr. Jewett delivered a suitable and instructive discourse from Rom. xii. 11: 'Not Slothful in business; fervent in spirit; serving the Lord.'" The *Boston Gazette* reported in 1768 that a number of women from South Kingston, Narragansett, had been invited to the "House of a Gentleman of the first Rank and Figure in the Town, to celebrate the New-Year Anniversary in a festival Manner; where they all appeared in homespun Manufactures." Reports from Providence, Salisbury, Byfield, Newbury, Rowley, Ipswich, Beverly, and Boston told of Daughters of Liberty gathering to spin in coordinated displays of "industry" designed to "save their sinking country." Harvard College's graduating class of 1768 wore homespun at commencement ceremonies. So did the graduates at Yale and the College of Rhode Island. The *South Carolina Gazette* described the appearance in Charleston of a gentleman "completely clad in the Product and Manufacture of his own Plantation." In Virginia, too, genteeler types dressed in home manufactures in order to register their dissatisfaction with English imperial policy in America. Robert Wormely Carter wore a whole suit of clothes made by a favored slave that became the envy of Williamsburg. At the House of Burgess ball in December 1769, men and women affected "a genteel appearance . . . chiefly dressed in Virginia cloth." And a Virginian declared that "the Whirling of our Spinning Wheels afford us the most delightful Musick, and Man is the most respected who appears clad in Homespun; as such a Dress is a sure Evidence of Love to his Country." In the *Pennsylvania Gazette* a "Freeborn American" was even more adamant: "The skin of a son of liberty will not feel the coarseness of a homespun shirt! The resolution of a Pennsylvanian 'should be made of sterner stuff' than to be frighted at the bug bear—fashion!"[2]

"The bug bear—fashion" that so exercised a Freeborn American was the thoughtless emulation of metropolitan style. It was fueled by love of luxury and was inimical to liberty. As "Brutus" explained in 1769, luxury bred immorality and excess, which made persons vulnerable to corruption. According to the *Virginia Gazette* in 1778, luxury had even precipitated the war. It "begot Arbitrary Power," which "begot Oppression," which, in turn, begot resentment and revenge. It was a credible genealogy. John Adams later recalled how "scarlet and sable robes, of broad bands, and enormous tie wigs" became the sartorial standard in Massachusetts's imperial courts exactly in the years when popular discontent with British rule intensified. The Yankee Doodle dandy, born a generation earlier as a British caricature of the uncouth colonial who could only dream of emulating a London macaroni, now proudly inverted his tastelessness into a symbol of patriotic simplicity.[3]

"Sterner stuff" was consequently required. For to resist luxury and so preserve their liberties Americans would have to forsake the "conveniences and superfluities" (Benjamin Franklin's categories in his testimony to the House of Commons in 1766) regularly imported from Britain. Were colonials capable of such sacrifice? Did they have the requisite virtue to "consider their interests as [in]distinct from those of the public"?[4] George Washington assured his London merchant in 1765 that once domestic manufacturing became widespread in the colonies, "the Eyes of our People will perceive, that many of the Luxuries which we have heretofore lavished our Substance to Great Britain for can well be dispensed with whilst the Necessaries of Life are to be procured . . . within ourselves." Franklin, polemicizing under the pseudonym "Homespun," promised that Americans would be able to give up their English tea and instead breakfast on Indian corn, which was no more "indigestible [than] the Stamp Act." Proof of their resolution was evidenced already by the innumerable calls to stop eating lamb and deliver the extra fleeces to colonial spinners. The logic, as the *Boston Gazette* explained, was simple. "Suppose that one half of the Woolen that is used in this Province is manufactured here of our own Wool: If therefore, they who keep Sheep would but double their Flocks . . . we might be enabled to make all our Woollen Clothing; and to prevent the Importation of any more from Europe." In such a spirit, the Cordwainers Fire Company in Philadelphia likewise declared that "whereas the Increase of our Woollen Manufactories will greatly conduce to the Benefit of this Country, it is therefore agreed . . . that we will not purchase any Lamb, nor suffer any to be purchased or used in our Families, during the Present Year."[5]

The industrious American householder thus confronted the empire simultaneously as the guarantor of popular sovereignty and of material independence.[6] Planting, harvesting, shearing, cleaning, drying, rippling, wetting, braking, hackling, dyeing, separating, and combing, and only then spinning for three weeks and weaving for yet another to produce the six yards of cloth necessary for a plain dress, to be made with material inferior to imported goods from England or the continent—this was the stuff of virtuous politics. The rhetoric of res publica thus became suffused with the less sublime grammar of skeins and yards. The *Boston Gazette*, surveying the progress of the patriot cause in 1767, congratulated Mr. Ebenezer Hurd of Connecticut for having made "in his own Family this present Year, by only his Wife and Children," no less than 500 yards of linens and woolens, "the whole of the Wool and Flax of his own raising," as well as Capt. Simon Newton, of Providence, for spinning and weaving 364¼ yards of linen cloth and for producing another 300 skeins of yarn that remained unwoven, "the greatest part of the whole (and all the fine) spun in his own house." William Attlee similarly reported to the American Philosophical Society in Philadelphia on cloth production in Lancaster, Pennsylvania, for 1769: 3,744 yards of striped cotton, 4,091 yards of flax linen, 4,232 yards of tow linen, 1,394 yards of linsey—in all, more than 30,000 yards of household manufactures, "so great is the Spirit for Home-spun among our good Females at present." Atlee identified each family "who had manufactured any Part of the above Quantity, and also the Number of Yards of each Kind manufactured by each of them . . . all digested in proper columns."[7]

Attlee's proper columns represented a political accounting that sought to put an end to business as usual—to the ever-growing volume of imported British manufactures reaching the colonies. This was the trade that led Adam Smith to call America "a nation of customers." In the early years of settle-ment, when the fulling mill (which finished, or "dressed," the homemade product) was a measure of civilization in the wilderness, individual colonies had organized cloth production in order to guarantee basic supplies. But America was soon too important a market for English textiles to allow colonial production to develop into a large-scale, commercial project. In 1660 Parlia-ment forbade the exportation of sheep from England, meaning that American manufacturing would be limited to the coarser qualities of goods. In 1688 the ascendent Whigs established a permanent Board of Trade to supervise economic activity in the colonies. In 1699, in response to complaints about American-made woolens reaching foreign markets traditionally supplied by English manufacturers, Parliament simply outlawed the trade. That, in turn, put an end to colonial bounties for woolen cloths. When, for instance, Rhode Island attempted to renew an incentive system for home production in 1751, the law was quickly repealed for fear that "it may draw the displeasure of Great Britain." In addition to such direct prohibitions, the British also in-stituted a system of drawbacks on duties. These effectively cheapened the cost of imports, again making American production less practical, as did the open toleration of smuggling. In these ways, America became integrated into the empire as exporter of raw materials and importer of finished goods from the mother country, woolens being the most important of the latter. Officials zealously protected this mercantile system. After seeing "Serge made upon Long Island that any man may wear," for example, Lord Canbury became concerned enough in 1705 to publicly fret about an American woolen manu-facture that "will hurt England in a little time."[8]

His fears proved baseless, however. Sir William Keith, the former gover-nor of Pennsylvania, reported in 1728 that the American colonies consumed more than a sixth of Britain's woolen manufactures and double its nominal value in linens and calicoes. After 1750 the tempo of this consumption rose

dramatically, as shopkeepers regularly advertised "broad-cloths, serges, cam-
bets, ozenbrigs, cotton checks, damasks, calicoes, cambricks, sattins, taffeties,
[and] highland plads" at prices that had been falling sharply since the end
of the previous century. Such inventories constituted well over half the goods
arriving from Britain, and an even higher percentage of the items shipped out
from port cities into the countryside for sale.[9]

Not only did this balance of trade satisfy mercantilist economics; it also
supplied English cultural refinement to a growing number of colonials. Indeed, the late-eighteenth-century surfeit of cloth was manifest in one of the
most important American cultural projects of the day: John Singleton Copley's hundreds of portraits of the New England elite that faithfully reproduced the plush interior tapestries and, most of all, the effusive materiality of
his sitters' raiment. Neither Copley nor, apparently, his contemporaries could
avert their gaze from all these fabrics. The 1769 portrait of the Boston merchant Nicholas Boylston thus emphasizes the heavy silk damask of Boylston's
voluminous morning gown. His beige silk waistcoat is opened just enough to
reveal the wide ruffles of the linen shirt beneath. Full white cuffs counterbalance the richer, darker silks. And a red velvet turban is angled high over
the brow so as to mimic and so call attention to the sweeping diagonals of the
background drapery and the folds of the gown. The fabrics, in short, were
the real subject of Boylston's portrait. Even Copley's portrait of the shirt-
clad Paul Revere, noticeably shorn of the usual layers of genteel outer dress,
the hand tools of an artisan ostentatiously arrayed before him, was a study in
the fineness of linen and the semiotics of sleeve ruffles.[10]

The growing relationship between commerce and culture so emphati-
cally evident in the improving standards of colonial dress did not signal
the obsolescence of domestic production, however. In fact, the economic
role of the household only increased in importance: yeoman farming proved
highly adept in responding to the pressures and opportunities of the commercializing times. The steady climb of prices for livestock and wheat after
mid-century generated a new division of labor within the family by which
men stayed outside feeding the herds, mowing the fields, planting clover for
feed, and building their barns while women assumed increasing authority
over "indoor" tasks such as milling, baking, gardening, dairying, and soap
making. But it was textile production, which began with planting the flax
patch and shearing the sheep and ended with cutting and sewing the cloth
into clothing—a sixteen-month cycle, for instance, in the case of making
a linen shirt—that emerged as the focus of the intensifying domesticity of
colonial householders. The operations were so varied, and required such a
wide range of skills, technologies, and physical resources, that it was usually

The Boston merchant Nicholas Boylston, as painted by John Singleton
Copley in 1769. Neither Copley nor his contemporaries could keep their eyes
off the clothing, which was arguably the main subject of all his portraits of
the colonial gentry.

unrealistic to carry out the entire process within a single household. Cleaning
the raw fibers, carding the results in preparation for spinning, the spinning
itself, then dyeing the yarn, warping the loom, weaving, and cutting—the
plethora of tasks were divided among family members or between neighbors,
or given to itinerants with the requisite skills, who worked in one's own home
or someone else's. Such household production, in short, entailed an elaborate division of labor organized largely through a local barter exchange that,
without too much effort, could be identified with republican notions of civic
cooperation.

Such homespun cooperation was not divorced from the trans-Atlantic
economy. Rather, the two systems became highly complementary, even sym-

biotic. Households were supplying more of their own basic needs at mid-century in order to free up resources to purchase more higher-grade imports. Similarly, homespun yarns and cloths were often exchanged directly for imported fabrics of finer quality, the homespun then being marketed elsewhere in the empire. In fact, those same households that were buying greater amounts of cloth on the market were also producing more cloth of their own. Consequently, these years witnessed an explosion in the number of spinning wheels and looms in the colonies.[11]

This was the context for homespun politics. Making cloth at home with the sole intention of wearing it, and it alone, was a pointed departure from colonial practice, economic orthodoxy, and imperial rules. However, the attendant sacrifice of the material benefits of the trade with Britain was not a protest against commerce per se. It was an attempt, rather, to reconstitute an American economy that would rest on the energies and skills of householders who had proven themselves up to the challenge. Thus, when in 1774 the first Continental Congress declared a general policy of "non-importation, non-consumption, and non-exportation," it was far less concerned with ascetic self-denial than with encouraging American arts and manufactures, "especially that of wool." Nonconsumption, in other words, was not synonymous with anticonsumption, and political independence rested not on the sacrifice of property but on its industrious, that is, its virtuous use.[12] Indeed, the homespun protest was an implicit acknowledgment that the world of goods had become integral to any discussion of public happiness.

- - - - -

The relationship between economic goods and the public good had informed remarks made in 1722, when a young Franklin already bemoaned the "Pride of Apparel" that had overtaken the colonies "ever since we parted with our Homespun Cloaths for Fourteen Penny Stuffs." The rise of fashionableness, Franklin complained, allowed persons with no real claim to social distinction to draw "Crowds of Imitators who hate each other while they endeavor after a similitude of Manners. They destroy by Example, and envy one another's Destruction." Fourteen Penny Stuffs, that is, spawned a miasma of social pretension and, with it, a betrayal of the civic order. The natural hierarchy was obfuscated by people dressing beyond their rank. "A Fall was the natural consequence."[13]

Franklin's eschatology drew, in part, of course, on a puritanical legacy. That was evident in "The Forefather's Song," which continued to circulate in the eighteenth century:

Our clothes we brought with us are apt to be torn—
They need to be clouted [patched] soon after they are worn—
But clouting our garments they hinder us nothing;
Clouts double are warmer than single whole clothing.

Puritans had welcomed such straitened circumstances as an opportunity to resolve the "dilemma" between success in this world and their more stringent obligations to the next. Franklin's jeremiad, however, contained no such metaphysics. His condemnation of luxury rested on a notion of civic sobriety and a view of the tensions between material advance and social stability that had nothing to do with the Calvinist sense of sin. Both the solution and the problem, as he understood them, were entirely of this world. Franklin, who eventually became the colonies' leading publicist for the distinctly nonpuritan idea that virtue could be acquired through regular habits, described the sartorial ideal he had in mind: "He appear'd in the plainest Country Garb; his Great Coat was coarse and looked old and thread-bare; his Linnen was homespun; his Beard perhaps of Seven Days Growth, his Shoes thick and heavy, and every Part of his Dress corresponding." What made such a dismal sight the object of universal respect? "It was not an exquisite Form of Person, or Grandeur of Dress that struck us with Admiration." In fact, it was the opposite. Authority would issue from the fact that "he always speaks the Thing he means." The virtuous, in sum, eschewed artifice as they did fashion, for these were the harbingers of corruption. They favored instead the "homespun Dress of Honesty," which Franklin associated with "the first Ages of the world." It was a foundation myth of simpler and more frugal times designed to help establish the basis for social order in a secularizing, postsumptuary world. A similar impulse informed the religious awakenings that swept the colonies in these same years. James Davenport notably instructed his followers to burn fancy clothing in addition to books. This would ensure that the accumulation of the ever-growing number of goods for sale did not "destroy" society. What appeared as nostalgic on Franklin's part, or as a reactionary religious impulse, was actually a new kind of response to a distinctly modern dilemma.[14]

One practical attempt to "virtuously" contain the effects of ambition in the New World took place in the newest American colony, Georgia. The colony's high-minded trustees, sitting in London, were most apprehensive about the nefarious effects of commerce on social life. But they also recognized that, because America offered unprecedented material opportunity, newer and freer forms of economic association were unavoidable. Perhaps, as the optimists among them hoped, such opportunities would actually present a way to reconcile what had become, since Hobbes, a proverbial tension between doing good for others and doing good for oneself. In Georgia the preferred method for striking that balance was to make everyone a primary producer. Even slavery was banned in the colony in accordance with that principle. Property would be widely distributed. The independent household was to be the predominant economic and social unit of the colony. And while production was thus facilitated, commerce would be strictly inhibited, and that because exchange was not to be the goal of the citizen's productive efforts. Credit was restricted and accumulation inhibited. In this way, it was thought, the luxurious aggregation of the householder's hard work would be avoided.[15]

Georgia exemplified the singular role America played in seeking answers to what was emerging as a central political question of modern life: how to reconcile the individual aspiration for material improvement with anxieties about its social consequences. Trans-Atlantic sentiment regarded America as a "middle landscape," no longer an untamed wilderness but not yet the site of refined artifice characteristic of Europe. It was where a "comfortable subsistence [without] the Pressures of Poverty and the Surfeits of Abundance" was uniquely possible. Plainness was the mark of this life, an aesthetic complement to grazing flocks, rural idylls, and industrious farmers. One finds it, for example, in the simpler, visually flatter copies of English engravings that circulated in the colonies during the first half of the eighteenth century, or in the political pastoral of "independent and hardy YEOMANRY, all nearly on a level—trained to arms . . . clothed in homespun—of simple manners—strangers to luxury—drawing plenty from the ground."[16]

But the Georgian experiment failed. The anticommercial zealousness by which the productive autonomy of each household was supposed to be maintained actually became an obstacle to the public happiness it was intended to nurture; and, anyway, the advantages of commerce proved irresistible. The problem was a basic one: while commerce served as the source of corruption because it made the pursuit of luxury possible, it was no less an agent of civilization. This was because the absence of material improvement was as much an affront to virtue as it was its guarantor. (It was also antithetical to the whole colonial project.) That contradiction was to be found in Adam Smith's new political economy as well, which assigned acquisitiveness a positive social role while recognizing that the public's general happiness depended on the restraint of wants. The conundrum begged for a homespun solution that would wed industry and frugality, personality and society.[17]

The household offered such a synthesis. While its origins lay in the distant past, it also proved to be thoroughly modern. In the mid-1760s farmers in Chester County, Pennsylvania, increased the size of their flocks. They invested in improved pasture lands and hired weavers to turn the resulting yarns into cloth. They were then happy to report that they had found "an encouraging small Profit" when selling their woolens in the Philadelphia market. These patriots certainly had no intention of replacing commercial relations with a simpler system of exchange. They accepted the reasoning of Maryland's Governor Sharpe when he assured the nervous Lords of Trade in 1767 that no one "will think much of Manufacturing for themselves while they can with the produce of their Lands purchase such Goods as they may have occasion for." But they now sought to turn such logic to their own advantage. Their aim was to replace imported commodities—and by mid-century most of the population of Chester County no longer wore clothing made at home—with American-manufactured ones. The market was their means for doing this, and the stuff of political economy was clearly now a constituent element of civic virtue.[18]

In fact, the patriotic boycotts of British goods organized in response to imperial reform acts opened up new opportunities for commerce in domestic manufactures. Homespun proved to be a business venture. In New York City, American-made woolens were rumored to be selling for three times their original value. And a Chester County farmer actually protested when the Stamp Act was repealed. "What security [will be] given us," he inquired of proponents of nonimportation, so to make the patriotic call to sacrifice materially viable?[19] Virtuous self-sacrifice, in other words, did not rest on the effacement of private desires but on their successful integration with public needs. Even Cato could be enlisted in the cause: "What is the public, but the collective body of private men, as every man is a member of the public?" The *Boston Gazette* gave this idea clear expression in 1768: "Every Man who will take Pains to cultivate the Cost of Homespun may easily convince himself that his private Interest, as well as [that of] the Publick, will be promoted by it." Or, as the same paper more pithily expressed it on another occasion, "SAVE YOUR MONEY, AND YOU SAVE YOUR COUNTRY!" Profit was the happy result of a virtuous coordination of private and public. The patriot cause could even be turned into an advertising strategy. Daniel Mause, a Philadelphia hosier, announced in 1766 that he had "lately erected a Number of Looms, for the manufacture of thread and cotton stockings and other kinds of Hosiery of any size or quality, hoping the good people of this and the neighboring Provinces will encourage this, his undertaking, at a time when AMERICA calls for the endeavors of Her Sons." In Virginia, where the nonimportation campaign found widespread support among the largest planters, home production facilitated a long-overdue economic reform intended to alleviate chronic debts by shifting the plantations to full seasonal labor, crop diversification, and a more profitable use of otherwise idle children and elderly slaves.[20]

A homespun economy would rectify imperial corruption by supporting an alternative commercial logic, monopolized not by government but by a civil society resting on the energies of independent householders who subsequently created a society, so it was believed, impervious to any monopolization at all.

The homespun imbued this public sphere with another novel characteristic: democracy. When sophisticates appeared in Boston and Charleston bereft of their figured silks and broadcloth woolens, they celebrated the coarseness that had traditionally been a sign of social marginality, the exclusive dominion of "Laborers & Servants." Typically, not too many years before, the colonial diarist Alexander Hamilton had described the homely effect of his landlady by dressing her in homespun and then barely containing his distaste at the sight. The young apprentice, Joseph Gilman, newly arrived in Boston, wrote home to New Hampshire in 1752 to request his mother send him additional garments, warning that if she dared include his homespun jacket, "I shall not wear it."[21]

Making the homespun a symbol of civic membership was thus a consciously leveling moment. Homespun erased the textured fineness of the cloth by which the "respectable Ladies" of Narragansett and Newport had traditionally maintained their status. "Rich and Poor all turn the Spinning Wheel," someone approvingly declared as a maxim for the times. The "indifferently cloathed," those heretofore considered incapable of virtue precisely because of their unpropertied and consequently dependent status, were now promoted to full citizenship by the homespun.[22] For the first time in the history of democratic thought, necessity—the desiderata of material subsistence—became a legitimate subject of political life. The long-denigrated *oikos*, or household, was transformed into the pan-gendered basis of sovereignty in which civic virtue rested on a person's very proximity to the production of basic necessities. This elevated the simple artisan to the same civic stratum as the philosopher-statesman.[23] That was unprecedented, even in America. When he waxed nostalgic in 1732 about lost homespun innocence, Franklin had actually bemoaned the mixing of the classes. And when, in 1748, the Pennsylvania Associators sought to express "the Union of all Ranks," they carried banners depicting three arms in a brotherly embrace—

respectively clad in ruffled, plain, and checked sleeves—or three associators marching abreast with shouldered muskets "and dressed in different Clothes, intimating the unanimity of the different Sorts of People in the Association." The Revolution's homespun ideology promoted a very different version of political unanimity, one no longer stratified into permanent ranks. Quite the opposite: the homespun now joined all on an equal footing in a manufacturing economy. And it prepared them for sovereignty by tying together their individual efforts through an ethos of *vita activa* that abolished, or at least suggested the abolition of, what had heretofore been an axiomatic division of humanity into the polite classes and the meaner sorts. As such, it was a most practical expression of what Jefferson would soon call the equality of all men.[24]

- - - - -

Nor did concerns about luxury and admonitions toward frugality abate after Independence. In fact, they escalated. Sovereignty brought Americans face to face with their republican revolution, and questions about how to institutionalize public happiness only assumed greater urgency. The homespun ideal proved no less relevant in the 1780s than it had twenty years earlier in searching for the answers. In the wake of a huge influx of British goods there were calls to renew the prewar boycott of British imports. Chastisements of the citizenry for "fluttering about in foreign dress" were common. In Philadelphia the fashion-conscious fop was a subject of scorn:

> His scarlet coat, that ev'ry one may see,
> Mark and observe and know the fool is he,
> With buttons garnish'd, sparkling in a row
> On sleeves and breasts and skirts to make a show.

Timothy Dwight opened his patriotic verse *Greenfield Hill* by comparing American simplicity to European pretense and locating the former in that "Farmer plain, / Intent to gather honest gain . . . / In solid homespun clad, and tidy."[25]

Mathew Carey's *American Museum* filled up with notices from Patriotic and Economical Associations from around the country addressing "those ladies, who used to excel in dress . . . [to] endeavor to set the best example, by laying aside their richest silks, and superfluous decorations [and] dress their persons in the plainest manner." The exhortations to plainness and sacrifice seemed to borrow verbatim from the previous generation's virtuous

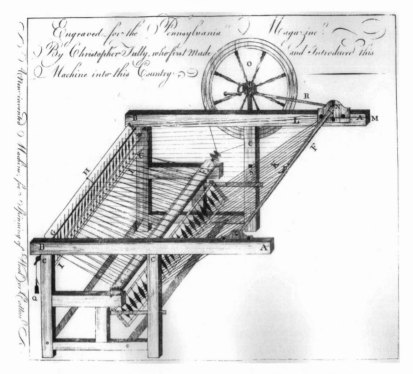

An exciting vision of the homespun future, as presented in the *Pennsylvania Magazine*, edited by Tom Paine, in 1775. (Courtesy of the William L. Clements Library, University of Michigan)

rhetoric. "No tax," the *New-York Gazette and General Advertiser* declared in discouraging women from adopting the new European fashions, "is more unreasonable and oppressive than that of Fashion." Or, as the idea appeared elsewhere: "Surely the man who is clothed in American manufactures, which he wears for the sake of enriching his native country, and relieving his fellow citizens, may be allowed to have some claims to patriotism, which is the most honorable garb that can be worn." Public spinning matches were reinstituted. "Oeconomy and Household Industries" were back in vogue. Tench Coxe promised that American manufactures would lead the country "once more, into the paths of virtue, by restoring frugality and industry, those potent antidotes to the vices of mankind, and will give us real independence by rescuing us from the tyranny of foreign fashions, and the destructive torrent of luxury."[26]

But Coxe, the assistant secretary of the Treasury, was no longer remonstrating against the King's ministers. He was nation building. And his good friend Mathew Carey was doing the same in proposing that all federal officers take an oath that they would perform their official duties "dressed principally in the manufactures of the united states." Carey actually called for the institution of a national costume. "We do not count it an honour to imitate the forms of government that prevail in Europe—why should we think it honorable to imitate the fashion of their coats!" A distinctly American dress would attach citizens to one another by forging a common identity, especially important since so much of American culture was inherited from a corrupt England.[27]

Carey did not describe what such national dress would look like, but his was not an entirely quixotic concern. From across the political spectrum, Thomas Paine also exhorted Americans to cease being "the servile copyists of foreign manners, fashions, and vices." The creation of a republican system of government clearly required the establishment of a commensurate civic culture. And so, when the Virginia state legislature commissioned a sculpture of Washington from Jean Antoine Houdon in the 1790s, a debate erupted over the subject's costume. An earlier commission by Congress of a statue of Washington had already resulted in a figure draped in classical robes. But Benjamin West now advised Houdon to dress Washington in contemporary garb. This would not only satisfy the romantic sensibility emerging in the arts but would also articulate a recognizably American point of view. In comparison, the new French republic had commissioned a design for a national uniform from Jacques Louis David that was supposed to be a sartorial representation of the new civic status of its *citoyens*. David submitted a thoroughly unmodern amalgam of Renaissance silhouette, medieval guild motifs, and classical drapery. His hybrid idealization of virtuous pasts apparently satisfied French notions of the republican present: the Committee of Public Safety distributed twenty thousand engraved copies of David's proposal throughout the country. American republicans looked elsewhere for inspiration in inventing their public life. Washington himself endorsed West's recommendation to Houdon and wrote to Jefferson, in questioning the togas popularly invoked to symbolize civic virtue, that a "servile adherence to the garb of antiquity might not be altogether so expedient." It was now necessary, rather, to face the "new realities of republican life."[28]

This is exactly what Washington did at his first inauguration, where his appearance excited considerable public comment. The *Gazette of the United States* wrote: "The President of the United States . . . appeared dressed in a complete suit of homespun cloaths; but the cloth was of so fine a Fabric, and so

Handsomely finished, that it was universally mistaken for a foreign manufactured superfine cloth. His excellency the Vice President, appears also in a suit
of American Manufacture and several members of both Houses are distinguished by the same token of attention to the manufacturing interest of their
country."[29] Washington had recently visited the Hartford Woolen Company
on a tour of New England. The company was a highly touted manufacturing
project and the subject of adulation not only by patriots but by the State of
Connecticut, which exempted it from taxation. While there, Washington so-
licited a sample of their best cloth. This was then made up into the suit he
so purposefully wore for the inaugural ceremonies, together with American-
made silk stockings and plain silver shoe buckles.[30]

The most significant aspect of Washington's sartorial embrace of the new
realities of republican life was the fact that the Hartford Company's commercial output was assigned the same status of homespun as the coarse product
of the householder's wheel and loom, flock of sheep, and patch of flax. That
equation underlined what had been implicit during more than two decades of
homespun politics: "domestic" had a dual meaning, simultaneously connot-
ing the household and the nation. Popular sovereignty, of course, was based on
the same equation of household and nation. As in the past, it was homespun
that gave material tangibility to such abstract notions.

All sorts of arrangements fell under this rubric. The appearance in Philadelphia's grand Federal Procession on July 4, 1788, of a Mrs. Hewson, together with her four daughters, all attired in homespun cottons under the
auspices of the city's Manufacturing Society, was one. The Hartford Company was another. So also were the several hundred spinning wheels put under William Molineux's charge in 1770, Molineux being a leader of Boston's
nonimportation campaign. The result was so much yarn that it became necessary to expand the project into an integrated cloth "apparatus" of warping and
twisting mills, weaving looms, a furnace, hot and cold presses for finishing the
goods, and a complete "Dye-House" with a large assortment of dyestuffs—
a protofactory based on mechanical innovations such as that which allowed
two boys to keep fifty looms supplied with yarn. These same patriot proponents of domestic manufacture had also made concerted efforts to secure
a working model of James Hargreaves's spinning jenny in the years before
Independence. Meanwhile, too, the traditional household remained a locus
of economic activity. Alexander Hamilton was the first to recognize the centrality of "family manufactures" to his postindependence development plans.
The family's ability to clothe itself, he wrote in his seminal *Report on Manufactures* in 1791, was important "both in a moral and political view." Flax became

a specific subject of federal encouragement precisely because of its role in household industry. "The ease, with which the materials can be produced at home to any requisite extent—the great advances, which have already been made, in the coarser fabrics of them, especially in the family way, constitute claims, of peculiar force, to the patronage of government."[31]

But manufacturing societies and woolen companies were ultimately not the same thing as households, and the axiomatic unity of all forms of domestic industry began to unravel. The end of the Revolution's homespun ideology, in fact, was discernible in the flurry of republican pageants—rife with imagery and symbol—by which Americans celebrated their new political order.

Boston's official reception for the president in the fall of 1789 was a testament to Revolutionary maxims. A military troop led the town's public procession. They were followed by town, county, and state officials, clergymen, and representatives of the professions. These notables were given no fanfares. They appeared without the accompaniment of a scarlet liveried guard, in telling contrast to monarchical British practice. Even more significant, however, was what followed, for marching behind them were Boston's tradesmen. These representatives of productive vigor and the common classes were, thanks to the homespun ideology, full participants in Washington's reception rather than the passive onlookers of yore. They marched in forty-six separate groups, organized by trades arranged in alphabetical order, from bakers to wheelwrights. Their presence turned the event into a popular demonstration of "industry and economy." True, each trade's representatives marched in a strict hierarchy of masters, journeymen, and apprentices, but this was indicative of corporate mutuality, certainly not yet of any class divisions.

In New York City, that same year, another procession "in honor of the Constitution of the United States" took to the streets. It, too, celebrated productive effort and located the citizen-craftsman at the center of the new political order. But in New York this was done in entirely different terms from those that guided the thinking in Boston. In New York, gentlemen of the bar, merchants and traders, the president and students of the college, clergy, physicians, and militia officers all marched. However, they took their place at the rear of the procession. At the front was the requisite military detachment. Behind the artillery pieces marched foresters attired in their work frocks, carrying axes. Then a figure representing Columbus appeared, recognizable by his antique dress. More foresters followed, and after them, in order, came a plough, a sower, a harrow, farmers, and gardeners. Once the land was thus symbolically cleared and the most basic subsistence ensured, the tailors came marching, suppliers of the other elemental necessity of raiment. And so it was that in New York, too, all the trades were conspicuous participants in the new social order. This was not, however, the static, neutral approach of Boston's alphabetization but a highly dynamic recounting of the material history of America, from European discovery to the present republican apotheosis. The procession narrated a story of progress, from pristine primitiveness, through productive effort, to the flowering of republican civilization as represented in the respectable personages at the rear of the parade. This was no less than a political economy acted out along Broadway.[32]

In spite of its conscious republican schema and embrace of the victorious homespun ethos, Boston's procession already represented an anachronism. The street drama in New York advanced a different homespun narrative, one recognizing that the same industriousness that had turned a savage wilderness into a bucolic middle landscape showed no signs of abating. This was an America, as Hector St. John de Crevecoeur observed, where "the idle may be employed, the useless become useful, and the poor become rich." Thus, for instance, what excited the most comment about Washington's homespun costume at his inauguration was not its domestic provenance per se but the quality of the American-made woolen, "so Handsomely finished, that it was universally mistaken for a foreign manufactured superfine cloth."[33]

The virtuous opposition between coarse and fine showed signs of fraying. Political sovereignty and the developing market destabilized homespun's meaning, pulling "industry" and "frugality" apart into separate, and even opposing, categories. The success in replacing imports with home manufactures now rested on the latter's relative fineness. John Chester, one of Hamilton's correspondents, wrote to convey the auspicious news from Connecticut that the state's more substantial farmers and mechanics had begun to wear Sunday dress made up at home. The improved quality of such manufactures, it was hoped, meant that the practice would become more common. An "American Farmer" could likewise still proudly declaim that in America there were none of "the works of luxury [and] the gorgeous temples" that characterized a decadent Europe. Underneath this familiar lexicon, however, was an altered grammar. "Those degrees of improvements will appear in time," was the happy prediction, once Americans cut down more trees and cleared more swamps. The difference was that in America, unlike Europe, the effort would not benefit "greedy landlords" but instead the toilers themselves. Similar indications of the changing meaning of homespun virtue were also discernible in Royall Tyler's *The Contrast*, the "first dramatic production of a citizen of the United States," staged in New York in 1787. Tyler created a plot centering on the familiar homespun opposition between the fashionable, self-centered

Procession.

AS this town is shortly to be honoured with a visit from THE PRESIDENT of the United States: In order that we may pay our respects to him, in a manner whereby every inhabitant may see so illustrious and amiable a character, and to prevent the disorder and danger which must ensue from a great assembly of people without order, a Committee appointed by a respectable number of inhabitants, met for the purpose, recommend to their Fellow-Citizens to arrange themselves in the following order, in a

PROCESSION.

IT is also recommended, that the person who shall be chosen as head of each order of Artizans, Tradesmen, Manufacturers, &c. shall be known by displaying a WHITE FLAG, with some device thereon expressive of their several callings, and to be numbered as in the arrangement that follows, which is alphabetically disposed, in order to give general satisfaction.—The Artizans, &c. to display such insignia of their craft, as they can conveniently carry in their hands. That uniformity may not be wanting, it is desired that the several Flag-staffs be SEVEN feet long, and the Flags a YARD SQUARE.

ORDER OF PROCESSION

MUSICK.

The Selectmen,
Overseers of the Poor,
Town Treasurer,
Town Clerk,
Magistrates,
Consuls of France and Holland,
The Officers of his Most Christian Majesty's Squadron,
The Rev. Clergy,
Physicians,
Lawyers,
Merchants and Traders,
Marine Society,
Masters of Vessels,
Revenue Officers,
Strangers, who may wish to attend.

Bakers,	No. 1.
Blacksmiths, &c.	No. 2.
Block-makers,	No. 3.
Boat-builders,	No. 4.
Cabinet and Chair-makers,	No. 5.
Card-makers,	No. 6.
Carvers,	No. 7.
Chaise and Coach-makers,	No. 8.
Clock and Watch-makers,	No. 9.
Coopers,	No. 10.
Coppersmiths, Braziers and Foundrers,	No. 11.
Cordwainers, &c.	No. 12.
Distillers,	No. 13.
Dock Manufacturers,	No. 14.
Engravers,	No. 15.
Glaziers and Plumbers,	No. 16.

Goldsmiths and Jewellers,	No. 17.
Hair-Dressers,	No. 18.
Hatters and Furriers,	No. 19.
House Carpenters,	No. 20.
Leather Dressers, and Leather Breeches Makers,	No. 21.
Limners and Portrait Painters,	No. 22.
Masons,	No. 23.
Mast-makers,	No. 24.
Mathematical Instrument-makers,	No. 25.
Millers,	No. 26.
Painters,	No. 27.
Paper Stainers,	No. 28.
Pewterers,	No. 29.
Printers, Book-binders and Stationers,	No. 30.
Riggers,	No. 31.
Rope-makers,	No. 32.
Saddlers,	No. 33.
Sail-makers,	No. 34.
Shipwrights, to include Caulkers, Ship-joiners, Head-builders and Sawyers,	No. 35.
Sugar-boilers,	No. 36.
Tallow-Chandlers, &c.	No. 37.
Tanners,	No. 38.
Taylors,	No. 39.
Tin plate Workers,	No. 40.
Tobacconists,	No. 41.
Truckmen,	No. 42.
Turners,	No. 43.
Upholsterers,	No. 44.
Wharfingers,	No. 45.
Wheelwrights,	No. 46.
Seamen,	

N. B.—In the above arrangement, some trades are omitted—from the idea, that they would incorporate themselves with the branches mentioned, to which they are generally attached. For instance—it is supposed, that under the head of *Blacksmiths*, the *Armourers, Cutlers, Whitesmiths* and other workers in iron, would be included; and the same with respect to other trades.

Each division of the above arrangement is requested to meet on such parade as it may agree on, and march into the Mall—No. 1 of the Artizans, &c. forming at the South-end thereof. The Marshalls will then direct in what manner the Procession will move to meet the President on his arrival in town. When the front of the Procession arrives at the extremity of the town, it will halt, and the whole will then be directed to open the column—one half of each rank moving to the right, and the other half to the left—and then face inwards, so as to form an avenue through which the President is to pass, to the galleries to be erected at the State-House.

It is requested that the several School-masters conduct their Scholars to the neighbourhood of the State-House, and form them in such order as the Marshalls shall direct.

THE Marine Society is desired to appoint some person to arrange and accompany the seamen.

The order of procession for two 1789 celebrations, one in Boston and the other in New York, both in honor of the new republic. These street dramas presented two distinct versions of homespun politics.

Order of Proceſſion,
In Honor of the Conſtitution of
the United States.

AT eight o'Clock on Wednesday Morning the 23d of July, 10 Guns will fire, when the PROCESSION will parade and proceed by the following Route, viz : Down Broad-Way to Great-Dock-Street, thence, through Hanover-Square, Queen, Chatham, Division, and Arundel-Streets ; and from thence through Bullock-Street to Bayard's-House.

No. 1.   2 Horsemen with Trumpets.
2.   1 piece of Artillery.

Firſt D I V I S I O N.

No.		No.	
3	4 Foresters in Frocks, carrying Axes.	12	A Band of Music.
4	Columbus in his Ancient Dress—on Horseback.	13	Taylors.
5	6 Foresters, &c.	14	Measurers of Grain.
6	A Plough.	15	Millers.
7	A Sower.	16	Inspectors of Flour.
8	A Harrow.	17	Bakers.
9	Farmers.	18	Brewers.
10	United States Arms, borne by Col. White, supported	19	Distillers.
11	Gardeners. [by the Society of the Cincinnati.		

Second D I V I S I O N.

20	Coopers.	22	Tanners and Curriers.
21	Butchers.	23	Leather Dressers.

Third D I V I S I O N.

24.   Cord Wainers.

Fourth D I V I S I O N.

25	Carpenters.	27	Hatters.
26	Furriers.	28	Peruke-Makers and Hair-Dressers.

Fifth D I V I S I O N.

29	White Smiths.	35	Windsor Chair-Makers.
30	Cutlers.	36	Upholsterers.
31	Stone Masons.	37	Fringe Makers.
32	Brick-Layers.	38	Paper Stainers.
33	Painters and Glaziers.	39	Civil Engineers.
34	Cabinet Makers.		

Sixth D I V I S I O N.

40	Ship-Wrights.	44	Block and Pump-Makers.
41	Black-Smiths.	45	Sail-Makers, and Rope-Makers.
42	Ship-Joiners.	46	Riggers.
43	Boat-Builders.		

Seventh D I V I S I O N.

47	Federal Ship Hamilton.	50	Marine Society.
48	Pilot Boat and Barges.	51	Printers, Book-Binders and Stationers.
49	Pilots.		

Eighth D I V I S I O N.

52	Cartmen.	60	Gold and Silver-Smiths.
53	Mathematical Instrument-Makers.	61	Potters.
54	Carvers and Engravers.	62	Chocolate-Makers.
55	Coach-Makers.	63	Tobacconists.
56	Coach-Painters.	64	Dyers.
57	Copper-Smiths and Brass-Founders.	65	Brush-Makers.
58	Tin-plate Workers.	66	Tallow-Chandlers.
59	Pewterers.	67	Saddlers, Harness and Whip-Makers.

Ninth D I V I S I O N.

68	Gentlemen of the Bar.	70	President and Students of the College.
69	Philological Society.	71	Merchants and Traders.

Tenth D I V I S I O N.

72	Clergy.
73	Physicians.
74	Strangers.
75	Militia Officers.
76	1 piece of Artillery.

By Order of the Committee of Arrangements,
RICHARD PLATT, Chairman.

Billy Dimple and the austere, upright Colonel Manly, who, characteristically, continued to dress in his wartime regimentals. Nevertheless, Tyler's contrast was no longer as stark or as elementary as it had once been. For while the foppish Dimple could never be a model of republican civility, Tyler suggested that Manly's naive, even puerile, self-abnegation promised no better a basis for responsible self-government. It was no longer as obvious with whom society's future best lay.[34]

The homespun had never been a utopian protest, frozen in time. Its prosaic, historical nature, in fact, was the key to its success as a symbol of the American Revolution. And that history, as New York's constitutional procession demonstrated, was now a distinctly linear narrative of commercial advance. Homespun augured progress. True, Franklin assigned it to "the first Ages of the world," but that was in relation to European finery. Aboriginal status really belonged to the animal skins of the Indians, whose atavism was measured precisely by their lack of a cloth-making tradition. In 1806, as president, Jefferson—who, in his *Notes on Virginia* of 1787, famously opposed all manufacturing, including the household kind, as a mortal threat to American virtue ("Let us never wish to see our citizens occupied . . . twirling a distaff")—lectured the Cherokee on the civilizing value of spinning and weaving their own raiment. By 1812, on the eve of another shooting war with England that had grown out of a trade conflict, Jefferson reconciled with John Adams on the basis of a homespun vision of commercial progress. As Jefferson wrote back to Massachusetts:

> I thank you . . . for the specimens of homespun you have been so kind as to forward me by post. I doubt not their excellence, knowing how far you are advanced in these things in your quarter. Here we do little in the fine way, but in coarse and midling goods a great deal. Every family in the country is a manufactory within itself, and is very generally able to make within itself all the stouter and midling stuffs for its own cloathing and household use. . . . For fine stuff we shall depend on your Northern manufactures. . . . The economy and thriftiness resulting from our household manufactures are such that they will never again be laid aside.[35]

This homespun was the same old celebration of productive energies and national improvement. It was still intended to mediate between material and political progress. However, the balance it now struck reflected a new kind of middle landscape, one in which luxury and virtue were no longer implacably opposed. That, for instance, was how the self-consciously refined members of the exclusive Sans Souci club in Boston countered familiar charges of "luxury, prodigality, and profligacy" directed against them in 1785 by Sam Adams and other veterans of the Revolution. Their cultural ambitions no longer signaled moral decline, they argued, but rather an ascent from primitivism to civilization.[36] Such logic was entirely consistent with the homespun values of production and national improvement. Indeed, luxuries could now become the best proof of liberty's success. "If you wish to separate commerce from luxury," a supporter of the Sans Souci wrote in the *Boston Observer*, describing the dismal alternative, "you expect an impossibility; let us break the bands of society, refuse all connection with the arts and sciences which live under the patronage of commerce and retire to the woods; let us learn of the savages' *simplicity* of life, to forget humanity, and cut each other's throats without remorse."[37]

In the new terms of this old debate, homespun admonitions about frugality now often served to freeze the social order and stem the democratic tide. When hard-pressed farmers in western Massachusetts protested in favor of tax relief, debtor protection, and greater amounts of circulating currency, their political opponents countered with apocryphal stories about thrifty farmers succumbing to their (wives') taste for silk and porcelain, which had eventually bankrupted them. "Luxury and extravagance, both in furniture and dress"—thus Abigail Adams analyzed the causes of Shays's rebellion. Concern for public virtue, in other words, expressed the wariness felt by some Americans of the ambitions of the less propertied. As Adam Smith explained, once "luxury" was accessible to the lowest ranks of society, "the labouring poor will not now be contented with the same food, clothing, and lodging which satisfied them in former times." The problem with luxury, one conservative complained, was that it confounded "every Distinction between the Poor and the Rich, [allowing] people of the very meanest parentages . . . if fortune be but a little favorable to them [to] vie to make themselves equal in apparel with the principle people of the place."[38] This was ironic mimicry of Franklin's plaint from half a century earlier about "Crowds of Imitators" who "endeavor after a similitude of Manners." The republican creed of government by the disinterested and uncorrupted was now threatened by the same industriousness and self-exertion that Franklin had considered to be the best safeguard against such corruption and social confusion in 1728. Franklin, in fact, supported the Sans Souci in the Boston *cause célèbre*. Others did not so easily update their homespun axioms to the new times, however. College orators debated "whether Sumptuary Laws ought to be established in the United States," and a last historic attempt at legislative prescriptions on dress—a vestige of a political order in which social arrangements rested on containing the effects of commerce, rather than vice versa—was actually made at the Constitutional Convention, where George Mason protested "the extravagance of our manners . . . and the necessity of restricting it." The convention appointed a committee to report on the question. It never did. Certainly, no such initiative found its way into the federal Constitution, which not only assumed that political sovereignty resided in the independent households of propertied citizens but also recognized the self-interested nature of their industrious independence. Popular government was thus tied to material improvement, as the homespun ideology had long signaled.[39]

By the time New York's Society for the Promotion of Useful Arts endorsed the importation of high-quality merino sheep in 1807—so that American cloth manufacturers, the vast majority still working in the family, would have an improved raw material during the embargo—the post-Revolutionary transformation of the homespun ideology was complete. The independence of American farmers, the society declared, is what has made it possible for them to advance beyond the mere necessities of life and aspire to life's "conveniences and comforts." ("Conveniences and superfluities" were what Franklin denounced as inimical to homespun liberty in 1766.) "Such men will take pride and pleasure in being dressed in clothes whose softness and pliancy give warmth to the body, pleasure to the touch, and grace to the wearer. And they will be doubly proud of this, if it is the product of their own farms, and of the industry of their wives and daughters."[40] Americans, in other words, still wore too many foreign clothes, and only their own industry could wean them of the bad habit. But such efforts should now result in prosperity, not frugality. "Softness," "pleasure," and "grace"—no longer "the coarseness of a homespun shirt"—were the basis of a proper civic life.

- - - - -

Not everyone was happy with this transformation. Discontent at the emergence of comfort as a guiding principle of modern life was most palpable in a centenary oration entitled "The Age of Homespun," delivered by the popular theologian Horace Bushnell in Litchfield, Connecticut, in 1851. Amid the industrializing vistas of nineteenth-century New England, Bushnell described a simpler, more virtuous time, free of the perpetual accumulation and striving of the present age. And here, in Bushnell's rendering of the homespun as the antipode of modern industry, the capitalist inversion of republicanism reached its apotheosis.

Bushnell conjured an older world of work and modesty. It was an age, he declared, when housewives made coats for children, sons built stone fences, and millers took an honest toll of rye. It was a time characterized by the "beautiful simplicity of nature." "Primitive and simple in their character . . . intelligent without refinement," homespun was the opposite of "all the polite fictions and empty conventionalities of the world." Bushnell reveled in a past in which persons appreciated the true value of things because they had produced them themselves. When no ready-made commodities were available, they understood just how much labor and effort were required to maintain their own material existence. "No mode of life was ever more expensive," he observed in sarcastic allusion to the bargain hunters of a wholesale age.[41] Homespun, the original ideology of production, had thus become by the middle of the industrial century a protest against the fate of man's productive energies in a world where industry and frugality were no longer complementary. For Bushnell, however, such irony had little meaning. He propounded a collective memory of an era before "affectation of polite living [and] languishing airs of delicacy and softness in doors, had begun to make the fathers and sons impatient of hard work out of doors, and set them at contriving some easier and more plausible way of living." As such, whether or not his idealized "home factory" ever really existed, it contained redemptive powers for a far more ambiguous age.

Bushnell's was not the only expression of homespun nostalgia. In a story entitled "Dependence; or What Made One Woman Meanly Penurious" that appeared in the feminist journal *The Una* in 1853, the heroine redeems her profligacy by rededicating herself to labor—in this case, to sewing, for no one seriously thought about spinning anymore[42]—and to its corollary, the rejection of fashion. In fact, the homespun ideology now seemed to unite disparate malcontents in the era of industrial revolution. Brigham Young declared in virtuous defiance that "I would rather wear gray homespun than your fine broadcloth. I would as soon wear a good home-made coat as a coat of the finest cloth in the world." And the radical, working-class *Subterranean* denounced the social sophistry of those polite types who wore white silk gloves and gracefully lifted their hat upon meeting an acquaintance. It presented an alternative image of "true politeness": "The man who lays aside all selfishness, in regard to the happiness of others . . . is a polite man, although he may wear a homespun coat, and make a very ungraceful bow."[43]

However, none of the protesters could escape the dialectics of homespun ideology. Even Bushnell, whose anticommodity fetishism ignored the homespun's important role in the colonial exchange economy, nevertheless acknowledged its relationship to the ethos of accumulation and market success:

> It is because they have gone out in the wise economy of a simple, homespun training, expecting to get on in the world by merit and patience, and by a careful husbanding of small advances; secured in their virtue, by just that which makes their perseverance successful. For the men who see the great in the small, and go on to build the great by small increments, will commonly have an exact conscience too that beholds great principles in small things, and so will form a character of integrity.

This was the same logic that guided the entrepreneur. "Although I realize only a small profit on each sale, the enlarged area of business thus secured makes possible a great accumulation of capital and assures the future," as A. T. Stewart, New York City's most renowned retailer in these years, explained his business success.[44]

Meanwhile, proponents of industrial revolution dismissed homespun as a distant memory. This is not to say they had forgotten its original importance to industry. "It was [British suppression of manufacturing], rather than taxation, that was the probable ground of the Revolution," as *Hunt's Merchant's Magazine* now interpreted the nation's founding impetus. "The colonists, simple in their habits of life, were contented to ride from farm to farm upon pillions, dressed in cloths woven from their own looms, and to acquire their subsistence between the handles of the plough." But the "progress of civilized nations" relegated homespun to the status of artifact. Its very antiquatedness, in fact, became a gauge of progress: homespun emerged as the negative reflection of productive achievement.[45]

This was most obvious in the escalating polemic between North and South. In his condemnatory travelogue of the Cotton Kingdom written on the eve of Civil War, Frederick Olmsted quoted a letter from an Illinois farmer published in the *New York Times* that disapprovingly observed the backward condition of citizens in a slave society. "For the most part, the people of these regions manufacture all their every-day clothing, and their garments look as though they were made for no other purpose than to keep them warm and to cover their nakedness; beauty of colouring and propriety in fitting are little regarded." Likewise, Olmsted himself wondered, how was it that while "in Ohio the spinning-wheel and hand-loom are curiosities, and homespun would be a conspicuous and noticeable material of clothing, half the white population of Mississippi still dress in homespun, and at every second house the wheel and loom are found in operation?"[46]

The slave was an obvious scapegoat for the death of the Union, but this
caricature, published in the *New-York Illustrated News* on the eve of
hostilities, suggests that the confrontation between North and South was no
less a fashion war. (Courtesy of the Collection of the New-York Historical
Society, neg. 75524)

If there was any doubt left about the contemporary identification of homespun with political reaction, one had only to observe how the coming of Civil
War provoked a rush of enthusiasm for homespun throughout the South.
When Carrie Long graduated from College Temple in Georgia in the spring
of 1861, her class chose homespun as the material for their dresses. "The
whole county praised the act." On that day everybody was singing: "Hurrah,
Hurrah! For the Southern girls, Hurrah! / Hurrah, for the homespun dresses
that the Southern Ladies wear!"Another popular song was even closer to
eighteenth-century origins: "My home-spun dress is plain; I know my hat's
common too, / But then it shows what Southern girls for Southern rights
will do." The governor of Alabama was reported to have appeared in a suit
of homespun made by a wife of one of the state's legislators, there being no
better "practical illustration of Southern Independence."[47]

And so homespun once again became a patriotic symbol of virtuous sacrifice in the face of a political and military threat posed by a corrupt economic

giant. And while the homespun ideology thus tied the Confederacy to the original Revolutionary impulse in a way the abolitionist Horace Bushnell would have had trouble explaining, or dismissing, the democratic North—which supplied its recruits with standard factory-issue blue kersey and flannels—had long since begun to buy its clothes at Brooks Brothers.[48]

2

A Clothing Business

In 1817 the economic journal *Niles' Weekly Register* devoted most of a single issue to showing that American agricultural production fell $128,459,000 short of paying the costs of clothing and feeding the nation. These were the same two standards of sovereignty applied by revolutionary patriots fifty years earlier, when Benjamin Rush proclaimed that "a people who are entirely dependent upon foreigners for food or clothes must always be subject to them." But *Niles'* now sought to use those criteria to prove that an agrarian economy could no longer sustain the republic and that the age of household industry was effectively over. That early conclusion was corroborated a generation later, in 1840, when *Hunt's Merchant's Magazine* enthusiastically reported that "the art of household manufacture is fast being totally lost." This meant that the farmer "was becoming quite as dependent for clothes upon the manufacturer, as the manufacturer is dependent for food upon the farmer." A transcontinental division of labor between farmers, factories, and factors had replaced the local efforts of carders, spinners, weavers, fullers, dyers, and bleachers as the source of the republic's all-important raiment. The 1860 census of manufactures—which was only published in 1865, ex post facto documentation of the industrial victory of the North over the Slave Power—gave this clothing revolution an official imprimatur: "Aided by cheap and rapid communication with all parts of the country . . . with all the advantages of large capital and machinery, [clothiers] supply every town and village with ready-made clothing, at the lowest prices."[1]

The "large capital and machinery" referred to by the census was the factory production of cloth, which, as we have seen, was an ongoing project dating from the previous century. The actual business of supplying "every town and village with ready-made clothing," however, was a relatively recent development. And yet, in spite of its novelty, the clothing business required none of the giant investments, corporate structures, or sublime machines that were the popular measures of industrial progress. Leaving to others what had always been, and remained, the far more complicated effort of making textiles, producers and marketers of clothing now situated themselves between the cloth and the consumer, who, in the past, had himself arranged to have the fabric turned into raiment. Clothiers profited handsomely from this niche in exchange. As such, they seemed to resemble an early-modern mercantile estate more than an industrial avant-garde. Indeed, an English survey of business opportunities conducted in 1747 had already observed that "the most general use of cloathing makes the Experience of their commodiousness almost universal." But what had been a logical inference in the eighteenth century regarding the commercial potential inherent in the general need to get dressed became a full-blown material reality in the nineteenth century. Clothiers' "arbitrage" between cloth maker and cloth wearer now entailed balancing the exigencies of a local retail and a distant wholesale market, coordinating long- and short-term credit cycles among disparate parts of the commercial world, and mobilizing a labor force in the country's cities by means of a system of subcontracting that the New York journalist George Foster began to call "sweating" in 1849.[2]

Clothiers staked out a heretofore nonexistent position in the developing networks of national and international exchange and, in so doing, helped to create those systems and equivalencies that industrialized the market. They integrated a textile revolution (the plethora of fabrics), a social revolution (the rise of wage labor in the metropolis), and a transportation revolution (by which canals, steam, and iron integrated a continental market). What's more, they operated at the intersection of the two great trading triangles of the age, where exports of cotton from the South and produce from the West met cloth and capital from the North and from Europe. No wonder, then, that there were 430 "clothing houses" doing business in New York City on the eve of the Civil War, compared to the twelve "slop sellers" purveying cheap garments listed in the city's *New Trade Directory* sixty years earlier. Their dramatic business success made clothiers the bearers of industrial-age abundance. When the New York Chamber of Commerce published its first *Annual Report* in 1858, it acknowledged the trade's contribution to the city's rise to commercial preeminence. "The appetite grows by what it feeds upon," these merchant princes, long indifferent to such ordinary pursuits, observed of the clothing trade's seemingly limitless elasticity, still a novelty in a world until recently circumscribed by Ricardian assumptions of implacable limits. "There is no telling the extent it may not reach."[3]

A contemporary watercolor depicting the American Institute's Annual Fair
in New York City, 1845. The progress of the arts was a manufacturing
phantasmagoria. (Painting by Benjamin Johns Harrison)

Material abundance, in fact, redefined the relationship between persons
and cloths and, with it, the very meaning of industry itself. The coat, Adam
Smith had explained in 1776, in illustrating the extensive social cooperation
required to make an ostensibly simple good, mobilized the "joint labor" of the
shepherd, the sorter of wool, the wool carder, the fuller, and the dresser. Notably absent from Smith's political economy was anyone who actually made
the coat. The omission was symptomatic of the traditionally marginal place
of garment production in the age-old economics of converting fleeces and
fibers into raiment. Thus, for instance, the homespun movement was all about
the virtuous production of cloth, not clothing. And thus, too, Henry Wansey
repeated Smith's formula in his widely circulated tract on cloth making published at the end of the century, again omitting any reference to the final stage
of the garment's fabrication. The same view resurfaced in a lecture at the
American Institute in New York in 1844. "To get at the cost [of a wool coat],"
Alexander Stuart explained, "you must estimate the value of the grass which
sustained the sheep, the labour and support of the shepherd whilst tending
the flocks, the labour of the manufacturers in spinning, weaving, dying and

dressing the cloth, including the support of their families whilst they were employed in these various processes." To these Stuart added the interest on capital, the profits of the manufacturer, rents, taxes, poor-rates, the cost of transportation, the profits of the wholesale and retail merchant, and other incidental charges "which it is not necessary to enumerate." How could it be that such a fastidious recital of modern commercial relations ignored the making of the coat itself, as if it were somehow incidental to the production process? How could Stuart, speaking in New York in the mid-1840s, fail to include in his list the hundreds of firms and tens of thousands of waged laborers in that city alone wholly devoted to nothing else but cutting and sewing cloth into clothing?[4]

In fact, Stuart's omission represented the reigning orthodoxy. That is why no figures for clothing production appeared in any official statistics before mid-century as well. Production statistics had a singular design: to identify the sites of industrial change—whole manufacturing sectors, such as textiles or iron—and then gather as much information about them as was bureaucratically possible. Such an approach informed Alexander Hamilton's landmark 1791 *Report on Manufacturers*. And it continued to guide all subsequent efforts. Even the ambitious manufacturing schedule of the sixth federal census of 1840, which generated an unprecedented statistical representation of the nation's economic life, adhered to the same epistemology whereby it investigated commercial activities that were chosen, a priori, for their presumed centrality to the political economy.[5] "Manufacturing" itself denoted the act that turned raw materials into "a form suitable for use." This meant the creation of something out of nothing, which was considered synonymous with the creation of value, a definition clearly rooted in the producerist sensibilities of the agrarian household. In this order of things, making clothing was an appropriation of the value already manifest in the production of cloth. It was, at best, a commercial elaboration.[6]

Then, in 1850, that commercial elaboration became the crux of industrial activity: clothing not only appeared in official statistics for the first time, but suddenly constituted one of the country's largest industries. This happened because Congress had instructed census marshals that year to record "the name of each corporation, company, or individual producing articles to the annual value of $500." The result was at once a more perfunctory and a far more exhaustive list of commodities than had ever before been compiled. It redefined manufacturing to mean no longer the physical transformation of nature, ex nihilo, but the manufacture of surplus values, for no one was going to be "producing articles to the annual value of $500" without intending to keep some of it for himself. The ambitious New York City merchant tailor George P. Fox, who opened a branch store in San Francisco in the 1850s, thus revised economic thinking: "Until the goods of the [cloth importer] have passed through the [tailor's] hands, their value is in a dormant state, and they contribute nothing to the embellishment or the utility of life." The official record of industrialization now became a business document. It reflected an entrepreneurial logic rather than a productive one, an industrial revolution driven by the pecuniary appetites of thousands of small firms and propriatary shops making up what they hoped would sell. Material activity had little meaning anymore outside the market, signaling the birth of a commodity system that gave clothing a wholly new value.[7]

- - - - -

If the clothing industry had an actual birth, it was in the emporiums and warehouses that appeared in New York and in other American seaboard entrepôts after the end of the War of 1812 and the reopening of European trade in 1815. Some of these businesses were run by tailors. Others were not. All responded to the unprecedented quantities and the low cost of cloths being dumped by British firms in the United States that allowed one to aggressively proffer the widest range of "fashionable apparel" for a varied clientele of "gentlemen." James Burk opened a store on still largely residential Wall Street in 1821, where he sold made-to-measure garments that featured the freshest imports: London cassimeres, William Hirst's superior blues and blacks, Sheppard's velvet cloths, real Tartain plaids, elegant Valencia vestings. Burk, a prolific copywriter, excitedly updated his inventory of fabrics in prolix and precise advertisements regularly placed in the *Evening Post*. There he listed the latest brand names, fabrics, and colors arriving from Liverpool, all of which he promised to make up "in the first style," appealing to the good taste of the self-consciously fashionable while offering them real savings of "$33\frac{1}{3}$ per cent on the amount of every six months clothing."[8]

Burk's store was no tailoring shop. Burk was not a craftsman selling his own skilled labor and hoping that the resulting income, less trade expenses, would leave a sufficient margin to support his household. A different ethos of accumulation informed his actions, guided by the anticipation of what would sell tomorrow rather than by what was available today. (In the twentieth century this behavior came to be called "risk taking.") The goods were now a means of generating capital rather than vice versa, and clothing was simply a current, and currently convenient, means for Burk to do so. He had formerly worked as an accountant and a commission merchant before this latest career

No. 1.—PRINCIPAL MANUFACTURES—Continued.

States and Territories.	Number of establishments.	CLOTHIERS AND TAILORS.					
		Capital.	Cost of raw material.	Male hands.	Female hands.	Cost of labor.	Value of product.
Alabama	19	$59,700	$49,800	72	21	$39,060	$107,050
Arkansas............	1	100	100	2	....	480	600
California............	....	....	....	....	....	....	....
Connecticut	155	361,515	900,885	428	3,766	473,556	1,519,433
Delaware.............	16	33,400	45,405	39	111	24,924	83,602
District of Columbia ..	45	82,250	163,031	160	244	97,656	297,900
Florida	1	300	400	4	....	960	1,600
Georgia	12	11,850	29,000	43	25	23,004	75,500
Illinois	61	162,550	201,276	351	249	132,432	441,897
Indiana	74	100,585	153,951	238	396	116,652	327,599
Iowa................	5	2,150	6,000	7	2	2,088	8,500
Kentucky............	131	353,530	563,224	787	781	325,428	1,058,877
Louisiana	75	114,300	128,675	163	194	125,136	339,830
Maine...............	93	173,650	555,075	232	1,469	232,344	917,311
Maryland............	267	632,340	1,339,781	1,641	3,689	855,876	2,694,377
Massachusetts........	333	1,758,155	4,763,470	3,626	10,702	2,799,480	8,757,156
Michigan............	33	71,710	97,628	191	176	78,024	212,300
Mississippi..........	9	19,980	14,570	23	5	11,700	32,550
Missouri.......	147	198,310	302,463	659	303	256,536	750,791
New Hampshire	85	134,100	358,149	185	721	174,624	616,233
New Jersey	137	646,910	1,568,787	1,360	3,545	679,104	2,484,594
New York............	976	4,011,622	8,603,388	16,148	24,923	5,067,036	16,007,534
North Carolina	22	34,930	37,551	79	15	25,128	76,144
Ohio	316	523,134	1,452,054	2,100	2,401	785,100	2,765,232
Pennsylvania	930	2,544,656	3,572,298	5,122	6,173	2,104,236	6,988,498
Rhode Island.........	22	79,750	189,252	255	577	166,944	422,372
South Carolina	23	25,460	24,600	68	14	16,896	60,075
Tennessee	76	69,742	115,033	227	29	73,776	241,356
Texas...............	....	....	....	....	....	....	....
Vermont	33	47,395	50,515	68	247	55,548	124,560
Virginia	138	186,227	303,078	512	590	209,856	615,857
Wisconsin	41	65,060	137,319	256	132	76,104	272,381
Minnesota............	....	....	....	....	....	....	....
New Mexico..........	2	3,800	3,500	5	....	2,652	10,000
Oregon..............	....	....	....	....	....	....	....
Utah	....	....	....	....	....	....	....
Total	4,278	12,509,161	25,730,258	35,051	61,500	15,032,340	48,311,709

By including any business "producing articles to the annual value of $500," the 1850 federal census effectively redefined industry to mean the making of profits rather than of things. As a result, clothing production appeared for the first time in the nation's official economic statistics. The clothing business, in fact, proved to be an industrial giant.

move, which began in his native Philadelphia in 1817. By the end of 1822 Burk opened a third clothing store, a mile or so up Manhattan in the growing village of Greenwich. Moving goods between his three stores facilitated an economy of scale that helped Burk realize his incessant exhortations to the public for "economy in clothing." At the same time, Burk's enterprise did not at all resemble the low-end "slops" shop, in which merchants with no artisanal pretensions sold cheap garments to a clientele of mechanics, sailors, itinerants, and other urban rabble. The unabashed commercialism of these "salesmen," as slops dealers were professionally known, was the traditional antipode of skilled tailoring. In Burk's case, however, that opposition made little sense.[9]

Burk's was not the only type of response to new business opportunities presented by British dumping. Samuel Whitmarsh—who, unlike Burk, was a tailor—opened an establishment on Broadway in these years where he insistently promoted "genteel . . . ready-mades," in contrast to Burk's decision to devote his store principally to the "Measure Business." Whitmarsh retained the traditional appellation of draper and tailor but called his business an "original." He promised visitors the standard rich assortment of cloths, "constantly on hand." But these would already be made up into garments. And instead of Burk's emphasis on economy, Whitmarsh offered an admixture of gentility and convenience. His store faced the City Hotel, a favorite meeting place for city residents and tourists located at the halfway point along Broadway's fashionable promenade. There they could buy complete suits available "at a moment's notice" and shop in spacious apartments expressly fitted to appeal to fashionable sensibilities. By the end of the decade Whitmarsh also carried a wide assortment of cravats, handkerchiefs, hosiery, suspenders, collars, undervests, and drawers—all in all "a splendid collection of Goods in his line," that line now being distinctly men's wear.[10]

A few blocks below Whitmarsh, also on Broadway, John Williams operated a Gentlemen's Fashionable Wearing Apparel Warehouse that he opened in 1816. Thanks to the full-page illustrated advertisement he ran for several years in the city's annual directory, Williams has allowed us a glimpse inside the store. His oversized entrance fronted the avenue's broad walk, a backdrop to refined male strollers in no hurry to get anywhere. Light floods inside, and we espy someone busy at work with his shears at the front of the shop. Is it John Williams? Perhaps. But Williams called himself a clothier, not a tailor, and so underscored his role as a seller rather than maker of clothes. At the same time, the facade of his Apparel Warehouse was dominated by a large window, not for display—finished garments advertising the store to passersby hung outside on the door frame—but to provide the illumination essential for sewing. Was Williams a tailor or clothier, a manufacturer or merchant? Or was such a distinction an artisanal artifact, no longer relevant in an expanding and increasingly variegated market?[11]

Another clothier, Henry Brooks, opened a store at the corner of Catharine and Cherry Streets in 1818, across from one of New York's busiest public markets and two blocks away from the bustling East River wharves. This was the city's old slops district. "What a tide passed through that narrow street in those days hurrying to the horseboats, hurrying to market, hurrying to the shops." It was an ideal retail site. Indeed, Brooks had been selling groceries at the same address several years earlier. When the War of 1812 interrupted his provisioning trade he retired to an upstate farm in Rye. With peace, however, Henry decided to return to business, though not to the grocery trade. He joined a younger brother, David, in the latter's clothing store on Cherry Street. In 1817 the two dissolved their partnership, but both stayed in the trade, with Henry moving a few blocks down Cherry, to the corner of Catharine Street, across from Henry Robinson's well-known clothing store. A year later Henry bought the building for the not inconsiderable sum of $15,250. In 1825 he opened a second store two blocks away, near James Slip, on the water. By then the business on Catharine Street was averaging sales of almost $50,000 per year. Unlike Burk and Whitmarsh, Brooks specialized in the pea coats, monkey jackets, duck trousers, and smocks made from cheap cotton and mixed cloths that were identified with the city's less genteel elements. Whereas in 1819 "extraordinary cheap" coats in the vicinity of Broadway were still being sold at prices ranging from $22 to $32, for instance, most of the coats Henry Brooks sold in these years cost less than $15. Nevertheless, he was taking advantage of the same new business opportunities as the more refined retailers in other parts of town.[12]

Burk, Whitmarsh, Williams, and Brooks each presented a distinct itinerary of entrepreneurial clothing success. Burk was a nontailor making clothing to measure. Whitmarsh was a tailor selling ready-made garments. Williams was a tailor manufacturing clothing to measure. And Brooks was a nontailor making ready-mades. All, however, were in the same business. What drove their enterprise was later described in an apocryphal story concerning A. T. Stewart, by then New York City's most famous retail merchant. One day in the early twenties, soon after opening his first store on Broadway, Stewart had turned for help to a veteran merchant. "A lady came into my store and asked me to show her some hose," he explained to his senior. "I did not know what the goods were, and I told her I did not keep the article. What did she

John Williams's clothing store at 212 Broadway, New York, in 1816. It was
unclear whether Williams was actually a clothier or a tailor, a merchant or a
manufacturer, or whether such distinctions had any meaning in the fluid
conditions of the industrializing market. (Courtesy of the Collection of the
New-York Historical Society, neg. 75520)

want?" Stewart, who had arrived from Scotland a few years earlier, was just
one of innumerable new men who now saw their chance to succeed in business
by buying cheap and selling at small margins. It clearly mattered far less to
them precisely what they were selling.[13]

Auction sales became the primary means of marketing the influx of English
cloth imports after 1817, the result of a decision by New York State to regulate the auction system in order to generate the revenue necessary to build
the Erie Canal. Once built, the canal then brought provincial merchants to
the metropolis in search of bargains at the very auctions that had financed
the canal to begin with, one of those tautologies characteristic of the emerging industrial market.[14] Auctions also became the focus of rabid controversy.
They were opposed by an unlikely alliance of veteran merchant houses nervous about losing their hold over importing, champions of American industrialization who dreaded the effect of so many cheap imports on domestic
manufacturing, and artisan mechanics who feared for their livelihood—all of

whom expressed their opposition in the nostalgic terms of "the mutual confidence and courtesy that subsisted in our better days." Now, they complained, business was characterized by fictitious bidding, false news, rigged markets, evasion of duties, and dishonest sales reports. There was a growing sense that too many taboos were being broken with impunity. Upstart merchants aggressively advertised in the "new papers" and exhibited none of the old mercantile qualms regarding commercial limits. They were impelled onward, as a visitor to New York observed in 1825, "by the fear of losing something that another man as quickly bestirs himself to acquire." In the fall of 1826, for instance, the market was flooded with English blue cloths, "beautiful to the eye," which turned reddish brown after a few days exposure to the air. It was representative of the general state of things, protested *Niles' Weekly Register*, a situation that victimized American tailors who were then "compelled to take back the clothes made of these goods, or disoblige and lose their customers."[15]

But there were obvious advantages here for makers of clothing. Half the fabrics reaching New York in these years sold at auction below wholesale rates. What's more, small lots were regularly available. Many were cottons, or cotton mixed with more expensive wool, such as the cassimere that was a staple of James Burk's business, a cheaper but respectable choice for one's coat and vest that helped make Burk's "experiment" in lowering the price of fashionable clothing possible. For that matter, the price of all-woolen cloth dropped throughout the decade, auctions remaining the cheapest way to acquire those fabrics as well.[16]

Such developments opened up new opportunities in a clothing trade that had evidenced considerable commercial ambition already in the previous century, when master tailors began to sell cloths in addition to their artisanal skills. That earlier business expansion had generated a commercial neologism—"merchant tailor"—who, by including the raw materials of his artisanship in his trade, succeeded in broadening his retail opportunities and exercising better control over his production schedules. Now, as commerce continued to expand and new markets beckoned, a New York journeyman tailor actually accused his employers in 1819 of being motivated by the sole objective of "accumulating money." Such avarice blinded them to the traditional rules of their craft, the journeyman complained, to the point where merchant tailors no longer hesitated in hiring women—to whom they paid a far lower wage—to execute a large portion of the sewing. By so doing, employers were able to shift labor from a fixed to a variable cost. Similar attacks on the "bastardization" of the craft were to be heard from the other side of the political and social spectrum as well. Charles Haswell, for instance, later recalled that it was during the 1820s that tailors' search for profits had effectively annulled the sartorial divide between gentlemen, whose garments were individually fitted, and the less genteel orders, whom he remembered as previously having dressed in slops.[17]

A new type of clothing entrepreneur now appeared on the economic stage, equally active in a second market, in addition to that of cloth: the buying and selling of labor. Thus, even when the garments were still personally measured for a specific customer, such as at Burk's store, that customer effectively purchased them from a middleman—whether he called himself a tailor or clothier—who mediated not only between the client and the purchase of the cloth but between the client and the terms of (others') garment making as well. This turned the product into a set of abstract inputs, to be properly—that is, profitably—manipulated. Balancing the cloth and labor markets so that they would yield the greatest return became the essence of clothing production. The clothier bargained with all the pertinent agents, those who were necessary for executing a given kind of work. He contracted to provide them a certain income and then appropriated the difference between the total cost of these contracts and the revenue from production. This made him a "windfall absorber" of the economic system. But he was also a new kind of "capitalist"—no passive investor of funds but the active coordinator of production. And thus the commercially ambitious divorced themselves from their craft in order to run their clothing businesses. By the early thirties the "draper and tailor" Samuel Whitmarsh was a busy wholesaler. Meanwhile, nontailors like James Burk could only dress the economic and fashionable gentleman as long as he hired "as good cutters as any in America."[18]

As Burk intimated, the industrialization of clothing was no local event. For all his self-professed devotion to the "Measure Business," in fact, Burk courted "Southern merchants and dealers in ready made clothing" by proferring at wholesale prices whatever quantity of previously made-up dress coats, frock coats, pantaloons, and vests they might require.[19] This far-flung clientelle constituted a third market, besides the markets in cloth and labor, integral to the industrialization of clothing. It came into existence as the trip upstream from New Orleans to St. Louis was reduced from three months to ten days by the steamboat, or, as the *Western Monthly Review* declared in 1827, when "a little Paris, a section of Broadway, or a slice of Philadelphia" began to reach "the very doors of our cabins." Thus it was that, upon reaching the frontier during his grand tour of America in 1842, Charles Dickens woke early one morning to ride out of St. Louis through swamp and bush for a glimpse of the proverbial prairie, the very edge of Western civilization. Along the way his riding party passed an abandoned wagon lodged in a miasma of mud and muck. On its side was printed the motto "Merchant Tailor." Dickens thought it highly ironic to meet with such modern commercial ambition in this forlorn landscape of wretched cabins and isolated villages. It was a distinctly American incongruity he left unexplained, if it was explainable at all.[20]

But the Mississippi and Ohio valleys were filling up with clothing businesses: Kennedy Foster's store across from Allen's Hotel in Louisville, John Torode's establishment on Main Street in Pittsburgh, James Waddell's "New, Cheap & Fashionable" clothing house in St. Louis, and R. Lusk's Emporium of Fashion on the south side of Nashville's city square, opposite Benson, Hunt & Co.'s clothing store situated on the north side. All were representative of hundreds of others, supplied directly from the east or through New Orleans, which had become the second-busiest port in the country in the 1820s as well as integral to New York's emergence as the busiest, and where by the early 1830s there were more than a hundred stores exclusively devoted to men's clothing. Indeed, while in 1822 New Orleans city boosters had rhetorically celebrated the four thousand miles of inland navigation connecting their city to New York in 1822 as "evidently intended to answer some wise purpose, as nature never exerts herself in vain," it was clothiers who now gave that putative "nature" its practical expression.[21]

Now, before leaving the city to the provinces, the cloths, or dry-goods, would be turned into garments. The added costs of the extra transaction were saved by manufacturers who marketed the clothing themselves, either to their own far-flung stores or to the legions of country merchants who travelled to the metropolis each year to restock. That vertical integration bypassed established dry goods jobbers and explains the early specialization of the men's clothing business, an innovation which satisfied traditional business reliance on a few trusted partners while also facilitating more modern desiderata of extended control, scales of economy, and efficiency. In such a specialized trade the provincial retailer could purchase in larger quantities. With fewer types of goods to attend, he was better positioned to discover cheaper sources of supply and to become an expert in his "line." And by buying and selling to greater advantage he undercut the retailing standard of old, the general store. Edwin Freedley, best-selling publicist of industrial progress, explained the logic: "Country merchants . . . have found that the sale of clothing can be effected with less trouble than piece goods [lengths of cloth], and without the serious drawback of remnants—that there is less competition—[and] that their daily receipts of cash are thereby increased."[22]

The cotton entrepôt of Augusta, Georgia, was illustrative of the national trend. A trading junction for a wide swath of the Georgia-Carolina black

A continental clothing market: the United States in 1860.

belt, Augusta sat at the head of steam navigation on the Savannah River. In exchange for the raw cotton sent out of the region, packets traveling up and down the Eastern seaboard regularly refilled the town's warehouses with manufactures, a significant portion of which was men's clothing.[23] That was evident to any visitor strolling down Broad Street in the mid-1830s, where a man could satisfy his sartorial needs at E. D. Cooke's newly relocated clothing store at no. 197 or at Price and Mallery's Clothing Emporium at no. 258, between the Globe and United States Hotels. If the inventories there were lacking, it was possible to continue down the street, to Francis Cooke's clothing house, or up the street, to Samuel Lane's men's-wear establishment. Still further, B. B. Kirtland & Co. offered an equally wide selection of garments right next door to Price and Mallery. Until 1834 one could also have visited Joseph Moss's store, at 305 Broad, but Moss had succumbed to the intense local competition. He closed up shop before his lease ran out, sold off his stock at reduced prices, and returned to his New York Fashionable Clothing Ware-House in Charleston. However, Mr. D'Lyon Thorp's "old and long-known establishment" was still doing business between Kirtland's and Moss's stores. Messrs. V. Durand & Co. were also to be found on Broad Street, next to the post office. The largest clothing inventory in town was not located on Broad Street at all. This was the store of Clarke & Holland, who regularly filled a whole column of advertising space in the *Augusta Chronicle and Sentinel* and ostentatiously declared the advertisement to be but a "partial list" of goods available for sale. But perhaps the most telling evidence for the clothing business's importance in Augusta's economic life was the fact that both Francis Cooke and B. B. Kirtland were elected city aldermen in 1837.[24]

Volume and variety were the sine qua non of business success in "a fluctuating market such as Augusta." As James Edney assured Francis Cooke in 1836, after having been sent by the latter to New York to oversee manufacturing for Cooke's clothing store, "I do not intend that you shall be behind any other shop in your market." A decade earlier Augusta clothier William Hills was still announcing that his "first quality clothing" was priced so low because it had been made the previous summer. By the thirties no such admissions were forthcoming, and Augusta's retail competition had become keen. Francis Cooke, for instance, had to quickly purchase an extra fifty or sixty coats in New York at the height of the season in October 1835, "even if we made nothing on them," in order to satisfy local demand.[25]

Advertisements boasted of new goods being received from the North every day, which might not have been much of an exaggeration. Francis Cooke regularly wrote to James Edney in New York to apprise him of local business developments and to request that he make up favorite styles and colors, often delineating price ranges and specific sizes. Edney, his workforce in place and under contract for the season uptown on Grand Street, would then search the city for the desired fabric, always checking the auction houses for bargains. The garments were ready by week's end, loaded into trunks, and sent south by steam or sail on packets that left New York every day for Charleston. From there they were shipped the nine hours by rail to Augusta, arriving in Cooke's store just a few days after leaving Edney's shop. Thus, within two to three weeks' time, Cooke could fill his shelves with clothing made up in New York to specifications for his Georgian clientele.[26]

Inventories were "manufactured . . . expressly for the Augusta market," which included a broad social and geographic range of provincial burghers and up-country farmers buying clothing for work or for their Sunday best. In the winter of 1837 E. D. Cooke—no relation to Francis—advertised both fine and common dress and frock coats in over ten different colors in the *Chronicle*. He also had a selection of overcoats made from mohair yarns, or from a camblet weave of German goat's hair, or a heavy, coarse Petersham woolen associated with the pilot coats worn by seamen and also by hunters. His stock of vests likewise contained a seemingly endless permutation of colors, yarns, weaves, and cuts, ranging from valentia, which imitated silk, to "common" blue and black cloths. Clarke & Holland offered the same cornucopia. True, they had no mohair goods in stock in January; Cooke apparently cornered the local market in mohair that winter. But the business principle was the same: figured silks and satins, superfine cassimeres, and merino woolens alongside negro cloth, kerseys, and cheap satinets. Up in New York, Edney simultaneously devoted his manufacturing energies to making up and shipping in the same week overcoats of expensive "drab" wool—to sell for "no less than $25"—and an assortment of "negroe" pants and vests, though of a "finer" grade. Indeed, the low end of the provincial market appears to have been as stylistically variegated as the upper reaches.[27]

Augusta lay on the Federal Road, a byway for families from the Georgia-Carolina piedmont migrating west, and the city's clothing merchants actively sought to extend their market as widely as possible. Steamboats regularly plied the Savannah River, and daily stages ran southeast to Savannah, northwest to Athens, southwest to Milledgeville and Macon, and northeast to Columbia, South Carolina, and, less frequently, to Greensboro and Fayetteville in North Carolina and to Chattanooga, Tennessee. The rail connection to Charleston was, for a passing moment, the longest railroad in the world, and in 1833 the Georgia Railway Company received its charter and began to build new roads connecting Augusta to the center of the state and from there to the Tennessee River and Knoxville. E. D. Cooke collected debts in Greene County, a hundred miles to the west, and Paulding County, which was all the way across the state on the Alabama border. Augusta clothiers also sold wholesale to general stores further inland as the latter began to keep several dozen men's garments on hand in addition to the more customary yards of uncut fabrics.[28]

The only ones not included in this expanding market were the bulk of the region's slaves, which comes as a surprise since the two million or so chattel field hands in the Southern states would seem a natural mass market for cheap, standardized wear. Most stores carried "Negro Clothing." But larger plantations often undertook their own cutting and sewing of the garments they issued seasonally to their slaves, buying the cloth directly from the North through their factors. Few produced their own cloth, since that required a considerable investment that would divert resources from the production of staple goods. Clothing, however, was easy to make, and the work could be done by pregnant or older slaves, under the supervision of the plantation mistress. The result was unfitted garments of the coarsest fabrics cut in two or three standard sizes, at best. This was what was universally recognized as the dress "crop negroes usually wear."[29] For that matter, the Northern textile mills themselves could send out their cloth to local householders to sew into coarse, unfitted garments for a modest extra cost. Such, for instance, was the practice of the Peace Dale Mill of the J. P. and R. G. Hazard Company in Rhode Island. The price was thus kept to a minimum, and no city-based clothing manufacturer could possibly compete. The same production process was occasionally used by the army, too, when it contracted for cloth for its enlisted men's uniforms. Both systems were certainly designed to mass-produce, though not in the same way that drove the commercial city trade.[30]

Meanwhile, Edney did his best to deliver Francis Cooke the fashionable goods the latter demanded—garments made of a popular cloth called honeycomb for the summer season, new vest patterns, extra pocket flaps, alterations in the extant styles of pantaloons, "$1.62 vests" and "$4 or $5 pants," or "plain buff valencias." Writing to Cooke, Edney declared that "I have been in intense anxiety to know what to buy for the spring trade, to know what articles suited, what articles did not suit, what was most wanted, what remained most on hand, sizes, quality, etc."[31] Production, in other words, seemed market-driven, attuned to demonstrated consumer preference and closely managed by the retailer in the best position to gauge popular tastes. Indeed, all the retail minutiae—the incessant advertisements for hundreds of varieties of coats, jackets, vests, pantaloons, and cloaks, not to mention shirts, drawers, collars, bosoms, hosiery, gloves, umbrellas, suspenders, cravats, handkerchiefs, hats, and shoes, "&c. &c. &c."—were an ode to abundance, a provincial "culture of consumption" manifest in Augusta and countless other towns, large and small. They represented the industrial transition to a world of plenty, where goods were not only desirable but attainable. What most impressed the public in these early years of industrialization was not the novel mechanized production processes anyway, but the unprecedented quantities of goods that resulted. This appeal to consuming sensibilities did not always make straightforward business sense, however. Edney complained about the wide range of goods Cooke requested for the store, specifically boys' clothing and women's cloaks (cloaks being the only women's garments that Edney made and that Cooke sold). There was an ongoing tug of war between retailer and manufacturer over such items. For Edney, they were an unwelcome diversion from the real business at hand—men's wear. They forced him into the market for small quantities of extra fabrics and patterns, which cost him time, effort, and money. For this reason, Cooke could not have made much of a profit on them. But Cooke knew they had a merchandising value not to be measured by any itemized bottom line. A range of goods brought customers into the store. Certainly, all his competitors offered the same for sale. And in the bustling retail market of the South, in which Cooke's markups ranged from 15 to 50 percent at best, a high turnover of goods was necessary to finance production that, in turn, was premised on a steady turnover. After all, Cooke had to finance Edney's salary and the much higher one paid to Edney's foreman-cutter, together with tailors' wages, rent, coal for heating, and the occasional emergency purchase of finished goods—sums that reached several hundreds of dollars a week during the production season—from his weekly sales in Augusta.[32]

But the plethora of goods obscured the other side of the equation, namely, that production exigencies did sharply delimit the nature of the commodities reaching market. Despite appearances, the seemingly limitless variety of fabrics was not necessarily a response to popular demand as much as an answer to the manufacturers' own production requirements. Mills would sometimes make a new fabric because it offered the most profitable use for their machines that year. One wonders, in any case, whether all those verbose clothing advertisements were meant to be read literally, item for item, or whether their real intent was to create a general aura of plenty, constituting an aesthetic of "capitalist realism."[33] Francis Cooke, for instance, eventually received "fancy drilling" instead of the honeycomb he asked for because the latter could not be had in New York. Edney found no substitute at all for the plain buff valencia; Cooke simply had to do without. In the fall of 1835 common grades of woolens became very expensive. Because the cost could not be passed along to customers looking for modestly priced goods, Edney substituted cheaper satinets for them. Presumably they found a market. But when satinets became scarce the next year, Edney simply made up no clothes in this class at all, even though they were a retailing staple. The situation provoked a crisis in his relationship with Cooke. Cooke demanded that Edney use cheaper labor in order to compensate for the higher cloth prices. Edney demurred. The result, he insisted, would only be "miserable trash . . . a hard bargain at nothing." Edney held his own, and Cooke was forced to acquiesce, though he remained unconvinced. Edney in fact suspected that his employment might soon be at an end.[34]

The differences between Cooke the merchant and Edney the manufacturer were based on the fact that the clothing business was still largely dependent on its cloth supply. Savings on labor costs, which had been a key factor in the business's early rise, were pulled taut. A skilled workforce was essential, and perhaps increasingly so as the growth of the market for fine clothing increased the number of fastidious customers. Cloth, on the other hand, was a highly fickle affair. It constituted not only the single largest expense by far for clothing merchants but the least predictable one at that. During the early

1830s the price of such domestic staples as flannel and "twill'd cloth," an important part of Edney's purchases, fluctuated by as much as 40 percent.[35] During the winter of 1837–38 Cooke made repeated requests of Edney to send him clothing made of mohair, camblet, "blanket," and green, brown, and black cloth, but he never received the goods, as Edney could not get hold of the fabrics. This was not because they were nowhere to be gotten. Edney's problem arose from Cooke's insistence on dealing with a single cloth supplier, Staples & Clarke, with whom he had a personal relationship. Edney protested that widening the circle of suppliers was essential for their business: the only way to make up for the inelasticity of labor costs was to enhance their ability to acquire the fabrics they wanted when they wanted them, and to do so on more competitive terms, namely, at lower prices or on longer credit arrangements. Cooke should have been the first to accept this reasoning. Who better knew the importance to retail success of a varied selection of goods? But Cooke was loath to complicate his exclusive relationship with Staples & Clarke, one of the new breed of dry-goods firms that specialized in the men's clothing trade. The firm sold tens of thousands of dollars' worth of cloths each season to Cooke, which he paid for with his personal notes on six months' time. The cloth supplier, in other words, was not just the source of the all-important raw material but of the no less indispensable long-term credit. Staples & Clarke consequently enjoyed great leverage over Cooke's business and even over his day-to-day operations. Mr. Clarke would travel to Augusta himself and observe business firsthand, apprising Edney upon his return to New York of what and what not to make up, advice that Edney suspected was informed more by Clarke's than by Cooke's interests. But there was little he could do. "You have placed me in your employ and have put both the employer and the employed in the grip and wholly at the will and entire disposal of Mr. Clarke." In the end, both employer and employee, Cooke and Edney, stood their ground. Neither cheaper labor nor cheaper fabrics were used to solve the conundrum, but the business prospered anyway. And Edney eventually learned an important lesson. When the high-flying economy crashed in 1837, it was Cooke's reputation as a careful and loyal borrower that allowed him to survive the panic and subsequent depression by opening accounts with other cloth suppliers, who knew they could trust him with their money during such stringent times.[36]

Cooke and Edney were everymen. Their clothing business was pursued in the same fashion all over the country, not only in Augusta but in Milledgeville and Macon, Tuscaloosa and Vicksburg, Dubuque, Peru, and St. Louis. As such, the industry's growth paralleled the integration of a national market, of "at least eight millions of white males over fifteen years old." By 1850 one of every two Americans lived in what had been unsettled wilderness half a century earlier. These pioneers never engaged in the extensive household production so characteristic of the preindustrial colonial era. Pulling flax to make their linens, carding and spinning the wool they sheared off their sheep's backs, not to mention the countless other stages in the "domestic manufacture" of cloths—all were largely unknown to nineteenth-century settlers, who relied, rather, on the cohering market to make their new life out west a better one. The frontier, in other words, might have served as an escape from the oppressions of waged existence in factory towns and Eastern cities, but it was certainly no escape from the market itself. The interested observations of *Hunt's Merchant's Magazine* in 1840 regarding the farmer "becoming quite as dependent for clothes upon the manufacturer, as the manufacturer is dependent for food upon the farmer" were not simply wishful thinking. "Whether one turned dried apples into nails, or salted hams into lumber, or bushels of wheat into bolts of printed cotton, the net effect was to link West with East, rural with urban, farm with factory," as the historian William Cronon has so effectively demonstrated.[37]

Hunt's recognized the revolutionary nature of this new industrial order. "Now, abundant harvests, barns bursting with grain, herds of fat cattle and fatter hogs, will not make a farmer prosperous," it observed in the same 1840 essay. A healthy exchange economy was required before the farmer could realize the value of his labor and the resulting fruits of the earth. This is when, in fact, the market was "transformed from something acted upon to something acting," in the words of the historian Winifred Rothenberg. Only an extensive system of exchange could convert the farmer's labor into the "great number of articles which habit has made essential to his comfort." America, *Hunt's* consequently declared, had become a "nation of shopkeepers."[38]

Tocqueville noted the cultural significance of such commercial achievements. "The man you left in New York you find again in almost impenetrable solitudes: same clothes, same attitude, same language, same habits, same pleasures." Thus, when a "great Ball" was held in Velasco, Texas, during the 1838 racing season, with confectionery and ornaments shipped from New Orleans, the gentlemen all wore clothes "brought from New York ready made and of the newest fashions." Clothiers created a ready-made product because it matched the exigencies of a far-flung, impersonal exchange system. Cloth marketed in the form of clothing allowed them to make provincial profits from city credit and labor. This not only lowered the price of apparel. It also ensured that the style and make would be the most recent "and therefore most

Although Robert Fulton developed his steamship on New York's Hudson River, he knew that its future lay on the Mississippi, where it would bring "a little Paris, a section of Broadway, or a slice of Philadelphia" to "the very doors of our cabins." (*Launch of the Steamship Frigate Fulton*, by Benjamin Tanner; from the Eno Collection, Miriam and Ira D. Wallach Division of Art, Prints and Photographs, The New York Public Library, Astor, Lenox and Tilden Foundations)

desirable." Indeed, Georgian fashions were informed by a bevy of metropolitan promoters of modern male taste. The *Spirit of the Times and Life in New-York*, the *New-York Mirror*, the *Knickerbocker*, the *Salmagundi*, and *Gentleman's Vade Mecum* all kept subscription agents throughout the state and all were regularly available in Augusta. Price and Mallery accordingly advertised an Augusta inventory that could "not fail to suit the tastes of the most fashionable or fastidious," selected as it was "by one of our firm now in New York." Francis Cooke, who upbraided James Edney for sending him "old fashioned pants" during the spring season of 1835, was clearly mediating an exchange of cultural goods as much as the latest style of pantaloons. Commercial and cultural success, as such, were united.[39]

The South emerges here as an important force in industrializing America. In fact, all the retail action in Augusta would seem to belie both contemporary antislavery rhetoric about Southern homespun backwardness and historians' more recent depictions of slavery's self-sufficient plantations and up-country moral economies. The clothing industry's marked success in the Southern market, in other words, raises questions about just how peripheral a patriarchal slave society was to capitalist revolution, to its new habits of consumption and new assumptions about material plenty. But in fact the intensive buying and selling of clothing in Augusta and elsewhere throughout the region reveals that the South was indeed "in but not of the capitalist world." For while its staple exports to the global economy allowed the South to import goods and credit at substantial levels, the fact remains that Cooke had to send Edney north in order to actually produce the goods, that is, to tap into a variegated and accessible pool of labor and an extensive wholesale cloth market, as well as into the day-to-day cash and credit infrastructure essential to a dynamic manufacturing economy. In this respect, slavery did indeed maintain a "near-colonial dependency" on the industrializing North, as its champions all but conceded when they compared their Southern cause to the homespun campaign of eighteenth-century agrarian colonies against the British empire.[40]

And so the history of clothing, like American capitalism in general, remains a largely "Northern story." This was nowhere more clearly manifested than in the frenzied dimensions of New York City's clothing production. Each day during the fall manufacturing season of 1835 the *New York Sun* showed how effectively the penny press served the industrial revolution by carrying employment notices advertising clothing work for thousands.[41] The *Herald* and the *Transcript* likewise printed scores of announcements each fall and spring promising "constant employment and good wages" for city needleworkers. In June 1836 Young & Van Eps sought four hundred sewers to make up clothing "in the best manner." A month later they were ready to invite clothing dealers from the South and the West to examine their "very large stock . . . in the latest fashion" and discuss credit arrangements. Hobby, Husted & Co. needed an extra three hundred tailors and five hundred tailoresses, in addition to six cutters "accustomed to southern work," to fill their wholesale orders that same spring. The cutters were to report to the firm's new store on Liberty Street, in the heart of the business district, where they had recently moved from the old slops district, William Hobby also for the first time separating his residence from his business. The tailors and tailoresses were sent a mile and a half uptown to just above Grand Street, not far from where Edney was busy manufacturing for Francis Cooke. There they received precut bundles of fabric and trimmings (buttons and such) in exchange for a cash deposit, taking the goods home or to rented work spaces to sew and thus saving employers the prohibitive expense of providing a workplace in the city. Two weeks before Hobby, Husted's call for eight hundred hands, twelve hundred "plain sewers" were immediately required at the corner of Chrystie and Stanton Streets, a few blocks away. Similar operations were to be found on adjoining Canal Street and on Grand Street, Division Street, and Madison Street. On Stanton Street, in addition to eight hundred good plain sewers, another firm required one hundred additional "girls . . . to do fancy work in the house." But the business was not restricted to a specific neighborhood. Nor was production confined to the city. In the mid-thirties, it was later recalled, every country village within a hundred miles of New York "became as busy as a beehive" with men and women sewing for the city's clothing houses.[42]

The scale of business is best grasped by looking again at James Edney's relatively modest operations in the mid-1830s. Having just arrived from Augusta in the late spring of 1835, new to both the city and the trade, Edney bought $20,000 worth of fabrics and paid $4,600 more in wages and rent to make them up. A year later, getting an earlier jump on production than he had in 1835, Edney purchased $50,000 worth of cloths between August and January. His volume had thus grown 150 percent from one year to the next. He employed nearly a hundred tailors to sew the cloth into garments. These were the not insignificant sums required to stock a single clothing store—just one of many—in Augusta, Georgia, for a single shopping season in 1836.[43]

The large wholesale businesses, of course, such as Frederick Conant's, who was a busy presence in almost every Southern state, manufactured for more than one store. They were engaged, in a way that Edney was not, in industrial production for an anonymous market. They had to think about advertising strategies, creative credit arrangements with buyers, and the risks inherent in any time lag between the commitment to produce (the purchase of the cloth) and the product's arrival to market, particularly in a market influenced by fashion. But while all these risks were compounded by the ambitious size of operation, volume also helped to ameliorate them.

Edney, for instance, could not compete with the wholesale prices of certain middle-range goods made of fabrics bought long beforehand, at auctions, and sewed with labor hired in the off-season when skilled hands were more available and less expensive. This strategy also allowed the large firms to provide the provincial market more economically with the wide variety of clothing it demanded, from the coarsest apparel to garments of the most expensive fabrics and cuts. Hobby, Husted's advertising motto encapsulated the business strategy: "Wearing apparel in great variety, adapted to all seasons and climates, and suited to every taste and condition." Young & Van Eps gave the slogan practical expression, listing a range of coats for sale from $5.00 to $25.00, pants from 69 cents to $11.00, and vests from 40 cents to $7.50. This made them suppliers of last resort for the whole trade, selling to other

Employment notices from the *New York Sun*, September 11, 1835. The penny press was one of the great democratic innovations of the industrial age. As such, it was integral to another great innovation: the city's anonymous labor market. (Courtesy of the Collection of the New-York Historical Society, neg. 75521) city clothiers who for one reason or another—usually an inability to acquire a certain fabric—couldn't manufacture the goods they needed. Edney, for instance, went to F. J. Conant's in early October 1836 looking for a mixed lot of long overcoats, which Cooke was anxious to have and which Edney would not have time to manufacture himself. Other firms competed for the business of country merchants who purchased their cloths from someone else. Kershaw & Co., operators of a wholesale clothing warehouse on Pearl Street, promised to manufacture goods from cloth bought elsewhere "at the shortest notice and for the lowest price." This arrangement would lower the profit margins but also the risks, and it opened up opportunities for smaller firms with less available credit. There was no lack of points of entry into the fast-growing business of clothing American men.[44]

In fact, the clothing business was almost too easy. In 1831 the *Working Man's Advocate* complained of the "hundreds" who knew nothing of the trade but had established themselves with their own money, hired cutters to prepare the work, and exploited the labor of impoverished seamstresses to sew the goods. A few years later, in the wake of the Panic of 1837, the *Philadelphia Public Ledger* condemned the hordes of "speculators" who had entered the clothing business because of the lure of quick and easy profits. These "mere mushrooms of bank credits" had been proliferating throughout the decade, to the point where the wholesale clothing trade was "running riot."[45] Edney, whom some might have wanted to include in this category, nevertheless gave voice to the opprobrium. Men "who knew nothing of the business," he wrote to Cooke, who were "entirely strangers to it in knowledge and practice," made up huge quantities of clothing. They then sold the goods to "Tom, Dick and Harry, here, there and everywhere," moving their giant stocks by extending credit for up to eighteen months even though they themselves often owed on notes that came due in half a year. No matter, for in the short run they showed a dramatic profit, which was enough to arrange another round of credit. Meanwhile, "the fool countrymen" coming to New York to buy their goods "got in the 'speculation' while they were here and saw fortunes staring them in the face." They bought up all the clothing offered at such easy credit. The cleverest converted that credit into land holdings in the West—the ultimate object of the inflated economy—so that when the bubble burst in 1837 they could leave their bankrupt stores behind for a farm or reestablish themselves in business with their land as collateral.[46]

Thus industrial success became available to those without any special claims to privilege or capital. Clothiers proved to be ideal men for the Age of Jackson. They were representative of a society, as William Ellery Channing not unambivalently described the times in 1841, characterized by "the tendency in all its movements to expansion, to diffusion, to universality" and "directly opposed to the spirit of exclusiveness, restriction, narrowness, monopoly, which has prevailed in past ages."[47] As a typical Revolutionary declaration defined American sovereignty in 1785, "If we are 'too young' for manufactures, we are too young for our independence." And, indeed, the republic seemed to be growing up with its economy. *Hunt's* thus concluded its 1840 paean to the commercializing nation by noting that "now the interests of everyone are all intertwined together . . . unit[ing] men everywhere into one society, having common interests, which can best be promoted by the joint prosperity of all." Edward Everett, one of the era's premier public intellectuals, concurred that modern society was held together by an "interminable succession of exchanges." No one pretended, of course, that the market transcended the clash of interests. Rather, the very fluidity of exchange prevented the creation of permanent power relations that would be "unsafe . . . arbitrary in nature, and liable . . . to great abuses." In this way, the reciprocity and even the mutuality required of civic life was becoming identified with the circular relations, and pseudosymmetries, of commodity exchange.[48]

Joseph Seligman's business career was representative of the social fluidity of the marketplace turned market society. He landed in New York in 1837, the eighteen-year-old son of a Bavarian woolens weaver and a mother who had managed the family's general merchandise store, and settled in Mauch Chunk, Pennsylvania. There he became a clerk and cashier and then the personal secretary of Asa Packer, who had recently begun to build his coal empire in the Lehigh Valley. Joseph soon went out on his own, however. After peddling for a year he paid the passage of two brothers, William and James, from Europe. In 1840 Joseph and William opened a store in Lancaster, while James went south to explore prospects. After the latter returned the next summer with $1,000, all three brothers, now joined by a fourth, Jesse, decided to relocate. They set sail from New York with $5,000 worth of general merchandise, landed in Mobile, discovered that they had insufficient capital to compete there, and so moved further upstate. Within two years the Seligmans were operating stores in Selma, Greensboro, Eutaw, and Clinton, in addition to peddling their merchandise throughout the surrounding region. By 1846, though, it was clear that the provincial market could no longer satisfy their ambitions.

At this point the Seligmans were firmly ensconced in the clothing business. William now left Alabama to open a clothing store in St. Louis with his brother-in-law, Max Stettheimer, who had previously sold clothing in

Natchez, Mississippi. Jesse went to Watertown, New York, and with a fifth brother, Henry, opening a clothing store there. Joseph and James, meanwhile, together with Max Stettheimer's father, Jacob, started a cloth-importing business on Pine Street in New York City. In 1850 Jesse and Henry left Watertown in order to open a clothing store in the boomtown of San Francisco. They were soon joined by William, while Max Stettheimer became a partner in the dry-goods firm of Seligman & Stettheimer in New York. In 1852 William picked up again and moved, now to New York, where he began manufacturing clothing for the San Francisco store and developed a general wholesale trade as well. The following year another brother, Isaac, was sent to Europe to broker the bullion Jesse was regularly shipping from California, which, in 1861 alone, totaled no less than a million dollars. The Seligmans then began to move into banking. In that same year, thanks to Joseph's influence in Republican Party circles, William secured contracts for army uniforms worth a million and a half dollars. In 1864 the Seligmans closed a circle, both in their family history and in the annals of global exchange, when Max Stettheimer moved to Frankfurt to open up a European branch of the family bank.[49]

The Seligmans' collective business career contained all the elements of the clothing revolution. Their expansion into dry goods addressed the crucial need for a reliable supply of cloth. The move to San Francisco merely followed the latest tributary in a network of exchanges governed by the country's commercial tides. And their peripatetic pursuit of profits—Pennsylvania, Alabama, Mississippi, St. Louis, upstate New York, New York City, San Francisco, and finally Frankfurt—was entirely characteristic of clothing's industrial geography. By the time a "country tailor" wrote to the *New York Tribune* in 1849 to protest how the "many pleasant and flourishing little villages which a few years ago sustained half a dozen tailors each . . . are now giving a scanty support to less than half the number, because the merchants, and establishments devoted exclusively to the business, are selling cheap ready-made clothing," the men's clothing business had become a national giant. I. M. Singer, for instance, marketed his sewing machines in Kentucky by promising local tailors that such machines offered the only chance to "realize a large profit themselves that now goes to the Eastern manufacturers." The tailoring journal the *Mirror of Fashion*, one of the country's first trade papers, worriedly advised its subscribers throughout the country to modernize their business and production practices in order to win the new mass market away from the clothing stores. *Hunt's Merchant's Magazine* waxed enthusiastic about "this branch of the manufactures of our country [that] has of late increased more rapidly and extensively than the great increase of our commerce and population would seem even to justify." And the *United States Economist, and Dry Goods Reporter* noted in 1852 that each passing season brought a further decline in the retail sale of piece goods suitable for men's garments. Writing to family in the East, a wife in Oregon summed it up quite matter-of-factly: "Your Father has as nice Cloathes as enney man both fine and corse. . . . It is cheaper to buy them Made up than to Buy the Cloath and Made them."[50]

Industrial success was not just based on the metropolis's wholesale incursion into the countryside. Clothiers enjoyed no less dramatic a success retailing in the city. As *Hunt's* further observed, "It used to be one job to seek for the cloth, and another to repair to the tailor, causing not unfrequently great loss of time and much vexation. We now see everywhere, not only the economist, but the man of fashion, saving his time and his money by procuring the very articles he requires all ready made to his hand." Daniel Devlin was exemplar of this new trend. Born in Ireland, Devlin had settled in Louisville in 1834, where he soon opened a clothing business. Ten years later he arrived in New York, married well, and began to manufacture for the family store in Kentucky. By 1849 Devlin's establishment on John Street in New York encompassed five floors organized into a city retail department, a cloth and custom department, a wholesale department, a cutting department, and a large basement for storing the "immense stock of woolens" and assorted trimmings of buttons, threads, and linings. All this meant, by the company's own excited admission, that they "must sell at least Half a Million, and that for Cash!" each year.[51]

At this point Devlin decided to create a new kind of clothing store. In 1852 he negotiated the purchase of a property on Broadway, kitty-corner from Stewart's famous Marble Palace. The asking price was over $100,000, a fifth of which was to be paid in cash, with the balance on a mortgage. Devlin did not lack for resources. Sales on John Street had reportedly exceeded $130,000 a year, and when Devlin dissolved that partnership his brother bought him out for $100,000. By now, Devlin had also acquired considerable real estate in New York and Brooklyn. That, together with the fact that his father-in-law was considered good for $200,000, made Devlin a safe credit risk. Nevertheless, interested observers considered the price for the Broadway property extravagant, and they became anxious that Devlin would quickly run up a debt of a quarter of a million dollars if he went through with the move. Their doubts did not abate when the deal fell through, owing to a feud among the heirs to the property, for Devlin was determined to acquire a Broadway address. His outright purchase thwarted, Devlin bought a twenty-one-year lease to the property instead. He quickly sold that lease for an advance of

$30,000 in cash and used the money to rent a new location just a block away for $28,000 a year, the basement of which he then promptly subleased for $9,000. "The store is entirely of white marble," it was approvingly observed. Its Corinthian columns and Italianate symmetries—interrupted only by the incongruous plain-lettered "D. Devlin & Co." sign hung between the third- and fourth-storey cornices—faced City Hall and the gated Park, a vision of neoclassical urbanity that became the firm's calling card, a lithographed likeness of the store embellishing its business receipts.[52]

With the initial year's rent covered and the financial risk thus eased, Devlin's efforts paid off immediately. In the first two years of business on Broadway his retail trade alone generated $4,000 a day. D. Devlin & Co. became "to the clothing trade what Stewart's is in the dry goods trade." It was a "mamouth establishment" whose size allowed it to "supply with expedition all wants and all fancies, even to the minute details of a wardrobe . . . [where both] the Quaker and the dandy can be furnished with every article of wearing apparel." Clothiers regularly boasted of having tens of thousands of garments in stock in seemingly limitless combinations of cloths, styles, sizes, and costs, able to furnish "tall men and short men, stout men and thin men, old men and young men, fast boys and slow boys" in a veritable democracy of body types, all of them with cash to spend. Size and volume were an important discovery for the clothing business, and an archetypally modern one inasmuch as the successful application of economies of scale to the unique, fitted body still had a distinctly anti-intuitive character.[53]

Devlin was followed by others. Wilde & Co., for instance, moved into a "new and beautiful edifice . . . of a pure white marble" a few blocks up Broadway "in order to keep pace with the progressive spirit of the age." Most impressive of all, however, was the project undertaken by Henry Brooks's four sons, three of whom had qualified for inclusion in Moses Beach's most recent enumeration of the city's wealthiest denizens. They had renamed the firm Brooks Brothers in 1850 but were still doing business at their father's original store on Catharine Street. In 1857, however, they built a new four-storey structure costing half a million dollars at the corner of Broadway and Grand Street, only fifteen years earlier the site of cheap sewing workshops but now an emerging center of high culture, and shopping, where two "magnificent hotels" had also recently been erected. The store's 100,000 square feet were "expressly adapted to the various requirements of their business." This included scores of six-by-twelve-foot mirrors, interior columns topped by golden capitals supporting a frescoed ceiling, and a broad staircase leading to the "rotunda" decorated with scroll work and emblematic painting. All combined to create "a most novel effect." Although the Brookses kept the Catharine Street store (which would be looted and burned during the city's draft riots in 1863) for another fifteen years, the move to Broadway was a clear indication of the ready-made clothing trade's emergence at the center of polite living.[54]

These "Marble Palaces" of grandiose proportion and genteel shopping for men, self-conscious fixtures of urban refinement at mid-century, were inextricably tied to the wholesale country trade. The broadcloth suit bought at one of the city's upscale clothing stores was, so to speak, joined at the seam with the Iowa farmer's smock or the California miner's denims. Local retail sales generated the cash that allowed clothiers to balance short-term expenses—salaries, wages, rents, and other overhead costs, as well as ad hoc purchases of production supplies—with the long-term credit rhythms of annual harvests. The city market, in other words, constituted the financial bridge by which ambitious clothiers integrated the two separate business functions of production and distribution. This is what so excited contemporary observers of the industry. Most manufacturing businesses in these early decades of industrialization relied on traditional jobbers or commission merchants to mediate between the two often-conflicting desiderata of making and selling. But clothiers took control of both and combined the traditionally distinct roles of the buyer of raw material, the jobber, the factor, the wholesale manufacturer, and the retailer. As a writer for the National Association of Wool Manufactures exclaimed in wonderment, the ingredients of this giant new industry were "so simple that the results to which they have led seem inconceivable."[55]

And so the ready-made revolution continued apace. Clothiers' tendency toward vertical integration now led them back into cloths. Since the 1830s an entirely new branch of the dry-goods trade devoted to supplying men's clothing producers had arisen. This included, for instance, Francis Cooke's cloth (and credit) supplier, Staples & Clarke. In the 1840s, clothiers—who had already combined production and distribution, and retail and wholesale—began to pull themselves out from under the control of dry-goods jobbers and establish control over the source of their raw materials. This was certainly the intention of the Seligmans, who, while opening clothing businesses in St. Louis, Watertown, and San Francisco, simultaneously established a cloth-importing firm based in New York. Similarly, Daniel Devlin's next expansion of his business in the late 1850s included two new partners who had previously operated a dry-goods firm based in New York and Charleston. Brooks Brothers, too, was importing its own cloth by 1850.[56] So was George Opdyke, a New Jersey native who first opened a clothing store in Cleveland in the

The commercial transformation of Broadway and Grand Street between 1830 and 1852. By the time Brooks Brothers built their new store here in 1857 the intersection lay at the center of one of New York City's premier shopping districts. (*Above: Broadway and Grand Street in 1830.* Publisher: Society of Iconophiles, 1907. Engraved by Walter M. Aikman, 41.62.70. *Facing: Broadway Looking North at Grand Street.* Engraving by Walter M. Aikman from a painting by R. Bond, 1852. Publisher: Society of Iconophiles, 1905. 41.62.62. Museum of the City of New York, The Arthur H. Scribner Collection.)

twenties, moved from there to New Orleans later in the decade, and then back east in the thirties. When he ran for Congress as a Free Soiler in 1848, Opdyke sold out to his brother-in-law, John D. Scott, who soon expanded the business, opening branch stores in New Orleans, Charleston, and Memphis. But Opdyke did not really leave the scene, having opened a cloth-importing business that supplied, among others, Scott and, a few years later, a nephew in the clothing trade in Chicago.[57]

Such ambitiousness provoked considerable resistance. In 1861 Philadelphia cloth jobbers organized a boycott of John Wanamaker after the latter went right to the source and began buying his fabrics directly from the mills. Dry-goods dealers also attempted to pressure the commission houses representing cloth producers not to sell directly to clothiers. But the clothing houses were simply too important by now to ignore. By the early 1850s the "wants of clothiers" had become a permanent fixture in weekly reports on the

state of the dry-goods market, and textile manufacturers increasingly catered to their needs, adapting their production schedules, for instance, to clothiers' seasons. Thus, manufacturers no longer made their "Spring Goods" on the approach of spring and their "Autumn Goods" just before autumn, the additional time being necessary because fabrics no longer went straight to the consumer but first "passed through the [sewer's] hands." The huge California market that opened up after 1849 gave this seasonal shift an extra push, since the garments required that much longer to make the trip to San Francisco.

And so the traditional relationship between cloth and clothing was inverted in this ready-made age as the latter increasingly came to dominate the character of the textile industry. Woolen mills, for instance, remained concentrated in the East even while their wool sources moved west because the clothing trade was likewise concentrated in New York and other seaboard cities. As mills began to produce specifically for the clothing trade, they made do with a multiplicity of smaller orders and learned to sustain a greater number of order cancellations. Diversity of product and small-unit orders became the conditions for their success, along with a far more strenuous production standard. All that "joint labor," of shepherd, sorter of wool, carder, spinner, weaver, fuller, and dresser, was now dependent on the clothier for its successful realization. For the first time in history, the making of cloth, or at least a whole branch of the woolen and mixed woolen-cotton industry, was subordinated to the production of clothing, not because of any direct technological or material changes but because of the changing economics of industrial revolution.[58]

3

The Reinvention of Tailoring

Ready-made clothing seemed uniquely modern to nineteenth-century observers. "Procuring the very articles [one] requires all ready-made to his hand" encapsulated the anonymity, the standardization, and the proficiency promised by industrial revolution. That impression was only strengthened by concurrent retail innovations—urban emporiums of grandiose design and an unprecedented volume of merchandise—and the fact that the goods were being made by the principal waged manufacturing force in the city, working on enormous scales of production.

The identification of ready-made with mass production had an important corollary: the equation of made-to-measure, or "bespoke," clothing with preindustrial practices. The distinction was perceived as an opposition, representative of the transition from a world of craft singularity to one of market-inspired standardization.[1] By the mid-nineteenth century the made-to-measure business had become known as the "custom trade." An old term that once described any customer, "custom" now denoted a certain type of consumption, namely, the purchase of goods made to personal order. By implication the appellation thus tied bespoke clothing to traditional practices. Of course, no such relationship necessarily existed. It was, in fact, more common in the preindustrial world than in the nineteenth century for a person to wear clothing originally belonging to someone else, or to leave clothing to others in their wills, or to adapt a garment and then readapt it through innumerable incarnations passed between family members and over generations.[2]

At the same time, the dichotomy between ready-made and custom clothing made sense in an industrializing context. The latter cost more, fit better, and had been associated with craft tradition ever since English tailoring guilds began fighting the encroachments of the ready-made trade in the seventeenth century. The ready-made garment was "a different species of make," recognizable by clumsy button holes or a "general misfit" justifiably blamed on the cost-cutting measures taken by proprietors of mercantile habits.[3] Its production was, in general, organized by "clothiers"—that is, merchants—many of whom had themselves never made a suit and whose artistry was manifest instead in the profitable coordination of cloth, labor, and credit. The custom suit, in contrast, was the product of a master tailor who measured his own customers, laid his palms on their shoulders in judging the shape of the shoulder seams, and then leisurely drew his hands down their sides, learning the customer's "form" in order to successfully model to that particular body a particular suit of clothes. This made custom the legacy of artisanal fastidiousness and seemed also to divorce it from the more aggressive and alienated expressions of commercial life. Rather than something gotten "much cheaper" from a big shop, it was "made expressly" for the customer. Certainly, the individual body personally attended by the skilled craftsman was an obvious antithesis to the anonymous wholesale trade in ready-mades.[4]

This opposition had other expressions as well. By the 1840s New York City business directories published two separate listings for men's clothing stores: clothiers' "warehouses" and tailors' "establishments." That bifurcation rested on a social taxonomy. Over a quarter of the city's clothiers were located in the distinctly lower-class venues of Chatham Street and the Bowery. Another quarter did business in the old slops neighborhood bordering the East River wharves. In contrast, a quarter of the tailors had Broadway addresses, and most of the others were to be found in the immediate vicinity. Only one clothier was listed on Broadway, for instance, in *Doggett's New York Business Directory for 1841–42*.[5] The distinction between custom and ready-made, then, appeared to be synonymous with the division between refined and coarse, between bourgeois and proletarian. That opposition reached its apotheosis in a company history privately printed by Brooks Brothers in 1918, celebrating the firm's centenary and staking a credible claim to be one of the oldest surviving clothing firms in America. The company account, however, reinvented Henry Brooks as a tailor, while in fact, as we have seen, neither Henry nor his brother David nor Henry's four sons knew how to make a suit of clothes—as distinguished from knowing how to make money from others doing the same. But such an artisanal pedigree allowed the latter-day firm, having since carefully nurtured an image as purveyor of sartorial refinement to the polite classes, to lay claim to a craft status otherwise refuted by the real nature of their lumpen origins selling low-priced ready-mades along the wharves of the East River. (The company version, however, achieved its aim:

the standard history of the early men's clothing business, Egal Feldman's *Fit for Men*, repeats the fiction.)[6]

In fact, however, the custom trade was the branch of the clothing business that underwent the most far-reaching industrial transformation in the middle of the nineteenth century. For while the ready-made commodity proved originally suited to the new conditions of a mass market, custom tailoring, which was no less exposed to market forces, had a far longer way to go in adapting itself to the economic facts of industrial life. Yet this it did. The result was a new regime of proprietary control over production and the labor force, unceasing competition among merchant tailors for a cut-rate cash business, the replacement of craft secrets with a burgeoning trade in new production technologies, and the attempt, by means of those standardizing technologies, to tap into the huge continental market. All these developments show custom tailoring to have been the full-blooded progeny of industrial revolution rather than the legacy of a less commercial past, and no less a part of the ready-made world.[7]

Tailors' achievements were no less social than economic. As we will see, in adapting their highly personal craft to the exploding market, tailors also effectively integrated the male persona into industry's ceaseless striving for system and predictability without forcing him to consciously surrender his uniqueness. The result was far-reaching. The personally fitted gentleman could now simultaneously embody abstract universal citizenship while honing his individuality, both important desiderata of modern life. Thus, industrial revolution, when it came, was not about the replacement of individual identities with standardized persons. It marked, rather, the simultaneous birth of both.

- - - - -

Edgar Allan Poe, who demonstrated an intuitive understanding of the mass character of private life, published a characteristically acerbic parable of commercial foibles called "The Business Man" soon after moving to New York in the early 1840s, one that exposed the modern nature of custom tailoring. The story was an abbreviated memoir of the insistent efforts of one Peter Proffit, utilizing the twin tenets of "system" and "method," to achieve self-made success. While some might consider Proffit's sundry schemes for enriching himself to more closely resemble business scams—and they included an Eye-Sore trade, an Assault and Battery business, and a Cur-Spattering operation—he himself had no doubt that the end of a country seat on the Hudson justified his unorthodox methods.[8]

Proffit's first venture was in the employ of Messrs. Cut and Comeagain, merchant tailors, who dressed him each morning and sent him out for a mid-day promenade in the city's more fashionable quarters. The "precise regularity" with which Proffit displayed his personage and brought his suit to bear to the most advantageous view "was the admiration of all the knowing men in the trade." Noon never passed without his returning with a new customer to Cut and Comeagain, anxious to be fitted to the same effect. Of course, once back in the shop a customer might be sold a far cheaper milled satinet instead of the broadcloth he had requested. Proffit was responsible for these prevarications as well, and he made certain to charge the tailors for each one he told while in their employ: 25 cents for a "second class lie," 75 cents for a "first class lie." In truth, Proffit's career as a "walking advertiser" of dubious ethics was the most innocent of all the hoaxes he perpetrated on his road to business success. "Tailors' tricks" were an old subject of popular suspicion anyway. But Poe knew that they no less belonged in his litany of modern avarice and that the new ethos of system and method, combined with commercial ambition, had overtaken such an apparently timeless relationship as that between a gentleman and his tailor.[9]

In fact, in the same year that "The Business Man" was published, the *New York Tribune* announced the arrival of a new era in tailoring: "Within the last few years a revolution in the price of Fashionable Clothing has been effected." Overcoats that not so long before had cost $40 could now be bought on Broadway for $15. What most impressed the *Tribune*, however, was not the low price of coats per se—"there were always plenty of shops where Clothing could be bought lower"—but that they were being sold at such prices in the center of bon ton, Broadway. Broadway tailors engaged "the best artists," acquired "the choicest qualities and most *recherché* styles of goods" from Paris and London, and turned out the very best design and quality of clothing. Nevertheless, they managed to do this "at prices which . . . opened the eye of the public."[10]

Even before the *Tribune*'s pronouncement of the dawning of a new sartorial age, Edward Fox, since 1841 the proprietor of the City Cash Tailoring Establishment at 202 Broadway, embarked on a campaign to refute "the impression that has heretofore existed in the minds of many that purchasers in Broadway are obliged to pay an exorbitant price for an article of dress." Fox kept a "desirable and choice" assortment of French and English broadcloths, cassimeres, and vestings in stock, fabrics that would be turned into garments by "none but the best cutters and workmen." Moreover, he promised to sell them at prices as low, if not lower, than those of any other house in the city.[11] Fox advertised in the *Herald*, however, and the *Tribune* preferred to puff its own advertisers. Its notice on the tailoring revolution thus profiled two other Broadway tailors, J. C. Booth and William Jennings. Booth had opened a tailoring business earlier in the decade on Fulton Street, a busy commercial boulevard that crossed Broadway just below City Hall Park and ran east to the Brooklyn ferry. There he offered savings "of at least 40 per cent from Broadway prices." He then moved himself to Broadway, a block below Fox, where "every article requisite to complete a Gentleman's Wardrobe of the latest styles and best fabrics" could still be had for the same low prices. The strategy proved successful. In 1848 observers estimated that Booth, who began in business with little means of his own, had pocketed close to $30,000. Such a reputation for success, of course, made it easier to pocket even more, and Booth had little problem financing the hiring of extra cutters and expanding the business.[12]

William Jennings, whom the *Tribune* actually credited with personally pioneering the revolutionary new price structure, had been tailoring in New York since the twenties. He was popularly considered one of the city's best and enjoyed the endorsement of the consciously fashionable *New Mirror*. Jennings's establishment was located in the American Hotel, at Broadway and Barclay Street, "opposite the Fountain," a manicured urban idyll peopled with well-appointed strollers that was made the centerpiece of his full-page advertisement in Sheldon's business directory of 1845. But such demonstrative gentility did not keep Jennings from matching the competition: suits "at a few hour's notice," winter clearance sales, an assortment of "FIRST QUALITY" ready-mades, a large selection of furnishings—scarfs, cravats, gloves, suspenders, "etc. etc."—and, of course, unprecedentedly low prices.[13]

According to the *Tribune*, the dramatic fall in the price of tailored men's clothing was not attributable to the depressed economy of the early forties. What had transformed tailoring, rather, was the conditions of doing business in modern times: the discovery of a giant market to be reached by lowering prices, or what Jennings pithily captioned "the system of small profits and quick returns."[14] The *Tribune* compared the change in tailoring to the birth of the penny press, which had made the heretofore excluded "carter . . . sitting on his cart; a barrowman on his barrow; and a porter at his stand" full participants in the age when they took a break in their workday to read the paper. A parallel could also have been drawn to the falling price of admission to the theaters. All three marked an unprecedented commodification of once exclusive cultural goods. George Foster, the *Tribune*'s most notorious exposer of aristocratic pretension, considered cheap theater a democratic revolution of sorts, a uniquely American success. And Nathaniel Willis, self-anointed

William Jenning's genteel location "opposite the Fountain" did not keep him
from championing a business system of "small profits and quick returns" in
his pursuit of the exploding market in men's clothing. (City Hall park
fountain, seen from the east, 1856; from the Eno Collection, Miriam and Ira
D. Wallach Division of Art, Prints and Photographs, The New York Public
Library, Astor, Lenox and Tilden Foundations)

copywriter for the city's Upper Tendom (that is, the ten thousand richest
New Yorkers) had to admit, albeit with barely disguised regret, that "the age
is, perhaps, forever gone by, when a privileged class could monopolize finery of garb; and of all the civilized nations, it were least possible in ours. I
have already seen a dozen at least of cheap-booted apprentices wearing velvet
waistcoats, which, a few years ago, would have delighted D'Orsay." The editor
of the plebeian *Aurora* rubbed elbows with the city's gentry at the high-society
ball held in Charles Dickens's honor at the Park Theater in 1842. Accoutered
in "faultlessly white" linens and a suitably black coat and pantaloons acquired
from Martin's tailoring shop, where one was taught that "economy is wealth,"
he mingled with the "beaux, exquisites, and the dandies at a positive saving
of 30 per cent."[15]

The aforementioned Martin did business on William Street, two blocks
east of Broadway, where he made garments "of the most stylish manner"
and sold them exclusively for cash. He was representative of scores of other
"Cash Tailors" who had recently capitalized the adjective in their appella-

tion into a proper noun and begun to aggressively fill the city's newspapers and storefronts with their wares. They could expect cash payment from a broad range of clientele as the urban economy and its waged occupations developed and the expenditures of city households grew steadily through the early decades of the century. Cash meant that there were fewer accounts to keep and fewer debtors to dun, and sometimes to sue. True, sales and gross profits declined in a cash business, but so did expenses and losses at the end of the year. The tailor no longer had to suffer the defaults of persons buying on credit, which was especially appealing in the wake of the 1837 panic. It was indisputably the safest way to do business. Retail advice in the 1840s was adamant on this point: "As he parts with these goods, again, he receives the money at once. Unlike the person who sells on credit, there is . . . very little risk of his losing his means by the dishonesty, incapacity or misfortunes of others." The consequent liquidity allowed proprietors to weather the regular downturns in the economy. Ready cash in a period of straitened business conditions even created opportunity, for one could then purchase a new stock of high-quality goods at low prices, turning a potential problem into a profitable situation.[16]

The savings were then passed on to the public. Cash "economy," in other words, was good for everyone, "most advantageous to [both] the manufacturer and consumer," as Arthur Levy, proprietor of the Broadway Cash Tailoring Establishment, asserted in his advertisements. "Purchasers will flock to [cash sales] as instinctively as sharks to a ship," *Hunt's Merchant's Magazine* predicted in 1839, an observation that William Ross repeated verbatim in his business manual a decade later. Ross pointed to those who had learned the hard way that one cannot do a large volume of business at a small profit margin and still give out credit. "The only inducement for reducing prices below an average standard is a certainty of payment." Reducing prices made sense because the market proved to be far more elastic than had once been assumed. This meant it was more profitable to broaden one's client base than to foster the loyalty of regular customers who were better trusted with credit purchases. Who could investigate every new customer's credit-worthiness anyway? Indeed, this "progressive reformation" based on cash and impersonal shopping was a democratic reform: "As none are credited, so there are none to take offense at a refusal." And it was just: "If Mr. Jones failed to pay for his coat," *Hunt's* explained in pointing out why good customers effectively subsidized the lapses of bad ones in a credit system, "Mr. Brown must pay double price for his, or the poor tailor must starve, steal, or beg." Cash tailoring, it turns out, served the Jacksonian hankering for hard money no less than it did the retailer's.[17]

The rush and competitiveness of cash tailoring was heralded by an otherwise unremarkable event. Ever on the alert for corroborative evidence of American industrial progress, *Niles' Weekly Register* had reported in 1822 on the results of a speed competition in upstate New York for producing a man's suit of clothing. A certain General McClure won a fifty-dollar bet that he [*sic*] could turn a fleece of wool into a coat, jacket, and overalls of satinet (a cheap staple of the American woolen industry) within ten hours. *Niles'* duly registered his success: first, the wool was dyed blue, which took 35 minutes; it was then carded, spun, and woven in another 2 hours and 25 minutes, and after that fulled, napped, dried, sheared, and dressed in 1 hour and 56 minutes. At that point someone ran the finished cloth three-quarters of a mile (in four minutes) to Mr. Gilmore's tailor shop, where the suit was completed in 3 hours and 45 minutes, with half a yard of cloth left over (thanks to Gilmore's economy in cutting out the pieces). Gilmore, it was noted, had been assisted by seven extra hands. Flushed with success, McClure offered to double the bet and to accomplish the same next time in less than eight hours.[18]

Could there be a more innocuous beginning to a world of stopwatches, splintered tasks, and the ceaseless rush to produce? For *Niles'* the effort represented a test of national character. For the locals it had a distinctly sporting air. But the desideratum of speed, together with its corollary of volume, also had a clear commercial application whose lesson was not lost on a clothing market that was becoming ever more competitive.

T. S. Arthur, a best-selling broker of antebellum sentiment, described the situation precisely in his story "The Seamstress":

> "Money don't come in hand-over-fist, as it ought to come," remarked Grasp, of the flourishing firm of Grasp & Co., Merchant Tailors . . . to the junior partner. . . . "A nimble six-pence is better than a slow shilling, you know. We must make our shears eat up cloth a little faster, or we shan't clear ten thousand dollars this year by one third of that sum."
>
> "Although that would be a pretty decent business these times."
>
> "I don't call any business a decent one that can be bettered," replied Grasp contemptuously.
>
> "But can ours be bettered?"
>
> "Certainly!"
>
> "How?"
>
> "By selling more goods."
>
> "How are we to do that?"
>
> "By putting down prices, and then making a confounded noise about it."[19]

Such an industrialization of tailoring is to be witnessed in the thirty-year span of Anthoney Arnoux's career. Arnoux opened his business in the twenties, announcing the fact in a notice in the *New York Post* written in French so that no one would mistake him for anything but the source of the most fashionable *habillements*. His posturing had apparent effect. George Templeton Strong, a recent Columbia College graduate and aspiring commercial lawyer with an acute sense of class entitlement, bought his clothing from Arnoux in the thirties. By the next decade, along with everyone else, Arnoux was emphasizing his "usual moderate prices" in increasingly prolific advertisements. The firm did almost all its "large and fashionable custom trade" in cash. They also announced their willingness to forward out-of-town orders to any part of the country. By 1851 they were soliciting customers in the South through advertisements in the *New Orleans Daily Picayune*. Arnoux & Co. took pride in the firm's sophisticated commercial operations: its organization into distinct "departments," each responsible for coats, pants, or waistcoats and each supervised by its own expert cutter. Arnoux, the self-proclaimed *Marchand Drapier et Tailleur*, had become overseer of production. In 1854, not surprisingly, considering Arnoux's business ambitions, the firm became embroiled in a nasty confrontation with the Journeymen Tailors' Society when it went outside the society's ranks in search of cheaper labor. [20]

Cash tailors did not make do with vague promises of unique savings. They filled the dailies with itemized price lists, outbidding one another for the business of the ever-growing public of shoppers interested in affordable prices. The new importance of the popular market was manifest in petitions sent by merchant tailors from New York, Boston, and Philadelphia to Congress in 1832 demanding a reduction in the duty on woolens. Tailors feared that the high price of cloth, which constituted their single largest production expense, was driving away business. [21] Interestingly, four years earlier, during the supercharged tariff debate of 1828, master, merchant, and journeymen tailors had similarly called for a revision of import duties. In 1828, however, their concerns focused on the insufficiently low tariff charged on ready-made clothing imported from Europe. The problem, as all three groups separately contended in almost verbatim petitions to Congress, was that while the duty on woolens had steadily risen over the years to protect American textile manufacturers from cheaper imports, the duty on ready-made clothing had stayed the same. This disparity actually made it cheaper to import many fabrics already made up into clothing, which could then be suitably altered, than to import the raw cloth that still had to be measured, cut, and sewn. In 1828 the profession had demanded, in the face of "total ruin," that the duty on ready-mades be raised to the same level as that on woolens in order to erase any incentive to import foreign-made garments. Congress complied. But four years later it was obvious that this had not solved the problem. True, the advantages in importing ready-mades were nullified. But the 50 percent duty on woolens kept the price of clothing in general too high. It was not enough to bring the two duties into line. The cost of imported cloth had to be reduced so that tailors could then lower their own prices.[22]

This did not happen, and so tailors turned to their next largest production expense—labor—in an effort to maintain their profit margin. T. S. Arthur's fictional account of Grasp & Co. explains what that meant:

> "But our prices are very low now."
>
> "True. But we may reduce them still further, and, by so doing, increase our sales to an extent that will make our business net us beyond the present income quite handsomely. But, to do this, we must cut down the prices now paid for making up our clothes. In this way, we shall be able to greatly increase our sales, with but a slight reduction upon our present rates of profit."[23]

Tailors, just like clothiers, were left having to rationalize production. A cash business required close management anyway. As profit margins narrowed and volume became the basis of tailoring success, that management increasingly focused on labor. The production process itself stayed the same. The division of tasks—measuring, cutting, basting, stitching, and pressing collars, forearms, coat fronts, and buttonholes—was unaltered. However, its social content was unrecognizably transformed. Class war broke out between masters and journeymen who, by the 1820s, were engaged in a struggle to determine how far property rights allowed one to command the conditions of another's labor. This archetypally industrial confrontation did not begin in those clothing firms that employed hundreds and even thousands at a time, busily mass producing coarse and mid-level ready-made goods for the national wholesale market. The strikes, protests, street confrontations, and subsequent conspiracy trials unfolded in the city's most exclusive tailoring establishments. It was here, in other words, in the highest reaches of the custom trade, that industrial change was most keenly contested.

The industrialization of the custom trade was clearly discernible in an 1827 strike by Philadelphia's journeymen tailors. In contrast to an 1819 turnout in New York provoked by the increasing use of female labor on the part of masters driven to "accumulate money" at the expense of craft traditions, Philadelphia's journeymen were less directly concerned by the disintegration of producerist mutuality. Indeed, their strike crowned an extended period of instability and work stoppages. Two years earlier, in 1825, an attempt had been made to settle outstanding issues. A carefully detailed bill of prices was drawn up governing payment by masters to their journeymen for work done. The breakdown of this agreement in 1827, however, stemmed less from differences over wages than from a more novel bone of contention: control of the work process.

David Winebrener, a Philadelphia merchant tailor, had assigned six of his journeymen to make up a single riding habit, "the notice being short" and merchant tailors often advertising the promptest attention to custom orders.[24] The habit was finished satisfactorily, and on time, but Winebrener remunerated the work at a lower rate than his journeymen had expected, namely that, they claimed, prescribed in the trade's recent bill of prices, which Winebrener had signed. Winebrener's journeymen protested by holding up further work until they were paid the difference. In response, Winebrener fired them. Their protest then spread to other shops as Winebrener farmed out his work while the Journeymen's Society sought to keep him from filling his orders. The subsequent conspiracy indictment of twenty-four journeymen tailors addressed the legality—and, by implication, the social legitimacy—of the journeymen's means of redress, namely, the cooperative effort by waged workers to hinder an employer's trade. However, the testimony at the trial itself focused far less on the stuff of criminal conspiracy than on the actual issue at hand: whether the manufacture of the riding habit should cost Winebrener six dollars, the price he sought to pay, or seven dollars, the price demanded by the journeymen. The problem was that the bill of prices was not clear on the matter. In the tradewide compromise of 1825 journeymen had acceded to their employers' insistent demand that differential rates for making up heavier and lighter garments be instituted. Accordingly, variable prices were listed for making up coats and coatees, explicitly distinguished in the bill of prices on the basis of the type of fabric. Riding habits, however—which were the only women's garments still made by tailors in the nineteenth century, since such garments were the closest in cut and style to men's clothing— were not similarly itemized as light or heavy. As a result, the bill of prices allowed each side its own interpretation. Journeymen could cite the letter of the agreement—namely, the prescribed price of a habit—while Winebrener could no less self-justifiably note its spirit, by which a riding habit made of pongee—a cotton fabric representative of so many of the new cotton or mixed cottons coming into the market for which the public was used to paying less— should cost him less to make up. The stakes were high. The informalities and irregularities characteristic of craft production and earlier market exchange had now become intolerable ambiguities for masters forced to compete in a quickly industrializing environment. Indeed, a new commercial logic could be discerned in these events, one that emptied traditional assumptions of their meaning. Thus, for instance, in seeking to strengthen the virtue of their position in the confrontation, the journeymen actually, albeit implicitly, conceded Winebrener's case. They called a series of expert witnesses to testify that making garments of light cotton fabrics entailed no less, and sometimes even more, effort on the part of the producer. This might have been true—it certainly was the crux of their case—but proportional effort was no longer the principle that informed the structure of their wages, a structure they themselves had agreed to when they signed the differentiated bill of prices in 1825 that was supposed to regularize and thus protect their wages. In any event, the trial resulted in a conviction, although on only one of the three charges brought against the tailors.

The next notable attempt by master tailors to enhance their control over labor occurred in a series of two strikes in New York City in the winter of 1835–36. The strikes marked the culmination of two mutually related processes: first, the heightened mobilization of waged craftsmen into political associations—such as parties or trade unions—that actively opposed the attempts by their employers to reorganize the trades along lines more congenial to market competition; and, second, the growth of a high-flying economy that made New York the country's leading manufacturing city and men's clothing one of the leading branches of manufacturing in the city. During the 1830s these two processes simultaneously pushed capitalists to attempt to "rationalize" production while giving the producers themselves considerable opportunity to resist those attempts. The result was an ongoing confrontation. Journeymen tailors struck continually throughout the first half of the decade, trying to leverage their craft skills into a suitable social position. By mid-decade it seemed they had succeeded. "Hands are scarce and work plenty," James Edney wrote in September 1835, upon realizing that his labor costs that year were going to be higher than ever before.[25]

Evidently trying to make the best of the situation, the Society of Journeymen Tailors carried out a long anticipated walkout in October 1835, at the height of the fall production season. The dispute was quickly settled, to the apparent satisfaction of both sides. Industrial peace, however, turned out to be illusory. In January the tailors struck again. This time the turnout lasted for months and was accompanied by vigils outside the shops, confrontations with the scabs hired to finish the work, intimidations and reputed beatings, newspaper denunciations, and police intervention and arrests—a spiral of mutual recrimination that escalated, at the end of May, into another trial for conspiracy. The trial, which took place in the city's Court of Sessions, resulted in a directed verdict against twenty journeymen tailors.[26]

The January strike ostensibly erupted over wage schedules again, triggered as it was by employers' attempts to pay below the rates agreed upon in October. Certainly, merchant tailors were keenly interested in lowering the costs of their skilled journeymen, upon whom they were dependent, inasmuch as there was still considerable resistance at the high end of the business to hiring women to make up fashionable apparel for men, despite the savings to be derived.[27] But this was not the whole story. Employers had a strategic aim that transcended their immediate interest in the profit equation. They were clearly unhappy with the strike settlement in October, and with their own easy capitulation to the journeymen's society. In response, they organized themselves into an employers' association. They prepared for a long strike and arranged to hire strikebreakers from the city's countless "irregular shops." One can credibly suspect that even the arrests for conspiracy "to the injury of trade and commerce" were not entirely unforeseen. In short, the January strike involved a concerted attempt to break the journeymen's society, not only in order to lower the short-term costs of labor but to affirm employers' singular control over the production process. That is why, for instance, the strike was characterized by "some features that had never before been presented to employers." Principal among these was the "slate rule." Judge Edwards explained the rule in passing sentence: "You [the convicted journeymen] would not work for any tailor . . . who would refuse to keep a slate hanging up in a public part of his store or shop, on which should be entered the name of every journeymen taking a job from his store, and that no journeyman should take one out of his turn. And also that no member of the said confederacy should go to any such shop for the purpose of getting a job, unless in his turn, under the penalty of forfeiting the price of the job." For Edwards, the wage workers' insistence on retaining the slate rule epitomized those "arbitrary by-laws, rules and orders" by which the journeymen's society sought "to govern not only [them]selves but other journeymen tailors, and persons engaged in the business of tailors," and which constituted criminal conspiracy. Their demand that a public roster of the shop's journeymen should alone determine the distribution of work within that shop—which had been a sacrosanct practice in the English trade for more than a century—clearly delimited the employer's discretion, let alone his control, over a business where he might consider it essential that a particularly important order be made up by his most skilled tailor.[28]

The Panic of 1837 and the depression that followed suppressed the self-assertions of journeymen more effectively than had employers' associations or conspiracy trials. The Union Society of Journeymen Tailors apparently ceased to exist. Or, in the least, its activities became invisible. But the return of prosperity in the mid-forties brought with it renewed agitation. New York tailors struck again in 1844. The main issue of contention was now quite explicitly the question of control over the work process, for which the wage rate was the principal means of expression. But employers were quite clear in the forties that their central concern was to secure an exclusive prerogative regarding the assignment of work to their hired laborers. Nor was the debate any longer confined to the slate rule's prescribed order of jobs. Merchant tailors now sought to combine control over job assignments with a differential rate schedule, whereby they would pay more to a tailor making up a coat of expensive broadcloth than to someone sewing cheaper satinet. The *Herald*, which was critical of the merchant tailors in 1836, was unequivocally understanding of their needs in 1844: "Where is the justice of compelling, even if the [journeymen] could, employers to pay the good and bad workmen the same amount of wages; or the same prices for every description of work? The same for making a coat worth thirty dollars as for one of forty or fifty dollars?" Thus the issues that first arose in Philadelphia twenty years earlier had reached their resolution. Clothing entrepreneurs—only rarely now referred to by the antiquated appellation of master tailors—could now ensure the highest-quality work on expensive goods while not simultaneously being obliged to pay the same high rate for making up cheaper goods. The importance of such an arrangement in a cash-tailoring business seeking to popularize its market is self-evident.[29]

Proprietary authority over the production process was not just necessary for controlling one's work force. It was essential for control over the product itself. This was especially important since male fashion in the nineteenth century was based on a singular, fastidious criterion: fit. "It is the cut," the *Mirror of Fashion* reminded its readers in 1855, "that decides the style." The matte surface of the woolens that were the standard fabric for men's clothing reflected little light, but what the garments sacrificed in color they gained in malleability. Wool was easily molded, stretched, shrunk, and shaped to fit the body in a way that silk, for instance, never could be. The goal was a proper fit that facilitated physical mobility and then smoothed itself when back at rest. "The main argument in favor of the personal appearance of the moderns, is utility," the *Mirror of Fashion*, that mid-century arbiter of a suitably industrial male aesthetic, continued. A properly fitted garment "discloses the shape of the figure, and yields to the conveniences of locomation without restraint to limb, muscle, or joint, and yet without the inconvenience of carrying a surplus of cloth." This was an apposite vision for the new middle class: "a quiet pose and graceful fall over the hips, which freedom from extremes generally lends to dress."[30]

Tailoring success depended on the quality of such a fit. No self-respecting bourgeois, or aspirant to such a status, could be seen in "spacious-hipped trousers." Nor could he risk them becoming "caught on the hip" and thus prevented from falling to his boots in gravitational poise.[31] A business built its reputation on little else but fit. In the competitive conditions of cash tailoring, in fact, a "warranted fit" became de rigueur. And a "warranted fit" on the "most reasonable terms" became an ubiquitous advertising slogan in the 1840s.

On one hand, there was little that was new in these promises. "Reasonable terms" had been a means of enticing custom since the previous century. And although guaranteeing a fit was a retail innovation of the forties, the promise only made explicit what had always been the traditional assumption of the trade. On the other hand, a contradiction between these two promises now seemed to manifest itself. Cheaper garments meant cheapening the cost of making them up, which employers achieved, as we have seen, by establishing an unprecedented authority over the labor force. But how could the drive toward cheaper labor be reconciled with promises about the quality of the fit when fit traditionally derived from the intuitive skills and practiced eye of the artisan? When the merchant tailor had been his own master craftsman there was little problem. But in an age of volume and speed, as J. C. Booth acknowledged, the "elegance and style for which the establishment has been so long celebrated" rested on "increasing our help in the cutting department." In fact, the "cutter"—who translated the customer's measurements onto the cloth and then cut out the pieces that would be sewn back together into coats, vests, or pantaloons—was the heart of the tailoring enterprise. "As efficient a corps of cutters as can be found in the country" was the key to success according to William Jennings. Sometimes the dependence was total, as Edney admitted, "considering the circumstances in which our business is placed, the manner in which it has been carried on, the means we have of keeping of it up, the danger that would attend a change of our cutter, the risk of getting one that would cut as well, the uncertainty of getting one that would be willing to devote his whole time to the business, and above all an honest man, one in whom confidence could be placed, in the house with the goods, and in case of my sickness one that would be capable and trustworthy to attend to our business."[32]

How could the artistic, discretionary nature of cutting be integrated into the fundamental logic of a cash business: a higher volume at narrower profit margins? How was the requisite good fit to be achieved when there was far less time to spend on perfecting it, and when repeated fittings were an unwelcome expense, particularly when it came to making up less expensive goods? As Joseph Couts explained in his *Practical Guide for the Tailor's Cutting Room*: "A gentleman calls to order a coat. He is just on the point of leaving town, or going to a party, and must have his garment ready at a particular hour. You have barely time to get the coat made before he requires to put it on. There can, of course, be no fitting on here. What is the cutter to do?"[33] What's more, how could a proper, fashionable fit be successfully marketed to the majority of American customers who still lived outside the cities?

Such production problems—such business ambitions—were solved by a new technology of drafting systems that came into use in the early 1820s. Each system offered its own patented technique for "taking the measure of man" and then drafting those measurements onto the cloth so as to achieve the best individual fit on a consistent basis using a minimum amount of cloth and for as varied a clientele as possible. Or, as J. M. Bostian declared in his *Directions for Measuring and Drafting Garments* (1850): "The author of this work, in presenting it to the public, does it with perfect confidence in its utility and easy application . . . which is most applicable in its various measurements of the human body, overcomes deformity, and renders symmetry symmetrical, approaches nearest to perfect, be it simple or complex in its application."[34] These systems were a far less dramatic means than strikes and conspiracy trials, but were of no less revolutionary significance in the transformation of tailoring into a mass production business working on a national scale. The number of drafting systems being patented and published proliferated steadily during the 1830s, and then jumped dramatically in the 1840s, by which time methods for drafting men's garments constituted a whole subsidiary trade of competing patents, legal entanglements, regional subscription agents, aggressive advertising, and price wars.

The drafting systems imbued the craft with principles of "utility and simplicity" that made it possible for "all who wish [to] be taught to be Practical Garment Cutters" to do so. William Stinemets, a veteran of the labor wars

THE

TAILORS' COMPASSES;

OR, AN

Abridged and Accurate Method of Measurement,

BY WHICH ALL THE NUMEROUS DIMENSIONS NECESSARY FOR ALL GARMENTS, IN GENERAL USE, ARE REDUCED TO ONLY **THREE.** FOUNDED ON
THE BEAUTIFUL SYMMETRICAL PROPORTIONS OF MAN; AND DEMONSTRATING WITH ACCURACY, AND IN A SIMPLE MANNER
BETTER LENGTHS AND BREADTHS BY PROPORTIONS, THAN ARE IN MANY INSTANCES TAKEN BY MEASURE.

Illustrated with Copious and Elaborate Tables and Explanatory Drawings.

TO WHICH ARE ADDED,

Extensive Tables of Divisions of Heighths and Breadths,

TO ENABLE EVERY POSSESSOR TO OBTAIN WITH TRUE PRECISION EVERY WHIM OF FASHION, IN A COMBINATION OF

UPWARDS OF 15,000 SIZES.

BALTIMORE:
PRINTED BY R. J. MATCHETT, CORNER OF GAY & WATER STS.

1829.

The title page of Gabriel Chabot's *The Tailors' Compasses* (1829). The
plethora of new measurement and cutting technologies transformed custom
tailoring into a mass-production industry, thereby incorporating it into the
ready-made revolution. (Courtesy of the Library of Congress)

of the thirties who gave up his Broadway tailoring business in 1841 to devote
himself to marketing his own system, advertised his desire "to divest the art
of all mystery, and in lieu thereof substitute simplicity and ease." This meant
that "a person of moderate capacity can, in a few hours, cut with ease and
elegance any of the various styles of garments now in vogue." All those who
wanted to get in on the action, whether on Nassau Street in New York, or
in Blountville, Tennessee, welcomed advice for "expediting the work and in-
suring the fit," as Allen Ward summed up the contribution of his system for
drafting the foreparts of coats when he applied for a patent in 1837. Ward's
business rival, Francis Mahan, who had unrequitedly challenged him to a
public demonstration of their competing drafting systems, quoted a letter he
had received from a satisfied tailor in Wheeling, Virginia: "After having given
your system a fair trial I must say it is superior to any system I have used, I have
been in business three years, and have tried Sagues, Chappell's, Williams's,
Wilson's and others, in using your system, I am always sure of a fit."[35]

Drafting technology was designed for the "cutting departments" of city
shops and for independent country tailors but not for amateur, that is, household, use. Sewing directions, for instance, were never included in the systems' copiously detailed instructions. As usual, the exceptions prove the rule.
A. J. Hunter designed his drafting system, which was published in Kentucky

in 1853, "for the relief of those who have small means, against the extortions and burthens of the professional tailor." But the focus of Hunter's system was women's clothing, which was more commonly made up at home than were men's clothes. Tellingly, only four of the 84 patents issued for drafting systems before 1860 included women's garments at all.[36]

Competition was rife among the inventors of these systems. In 1841 William Fitzmaurice advertised lessons in measuring and drafting techniques "in the Parisian and London styles" to merchant tailors and clothing manufacturers, supplying vest and pantaloon patterns of "every size, shape, and style." In the same year Thomas Oliver touted the popularity of his plan of measuring and drafting among many of New York's leading merchant-tailoring shops. In 1842 the American Institute awarded a prize at its annual industrial fair for the first time to "the best system for drawing garments." Oliver, a Broadway tailor, was the honoree, which he must have found particularly gratifying since he was engaged in a bitter public battle with Genio Scott and James Wilson over their accusation that Oliver had infringed on their system. Meanwhile, notices for the second edition of Stinemet's drafting system included a highly reputable list of endorsers from among the city's tailoring elite, and Amos Sherman, author of the *Tailor's Instructor, Professor and Teacher of Cutting*, bragged the next year that his measurement system was used extensively in New York tailoring shops.[37]

The possibility that, as Stinemets already put it, "a person of moderate capacity can, in a few hours, CUT WITH EASE AND ELEGANCE any of the various styles of garments now in vogue" not only suited metropolitan producers anxious to improve control over, speed up, and reduce the cost of production. It also facilitated provincial initiatives designed to take advantage of the industrial surfeit of cheap cloth, credit, and labor. Sanford & Knowles, Broadway merchant tailors, would send custom suits "to any part of the United States" as long as customers left their measurements with them. Diagrams for self-measurement began to appear in advertising circulars, so that even those unable to visit the city could nevertheless partake in the sartorial distinction of having one's own custom tailer in New York or Philadelphia.[38] But the main effort came in marketing, not the suits, but the technology. Genio Scott had 136 agents spread over twenty-three states and in Canada selling subscriptions to his *Mirror of Fashion*, which, while peddling urban male style and culture, was also the principal vehicle for Scott in promoting his assorted patented drafting systems. The Wards, in turn, reprinted testimonials from satisfied tailors working with their system in, among other places, Cornesburg, Ohio; Winslow, Indiana; Lexington, Iowa; Rogersville, Tennessee; Little Georgetown, Virginia; Galveston, Texas; Vienna, Georgia; Rutland, Vermont; Watertown, Massachusetts; and Cherry, Pennsylvania. The technologies not only supplied tailors in more remote locations with new economies of production; they also bolstered their businesses by supplying "the newest fashions from Philadelphia and New-York." The direct association with New York, and, by implication, with Paris and London, provided popular cachet, and the *Mirror of Fashion*, a trade journal by any other name, adopted a self-conscious tone of high urban sophistication in soliciting the business of America's far-flung tailoring trade, explicit in the hope that its subscribers would "become the principal teachers of cutting in this country." Scott began his publishing venture in association with James Wilson, who received a patent in 1827 for inventing a "Square Rule System." Together the two had since bought up related patents and used the *Mirror of Fashion* as the means to market their resulting *Treatise on Cutting Garments to Fit the Human Form*, or their new "Tractates Nos. 1 and 2," which contained "a series of descriptions and illustrations for measuring and drafting."[39] The reciprocal circulation of fashion and its system of production—the powerful mutuality between the economics and the aesthetics of tailoring—is what contemporaries must have meant by all their talk about the "utility of fashion." It certainly makes literal the notion of the mass production of culture, and shows self-fashioning to have been entirely rational, predictable, and constant, and thus potentially common to all.

This trend was already evident in the 1820s as the fashions, like tailoring standards, and together with them, circulated en masse throughout the country. James Douglass, for instance, set up a tailoring business at the west end of Superior Street in Cleveland in the fall of 1825, announcing that "he has made arrangements to receive the newest fashions from Philadelphia and New-York." John Wills, another Cleveland tailor, received quarterly reports of the latest fashions for gentlemen's clothing from New York. In Milledgeville, Georgia, A. Cumming regularly acquired "the latest New York fashions" during the fall of 1827 and promised that his work would be executed according to their designs. One of Scott's agents in Buffalo promised potential subscribers "New York Fashions at Four Dollars a year only, and including a paper published monthly, and the London plates of Fashions, together with cuts in your paper, representing the Paris Fashions, and the various changes in your city—the whole included at Six Dollars a year." J. H. Bancker of Nashville sold A. F. Saugues's *Report on Fashions* to tailors in the area "at the New York prices," together with squares, scales and a book of diagrams, and inch measures. Samuel and Asahel Ward made their color plates available separately, at a dollar apiece, for adorning the windows of tailoring shops. The new measuring and cutting technologies, while deskilling, or decreasing the need for skilled craftsmen in urban areas, actually gave provincial tailors a new lease on business life. And, of course, the advent of these standard technologies potentially brought customized fashion to the entire citizenry. No wonder, then, as Tocqueville had observed, "the man you left in New York you find again in almost impenetrable solitudes: same clothes, same attitude, same language, same habits, same pleasures."[40]

Drafting systems, by their nature, emphasized quantifiable exactitude over subjective judgment. They signaled a new age of "literacy" in the tailoring craft. Thus, Gabriel Chabot's *The Tailors' Compasses; or, An Abridged and Accurate Method of Measurement* was "illustrated with Copious and Elaborate Tables and Explanatory Drawings; To which are added Extensive Tables of divisions of heights and breadths to enable every possessor to obtain with true precision every whim of fashion, in a combination of Upwards of 15,000 sizes." Numbers became the standard of measure, replacing the tailor's personal observation of spatial relations. Deduction of the "mathematical proportions of the material man" by "the rule of mathematics" was what distinguished modern times from "the fantastic days of Elizabeth, or Louis XIV," as B. Read and H. Bodman, highly reputable London tailors who operated a branch store on Broadway, asserted in their *New Superlative System of Cutting*. Public enthusiasm for such scientific conceits was high in the antebellum years, and tailors were in a position to bring the progress of the age to that most popular level—each man's body. One need only look at how these systems promulgated a cartographic ordering of that body into so many discrete provinces of waist, hip, shoulder, back, neck, arm, and leg to understand that the claim to scientific progress was no matter of hyperbole. In fact, science and system were now the determinant principles of the tailoring craft. It was what Poe had made fun of in his annals of Peter Proffit, except that the pronouncements of patent holders and system sellers were no hoax. Behind all their self-promotion was a basic truth: that tailoring was being driven by the same desiderata of standardization and commercial efficacy as any other industrial-age business.[41]

Prior to that age—in the not too distant past—tailors had each kept their own exclusive set of "patterns," variably sized and styled paper or cloth cutouts of the constituent sections of sleeves, collars, breasts, and so on, belonging to the various types of garments they regularly made up. When cutting the cloth, the tailor traced designs from the pattern that best matched his customer's size and shape, using the client's personal measurements to particularize the draft. A tailor developed his collection of patterns over the

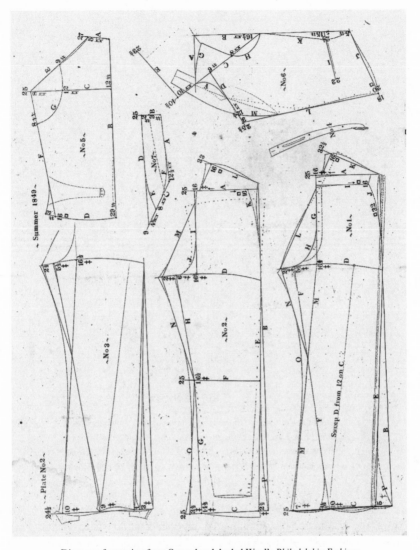

Diagrams for cutting from Samuel and Asahel Ward's *Philadelphia Fashions and Tailors' Archetypes* (1849). (Courtesy of The Winterthur Library, Printed Book and Periodical Collection)

A cartographic ordering of the male body into standard provinces of neck, shoulder, arm, back, waist, hip, and leg. An individual fit was achieved by applying universal truths. (From Scott and Wilson's *Treatise on Cutting Garments*; courtesy of The Winterthur Library, Printed Book and Periodical Collection)

years, the product of his accumulated experience and artistic talents. They were unique to him, although he did occasionally sell patterns and would pass on copies to apprentices at the end of their service. The success of the patterns formed the basis of his own reputation, since they were what translated measurements into a fit. As such, they were carefully guarded trade secrets. Consequently, too, tailors had no need for standard units of measurement. A tailor recorded the length of a person's arm or the circumference of his chest by making notches on a strip of parchment or paper. That strip then contained all the sizing information for a particular customer and could be kept for future reference.[42]

The adoption of the inch tape measure by tailors after 1820 was thus a watershed in the craft's history. Curiously, there is no satisfactory explanation of why the inch measure came into use when it did: the technology was old and was common among other crafts. Nora Waugh, a careful observer of the social details of dress, has argued that the tape measure was invented when it was because it "drew attention to the comparative relations that exist between the various parts of the body." This made it integral to a general ethos of interchangeability and proportionality, the systematization of the body requisite for the mass production of raiment. But Claudia Kidwell, the preeminent historian of the nineteenth-century clothing revolution, has pointed out that an awareness of comparative relations between body measurements was nothing new. Such knowledge formed the basis of the system of patterns utilized by colonial tailors in their clothing production. Having made that correction, however, Kidwell does not then offer her own explanation for why this technology emerged when it did. She is satisfied with vague allusions to the search for system inherent in a statistical age, an argument curiously akin to Waugh's own.[43]

The truth is that a standard measure was necessary for circulating information in an age when secrecy was no longer good for business. It made it possible to sell what had once been considered trade secrets but now constituted a new opportunity to make money in the exploding clothing market. The practical effect, as Kidwell and Christman have pointed out, was that "instead of each tailor having his own unique set of markings, now anybody, by following the set procedures for measuring and drafting, could cut for anybody." An "American system" of interchangeability had overtaken one of society's oldest and most personalized crafts. Thus, Scott and Perkins could claim that their *Instruction in the Whole Art of Measuring and Cutting* (already in its seventh edition) marked the entry of the "ordinary mechanical professions" into the same realm of "useful and practical improvements as steam-driven multiplication and combination of physical power," as contemporaries strained to describe new industrial divisions of labor, even though the physical process of clothing production—the tools and tasks—was actually unchanged. What had changed, of course, was the economic context of production: one now measured and cut garments as part of a new commercial system emphasizing mass volume and speed. This was manifest not only in the escalating number of patents issued for measuring, drafting, and cutting men's clothing but in the clamorous marketing of them. Thus, Samuel and Asahel Ward offered not only their *Quarterly Reports* of the new fashions for sale (an annual subscription costing five dollars a year), but, for an extra dollar, would include colored

plates each spring and fall. They also offered extensive alteration information that allowed for updating fashion details, such as widening the lapels or
elongating the skirts of coats. Instructions for learning the Wards' "Protractor System of Garment Cutting" cost another five dollars. The protractors
themselves were 25 cents, the essential scales of measurement 75 cents each.
The special ruler cost a dollar. The Wards also advertised inch measures, tailors' crayons, measure books, shears, trimmers and points, yardsticks, eyelets,
squares, scale boxes—all the manufacturing paraphernalia, and all for cash,
of course. It is not clear how many provincials in 1853 actually ordered new
riding or promenade coats, the kind with large sleeves and edges bound with
twilled galloon to match, made of a new style of cashmerette called *constelle*
that, the *Mirror of Fashion* reported, had just appeared in Paris. But the trend
was clear, and it was on view in Cleveland, or in Memphis, or almost everywhere else, thanks to Thomas Oliver's "superb steel plates" that presented
unrivaled color illustrations of the latest fashions.[44]

A growing percentage of the drafting technologies were based on the principles of proportionality, whereby only a minimum number of measurements
were taken directly from the customer, the rest being extrapolated from them
by means of a patented set of scales or tables. Competing systems touted the
superiority of both their actual measurements—which limbs they measured,
and with what devices—and the subsequent extrapolations. In a proportional
system a tailor would be satisfied with two or three measurements, and sometimes just one. Proportionality, of course, saved time, although just how much
time was open to question. More significantly, proportionality seemed to be
the basis of mass production, since its logical end was in ready-made clothing,
whose sizings were extrapolated from no direct measurements at all.[45]

Standardized production did not have to assume the guise of proportionality, however. A considerable number of the patented drafting systems being
published in these years were based on the principle of direct measurement,
according to which the tailor eschewed proportional shortcuts and personally
took each specific measure, which for a full suit of clothes might reach thirty
or forty. On the one hand, these systems approximated popular notions of
artisanal tradition. The most exacting personal tailors all claimed to work
with direct measurements, which they then favorably compared to proportionality's lazy reliance on patterns and eschewal of fittings—a slothfulness,
as one proponent then declared, that reduced the tailoring trade "to the level
of clothes-pin making" or, even worse, made it indistinguishable from dressmaking. But while it assumed for itself the mantle of a higher standard of craft,
there was, in fact, little that was traditional about direct measurement as it was

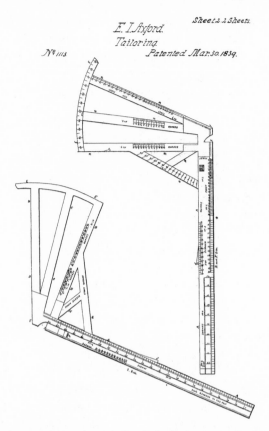

Sheet.2. 2 Sheets.

E. I. Axford.
Tailoring

Nº 1113

Patented Mar. 30. 1839.

A newly patented measuring tool, 1839. Each tailoring system offered its own technique for "taking the measure of man" and then drafting those measurements onto the cloth so as to realize the best fit on a consistent basis for as varied a clientele as possible, while using the least amount of cloth.

practiced in the nineteenth century. We have seen how patterns and proportionality predated the industrial age. At the same time, systems of direct measurement were increasingly informed by industrial priorities. They rested no less than did proportionality on newly discovered standards—universally applicable, commodifiable, and aggressively merchandised throughout the land. They represented no less of a systematization of the craft for commercial advantage, promising as they did to deliver a "definable, repeatable . . . procedure" that was utterly at odds with the practices of tailors in the previous century. J. O. Madison, for instance, insisted that taking the measures for a coat using his nonproportional system would entail less than a minute of time and that the entire subsequent drafting could be completed within five more. The promised result offered a distinct commercial advantage: a more reliable fit utilizing less fabric. Madison went on to explain how direct measurement technologies relied no less than proportional ones on an anthropometric mapping of the human body:

> The body has points that divide the surface; therefore, every point requires a separate measure and each measure must shape the cloth for the part over which the measure was taken; consequently, the envelope for the shoulders and body, like the covering of a ball, must be cut in separate pieces; and then, the great desideratum is to join these several parts or pieces together, in a manner that will produce harmony among the different sections, so that each part will rest at ease without struggling to displace its neighbor.

"Knowledge of the human shape, and . . . mathematical science" uncovered anatomical correspondences of a fixed nature that, in turn, became the key for cutting and then reconnecting the cloth so that it matched the individual contours of each body.[46]

And so the myriad drafting technologies all sought to discover the immutable laws that would allow tailors to treat each body as unique while mass producing its raiment faster, cheaper, and more anonymously. This meant that in the new conditions of capitalism, a personalized fit, one that started from measurements taken directly by a tailor, was no less based on a systematization of the buying public—"whereby much labor and expense is saved"— than was the ready-made. Proponents of direct measurement, in fact, made claims that suggested their method was the one ideally suited to a mass market. Proportional measurement, they pointed out, was based on stereotyped patterns. These stereotypes were, by definition, a predetermined assortment of postulated shapes and sizes that did not actually exist in nature. The result was a garment that might or might not fit. For while systems of proportionality rested on the assumption of variation (and thus they needed to establish as wide an assortment of shapes and sizes as possible), their result was singular, that is, a fixed stereotype. The tailor working from "a successful system" of direct measurements proceeded by the opposite methodology. His system postulated a single standard, a model applicable to all, that, when applied to various persons' measurements, would again and again yield a properly idiosyncratic fit. That is, having uncovered universal truths about body shape, it was capable of suiting everyone. The new tailoring regime thus made a signal contribution to the emerging industrial order by rationalizing that most natural of subjects, the human body. Not only did the personally measured suit, in other words, represent the acme of technological standardization, but standardization proved to be no less than the means of achieving individuation. That individuation, in turn, was what tied the person to the mass market—was what integrated the private body into that market—since it was what made him profitable. If the antebellum economist Henry C. Carey wrote that "the highest civilization is marked by the most perfect individuality and the greatest tendency to union," it was the custom-fitted suit that in daily practice actually wedded self and society. It did so by a commercial logic that was replacing older, homespun versions of a common identity.[47]

Dressing for Work

Pantaloons, vests, and coats constituted an assembly of cylinders and planes that simultaneously realized the values of "mathematical utility" while also achieving a "quiet pose and graceful fall over the hips." The suit, it could thus be said, aspired to wed dynamism to self-control, two latently conflicting principles whose unity was fundamental for industrial success. Male appearance consequently contained a structural tension endemic to the market's incessant drive toward standards and control, on the one hand, and its equally strong tendency "to expansion [and] diffusion" on the other. In the years following 1820 this tension was personified by a new "white-collar" class of business clerks who.had come to the city to administer the banks, insurance companies, importing firms, wholesale trading houses, retail stores, attorneys' offices, and whatever other enterprises were necessary to the workings of industrial society. Typically, the clerk had left farm and family behind in pursuit of a business career whose success rested on a "genteel appearance, and passing address," qualifications that were deemed essential for a job that entailed waiting on customers, receiving and arranging stock and inventorying it at the end of the season, making visits to collect payments, discounting notes, and keeping accounts. Living an unsupervised existence in the anonymous conditions of the metropolis, the clerk was a leading protagonist in the demise of homespun patriarchy: he preferred the city to the country, "counter-jumping" to plowing, and selling to producing. As such, he effectively repudiated all that the agrarian republic once held dear. Indeed, the clerk was living proof of the 1850 census's redefinition of industry as being about making a profit more than about making things.[1]

Dressed in "the cast-off graces of the gentry," as Poe disparagingly rendered their cultural ambitions, these clerks appeared on the historical stage at

the same time that a replaceable collar was invented, which made the once exclusive white linen of the gentleman a commonly available good. The timing
couldn't have been better for such a socially ambitious but poorly remunerated group of young men on the make. And yet the transposition to the industrial age was not an entirely smooth one. The clerk's white-collared plasticity
also seemed to recapitulate the social confusion that Franklin had discerned a
hundred years earlier, "ever since we parted with our Homespun Cloaths for
Fourteen Penny Stuffs." It was clear evidence of the democratic free-for-all
Tocqueville worriedly depicted as driven by "desires inspired by equality"
that had nothing to do with public virtue. The result was distinctly modern:
the clerk's enthusiastic enlistment in the propertied order was at once perceived as a threat to that order.[2]

- - - - -

The clerk came of age in those years when New Yorkers were congratulat-
ing themselves on the great advances made in their shopping life. "The majority of our readers," the *New-York Mirror* wrote in 1836, "doubtless remember the dingy, comfortless, uncarpeted appearance of the shops some
fifteen and twenty years ago, and the contrast of their then condition with
the splendour and magnificence of the present day." Broadway retailers had
begun to accoutre their interiors with lamps, fine carpets, and easy chairs,
thus winning the inclusion of their stores among the "new age's new cultural amusements." Meanwhile, "commerce pour[ed] forth her glittering and
costly wares." Awnings were hung to protect strollers from sun and rain and to
encourage them to bide their time peering through the large plateglass fronts
being installed on an increasing number of Broadway facades. Well-dressed
women were seen moving "with that lingering, hesitating step which threat-
ens to terminate at every dry-goods or jeweler's store." Inside, "recherché
dressed persons stand bowing and obsequious, ready to fly at your merest
whim, and anxious to gratify every caprice." A montage of display windows,
pavement tablets, placards, lettered signs, and countless other advertising tac-
tics replaced the residential still life that had once characterized Broadway and
other downtown streets. Indeed, the fluidity was palpable:

> A general and undistinguishable hurry and confusion. The carmen halloo and
> lash their horses . . . the omnibuses whip and hurry to pass each other. . . .
> Slight, airy figures . . . pass you at every step; well-dressed men of all ages,
> and foreigners of all complexions, and fashion of apparel and manner, throng
> the way; the shops look like drawing-rooms on a bridal morning visit, and the

whole scene is gay, and dazzling, and delightful. Broadway against the world—
we allow it!

The city's vaunted Knickerbocker proprieties of yore were giving way to a far
less patient ethos of accumulation, speculation, and display.[3]

The era's transformations were plain to see in New York City's popular
iconography. Theodore Fay, editor of the *New-York Mirror*, published a series of engraved views of the city in 1831 whose principal subject was the city's
architectural landmarks. These views taught the well-to-do subscriber—for
the engravings were costly—that the metropolis was a stable edifice and that
urban nature was static. The human landscape was limited to groups of prom-
enaders or carriage riders who provided a sense of scale to the buildings,
which appropriately dwarfed them.[4] Within a few years, however, a new style
of cityscapes began to appear. Aquatints with a far more vibrant tonal range,
they also circulated in far less expensive lithographic reproductions. Most
significantly, they presented a different view of the city, a perspective that
shifted the observer's focus from the monumental grandeur to the incessant
human activity in the street below. The subject of Thomas Horner's well-
known series of prints published in 1836, for instance, was the very busy-
ness of daily life. Broadway was now crowded with persons, walking, sitting,
slouching, strolling, arguing, rushing—and all caught up in their own affairs.
Goods were everywhere as well in Horner's pictures. They filled up shop
windows, sat perched on sidewalks, or waited to be transported across town.
To be sure, this perspective was no less idealized than its more staid predecessor. Horner depicted prosperous avenues of smoothly coordinated traffic,
industrious laborers, and fashionables strolling on immaculate sidewalks. But
their ceaseless activity constituted a far more dynamic ideal, a kaleidoscope of
movement in which the city not only was the backdrop for the human business
at hand but, like that business, was itself a *mobile perpetuum*.[5]

"Half the city is being pulled down," *Putnam's Magazine* reported in
1853, practical corroboration of what the young millinery store clerk, Henry
Southworth, had heard at a lecture at the Mechanics Society not too long
beforehand: "The last fifty years which have just expired have formed the
most eventful half century that has ever been known since the creation of the
World." "Hardly had [the old] disappeared, before the foundations of new
buildings were laid," another observed of the times. Brick tenements were
cleaned out. Narrow windows were widened. Impractically small doors were
replaced. "Groups of dilapidated wooden hovels, intersected by dark, narrow,
and filthy lanes, the abode of squalid misery, are continually passing away, and

giving place to broadened streets and lofty mansions." "Broadway was fast becoming a street of palaces," George William Curtis observed in 1854, the European imagery no longer such a pejorative. But such "modern improvement" was not to be compared to Haussman's state-sponsored reconstruction of Paris during these same years. New York was undergoing a market-inspired drive toward a business grandiloquence of marble, brown freestone, and black walnut. It was a group of Broadway merchants, for instance, who created a fund in 1854 to ensure that the street between Bowling Green and Union Square was swept every day before 7:00 A.M. Degraded neighborhoods were "redeemed" by being "thrown open to the activities of trade, [their] rookeries replaced by marble palaces." "The mania for converting Broadway into a street of shops is greater than ever," Philip Hone observed at mid-century, as the city became as much a subject of consumption as a place to live. The floor of Hone's own former residence on Cortlandt Street was lowered and the rear of the building extended back twenty feet in order to enhance the property's potential as retail space. *Putnam's* continued: "It is startling to enumerate the number of churches which have been pulled down and displaced to make room for the great business which spreads with such astounding rapidity . . . utterly obliterating everything that is old and venerable."[6]

Like ownership itself, brick and mortar proved to be a highly conditional thing in industrializing times. The rush of improvements inspired a sense of bewilderment no less than it did enthusiasm, as the "most eventful half century that has ever been known" continued to unfold. "The history of New York for the last three years is comparable to nothing but the explosion of a pack of crackers—pop—pop—pop—one after another they go off and all their substance vanishes in fumes," the young conservative George Templeton Strong wrote during the depression of the early forties, anticipating by a few years Marx's own dictum according to which "all that is solid melts into air." "Things change so fast here that the city does not seem like home to those who own it."[7]

Out of this escalating tide of people, goods, and buildings men's clothing emerged at the center of retail life. The gigantic scale on which clothiers did business might seem to belie the ephemeral nature of the city in the age of capital, but their Marble Palaces actually were the cultural expression of speed and volume. Brooks Brothers & Co., which built its new store on the site of the old Whig Party headquarters at Broadway and Grand, filled four storeys and 20,000 square feet with a sales force of two hundred responsible for administering custom, city, and wholesale departments of coats, pants, vests, shirts, and a full complement of men's furnishings in search of the broadest market possible. While size was the basis of profits, it was no less a prerequisite of refinement, a key to the "beautiful thoroughness" that was now integral to "our national character." The Brooks's black walnut interiors, which so dramatically highlighted the golden detailing on the building's interior capitals, invited the promenade to move inside from the street, much as did Daniel Devlin's Corinthian columns and Italianate symmetries a few blocks down Broadway. In this way the economic priority of volume was wedded to polite culture. "Grandiosity" became at once a business principle and an aesthetic.[8]

Since footage was more expensive when it fronted a shopping avenue, these clothing palaces were long and deep spaces. Wilde & Co., for instance, squeezed into a 176 × 30 foot lot. Even the Brookses, who obviously spared no expense, had one hundred feet on Broadway and two hundred on Grand. The proliferation of looking glasses along the walls addressed any sense of undue narrowness—while, at the same time, "doubling the wealth"—as the shopper proceeded under high ceilings and chandeliers along a wide aisle into the heart of the store.[9] In the evening and during the winter months the interiors were illumined by artificial light whose glow was intensified by the many mirrors. Lewis & Hanford boasted of no less than 112 gas lamps on their premises. Long tables piled with neatly folded pantaloons lay on either side of the central aisle. Other surfaces were more sparsely laid out, allowing one to better inspect the garments. Coats were hung from hooks on the walls, perhaps on the "coat forms" recently patented by William Olds, which were "particularly well adapted for exhibiting garments in stores" since they did not draw up on the collar and injure the coat's shape. Other tables supported display cases tilted at a soft angle to show off shirts and furnishings, a salesman at hand to retrieve the desired goods from shelves lined with carefully labeled boxes organized by price. Clerks attended to the tables and devoted personal attention to customers by assessing a fit in front of the mirror, examining the stitching of a lining, or recommending the quality of a fabric. Upon a sale they would write up a receipt that the shopper then brought to the cashier's desk. Only there did money exchange hands.[10]

The shopping resort, then, was simultaneously an arena of refinement and the location for the baser quest for profits. But there was no confusion. Gentility, of course, traditionally eschewed any explicit identification with the active pursuit of riches while having always rested on a generous material base. Homespun industry inverted that indifference to the profanely material, turning it into productive virtue worthy of the gentleman citizen. And now that there was no production without profit, enrichment could be the unabashed end of male effort. Thus capitalist gentrification was no longer an

This is the splendid stock in trade,
Comprising rich clothing, all ready made,
Of every fashion, rank, and grade,
Sold by the clerks, who faithfully work
In the famous Oak Hall, in North Street.

5

An interior view of George Simmons's Boston clothing emporium, Oak Hall, in 1854, accompanied by a rhyming advertisement. (Courtesy of The Winterthur Library, Printed Book and Periodical Collection)

oxymoron. Nor were consumption and production yet antipodes in a world whose denizens, including the most effete among them, were intimately familiar with the material provenance of the commodities they purchased. The particulars of mass production, in fact, were no less a part of the new "phantasmagoria" of material plenty. Daniel Devlin's copywriters assigned two exclamation marks to the "near 2000 hands!!" who produced his giant inventory of coats. James Wilde, Jr., another Broadway clothier, bragged in an advertisement in Gobright's *New-York Sketch Book* that his firm provided employment to "twenty-five cutters and . . . a force of from fifteen hundred to two thousand work hands." True, these notices were primarily directed at commercial buyers from the provinces. But when in 1861 the young Sally Shephard visited Brooks Brothers with her father, who had come to buy underwear, she too was no less impressed by the four hundred persons cutting and sewing on the premises than she was by the bronze pillars and the painted rotunda.[11]

Shopping, in other words, was an unmistakably industrial experience. In an age of accelerated turnover and narrowed margins, the comings and goings of customers were no longer carefully regulated. A person now entered the store unhindered, was left alone with the merchandise, and could even leave without buying something. The store, in this respect, clearly became an extension of the street outside. This made it a new locality of public life, one organized under the aegis of retail and consequently representative of a specifically "commodified" form of citizenship. A new lexicon was consequently required that could mediate between the gainful requirements of those in business and the as yet uncommitted relationship of the anonymous shopper to the goods. Uniform pricing became that modern vernacular. Alfred Munroe & Co.'s language was typical: "The price of every article is marked in plain figures upon a ticket attached to it." Each item now had its permanent and predetermined price, a function of a rational economic process that replaced an earlier practice of seeming arbitrariness and deceit. One-price shopping marked the end of haggling, which then obviated the need for trickery, especially since private markings decipherable only by the store's clerks were also disqualified. The relationship between buyer and seller would now be conducted without any subterfuge. "Gentlemen," Silvers & Armitrage advertised, "will be capable of judging for themselves relative to the [clothing's] cheapness."[12]

Such honesty was good for business. "Truthfulness is a trump card" in the retailer's hands, Edwin Freedley wrote in his *Practical Treatise on Business*, since the seller's great object must be "the *confidence* of the public." This allowed buyers and sellers alike to let down their guard. Truth and convenience were simultaneously served. The single price, as the impresario merchant tailor George P. Fox wrote, "thereby render[ed] interchange of commodities of an agreeable and sincere character, performed in the courtesies that are usually practised in polite society." This was a commercial victory of the gentleman over the trickster as the former sought to diffuse the antagonisms inherent in exchange. Indeed, the claim of the single price to serve the common interest almost seemed to resurrect a precapitalist rhetoric of a "just price." At the same time, one-price shopping rested on a far more impersonal form of justice. For by avoiding the need for haggling, exchange became focused on things rather than on persons. This, of course, matched the ethos of a ready-made age, as it did tailoring's very codification of the male body by means of new drafting systems. Not only was civility placed on a standard of predictability, but the result was distinctly modern: "Comfort is brought to

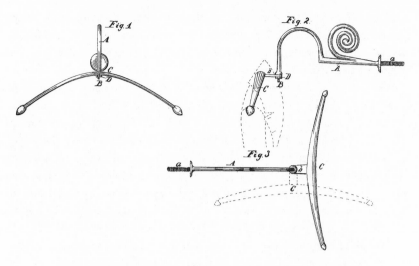

Illustrations from patent number 8,858, issued April 6, 1852, for William B. Olds's "revolving coat form," designed to display the garment to its best advantage in the anonymous conditions of ready-made shopping.

the household of every customer when he feels confident that he can send a child or a servant to make a purchase, and he will be sure not only of getting the article he wants, but of obtaining it on the same terms if he were to go himself."[13]

Popular suspicions of being cheated were not, of course, automatically assuaged. Many wondered whether a single price meant not the same cost to all, but the salesman's determination of a price appropriate to each customer and his refusal to then budge from it. However, as stores grew bigger and the management of their inventories became an increasingly complex enterprise, the desire for reliable standards became ever more real. If P. L. Rogers was serious when he announced that every article was "put down to the lowest figure which an immense trade will justify, and from it there will be no deviation," it was necessary to take pricing out of the hands of the clerks and establish a reliable system of product-inventory control. One-price practices were, in addition, necessitated by the increasing popularity of cash sales. "Rakes are in the habit of buying on credit," Charles Stokes & Co. declared in explaining the company's two mottoes "that ensure but one class of customer . . . 'one price' and 'terms cash.'" If no one was buying on credit, there was no reason for retailers to demand variable prices. The introduction of return policies, born of the guarantees of cash tailors as well as the very nature of buying ready-made items "from the shelf," also required a fixed price, especially now that fitting rooms were being provided in the stores, which left "the responsibility of not being suited entirely with the customers." There was consequently no reason to disbelieve Alfred Munroe & Co. when they announced that "NO DEVIATION from the price in any instance [would] be made." In fact, all the large clothing firms proclaimed their support for "One Price" shopping. For the Smith Brothers, who sold half a million dollars' worth of clothing a year, the single price was no less than the subject of bragging rights, as the firm presented its adoption of the system as testimony to its progressive spirit. It was a credible claim. Since the Smiths also announced that they would satisfy themselves in business with "a profit of a homeopathic character," their margins had to be closely managed by means of a system that controlled the conditions of sale. [14]

The Smith Brothers also presented themselves as an alternative to "those mansions of marble." They did business on Fulton Street, a busy commercial artery running from Broadway to the ferry on the East River, home to a plethora of offices and hotels catering to merchants, jobbers, stockbrokers, and commercial lawyers. This was where Daniel Devlin's first New York store was located, not far from the law office where Bartleby, Melville's "pallidly neat" clerk, was hired to copy documents. While satisfying the twin goals of "economy and elegance," the Smiths specialized in a wide variety of wardrobes "for promenade and dress; for the workshop, the country room and ball." Like the Broadway houses, the Fulton Street firms did a high-volume combined retail and wholesale business. In fact, grandiosity was no less valued on Fulton Street than it was on Broadway. Typically, P. L. Rogers described his "Union Hall," situated at the corner of Fulton and Nassau, as "the most extensive house of the kind, in America or Europe." If the hyperbole was commonplace, it was excused by the fact that the chances were probably very good indeed of finding whatever one needed in stock at Rogers's store. In his case the self-advertisement was also invested with political meaning. As the *Irish American* proclaimed, Rogers's success in the clothing business was proof that in America Irishmen could no longer be sneered at by the aristocrats of the "ancient world." [15]

Clothing was in abundance further uptown on the Bowery as well, where emporiums were "stacked high to the very ceiling, and hung thick along the shop fronts with great Bowery overcoats, blazing waistcoats, and everlasting pants." Here, too, clothiers claimed to have the largest establishments in the city, whose magnificence "equals, if not surpasses any Broadway establishment in point of quality, excellence of material, and superiority of workmanship." The Bowery, the principal avenue for working-class shopping, was lined with men's clothing stores: J. G. Sperling at no. 2, Silk & Wise at no. 4, W. L. Conklin at no. 8, Smith & Conant at no. 12, H. M. Lockwood & Co. at no. 14, Mauritz Linds at no. 18, Crosby & Sackett at no. 22, Rac & Scofield at no. 24, Jacob Anhalt at no. 26, Thomas Ogilvie at no. 28, Boace Levy at no. 34, John Dolan at no. 38, Eugene Brown at no. 56, H. S. Sloan & Co. at no. 58, H. Levy & Co. at no. 64, Samuel Fox at no. 66, Solomon Rich at no. 72, E. J. Olssen at no. 74, Bernhard Ditterhoefer at no. 78, Andrew Chadeayne at no. 80, Myers Londoner at no. 88, Aaron Chichester at no. 98, G. C. Jeffries at no. 106, Elisha Davis at no. 108, A. L. & W. S. Woods at no. 110, Jonathan Haight at no. 114, and Harbutt Cooper at no. 118. By now one stood at Grand Street, seven blocks east of the Brooks Brothers' new palace, a half mile that became a favorite gauge of the era's developing class schisms. On the Bowery, for instance, there were no plate-glass windows, no "gorgeous jewelers' shops," no huge furniture establishments. Business there was euphemistically conducted "with more of an eye to comfort than splendor." Nevertheless, working-class men had ample opportunity for genteel stylization. Nathaniel Willis, torn as he was between his apprehensions concerning the market's democratizing tendencies and his embrace of male color and ornament, made note of "the much more violent array of those gorgeous stuffs" to be found on the Bowery. "The small tailors' shops in these Alsatian quarters are quite in a glow with the display of cravats and waistcoats and their catering for the taste of their customers is, of course, careful and well considered."[16]

In fact, the clothing revolution was everywhere: on Broadway, Fulton Street, the Bowery, in Chatham Square, on Cherry Street, and along the docks of West Street. The city had simply filled up with places where men could buy a suit. By mid-century there were over a thousand establishments regularly listed in the city's business directories. As Willis admitted in barely disguised regret, "the age is, perhaps, forever gone by, when a privileged class could monopolize finery of garb; and, of all the civilized nations, it were least possible in ours."[17]

This material explosion ushered in a fashionable bias against what became known as the "shabby-genteel look." A half-worn coat, even one made of the finest cloth, was no longer considered appropriate even as less formal daytime wear. If anything, it signaled a certain eccentricity, an "indifference" to progress and improvement. New clothes were a conscious disavowal of the paucity of the past, which was still evident in less civilized provinces where they "wear the coats they have until they are worn out. . . . One shirt on your back and the second on the wash line are sufficient." Since so many

A street map of New York City in 1852 (showing Brooklyn as well). As the source of labor, cloth, and credit, the metropolis was deeply implicated in the creation of ready-made democracy. (Courtesy of the Collection of the New-York Historical Society, neg. 75522)

mass-produced garments were also made up from less permanent qualities of cloth that could cause one's pantaloons to become "bulged and strained" or one's cravat to be "frayed and brownish," buying new was a practical fashion as well. The imperative was not to look like some poor country parson living on $300 a year, betrayed by a well-worn broadcloth coat, a fur hat that had undergone its nine-hundred-and-ninety-ninth ironing, and boots that glittered suspiciously in the morning sun from the effects of "an extra coating of Day & Martin's best, well laid on." Worse yet was to be so antiquated in style and condition as to resemble one of the Pilgrim Fathers, "as they appeared when they first landed from the Mayflower." Americans, the *New-York Mirror* insisted in its premiere issue, were "perpetually in search of something *new*," and tailors and clothiers collaborated in promulgating an ethos in which "every thing that tells of hoary antiquity" was suspect. The man who did not manifest progress in his sartorial habits was marked. "The observers point him out among the multitude—'There is a sample of old times'—'There goes a miser who can't afford a new coat.' . . . Thus to be out of fashion a man is generally regarded as wanting in spirit or purse."[18]

The *Ladies' Companion* presented the corrective: "The sun was shining brightly; all the world was abroad but I did not meet with one whose coat was so new as my own. I felt my superiority; I perceived that I was an object of universal attention."[19] Of course, the coat was merely representative of the whole ensemble. Without an equally fresh vest and pair of trousers—which were not, however, always purchased together, or made from the same fabric—the coat was only a transparent pretense, no better than a patch. This esteem for the new was not just a function of fashion's generic interest in novelty. Nor was it necessarily an attempt by the arriviste to close the door to polite status to others after him and so accentuate his own success. Newness had direct relevance to the age of abundance and to the general availability of goods. Even pioneers, the *American Gentleman's Guide* insisted in 1857, no longer needed to don an old dress coat and a half-worn satin cravat. "A cutaway coat . . . with ample pockets, loose, strong, and warm," specifically made for pioneering activities and generally for sale most everywhere, was to be preferred.[20]

Whereas in the past one could demote aging dress suits to day use, the requirement was now for pristine garments around the clock. In a family of restricted means, "where the father is obliged, by his line of life or connections, to keep up what is called a respectable or genteel appearance," a man's old suits could no longer be adapted for his sons' wear. The neighbors would certainly look askance at such "meanness." Instead, the children were all attired in new ready-made garments. For the same reason, an English gentleman, now considered an appropriate model for emulation by the *American Gentleman's Guide*, was never to appear "in the morning"—the portion of the day that lasted until evening and was devoted to either business or outdoor amusements—in the "half-worn coat of fine black cloth . . . but in some strong-looking, rough, knock-about 'fixin,' frequently of nondescript form and fashion, but admirably adapted both in shape and material for use—for work."[21]

These new work clothes were what Henry Southworth couldn't peel off fast enough upon returning home on a hot July evening in 1851, after spending all day in a heavy woolen coat attending customers at Beard's millinery store. Such attire in fact constituted a new category of male fashion that was coming to be known as business dress. "In the counting-room and office," Samuel Wells advised in his "manual of republican etiquette" in 1856, "gentlemen wear frock coats or sack coats. They need not be of very fine material, and should not be of any garish pattern." "Pantaloons for full dress fit quite close, while those for morning wear are cut more easily to the figure," the *Mirror of Fashion* explained in describing the utilitarian qualities of dressing for work. Indeed, "business coats," "business surtouts," "business paletots," and sundry other "office" attire were an increasingly conspicuous presence in male fashion plates: "Fig. 2 represents a person, who, having returned from his counting-house, is taking a quiet seat in his back yard, intending after tea to change his habit to a demi-toilet and go with his family to the Opera at Castle Garden." Meanwhile, he remained in his business dress, "a la mode and comfortable." Degroot sold business coats on Fulton Street of Drab d'Ete, cashmerette, erminette, alpaca, bombasin, croton cloth, and tweed, "in every style," for as little as $2.50. His neighbor, P. L. Rogers, had a selection of "office" and "business" coats that started even lower. Mann & McKimm, doing business farther uptown, appeared to make a specialty of business dress, manufacturing for other city retailers. The Broadway tailor J. C. Booth made office coats the lead item in his advertisements starting in the late 1840s. Business clothes were the only kind of ready-made garments P. Mulligan specified for sale at his tailoring shop, and they were the only ready-mades that James Lacy, a John Street draper and tailor, would sell at all.[22]

Business fashion emerged as "countinghouses" began to give way to "offices," and banks, insurance companies, railroad offices, wholesalers, and the city's ever-growing retail sector recruited an unprecedented mass of clerical labor to administer their expanding operations. Earlier in the century there had been little need for such a workforce. "There are here no very large concerns, and most men are capable of attending to their own business," Henry Fearon testified in 1819. By the next decade, however, "General Information" companies were busy placing young men in "offices and stores." In the thirties, the *New York Herald* targeted "the clerk and his principal," together with the journeyman and his master, as part of its new mass readership. By the early forties, the *Tribune* identified "all clerks in the city" as a permanent constituency of urban life. Indeed, they were the city's fastest growing public. When A. T. Stewart opened his Marble Palace in 1846 he already employed a hundred of them. As Asa Greene observed, "in a large and fashionable shopping establishment, there must be a large number of clerks, to wait promptly on the ladies; otherwise there will be pouting, fidgetting, and withdrawing of patronage." By 1853 the number of clerks in Stewart's employ had tripled. It was representative of a trend. Even in a manufacturing city like Philadelphia a third of the labor force was employed in nonmanual occupations by 1860.[23]

George Foster saw these clerks commuting downtown each day on the morning omnibuses, appareled in self-conscious contrast to the straw hat and lime-colored blouse of the proletarian sitting alongside. They signaled the birth of a world of socially ambitious newcomers to the city, epitomized when Henry Southworth, the millinery clerk, rushed home in the middle of another busy morning of sales to put on a clean collar. Detachable shirt collars, which had been available since the twenties, offered a uniquely convenient way to display one's "immaculate body" on a consistent and affordable basis, for they were much cheaper than maintaining and cleaning a large wardrobe of fine linen shirts. Such economy was of no small consequence for these politely attired but poorly remunerated clerics of the new order, who not only administered the industrial revolution but embodied it. From behind the desk or the sales counter they represented commercial culture to the citizenry in its everyday encounters with the market. "The appearance and demeanour of those who stand behind the counter have frequently much to do with converting a casual customer into a regular one," went the popular wisdom. Indeed, they did not just market the exploding volume of goods; they no less notably consumed them. Thus the growth of the collar industry directly paralleled the rise of this huge class of modestly waged market bureaucrats. In the 1850s a half-dozen collars of medium quality cost $1.50 at Brooks Brothers, half the sum of an inexpensive shirt. One saved on laundry bills as well, since shirts did not then have to be washed as often. By this time an even cheaper option was also available. A paper collar had been invented whose imitation stitching and cloth veneer effectively resembled the "real" imitation but that sold for less than it cost to wash and starch a linen collar.[24]

Clerks required a fine appearance and the least costly way of achieving it. As James Edney complained to Francis Cooke in the spring of 1836, "my board and washing thus far has cost me $188 and my clothes, etc. have cost me so much that I am now $17 in debt and hardly decently dressed. At least, not so well as a respectable situation demands." When Asa Greene arrived in the city in the 1830s in search of a clerkship, he owned two pairs of stockings, one vest, one pair of pantaloons, one dress coat, one surtout, three cravats, one pair of boots, and "apologies for a shirt." He knew he quickly needed to supplement his wardrobe. James Talcott also felt that his initial attempts at finding a jobbing position in the city were hindered by his country appearance, and he soon went out and bought himself a plug hat and a closely buttoned frock coat made of broadcloth.[25]

As such, the clerk was representative of the new urban market: the half million new New Yorkers who came to reside in the city between 1840 and 1860. Edward Tailer, a twenty-year-old "entry clerk" for the dry-goods firm of Little, Alden & Co., was probably a typical customer when he stopped into Brooks Brothers to buy an overcoat on his way back to work on a November afternoon in 1850, shopping that day in the "city department," where those either too busy or too budget-conscious to engage a personal tailor bought quality ready-mades. "Cheapness, and at the same time a certain elegance," were the twin requirements of these self-consciously outfitted paragons of the market revolution. George Simmons, Boston's largest clothier, explicitly addressed the need to attract the business of what he called "men of moderate income . . . whose patronage is always desirable because this class of the community compose the mass of customers." The *Mirror of Fashion* publicly fretted about the tailors' loss of business to the "ready-made-clothes-man." As Alfred Munroe & Co., exhibitors of ready-made wear at the Crystal Palace Exhibition of Industrial Arts in 1853, explained to readers of the exhibition's advertising circular, the time had passed "when every man or boy in want of a new coat or other garment, must resort to his tailor, and pay exorbitant prices in order to be satisfactorily suited." This was the point behind J. C. Booth's claim to a ready-made inventory "in every respect equal to those made to order" or the Jacobs brothers' confidence that "gentlemen wishing apparel for immediate use, can rely upon being as well fitted from the shelves, as if furnished to order." "ECONOMY AND COMFORT," exclaimed W. H. Degroot (whose Fulton Street clothing store shared a building with Freeman Hunt's editorial offices) in the most pithy incantation of a shopping credo that was becoming a social ethos.[26]

A ready-made wardrobe did not necessarily come at the expense of a custom-fitted one, however. As in the business of making and selling a suit, so, too, in wearing it the two were complementary. Whereas gentlemen once had no choice but to turn to a tailor, now they had the opportunity to acquire extra suits at less cost. This meant that purchases from the clothiers' city departments had not yet replaced the tailor. They supplemented him. This we learn, for instance, from the notebook in which A. L. Sayre diligently recorded all his expenses (beginning, of course, with the thirty-eight cents expended on the notebook itself) he incurred over the course of 1849. Considering that Sayre's annual disbursements totaled $416.15, he was representative of the modest gentility of so many of the city's retail customers. On April 22 Sayre bought himself a vest. On May 13 he bought a dress coat. On June 10 he acquired a light linen coat and a vest. On August 16 two new collars were added to his wardrobe and on September 29 a cravat. On November 4 he bought another vest. Four days later, in anticipation of the upcoming winter season, he purchased an overcoat and a third vest. More collars and cravats followed in December. Together with these ready-made, "city department" purchases, Sayre also bought several yards of linen cloth in July that he then took to a tailor to be cut and then to a third person who would sew the pieces up into two new pairs of pantaloons. [27]

- - - - -

Clerks were, as one contemporary remarked, "Bright youths generally, who liked the idea of wearing 'appearing out clothes' on weekdays as well as Sundays, and hoped to advance in the world, [and] saw that the successful merchant was a man of influence and substance." Walt Whitman espied them walking to work down Broadway, constituting a distinctly different procession from the republican celebrations of yore: "a slender and round-shouldered generation, of minute leg, chalky face, and hollow chest—but trig and prim in great glow of shiny boots, clean shirts—sometimes, just now, of extraordinary patterns . . . tight pantaloons, straps, which seem coming a little into fashion again, startling cravats, and hair all soaked and 'slickery' with sickening oils." [28]

At Lord & Taylor's new store on Broadway and Grand, across from Brooks Brothers, no one was employed "who is not a gentleman both in education and in manners." The more ambitious learned bookkeeping techniques at evening classes in schools for business that began to appear after 1820. ("I cannot easily buy a blank-book to write thoughts in; they are commonly ruled for dollars and cents," Thoreau complained.) They deposited their accumulations at the Clerks Savings Bank. And they were the primary audience for the era's proliferating manuals on etiquette, which, as *Burton's Gentleman's*

Magazine observed of the recently published *Manual of Politeness*, were "for the use principally, of the uninitiated youth who possesses a desire, or what is more to the point, an opportunity of figuring in good society, and [is] ignorant of the style of dress required." Indeed, the clerks' fealty to polite culture was obsequiously sincere. When New York City's Dry Goods Clerks' Association struck for shorter hours in 1841, they actually justified their impudence with paeans to the employer class. Their aim in demanding that stores be closed by eight, these aspirants to gentility insisted, was to win a place for themselves in the same good society of "reading rooms, lecture rooms, libraries [and] churches which have been open evenings for religious instruction."[29]

Such unabashed enthusiasm for the bourgeois order provoked the suspicions of contemporaries. In this respect, the replaceable collar was a fitting metaphor for the fluidity of the social conditions that had given birth to this new class to begin with. Certainly, Whitman meant nothing nice in his remarks about the clerks' shiny boots and clean shirts, which were too transparently the stuff of performance. Of course, Whitman himself wore a sailor's pea coat around town in an ostentatious display of contempt for the business class.[30] But employers were no less concerned than was Whitman about these exemplars of the new industrial order. "How frequently are cases brought to light, where young men led on little by little in a train of extravagance, have at last been obliged to defraud their employers, in order to sustain their style of living?" the *United States Economist, and Dry Goods Reporter* wondered. "They seem fine youths, those silk-and-suavity venders. Who knows what is their pay and prospects? How can they afford such good manners and fine waistcoats? What is the degree of friendly acquaintance bred between them and the ladies in the course of a bargain? Have they legs (below the counter?)?" the *New Mirror* added. In his *Bible in the Counting-House*, H. A. Boardman nervously italicized his insistence that "*every clerk should identify himself with the house he is engaged in.*" And *Hunt's Merchant's Magazine*, devoting increasing attention to the clerk's place within the firm, identified a problem that resulted from "the sons of persons resident in the country, who, left to themselves in a large city, have been dazzled by the gayety, and ruined by the profligacy of others." Indeed, the notoriously strict A. T. Stewart boarded his clerks in a residence around the corner from the store and supplied them himself with a library to fill their leisure hours.[31]

Such talk of profligacy revealed the anxieties aroused by the emergence of such an impermanent, interchangeable population—a new type of anxiety that was discussed in a traditional vernacular of virtue versus corruption. As Mrs. C. H. Butler remarked in a 1847 story, "The Merchant Clerks," which she published in the *Columbian Magazine*, "I have always thought it impossible for a man to be very wicked in the country." *Hunt's* observed that "country boys, who come to New York to get situations in stores, make very great mistakes. They had better learn a trade, or stick to the farm." And Emerson meant the same when he contended that "a sturdy lad from New Hampshire or Vermont . . . is worth a hundred of these city dolls." Most of these lads were indeed far from home. The clerk's transience, in fact, was both an emulation and a function of the growing placelessness of the industrial market, and contributed to the fluid, unpredictable, and individual character of the social relations that resulted. "I am alone in this city . . . and in fact I am alone in the world." Or, as Poe described the disorientation of metropolitan life in "The Man of the Crowd," one experienced a "solitude on account of the very denseness of the company around." The clerk was no longer considered a member of the merchant's household, or indeed of any household. He was said, rather, to board in houses of "large and miscellaneous" character, divorced from a maternal domesticity that would keep him out of "theaters, gambling houses, saloons, clubs, [and] a thousand dazzling attractions." Richard Robinson, a city clerk who inspired a new style of cap during his 1845 trial for the murder of the prostitute Helen Jewett, defended himself by appealing to these very anxieties: "I was an unprotected boy, without female friends to introduce me to respectable society, sent into a boarding house, where I could enter at what hour I pleased—subservient to no control after the business of the day was over."[32]

Clerks were not only caught between country and city, that is, between virtue and profligacy. They also found themselves in an ambiguous situation vis-à-vis the emerging balance of social classes in the marketplace. When in 1850 the Dry Goods Clerks' Mutual Benefit and Protective Association appealed again to city merchants to end the "present Long Hour System," they also made certain to announce that "no principles are advocated at our meetings which, if carried out, would not benefit the merchant as much as the clerk." Nevertheless, the *New York Tribune* regularly included the Dry Goods Clerks' Association in its list of labor movements on the grounds that, like all working-class organizations Horace Greeley considered worthy of the name, they sought to regulate their work hours. The city's Industrial Congress also publicly supported the successive attempts by these "mercantile wage-workers" (as Marx insisted on calling them, despite their pretenses) to reduce their hours. Observers remarked on the contradiction between the loyalty and trustworthiness required of clerks and the low salaries they were paid in return. What's more, no one could guarantee their future prospects.

"Fond parents, who fancy that white hands and a well-tied cravat are the signs of gentility, manage to get their sons into a store, and seem to imagine that they must be in the road to fortune and respectability," Edwin Freedley complained. "One in fifty is a fair estimate of the number of clerks that succeed in business for themselves," *Hunt's* warned.[33]

The clerk was trapped "between monkeyhood and manhood." That, at least, was how the *New-York Mirror* conjured the pressures of having to convey the appearance of respectability without having yet acquired respectable status. This might seem one of the more trivial contradictions born of capitalism's remaking of modern life. However, it was indicative of the "epistemological instability" signaled by the clerk's appearance on the historical stage, for he was at once essential to the new production economy while he did not actually produce anything himself. The ensuing confusion was manifest in contemporary attacks on the clerk that were formulated in the proverbial terms of the modern city's corruption of homespun virtues by anxious urbanites themselves. The fact that they used eighteenth-century country ideology to explain the clerk's nineteenth-century condition suggests that the clerk stood—for he was no longer allowed to sit on the job—at the center of the republic's great industrial transformation.[34]

The clerk was at once a creation of America's capitalist revolution and a repudiation of capitalism's claim as heir to an older tradition of virtuous industry practiced by independent, propertied men. Employers looked their clerks in the eye, in other words, and found themselves staring down their own Faustian bargain: that their own industrial success rested on an increasingly naked pecuniary self-interest. It was no wonder that the clerk's refined but obsequious style—so pithily expressed in his (detachable) white collar that had once been (and, he hoped, still was) the exclusive sign of the gentleman—provoked such suspicion and criticism, for it signaled the passing of homespun certainties. The clerk, in fact, embraced a wholly new kind of industry. "Speak to our Young Men, and tell them not to be so anxious to exchange the sure results of labor for the shifting promise of calculation," Sylvester Judd implored in his 1850 novel, *Richard Edney and the Governor's Family*. "Tell them that the hoe is better than the yardstick." Meanwhile, Edwin Freedley, that indefatigable promoter of industrial progress, explained in an anecdote he published in his *Leading Pursuits and Leading Men* in 1854 that the "shifting promise of calculation" was no longer antithetical to productive labor: "A celebrated merchant, himself a very active hard-working man, was associated in business with a brother, who seemed to pass his whole time . . . in watching the progress of the other's industry. A neighbor jocosely remarked upon what he conceived to be a habit of indolence, when the busy brother exclaimed, 'I wish I could be as idle: why, John makes more money for us with those gray eyes, than I could make with four pairs of hands, and feet to match!' "[35]

Freedley's exposition on the value of the seemingly idle manager was an attempt to address what he considered an anachronistic, but still prevalent, concern about the indolence and corrupting luxury that resulted from commercial ambition. John Trumbull's 1773 account, in his poem "The Progress of Dulness," of Tom Brainless, a country fop who finds success in the metropolis, already anticipated the next century's trope regarding the clerk. In 1782 the Jeffersonian journalist Philip Freneau similarly mourned the "simple husbandman" who had given way to "the idle, scheming citizen, who sits perpetually behind his counter, like a spider in the web, watching his commodities." Charles Brockden Brown's novel *Arthur Mervyn* likewise described its hero in 1799 as reluctant to take a job as a clerk or copyist because "he could not part with the privilege of observing and thinking for himself."[36] But others, expressing concern for the nation's future progress, recognized the need for someone to watch over the commodities, lest society find itself "retir[ing] to the woods" to "learn of the savages' *simplicity* of life." A young man from upstate New York noted in the 1830s that, "as to the mechanic arts, I could not help seeing that those who followed them could never obtain a cordial admission into what was accounted good society." He now openly preferred the latter option. In fact, the ideologue of homespun tradition himself, Horace Bushnell, decided to join the ministry in the 1820s when it became obvious that there was no point in pursuing his father's profession of weaving. By the time P. T. Barnum looked back in the 1850s and credited his abandonment of the family farm in Connecticut and arrival in New York to his "settled aversion to manual labor," the pattern was well established: personal success and social progress were no longer grounded in agrarian truths concerning the physical production of things. Henry Southworth attended a lecture on the subject of "labor" one evening in 1851 at the Mechanics Society—whose name was an artifact of the homespun past—where he heard the Reverend Dr. Adams explain that a worker was anyone who produced anything, whether it be the result of his thought processes or of tilling the land. This redefinition of industry to include those who, like the clerk, produced nothing but profits also informed Edward Everett's reminder in these years that capital "was, itself, originally the work of men's hands." Perhaps the most striking expression of the changing meaning of work was the ubiquity of the term "loafer," a favorite epithet of both Walt Whitman and George Templeton Strong, who, though cultural and ideological rivals, were equally mindful that the once transcendent value of productive labor had been uprooted.[37]

In 1820 dry-goods clerks stoked fires, carried and piled wood, and trimmed the lamps. They were still responsible for the tasks given over a generation later to Negro porters. By 1849 Edward Tailer's principal activity was "opening the Yards" each morning at Little, Alden & Co. and arranging the lengths of fabric one upon the other, "so as to display to the greatest vantage." Tailer visited the post office at least once a day, faithfully placing letters from correspondents on the desk of Mr. Alden for his perusal. He distributed bills and business cards at the Astor House hotel and at Delmonico's restaurant, as well as to jobbers and other buyers throughout the city. Bills were made out from the sales book, and each entry double-checked. Newly arrived cases of goods had to be divided, and the measurements of each piece of fabric recorded and then added up, to ensure that the yardages listed in the sales book were correct. Tailer also visited the banks after twelve o'clock, and sometime after four in the afternoon he usually carried "the Boston letter" to the boat. From then until closing he tidied up the goods, the patterns cards, and the cartons that had been tossed about by customers and salesmen during the course of the day.[38]

Writing in 1834 about the "perils" and "dangers" of commercial ambition, Asa Greene offered this description of the successful man of business:

> His hands were soft and white, as though they had been steeped in new milk; and so delicately did he handle the silks, the lace and the muslins, that he barely touched them with the tip of his thumb and finger. In addition to all these admirable qualities of look and motion, the ladies declared that he smelt delightfully; that his whole person seemed to exhale perfumes; and that, when they were in his shop, they could not help fancying themselves in the midst of Arabia the Blest.

It was not only impossible to discern any trace of the virtuous yeoman in such fawning, perfumed surroundings; it was not even clear who actually was a man. This was rather the world of "namby-pamby clerks" serving the whims of "sauntering Queens, Duchesses, and Countesses . . . endeavoring by the help of finery which they do not want, to stimulate their jaded and satiated tastes and ambitions."[39] Thus, George Foster continued, the times could be described as an "inverted age" of human energy and activity. In an urban market society, he complained, all energies were channeled to the acquisitive faculties rather than the productive ones. "The slightest rumor of a change for the better or the opening of a fresher and more attractive field, instantaneously excites . . . the entire community to a state of partial insanity." At best, one would now go and exercise one's muscles in digging for gold in California.[40]

However, most of the acquisitive talent came to New York. "To this place there seems to tend all the unsettled spirits of the nation; men who have devised schemes of usefulness or of mischief, and who expect to reduce them here into some practical form." Isaac Mayer Wise recalled his arrival in 1846: "The whole city appeared to me like a large shop where everyone buys or sells, cheats or is cheated." Salesmen showed a customer their poorest goods first so that the more costly ones would appear to be that much better. Or they shuttered rear windows and doorways so that the shadows would obscure lowly quality and poor color. "No wonder the ancients harangued the people from the market-places," the *New-York Mirror* observed in an essay devoted to classifying a new urban type it called the "New York sharper." Such ambitions, however, were now the common denominator of public life. As George Templeton Strong ruminated in his diary: "I'm beginning to feel a desire to make money. . . . In this city the feeling is necessary to enable one to sympathize with the rest of mankind and be sure of his common humanity with the people about him."[41]

The desire to make money was a nervous basis for social intercourse, and not just because exchange "yoked partners together in a rhetoric of reciprocity while dividing them by means of a logic of mutual indifference." Some of the more obvious tensions were addressed by the retail innovations in one-price shopping, as we have seen. But business in the city of "Got-him" provoked a deeper anxiety, one that could not be resolved by a new lexicon for buying and selling. As that perspicacious visitor from New England summarized after a visit to New York City in the mid-twenties: "One man is impelled onward by the fear of losing something that another man as quickly bestirs himself to acquire." And Herman Melville, while ostensibly describing life aboard a U.S. Navy man-of-war, explained how this commercial circularity generated its own kind of truth: "With some highly commendable exceptions, they rob from one another, and rob back again, till, in the matter of small things, a community of goods seems almost established; and at last, as a whole, they become relatively honest, by nearly every man becoming the reverse."[42]

Burton's Gentleman's Magazine claimed there was "something extremely laughable in the multiplicity of 'books on good manners,'" but nevertheless could not dismiss the phenomenon, and conceded that the massive presence of the new clerical class in the book-buying market proved that social position was a man-made thing and that there was nothing innate in being a gentleman. Such social flux was the driving force of Genio Scott's *Mirror of Fashion*, which simultaneously functioned as a trade journal overseeing the mass production of tailored suits and as a fashion connoisseur of their tasteful consumption. Scott labored to make tailoring's connection between polite culture and commercial advance self-evident. He modeled his journal on Willis's *New Mirror* and other aristocratic shilling literature of the Upper Tendom. Fine arts and leisure culture filled its pages, which not only included fashion plates and instructions for making up "shooting dress," "fisherman's toggery," and other hunting clothes, but narrative accounts that illustrated the sporting life as well: mountain climbing expeditions or visits to "first-rate gambling houses" in the city. Nevertheless, fashion and commercially driven democracy did not always make a convenient marriage. Was it not true, the *Mirror of Fashion* itself pointed out, that in lands where the right of kings was considered divine, the art of tailoring was the most developed? Scott was conscious of the problem. He aggressively defended his cultural program against homespun-inspired critiques of luxury voiced by "all the leading reformers who seek to transform society by throwing its elements of social order into chaos [and who] make a home thrust at the art [of tailoring], as being the medium through which many of the social distinctions are maintained." He pursued his counterattack by claiming the homespun mantle for himself. The *Mirror of Fashion*, it was declared, rejected the "freaks and follies of foreign fancy" in favor of those fashions "strictly consonant with American feelings and predilections." Meanwhile, Scott had to apologize for the white servants dressed in livery who kept appearing in the fashion plates he imported from Europe.[43]

All this posturing was revealing of a difficult contradiction. The *Mirror of Fashion*'s raison d'être was to market metropolitan fashion to the largest possible number of potential consumers. How was this to be achieved if it was equally important to accord fashion an aura of genteel exclusivity? The *Mirror of Fashion*, for instance, declared its preference for the rural farming idyll over the cosmopolitan relativism of the city even while its business relied on a provincial population that eagerly mimicked the sophistication of urban culture. It was self-consciously "conservative" on political and social issues of the day but embraced the perpetual novelty of fashion, each month inventing new styles that would generate new business. It approvingly quoted Carlyle on its masthead—"Thus in the one pregnant subject of CLOTHES, rightly understood, is included all that men have thought, dreamed, done and been: the whole external Universe and what it holds is but Clothing; and the essence of all science lies in the PHILOSOPHY OF CLOTHES"—but preferred not to read further in Carlyle's *Sartor Resartus*, which ultimately condemned the very centrality of the sartorial. So unnerved were these bourgeois revolutionaries by their own modernity, in other words, that they needed to dress it up in traditional garb. The *Mirror of Fashion* labored, in the words of the historian Jean-Christophe Agnew, to "purify the meanings that the market had so promiscuously mixed together," while the journal's very existence was proof of polite culture's corruption by the new economy and of the fact that propriety still could not be divorced from property. Ultimately, in the wake of New York's Astor Place riot in 1849, when a mob of lower-class rowdies attacked the city's upscale theater, the *Mirror of Fashion* upbraided that very leisured ethos it at once sought to make its own, quoting the *Herald* in condemnation of nabob exclusiveness and criticizing the way the fashionable classes "planned the [Astor Place opera] house upon the namby-pamby, picaune principle of themselves." The reason for this apparently contradictory attack was obvious. One could not propound the interests of the tailoring trade while trying to maintain a veneer of studied indifference to industrial reality. If the *Mirror of Fashion* was genuinely "devoted exclusively to the best interests of THE TRADE," it had to do its best to include the less genteel classes in the world of custom refinement. Everyone should dress well in a "nation of free men," it asserted, most especially those waged constituencies who would otherwise take their business to the ready-made clothing stores.[44]

And so it was that anyone could be a gentleman. As Alexander Bryan Johnson, a banker from upstate New York, remarked in proffering advice to his son: "Mark out for yourself such a character as you desire to possess, and by speaking constantly thereto, you will attain the desired character as certainly as you will a coat, by going to your tailor and ordering it."[45] The city filled up with all sorts of gentlemen, for there was no longer a single, unequivocal model to emulate. That became apparent in 1835, when the *New-York Mirror* asked, "What is a gentleman?" and couldn't find an answer. "Is it that suit of broadcloth drawn smoothly over a well-formed figure, strutting Broadway?" The criteria were proved equally elusive when the *Ladies' Companion* sought to bring some order to the age's centrifugal tendencies:

"That is a gentleman of fortune, but a very proud unprincipled fellow."
"That is a modest, unassuming gentleman, but badly off in his pecuniary affairs."
"There's a silly good-for-nothing of a fellow, but gentlemanly in his conduct."
"He's clever and talented, but cannot be termed a gentleman."

"That's a regular sponge—he would sell his conscience for a dinner, and his
   soul for a play ticket, but he is most gentlemanly in his manners."
"There's a mean, miserly fellow in business, but a gentleman in his own house;
   and charitable to the poor."
"That's a purse-proud ignoramus, with nothing to recommend him but money;
   petted in his childhood and indulged in his growth. He spends his money
   like a gentleman."[46]

The *Tribune* noted that Joseph Morse, suspected of murdering the Beautiful Cigar Girl Mary Rogers, was "very neatly and fashionably dressed."
And the South Carolinian, William Bobo, who was generally suspicious of
the Northern cult of industrial progress, watched the parade of refinement
along Broadway in 1851 and exclaimed, "Trust it not, it covers—what? All
that horrible, despicable, mean, heart-breaking, and agonizing." "Go to the
hotel," someone else pointed out, "in a homespun coat, in cowhide boots . . .
and they will thrust you into the garret. . . . But open your trunk, put on your
broadcloth, and don't forget your straps, and they will say give the stranger,
it may be a parlour, for *he* is a gentleman." Unsettling stories of disembodied
clothing appeared in the *New-York Mirror* and *Godey's Lady's Book*, pointing
to a new genre of fetish and anxiety in which the garment took on a life of its
own or, more horribly, assumed the wearer's identity, so skillfully "melted on
to a shape" was it by the tailor and dressmaker. This was a reality in which
"a gentleman wears a clean shirt, and white gloves, some one says, and *dress*
thus makes the gentleman." But in these terms Henry Clay was no gentleman,
known as he was to be a sloven. And Andrew Jackson and John Marshall also
failed to qualify for inclusion in that category, for the same reason. Pickpock-
ets, however, were fine-looking gentlemen, with ruffled shirts, kid gloves, and
gold chains. And "tailor-boys are always the best dressed men in the world,
and ergo, the most of the gentleman."[47]

Did democratic standardization beget this social and moral obfuscation?
Joseph Scoville, for instance, a veteran Gotham merchant who mourned the
passing of an older, more personalized way of doing business, complained of
the piety game of "the society of young clerks [who] boarded generally at
twenty shilling boarding houses, curled each others' hair on Saturday night,
went to Sunday school as teachers, and became members of the Presbyterian
Church, which had the richest members and the prettiest daughters." They
were representative of the circumlocution and pretentiousness—the corruption and deceit—that now threatened to dominate all intercourse. If, in the
1820s, observers complained of shopkeepers who made themselves "all things

to all men," the appearance—the epiphany—of the "confidence man" as a new social type in the 1840s suggested that things had indeed gotten out of hand and that market society was a self-referential quagmire of unknowability or, worse yet, that the truth, even if it were recognized, might have no moral worth anyway. As again Melville, that most acute of modern American prophets, remarked: "Supposing that at high 'change on the Paris Bourse, [the Jewish demon] Asmodeus should lounge in, distributing hand-bills, revealing the true thoughts and designs of all the operators present—would that be the fair thing . . . ?"[48]

The appearance of a class of young men in the city, loyal to the social order while at the same time taking advantage of its fluidity and disorder—at once dependent on their employer and their social betters but independent of traditional forms of social control (and in both instances violating republican propriety)—encapsulated the chronic instability. James Edney gave this situation a clear, if unintentional expression, when he wrote to Francis Cooke back in Augusta to ask for a raise, phrasing his request in a white-collar vernacular of sycophancy, self-effacement, and politesse designed to obscure the personal ambition that drove it: "I do not wish by this intimation to tax your well known liberality nor indulge my sensuality or miserly conceit at the expense of your hard earned accumulations, but merely to solicit of you what I think (and not only I but others) just and reasonable," as Edney carefully broached the subject. But then he seemed to inadvertently reveal his real opinion, and with it the disingenuous nature of his delicately rendered humility: "If you can on the contrary produce as many reasons that are cogent to justify you in refusing me what I here demand . . . I will through myself upon the liberality of your better judgment and abide by the consequences." One may suppose that by a slip of the pen Edney threatened to be "through" with his dependence on Clarke's better judgment rather than "throw" himself upon it, thereby exposing his insistent loyalty in all its base interestedness.[49]

The clerk's redefinition of industry entailed the replacement of that republican nemesis, luxury, with the far more private problem of desire. "Young men, especially young men in our cities, walk in the midst of allurements for the appetite," Horace Mann lectured an audience of clerks at the Boston Mercantile Library Association in the early 1840s. Driven by the same concerns, American physicians had a few years earlier identified a new medical condition they diagnosed as "moral insanity," a term used of persons who failed to restrain their passions. It was a distinctly postpatriarchal disorder, born of an age "of the first person singular," as Emerson described it. Noah Webster accordingly added sixty-seven new words to the second edition of his *American Dictionary* in 1841 that all began with the prefix "self." This was convincing, if circumstantial, evidence of the transformation of Americans' personal sovereignty. Self-government now acquired a new, and newly private, meaning. It was the clerk's historic task—and this was one reason why so much anxious attention was directed his way—to show that desire could be checked in an age of freedom and that the democratic citizen could police himself.[50]

The clerk's success in doing so would prove that ambition and self-control were compatible, and that industrial abundance was not equivalent to the republican problem of luxury, for it did not lead to personal corruption. That, in turn, would mark an important revision of property's relationship to virtue, while also legitimating the new, post-homespun meaning of industry as embodied by the clerk who produced nothing (while enticing others to buy) but still demanded a privileged place in the new production regime. This, in turn, would resolve the proverbial political tension between individual ambitions and their social consequences, which is what the ideology of homespun had itself sought to do in tying household to nation.

Thus the problem of social order in such revolutionary times both began and ended with the self. Edwin Freedley, in yet another volume of industrial advice, encouraged the business class to meet the threat that the class itself posed: "Serenity of temper is a virtue of which all men cannot boast . . . but it is a fundamental constituent in the character of a clerk and a business man. To command the temper is one of the first great lessons to be learned in practical life." Only self-government, or one's "serenity of temper" as Freedley called it, could replace the family commonwealth as a source of stability in light of the wholesale migration of farm boys to the metropolis and their subsequent repudiation of their fathers' version of masculinity and industry. The advice was dutifully put into practice by William Hoffman upon his departure from the family farm near Clareack, New York, in March 1848 in search of a clerkship in the city. Warned of the lures that lay in his path, William assured his friends in a clear echo of republican virtue: "My mind is as it always was—that I always held an aversion of the strongest kind against anything that would tempt to moral depravity and disregarded looseness."[51]

But such self-government was a specifically capitalist solution, becoming as much a personal motto as it was a form of political sovereignty. It actually inverted republican prescriptions of virtue in that the private self was now responsible for policing the corruptions of public life. In fact, not only did private experience become morally superior to public life, it became the model for public life. This was not comparable to Bernard Mandeville's early-eighteenth-century embrace of private vices as the source of public benefits, a notion whose inverted logic remained rooted in, even while taunting, the paradigms of moral economy and patriarchal hierarchy. The goal now was rather to give self-interest itself a good name. This would then make democracy, which in America was explicit in promising abundance to all, a viable principle of governance. The man on the make, in other words, could still be a good citizen. Such reasoning was evident in the arguments defending the liberalization of the voting franchise in the 1820s, which contended that universalized access to state power would pose no threat to private property—that is, the newly enfranchised masses would not rewrite the tax laws—because they no less wanted a piece of the same pie. A generation later, Philip Hone was still not entirely convinced. "Several of the windows on the first floor of [Stewart's new Marble Palace] are formed of plateglass, six feet by eleven, which must have cost four or five hundred dollars each, and may be shivered by a boy's marble or a snow-ball as effectually as by a four pound shot; and I am greatly mistaken if there are not persons (one is enough) in this heterogeneous mass of population . . . bad enough to do such a deed of mischief." Hone was proven a needless pessimist. The "heterogeneous" public showed itself to be far more respectful of property, and more self-disciplined, than he gave them credit for.[52]

This discipline was the crux of self-government. Thus the *New Mirror* described the making of gentility in an ungentle age: "An habitual self-possession determines the appearance of a gentleman. He should have the complete command, not only over his countenance, but over his limbs and motions. In other words, he should discover in his air and manner a voluntary power over his whole body, which, with every inflection of it, should be under the control of his will."[53] It was indeed a distinctly physical effort. Henry Southworth, the clerk at Beard's millinery store, deliberately started each day with a cold water wash. Edward Tailer, the entry clerk at Little, Alden & Co., visited the gym before work every morning at a quarter of six. Both could have been training themselves for the manly adventures featured each month in the *Mirror of Fashion*. More likely, however, they were simply putting into practice Charles Follen's program, popularized in his *Lectures on Moral Philosophy*, that identified "methodical exercise of every part of the human frame [as] the only way to make the body a sure and well-trained servant of the mind, always ready to obey its master's call." Follen gave voice to a widespread concern over the cultural consequences of the clerks' sedentary existence, so far divorced now from manual labor. So did the *American Review* in 1845 when it observed that the "anxious spirit of gain" had turned palor into the national complexion—and the *Manual of Self-Education* was representative in encouraging "bodily sports of a healthy and animating description" as a remedy. In so animating their bodies, Henry Southworth and Edward Tailer, "just like hundreds of the rest," incorporated traditional male physicality into their "strenuously idle" lives.[54]

The private body thus became an insistently public subject. Clothing entrepreneurs, of course, already knew that. Indeed, the "disciplinary economy" of the clerk's life was analogous to tailoring's standardization of his individual body. The goal was likewise the same, namely, to integrate that body into a general system (in both instances a system of profit). Again, the ultimate aim was to reconcile the two great impulses that drove industry: individuation and standardization. And if the body was a central means for fashioning the industrial persona, what was more fitting than to suit it in one of industry's leading commodities? The self-governing citizen and the mass-produced suit, in fact, both claimed a provenance based on a new and truer reading of the body's nature. William Stinemets's "easy and elegant appearance" that would result from the proper application of his *Complete and Permanent System of Cutting* ("Scarcely does [the coat] get to its destined place than the figure of the trier on seems to have wholly changed") could thus be genuinely described as a natural fit—regardless of all the technological manipulations employed in realizing it. This was a nature that united "materiality and meaning" and so ensured a measure of cultural stability during an industrial revolution in which "things change so fast here that the city does not seem like home to those who own it."[55]

Men's dress, part of the problem to begin with, thus also had an important role to play in ameliorating the tensions endemic to the age. To this end, the *Mirror of Fashion* explained how the "utility of fashion" had two aspects. On one hand, "it inspires modesty, self-respect, a love of personal readiness, decency and morality." On the other, "it loads the ship, it endows the waterfall with powers of beneficence, [and] it digs up and gives life to the otherwise dead and useless coal-bed."[56] In short, clothing really did constitute a link between self and society: that basic homespun postulate had not changed. In democratic times, however, when civic virtue rested on self-government, a particularly disciplined and predictable costume was required. Circumstances would not suffer the kind of caprice that so perturbed Philip Hone upon seeing Daniel Webster one morning on Wall Street attired in a bright blue satin vest sprigged with gold flowers. Much nearer Hone's ideal, no doubt, was the rendition of New York's Merchant's Exchange included in Fay's original series of city views and republished in the *Ladies'*

Companion in 1836. There, in the presence of the sartorially hybridized statue of a mythic Alexander Hamilton arrayed in colonial breeches and classical toga, the city's industrial class met to conduct its business. No more tangible expression could be found of the regularity—and notion of equivalence—these broker-citizens sought to bring to the industrializing market and to the social relations growing up around it than the uniformity of their "well broad-clothed" appearance. The monochromaticity of the dark suits and white linen of their single-priced "business attire" constituted a capitalist aesthetic. It helped these individuals to recognize each other's "utilitarian" fit as their own, and made every body a reproduction of the next one. It was indeed a ready-made age.[57]

These suits now became that specifically American civic uniform that early nationalists like Mathew Carey had hoped to use to forge a common social life. Indeed, the scene Fay depicted at the Merchant's Exchange kept reappearing throughout the city. Willis looked out his window across from St. Paul's at nine o'clock one morning and saw "a rapid throng of well-dressed men, all walking smartly, and all bound Mammon-ward." These were the same "compact rows of attentive, orderly, and well dressed gentlemen, in their dark habiliments, and white linen" observed by the *New-York Mirror*, and the same "solid mass . . . of glossy broadcloth" in its Sunday procession from Grace Church to the Battery described by George Foster. They constituted an industrial spectacle that brought social order to an otherwise disordered situation.[58]

5

Ready-Made Labor

The largest labor protest in the history of the clothing trade, and in the history of New York until that time, broke out in July 1850. Several thousand waged journeymen struck the city's clothing firms, demanding that their pay be brought into line with the rising costs of living and with the rising profits of their employers. Open-air meetings were organized, as were actions against manufacturers who attempted to bypass the strikers by putting out their work to other sources. Tense confrontations between journeymen tailors, on the one hand, and an alliance of employers' men, "loafers," and the police, on the other, became weekly occurences. These often developed into running street battles, the most serious of which took place on August 5, in front of Frederick Wartz's house uptown on 38th Street. Wartz was suspected of working for a boss under the prices. The accusation brought out two hundred striking tailors, who began "breaking windows and raising a great disturbance," as police sources later described the scene to the *Tribune*. The ruckus soon spread to adjoining streets. Arrests were made. Shots may have been fired. What is certain is that two of the strikers were beaten to death by the police and scores of others were wounded. "The blood flowed in profusion over the faces and clothes both of the police and tailors." The "June days" of Paris seemed to be repeating themselves in the New World.[1]

Comparisons to European class insurrection were wholly relevant, as some of the rhetoric made explicit: "Many among us have before been engaged in fighting for liberty in [the] Fatherland. Now, brethren . . . it is time to fight again." The riot in front of Frederick Wartz's house was the exclusive action of German immigrants. German tailors were also the overwhelming majority at an earlier confrontation that ended in a violent demonstration against C. T. Longstreet & Co. on Nassau Street on July 22. The unfounded view that the tailors' strikes of 1835 and 1836 had been "instigated by a set of vile foreigners," as Philip Hone wrote in his diary at the time, was now, in 1850, incontestably true.[2]

The strike proved how trans-Atlantic exchange not only supplied the millions of yards of cloth required by the industry, but also the tens of thousands of hands needed to turn it into clothing. As Robert Albion observed in *The Rise of New York Port*, which remains the best history of New York City's industrialization: "Whereas New York became the nation's richest city by managing to disperse most of its commercial imports throughout the country, it increased its lead as the nation's biggest city by keeping a much larger share of its human imports within its own environs." The Germans were organized in their own journeymen's society, which did not meet with the Tailors' Society at the Sixth Ward Hotel, but at Hillenbrand's Mechanics' Hall on Hester Street in the Tenth Ward. There they conducted their business in German. And when thousands demonstrated in the Park fronting City Hall, they did so in separate societies. Only after the speeches and testimonies did the Germans join forces with the "English Branch" for a march up the Bowery. Meanwhile, the English Branch itself was predominantly Irish—tailoring being one of the traditionally better organized trades in Ireland. Dickens saw two of them strolling down Broadway in holiday clothes in 1842 and couldn't resist a sarcastic aside: "Irishmen both! . . . It would be hard to keep your model republics going, without the countrymen and countrywomen of those two labourers." By the mid-fifties over 80 per cent of New York City's manual labor force was reportedly foreign-born. In fact, the proportion of immigrants working in the city's largest manufacturing industry may have been even higher since the wholesale clothing houses recruited their labor power from those populations with the least bargaining power in the market. In so doing, they began that tradition by which newcomers shouldered "for a time . . . the responsibility for clothing the people among whom they settled."[3]

There were other important differences between the 1850 strike and all that had preceded it in the trade's history. In spite of the familiar nomenclature, for instance, "journeymen" of 1850 were no longer the craft elite working for the city's most prestigious shops, those who had been leading labor protests since 1768, when New York tailors first walked out against city masters in what was possibly the first labor strike in America. "Custom men" in fact remained aloof from the 1850 protest, although they, too, took advantage of the improved economy to organize. Rather, 1850 marked the first tradewide action directed against the ready-made firms—against the "Southern trade" and the "clothing houses"—that now dominated clothing manufacturing. As such, the strike was fitting testimony to the escalating processes of industrialization and proletarianization. It came, as if on cue, in the same year that the federal census redefined industry to mean the making of surplus value, an activity that rested on the emergence of the market as the principal means of organizing the labor force (including the labor of those, usually women, not yet collecting a wage of their own).[4]

Indeed, when the vital statistics for all companies "produc[ing] articles to the annual value of $500" were first assembled in 1850, the sheer volume of wage labor in the clothing industry became strikingly obvious. Census marshals counted 29,995 "hands" making men's clothing for a living in New York City. At the same time, because the census appropriated its categories from the businessman's ledger, it presented little more than a balance sheet of gross inputs and outputs. These numbers revealed nothing of the multifarious hierarchy of foremen, general cutters, Southern cutters, specialized cutters, journeymen, "irregular" men, coat makers, pantaloon makers, sweaters, "plain" and "fancy" needleworkers, in-house girls, put-out labor, spongers, embroiderers, basters, and finishers all busy transforming cloth into clothing for an equally multifarious hierarchy of wages. The single distinction that the official enumeration made in the giant monolith of labor power was between male and female. Of course, that detail was highly pertinent to the bottom line. Women were paid, on average, half of what men earned. More importantly, they performed the least remunerative work. However, sexual difference was not the only relevant social fact that informed the industry's hiring practices. Distinctions between organized and unorganized workers, between immigrants and native-born, between Germans and Irish, and between the poor ("that class whose living absorbs all their earnings") and wage earners enjoying a "comfortable subsistence" also proved integral in matching living and breathing "hands" to the highly variegated production needs of the business. The fact that these were also some of the most fundamental social categories of urban life in general suggests how much the clothing business was implicated in the life of the modern city, and how much the modern order, in turn, served its hackneyed needs.[5]

- - - - -

No one really knew the size of the largest manufacturing work force in the country's largest manufacturing city. Efforts at strikebreaking in 1850, for example, utilized a myriad of informal avenues for getting clothes made up, both in and outside the city. Bundles of precut fabrics were distributed to neighborhood storeowners, to the local church, or to independent operators in Newark and Williamsburg. In 1857 the *Herald* estimated that city clothiers employed close to 60,000 persons, half of whom lived outside the city "for a circuit to perhaps five hundred miles."[6] Neither official tabulations nor well-informed conjecture, in other words, could definitively establish the size of the industry's work force. Buying human labor power proved far less quantifiable than the purchase of yards of cloth or the resulting crates of frock coats. Still, the gross numbers are enough to confirm the basic point: the clothing trade, born of a mercantile constellation of trans-Atlantic and intracontinental exchange and dominated by innovative wholesale and retail merchants, remained a uniquely labor-intensive project.

At the same time, the capitalist production of clothing was technically no different from the precapitalist version. The technology of a needle drawing thread through a hole it simultaneously created dated back to Paleolithic times. Granted, the sewing machine, introduced in the early 1850s, succeeded in combining two distinct hand movements into a single mechanized one and thereby dramatically increased productivity. But it effected no reorganization of production. In fact, the labor history of men's clothing presents a far-reaching example of proletarianization that was effected without any fundamental redivision of labor or rise of a machine culture.[7]

"The least difficult parts of the process of turning a piece of cloth into clothing are readily taught," it was observed, "and the busy tailor could increase his output by handing over this part of his work to semi-skilled labor." Indeed, mothers and daughters in the countryside had long sewed up what they had paid the itinerant tailor to skillfully cut, thus saving the family money. The eighteenth-century merchant tailor adopted the same division of labor, and for the same reason. The custom shop was organized around a hierarchy of tasks of escalating difficulty and acquired skill. Stitching the edges of collars, felling linings, sewing and then pressing seams, putting on bindings, basting seams, making and putting in sleeves, stitching inside seams and then the more conspicuous outer ones, and attending to the finishing of linings, buttonholes, and the garment's front were all discrete tasks that were distributed on the basis of experience and expense. In making up a coat, for instance, an apprentice would be given the pieces of a collar to sew, a relatively simple task, the pieces having already been cut in the prescribed fashion by the master. After completing the stitching he returned the collar to the master, who then gave it shape by applying a dark brown soap into the open texture of the padding and molding it with his hot iron, or "goose." Thus finished, the collar was handed over to the shop's journeyman who attached

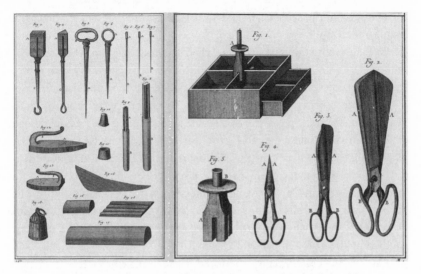

The tailor's tools, as illustrated in Diderot's *Encyclopédie* (1763). Industrial revolution did not change the picture, as mass-producing Cash Tailors and ready-made clothiers continued to work with the traditional appliances of the trade.

it to the rest of the garment. This system proved directly applicable to the ever-escalating scales of production. At Lewis and Hanford's, for instance, which made over $300,000 worth of goods in 1850, the cloth was still cut into suitable shapes by a highly trained artisan and then sewn back together by someone paid considerably less to do so. Separate sewing tasks were also often divided, as they had been in the master's shop. The same modest, portable collection of tools—shears, needles and bodkins, a sleeve board, a goose—that had been in use for centuries were still employed. The garment itself included the same constituent parts: a relatively expensive outer fabric, cheaper materials used for inner linings and for unexposed sections, buttons, threads, and the like. John Shephard's daybook of 1786—in which he recorded 3½ yards of superfine broadcloth, 2½ yards of rattinet, linen for stay pockets and sleeve linings, buckram, silk, twist, thread, Naytom, and large and small buttons— read, despite some minor difference in details, much like the business ledgers produced almost a century later.[8]

The mass manufacture of clothing, then, rested on a material logic inherent in the making of garments as much as it rested on commercial desiderata that dictated the most profitable exploitation of labor. Moreover, inasmuch as this logic of production appeared to make material and commercial behavior twin aspects of the same transcendent, natural process, it had an ideological signficance as well.

In fact, production tasks retained their technical content while acquiring new social meanings. In this way, "cutting" was reinvented as a new profession, a separate category in the newly organized occupation statistics compiled at mid-century. Employment notices for cutters began to appear in the general and the trade press. In 1855, for example, a young married man sought a situation as a "salesman and cutter" through an ad placed in the *Herald*, promising to influence $5,000 worth of "good trade" and asking in return a salary and a percentage of the firm's custom. "Be independent, but not impertinent" was a maxim of the new profession, which was dominated by the native-born or by those of a similar Anglo ethnic extraction. In 1855 there were only seven Irish-born cutters living in the seven New York City wards studied by the historian William Devlin.[9]

Cutters, the craft elite, were situated between the contractual obligations of a waged employee and the self-conceits of a proud artisan. The combination of craft work with retail responsibilities was revealing of the middle-class nature of cutting. Cutters were in a position to benefit from the fluidity of the industrial market, from the impermanence of traditional labor hierarchies, and from the dramatic growth of the clothing business. James Edney, the novice sent to New York to keep Francis Cooke's store in Augusta supplied with clothing, was, for example, completely dependent on his cutter. When Edney could not pay him the thousand-dollar salary he commanded—nearly twice what Edney himself earned—the cutter arranged for Edney to hire his brother, "equally honest, attentive, and competent," at a salary of $800. The *Mirror of Fashion* identified these artists "of great skill and refined taste" as being no less than responsible for the appearance of mankind, thus justifying salaries that by the 1850s could reach $2,500 a year. Meanwhile, there were many, such as C. A. Hughes of Arnoux & Son, or R. B. Valentine of William Jennings's firm, who used their situation as a valued cutter as a springboard to partnership.[10]

Not all cutters were created equal, however. At the higher end of the market the cutter took measurements, cut cloth, superintended the construction of the garment, and perhaps became a partner in the firm. But there was another class of cutter who did nothing but cut. These included the hands "accustomed to southern work" whom Hobby, Husted & Co. sought at the height of the 1836 spring season. By the 1850s there were over a thousand such cutters working in the city. They might be paid fourteen dollars a week, which was a respectable income, but it was earned for cutting 150 coats. This was an average of less than ten cents per garment, a wage far below custom rates, even in the countryside. These cutters did no designing and no measuring and had no contact with customers. They worked in a central shop where the continual clip of shears could be deafening. They could be speeded up. They were even occasionally given knives in place of the proverbial cutter's shears in an attempt to raise productivity, since a knife could cut through several thicknesses of coarse goods at once. They often cut not from the custom-designed patterns of a master tailor but instead from standard patterns placed on the cloth by someone responsible for generating the maximum number of garments that could be extracted from a given piece of fabric. As such, they represented the most ambitious application of the new tape-measure technology, which had originally detached drafting from cutting.[11]

Cutting rooms became "cutting departments." *Hunt's Merchant's Magazine* reported how Daniel Devlin's cutters were assigned respectively to the firm's coats, pants, vests, and trimmings departments, each overseen by a foreman responsible for keeping the cutters supplied with materials, thus ensuring a steady work flow. Arnoux & Son bragged in advertisements about its systematic subdivision of cutting into separate operations for coats, pants, and vests, while Edwin Freedley marveled at how "every thing is carried on with the regularity of clock-work" in these clothing firms. On another occasion *Hunt's* congratulated Lewis and Hanford for their economic rationality: "[The cloth] is made up into a lot, and one ticket placed upon it stating the number of pieces in the lot, the kind of goods, and number of yards, the cost, width, and of whom it was bought. Another ticket is passed to the head man in the cutting department, who enters the ticket in the cutting account book, giving it a certain number." It was the department's "head man" who then organized the cutting of the cloth per order. The cutter thus became the subject of the "lot system," as the *Bulletin of the National Association of Wool Manufacturers* later called the production principle underlying the clothing revolution. In a way, the *Bulletin* had simply given a formal title to Edwin Freedley's comment regarding the manager "who seemed to pass his whole time . . . in watching the progress of the other's industry" but who was in fact more responsible than anyone else for increasing the firm's profits, since he best knew how to organize others' work. Cutting—and pressing—were thus closely supervised. Silk, cotton, worsted, overcoating, and more standard woolens all needed to be spread and cut differently, which involved varying amounts of time and material, while plaid and striped patterns had to be carefully matched since the buying public was becoming increasingly demanding. And because cloth continued to be the principal expense of business, all this work was trusted only to in-house employees.[12]

Cutting cloth into the constituent parts of a coat required several minutes. Sewing the pieces back together into a garment took far longer. "One cutter will cut as many garments in one week as three hundred persons can make up in the same time," went the contemporary estimate. "Oh, my! it is an undertaking," a young diarist agreed, upon being asked to stitch a linen shirt-bosom, wristbands, and sleeves. "I have to pull the threads out and then take up two threads and leave three. . . . The stitches must not be visible to the naked eye. I have to fell the sleeves with the tiniest seams and stroke all the gather and put a stitch on each gather." There were 25,243 stitches in a man's coat, constituting two days of work in "journeymen's hours," according to *Niles' Weekly Register*, for whom such numbers were a part of its tireless campaign on behalf of the rationalization and system befitting an industrial society. Of these, 782 stitches were required for the basting; 5,500 for the edges; 7,114 for felling edges and faces; 1,982 for the pockets and other out-of-sight places; 3,056 more for the collar; 5,359 for the seams; and 1,450 for the holes. The ennumeration broke the activity of sewing down in terms of a standard denominator, the stitch, which could then be translated into time, into piecework, or into specific tasks. And even though all the breathless accounts of the new lot system of management treated sewing as almost incidental to the industrial production process, the work of sewing was clearly the basis of the industry's giant labor needs. Not only that, but "a great deal depends upon the sewer," as Joseph Couts wrote in his *Practical Guide for the Tailor's Cutting-Room*. Fitting the pieces of cut cloth back together was hardly a perfunctory matter. "The subtleties of inter-linings, padding, pressing, sewing" were no less integral to "the whole art" of tailoring than was the cutting. That fact became immediately obvious to James Edney, who was chronically late in entering the labor market in the mid-1830s and was subsequently frustrated by his failure to hire sewers with the requisite skills, or keep in his employ those who had already become experienced with his patterns.[13]

At the same time, sewing was categorically separated from the rest of production. Lewis and Hanford, for instance, employed 72 persons on the premises and hired an additional 3,600 outsiders, "a large portion of whom are women and girls," to actually sew up their goods. Far more than the cutter working under the lot system, these tens of thousands of sewing hands signaled the creation of an anonymous mass of labor power operating in a buyer's market, one in which the techniques of production had undergone only minimal transformation and in which those selling their labor had little chance of gaining any control over the terms of exchange. The almost ad hoc nature of sewing employment was no hindrance to rationalizers and system-izers. For if they were by no means incidental to production, sewers almost always proved to be interchangeable—a floating public of men and women dispersed throughout the city and its hinterland whose cash needs made them easy recruits to the metropolis's largest industry.[14]

Since businesses strove to offer inventories "adapted to the means and wants of all classes of society," sewing requirements were highly varied. Bet-ter garments, for instance, were constructed with finished edges, with pockets that matched, or with darts and tucks similar in length. Some seams were double-stitched—which, of course, required far more labor time—or back-stitched with fine linen thread. The top of the back of a more costly pair of trousers might be faced with cotton twill sewn in place before the center back seam was finished and the hem of the legs secured with silk bias tape. Formal and evening wear was often braided along the outside seams of pants. Some-times pockets would be added on the breast of the coat, or a button would be put on the watch pocket, or three buttons sewn onto the cuff of the sleeves. All these variations belonged to the innumerable permutations of style and construction adapted to a highly segmented market, each of which required more or less time, expertise, and experience on the part of the sewer. How else could Lewis and Hanford, employing 4,000 persons in an average week, prof-itably issue a spring catalogue in 1849 listing four distinct "qualities" in which each of hundreds of separate styles of garments were available? Messrs. Lewis and Hanford had to be able to order up labor much as they did their cloth.[15]

Such "elasticity" in production meant heterogeneity in society. The co-ordination of variable labor costs with the business's multifarious markets was, first and foremost, a social process. Hierarchies of in-house trimmers, Southern-work cutters, vest embroiderers, journeymen sewing surtouts with side linings creased in half-inch blocks, and "plain" shirtmakers hired on a subcontract and earning what contemporaries acknowledged to be starvation wages—all were expressions of how the material facts of production were ap-plied to a social reality of classes, genders, ethnicities, and families, and how that social reality was integrated into production. When there were no ma-chines increasing productivity or technologies redividing the labor, when the product itself underwent no physical transformation to speak of but became a commodity in every respect, industrial production could only be organized through a proper manipulation of the existing organization of society.

This organization included a geographical aspect. In 1834 a provincial entrepreneur advertised in the *Journal of Commerce* for precut cloths that he would then distribute for sewing to "a number of industrious young Ladies in a country village." As his offer suggests, New York firms sent sewing work to New Jersey, Connecticut, and upstate counties on a regular basis. In Newark alone they employed some two thousand women by the 1850s. Clothing firms in Boston, another important center of the industry, likewise spread their manufacturing work over a wide swath of hinterland in New Hampshire, Maine, and western Massachusetts. "By means of . . . expressmen to the most remote towns and villages," Boston's Board of Trade reported, "the wives and daughters of mechanics, farmers and fishermen, are continually supplied with fabrics by the dealers in clothing here." Production, it turned out, traveled the same rivers, canals, and railroads by which the finished goods subsequently circulated. Indeed, labor was famously now no less of a commodity itself, and its wide geographical base helped to deflate labor prices back in the city. Farm women, in other words, had not stopped sewing men's clothing. But now they were often paid a wage by city clothiers to do so. Like cloth, credit, and transportation, household labor fell under metropolitan control as well. And because householders were usually hired to sew up less stylish goods or work clothing, many of these same garments then came back from the city for sale in the provinces.[16]

The industrial production of clothing also contained an important temporal element. "The tailors have sometimes work, and sometimes not. Most of them are out of work sometimes and some of them very frequently." Custom tailoring shops were at their busiest for about half the weeks out of the year, in the late summer and fall, and again toward the end of winter and through the spring. During these seasons their journeymen had no shortage of work, and extra hands were hired to keep up with demand. During the rest of the year the latter were let go, many of them finding employment with the wholesale trade at a lower wage rate. Because they were paid by the piece to make up ready-mades, however, their earnings did not necessarily fall. They could instead devote less time and effort to each garment, thereby increasing their output. Ready-made production in general had a longer season than custom manufacture, unless the ready-made firm produced for a highly specific market. The longer season was, of course, a function of the prefabricated nature of the goods, which allowed clothiers to spread production out over time. In addition, garments had to be ready for shipping earlier so as to reach provincial stores by the beginning of the shopping season. But wholesale production had its seasonal caprice as well, expanding and diminishing operations in accordance to market demand. Ready-made firms also "curtailed" hands over the course of the season as part of their strategy to keep stock at a minimum and avoid sinking more capital than was necessary into wages. Those employees who were kept on year-round were usually paid a lower wage in exchange for the steady work. Almost all were released for up to two months each year anyway, in mid- or late summer and again in late winter (a difficult time of year to be out of work), when orders were sparse and new fabrics for the upcoming changeover of seasons needed to be prepared.[17]

The best way for businesses to address the geography, seasonality, and variety so characteristic of clothing production was by putting out the work. Such a timeworn practice answered the need for a fluid, flexible, and gigantic work force that could be immediately forthcoming when necessary. Putting-out addressed the important spatial and temporal nature of production, a success made all the more significant by the widening social distances between citizens in an age of industrialization and by the market's role in reconnecting them. Putting-out allowed manufacturers to coordinate supply and demand in a way that avoided fixed costs or expensive long-term investments. It enabled them to adjust the labor force to their variable production needs. It saved them money by allowing them to pass expenses and risks along to labor, including the costs associated with unemployment and "unused" capital, principally in the form of work space but of tools as well (threads, needles, and candles, not to mention wood for heating). What were inhibiting factors for other large industrial enterprises in the city—the lack of a power source, high rents, and social fluidity—were incentives for clothiers. Clothing once again proved ideally suited to the exigencies of metropolitan profit making as clothiers avoided the more rigid, and costly, social obligations—overall responsibility for their laborers' subsistence—once expected of employers. The employment relationship was put on an entirely adventitious footing: it was another version of one-price shopping.[18]

Labor was consequently left to make its own arrangements. Alongside the proliferating notices for clothing hands in the 1830s another kind of advertisement thus appeared: "To journeymen tailors: 10 or 12 journeymen can have seat room in one of the best rooms and locations in the city, by applying immediately at 76 Maiden Lane, junction Liberty St., upstairs." Others could reserve a seat for fifty cents a week at the junction of Elm, Orange, and Spring, midway between Broadway and the Bowery, the city's two principal shopping arteries. There were also individual work spaces for rent at the same price near the downtown clothing firms, at 65 Exchange Place. This system of freelance workshops could not supply all the industry's needs, however. The bulk of mass producers, particularly women, had no choice but to work at home.[19]

The cloths that were cut in-house were distributed by the foreman as bundles of pieces—backs, sides, fronts, front panels, skirts, sleeves, collars, and so on—for sewers to take home, lay out, and sew up. Attaching the pockets to a coat was usually the first task. This alone took about two hours. Then came the two foreparts, excluding button holes, which were best left for a time when the eyes were freshest, especially if one was working on a double-breasted jacket. Once the body of the garment was done the sleeves were ready to be put in. Then the back and shoulder seams were sewn up, after which the collar could be attached. Various types of needlework were applied to each garment. Plain sewing was used on the bodies. Neater stitching was required on the more visible front panels, wrists, and collar. Finishing, which entailed a great deal of gathering, involved yet another technique, as did the stitching of button holes and the sewing on of buttons, which was one of the first sewing jobs that employers set apart as a discrete task.[20]

Such out-work was paid by the piece, since there was obviously no one to supervise the clock. Each style of vest, shirt, coat, or trousers had its own price. That was made plain in the bills of prices presented by striking journeymen to their employers in 1850. Tailors demanded $2.50 for making a frock coat of cloth or cashmerette that included eight rows of stitching across the shoulder and six in the side lining, five button holes in the breast and two in the cuffs. Padded lapels cost $12\frac{1}{2}$ cents extra; side edges (half- or full-length), $18\frac{1}{2}$ cents; "stitching front edges with side cuffs," $37\frac{1}{2}$ cents; silk or alpaca neck pads not exceeding six rows of stitching, $6\frac{1}{2}$ cents; silk or alpaca skirt lining, creased diagonally, $12\frac{1}{2}$ cents. These were just some of an intricate system of extras that could double the price of a job. Similarly, extensive lists were compiled for merino coats, overcoats, and sack coats, and for a wide range of pants styles as well.[21]

Piecework, however, was not limited to put-out employees of the ready-made trade. Although in England opposition to the piece system was fierce during these years, the system had become universally accepted in America as early as 1800. When Baltimore tailors won a price advance in 1805, for instance, the new rate was calculated per job, with a system of extras used to further enhance their gains. In fact, the splintering of tasks usually equated with industrial deskilling was, in the case of clothing, especially characteristic of the upper levels of the craft as well as of the most remunerative in-house work. When David Winebrener assigned the infamous riding-habit job to six of his journeymen in 1827—the same riding habit that resulted in their conviction for conspiracy later that year—one of them was, for example, made responsible for the sleeves, the breast, the vents in the cuffs, and part of the wadding. Since the journeyman was paid directly for his output, this piece-work actually resembled independent artisanal production, a well-established American value, though such artisanal independence should not be confused with an artisan's construction of the whole garment by himself. At the same time, it was becoming necessary to translate these production tasks into labor time in order to coordinate between the business's cash logic and the exigencies of its workers' subsistence, which is what prompted *Niles'* to determine that 25,243 stitches were equivalent to two days of work for a journeyman.[22]

Most of all, though, piecework proved to be a most effective method of ensuring discipline among an unorganized, variously skilled labor force working unsupervised off the premises. Put-out workers kept themselves hard on the job in order to maximize the number of garments they could finish in a week, the prices for each piece being set at a level where only such concerted effort would earn a decent subsistence. The arithmetic was simple. White or checked cotton shirts, the common variety with five seams in each sleeve, paid 6 cents each in the mid-1840s. A "common fast semstress" could make two per day, and the swiftest hand could possibly make three if she worked an eighteen-hour day. In the best of circumstances this brought in $1.26 at the end of the week. Rent for a single room in a working-class neighborhood was $4.00 a month in those years. Duck trowsers, overalls, and other cheap working clothes paid a little more per piece—8 to 10 cents each—but because of the greater intricacy of their construction they generated no greater weekly wage. On the other hand, provided she had the requisite skills and could convince an employer of the same, the same seamstress might receive fine linen shirts with plaited bosoms to make up the following week. These paid 50 cents apiece and could be finished at the rate of about one every two days—$1.75 a week, well beyond bare subsistence. Better yet, three cloth roundabout jackets, each paying 50 cents, could be made in two days. All these weekly rates assumed that one assignment immediately followed upon another. They did not take into account the half a day often required to pick up work or to deliver finished goods and then receive one's payment. These figures also presumed maximal productivity—that the "15 to 18 hours of steady work by the best hand" would not be interrupted by children, washing, cooking, and other household chores, or by illness or exhaustion. They also ignored seasonal lay-offs and regular economic downturns, which, in the mid-1850s, for instance, resulted in a deflation of up to 40 percent in sewing prices.[23]

"An industrious sewer can get along pretty well upon a pinch," contemporary apologists claimed. In fact, something of a public relations game developed around the question of wages in the clothing industry. One foreman told Virginia Penny, the era's most systematic investigator of "women's employments," that in good times there was enough work for all the tailoresses in New York. He himself paid "good operators" of sewing machines five dollars a week for ten-hour days (which also meant that he paid other operators less). The truth is, however, that the highly variegated inventory and the wide range of jobs yielded an equally broad variation in wages. The Society for the Relief of Poor Widows reported in 1859 that prices for sewing "vary so much, in the quality of the work required, that figures would give a very inaccurate idea of the value received."[24]

Such a system was not without its risks for employers. The same low piece-rates that sped up the work and allowed the absent boss an impressive degree of control also raised concerns that temporary hands would disappear with the goods. Hard-pressed wage earners in the city, for instance, not only pawned their own clothing to raise cash for rent or groceries; they also pawned the garments they made up for the firms, redeeming them with a new job when the previous one was due. In this way, they could keep turning over their debts using a cycle of ostensibly free credit borrowed from their employers. In fact, however, payment was exacted. Clothing houses soon required deposits of up to several dollars—the value of the whole job—from those taking pieces home to sew. The money was returned when the finished goods were delivered and approved, although that, too, might depend on the cash flow of the clothing house rather than on the fact that the work had been delivered. Stories abounded of employers postponing payment, withholding wages until alterations were made, or even pocketing deposits under the pretext that substandard work had ruined the value of the cloth. If a deposit was not required, then references were. Pieceworkers kept their own ledgers of past jobs that constituted an employment history available for the perusal of each new boss. Naturally, records of all incoming and outgoing work were also maintained by the firms. Without such documentation it would not have been practical to organize put-out production on a mass level. In that respect, the neutral ledger gave employers a structural advantage in the system.[25]

Their advantage rested, in addition, on the city's own commodification. As the political economist John Dix observed in 1827, the island of Manhattan had become, "by means of hypothecations familiar to the common course of trade, . . . a circulating capital, which is constantly changing its form, and yielding at every conversion a profit to its employers." New York City, in other words, was also not a neutral setting where businessmen happened to accumulate their surplus values. It was "a form of capital itself, and one of the most effective."[26] At first glance, the birth of a real estate market, with its characteristic speculations and frequent fluctuations, would seem to be antithetical to manufacturing's requirement for stability. But the continual enhancement of land values in the city pushed the cost of independent artisanship in Manhattan to prohibitive levels, thereby encouraging waged outwork. At the same time, the construction of tenement housing, motivated by the desire of employers to also profit from land values, created the dense urban geography that also favored putting-out. Thus the whole city became the industry's workshop, and the proverbial needleworker became pathologized, living and working in a "single room . . . in the upper story of some poor, ill-constructed, unventilated house . . . for [which] the tenants never pay less than three to four and a half dollars per month—and pay they must do." There is no evidence that New York clothiers deliberately built the very tenements that housed their workforce. But like all businessmen, they shifted their manufacturing profits into real estate at the earliest opportunity. And this investment strategy, along with its resulting social geography, contributed to their control over an otherwise unwieldy labor force—a control effected, again, not by any machine technologies or novel divisions of labor but by an even more basic industrial phenomenon: the very alienability of all things— land, labor, and the results thereof—to the highest bidder. Not only was the home sewing of tailors and tailoresses a source of profit, then, but so was the very fact of their tenancy, indeed, their very presence in the city.[27]

Real estate investment in urban tenements was a novel aspect of economic success. A more familiar ingredient was clothiers' mobilization of the most traditional production unit of all, the family. In 1854 Angela Heck wrote back home to the Rheinland to report that her tailor-husband had been hired right off the boat upon their arrival in New York. So anyone planning to follow her to the New World, she advised, should make sure first to get herself a tailor.[28] Frau Heck probably had more to do with her husband's success than she let on. A couple of years later, for example, a young German tailor hired a seamstress from the Five Points House of Industry. Overcome by pity for her impoverished situation—that, at least, being how the House of Industry's patrons subsequently explained his actions—he resolved to marry the poor woman and so "save her reputation." Having, in addition, plenty of work, the tailor "was sure that instead of being any hindrance, she would assist him in making a living." Regardless of his fundamental motivation, the fact is that such intrafamily industry was commonplace in clothing production. Everyone in New York knew that "a tailor is worth nothing without a wife and very often a child." Almost a fifth of the seamstresses living in the city's Fourth Ward in 1855 resided with male kin who worked in the tailoring trade, a figure that likely excluded most wives, who frequently did not report a profession to the census marshal. Theodor Griesinger, writing to Germany about work prospects in New York City, described the tailor's road to success in America: "The first thing he does upon arrival is to marry. Then he sets up shop, goes to a clothing merchant and gets pre-cut cloth to sew. His wife's assistance is essential in this work, but they get along well." Virginia Penny reported that a clothing merchant on the Bowery had a family working for him that sometimes earned the astronomical sum of thirty dollars a week. The story might have been apocryphal, but the point was real. In the early 1860s a tailor taking home piecework and laboring one hundred hours a week was said to earn seven dollars. With his wife assisting him his earnings rose by almost half, to ten dollars.[29]

Putting-out provided access to this cheapest labor source of all, domestic women. And that was made possible, in turn, by the fact that all girls learned to sew. It was a skill integral to their self-identity. Lucy Larcom recalled a moment in her childhood when "I lifted my eyes from my father's heels to his head, and mused: 'How tall he is! and how long his coat looks! and how many thousand, thousand stitches there must be in his coat and pantaloons! And I suppose I have got to grow up and have a husband, and put all those little stitches into *his* coats and pantaloons. Oh, I never, never can do it!" John Pintard paid his daughter, who was "exceedingly expert with her needle," half of what it would have cost him "at a store" in 1819 to have vests, pantaloons, and a short coat of India gingham sewn up. Forty years later Samuel Edgerly spent a typical winter night reading aloud to his fiancé from the *Home Journal* while she "pursued her labors," making fringe for a short-sleeved shirt and mending his coat, as well as that of a friend. As Catharine Beecher advised in her *Treatise on Domestic Economy*: "Every young girl should be taught to do the following kinds of stitch, with propriety: over-stitch, hemming, running, felling, stitching, back-stitch and run, buttonhole-stitch, chain-stitch, shipping, darning, gathering, and cross-stitch." Thus Beecher prepared women for the practical exigencies of the domestic ideal while also training them for waged existence.[30]

Clothing entrepreneurs sought the same savings as these householders. In 1819, the same year that New York's journeymen tailors went out on strike to protest the growing use of female labor by the city's master tailors, almost 90 percent of the hands hired by Henry Brooks to sew for his Catharine Street clothing store were women. That is not to say that Brooks did not also apply a sexual hierarchy in dividing the labor. His pricier items—coats and surtouts, which required the most time and greatest skill to make up—were invariably given to men to sew, while shirts and drawers and cheap nankeen trousers were exclusively assigned to women. Nevertheless, there was a large inventory of goods, constituting the bulk of his sales, that were not restricted to one sex or the other and for which Brooks paid the same prices to both men and women for making up.[31] Women were clearly available for every sort of tailoring. During a strike by the city's seamstresses in 1831, one merchant tailor defended himself in the pages of the *New York Sentinel* by claiming that he and his peers paid "a liberal price for work, sufficient indeed to support an industrious female genteely, without resorting to any thing degrading." In the middle of the season in 1835 Edney became pressed for labor, using "all means to obtain hands." The avaliability of women saved his situation. In 1836 Louis Levy advertised in the *Morning Courier and New-York Enquirer* for fifty good tailoresses to do city-department and custom work. And in 1841 the *Herald* complained that it was no longer possible to find a pair of pantaloons in New York made by a man.[32]

There was a powerful social intersection between the casual nature of this work and commercial priorities. Married women, for instance, often entered and exited the labor market in accordance to their family's material needs (not that those could be divorced from general economic conditions or from the business cycle). They sold their sewing skills when income from other sources fell short of needs: when a doctor's bill was due, new shoes were needed, or their husband was out of work. Sewing generally complemented a woman's unremunerated responsibilities. It could be picked up and put down at home while she was caring for children, preparing meals, cleaning house, and otherwise managing the family's domicile (and attending to any boarders)—the same practical advantage that helped define spinning as women's work in an earlier age. Sewing was, for example, the favored source of income for widows with small children in New York's working-class Sixth Ward in 1855. As they, and their children, aged, these widows usually tried to move on to other employments, largely because income from sewing was clearly intended as a supplement to family income. Such work paid less than what house servants, cooks, or washerwomen earned, all of whom also received meals and often lodging. Instead, sewing was meant to generate the extra cash needed to buy blankets, furnishings, and even clothing, especially after children were born, cash needs not limited to the poor or to the city. The supplementary nature of sewing work also explains why the seamstress-widow became a favorite subject of charitable concern in these same decades, falling as she did through the cracks by having to earn a living wage in a profession designed to provide no such thing. In fact, while complaints were often heard in other industries about the transience of female labor, and particularly about the unreliability of married women's employment, clothiers made few such noises. Of course, this meant that women searching for full-time employment in the trade often had a problem.[33]

In fact, the industry's entire wage structure rested on the savings to be derived from employing women. The *Emigrant's Dictionary* of 1820 warned English journeymen who were thinking about relocating that New York's tailoring trade was "much injured by the employment of women and boys, who work from twenty five to fifty per cent cheaper than the men." Henry Fearon had published similar figures two years before. The average weekly wages paid by clothiers in Boston four decades later suggested that little had changed:

Overseers	19.45
Cutters	13.92
Trimmers	11.06
Pressers	9.17
Basters	6.32
Machine operators	5.53
Finishers at home	4.00
Finishers in shop	4.56
Finishers, custom	6.00
Makers of custom pantaloons and vests	5.58

Women never rose higher than basters on this scale. They were still restricted, as they always had been, to the less remunerative work. Moreover, the Boston figures may even have been on the high side. Two separate investigations in New York a few years earlier found that twelve-hour days of sewing vests, pantaloons, and light coats for the summer season earned seamstresses less than two dollars a week. And only one in ten shirt sewers brought home a viable income of six dollars a week.[34]

That which made waged sewing so convenient for women seeking to earn extra cash made it problematic for others, however, a situation that employers exploited to their advantage. As Virginia Penny explained: "The nature of the employment is such that no woman could enjoy health long, who did nothing else, and the wages are so small that anyone must work all the time to make a living; hence the work does not suit any, except those who have homes and have recourse to this as a secondary employment." But the foreman at a large clothing manufactory told Penny that "those that are dependent on their work for a living, do their work better than those that merely do it for pocket money." Seamstresses who needed to support themselves by sewing were more disciplined employees. They did not waste material and worked more steadily. In other words, while the wage women earned for piecework was designed to be supplementary income, the industry preferred primary earners.[35]

And these there were in abundance. It was not only farm boys who were migrating en masse to the industrial metropolis. "Hundreds [were] daily attracted to the Cities by vague hopes of doing better," as the *Tribune* observed in 1845 of the market that had developed in sewing skills. "Sewing girls" were consequently seen passing down Broadway a good hour each morning before the clerks commenced their procession. The *Tribune*'s announcement in 1845 of a revolution in city tailoring actually opened with a comment about the prevalence of women in the trade "who work for such prices as they can get." In 1860, according to one estimate, 42.9 percent of all women employed in New York City worked for manufacturers of men's clothing. The 17,000 women counted by the 1850 manufacturing census constituted well over half of the industry's waged employees, a percentage that obviously left out the considerable number of nonwaged sewers, that is, wives and daughters sewing for tailors in the family. Only domestic service might have commanded a greater number of female workers in antebellum America than the needle trades.[36]

The increasing commercial importance of the sexual division of sewing work made sewing's gender increasingly important as well. Man could be taught to sew just as women might be instructed in science, the *Lady's Book* pronounced in applying the emerging sexual ideology of gendered spheres to the industrial revolution in 1828, "yet revoltings of the soul would attend this violence to nature; this abuse of physical and intellectual energy; while the beauty of social order would be defaced, and the fountains of earth's felicity broken up." This was essentially the same argument used a decade earlier against the journeymen who protested their employers' increasing use of female labor. "The original cause of casting odium on the occupation of a tailor," an opponent of the strike explained in the *New York Post*, "arose . . . about two centuries ago [when] this trade of a tailor was performed wholly by women; it was scandalous and effeminate, for *men* to work at the needle." The journeymen tailors were thus deprived of any claim to traditional artisanal status, and their cause was presented as no less than a violation of the natural order (a natural order that also happened to favor their employers' pursuit of wider profit margins). It was a complicated argument, for as long as sewing was a noncommercial household activity, it was indeed a female monopoly.

Only when it became the subject of economic exchange—when tailors were paid to make clothes—had sewing traditionally become a male occupation. Now capitalists sought to do away with the sexual segregation of labor and normalize women's place in the sewing market. As such, they were simply taking women's natural position as society's premier sewers and updating it for a market economy. Thus, it was Brooks's vision of a gender-neutral production force rather than the male exclusivity of the Journeymen's Society that became the general practice throughout the trade.[37]

But because capitalism was far from being the exclusive source of social values, women's production role in the clothing industry—or in almost any industry for that matter—continued to generate ideological controversy. As Virginia Penny observed, everyone still pretended in the early 1860s that the most fashionable coats on Broadway were not made by women. It remained culturally important that clothing production was sexually bifurcated. Accordingly, a woman's wardrobe became the exclusive purview of the dressmaker—there was nothing more insulting to nature than a "male milliner," for instance—while gentlemen were to be exclusively dressed by men.[38] Only the lower orders, such as those who bought "slops" from Henry Brooks, wore clothing of ambiguous sexual provenance, further evidence of their lumpen status. Thus, that self-styled arbiter of male fashion, George P. Fox, announced in newspaper advertisements that he employed no tailoresses at all. His reason—the "scientific cut and peculiar improved constructed coat, vest and pantaloons"—actually obviated the need to hire only the most highly trained journeymen. But the niceties of logic were clearly less important than the tailors' embrace of the male values of science and technical improvement, and their special relevance to men's bodies. Meanwhile, economic logic itself followed a separate trajectory: of the 119 New York custom tailors visited by census marshals in 1850, only eleven reported hiring no women.[39]

– – – – –

"Sewing enters largely into the construction of every thing [persons] wear," Elias Howe's lawyer wrote in applying for an extension of Howe's sewing-machine patent. Why, then, was it not a sewer's market? Why, as the *Tribune* resignedly observed, "will [there] never be a lack of Seamstresses while the world remains essentially as it is, and the great mass of them will always be meagerly paid?"[40]

Sewing was at once a lowest common social denominator—all women sewed—and a lowest common production denominator—most of the city's manufacturing industries needed to sew their goods. "If any girl . . . wants to stop working at those prices," a clothier announced, "she's perfectly welcome to stop; there's a dozen wants it, where one gets it." This coincidence engendered a horizontal promiscuity that only further cheapened seamstresses' labor. Not only did she make linen shirts for one firm one week and woolen pantaloons for another the next week; she also moved between one industry and another. When needlewomen protested their employment conditions in a public meeting in 1845, for instance, straw workers, tailoresses, plain and coarse sewers, shirtmakers, book folders and stitchers, cap makers, dressmakers, crimpers, and fringe and lace makers were all represented. Apart from clothing, countless other commercial goods required sewing skills as well: pillowcases, towels, artificial flowers, belts, bonnets and bonnet ruches, dress trimmings, embroideries, feathers, hoop skirts, muslin sets, parasols and umbrellas, furs, children's clothes, cloaks and mantillas, costumes, headdresses, fans, ladies' underwear, cravats, gentlemen's hats, and suspenders. In addition, used-clothing establishments, clothes-dyeing shops, and cleaners all performed repairs and renovations that required a sewing force.[41] Not all this work, of course, was identical, let alone interchangeable. Men's clothing alone demanded a wide array of skills and levels of experience. But many of the skills were transferable, a fact that ostensibly worked to the advantage of sewers, who could then move out of a depressed industry to one in which jobs were available. In fact, their actual activity—whether they were sewing vests, or pillowcases, or caps—had lost any specific meaning. The value of their labor issued from the sewers' general availability in the market. A city filled with women working at home, in other words, not only saved employers overhead expenses; the labor itself came cheap, having required no prior investment on their part. The "numerous thousands [who] ply the polished shaft for support," as the Association for Improving the Condition of the Poor described them in its annual report of 1852, were not just anonymous objects of charitable pity. They were a truly abstract mass of labor power. They were ready-made labor.[42]

The seamstress was the clothing industry's analogue to the machine: she lowered the cost of production while enhancing the capitalist's control over labor. As was often the case with machinery as well, she was also considered by many to be the cause rather than the consequence of changes in the craft. William Sanger provided a stark account in 1859 of the sexual power structure of sewing for a living:

The person who delivers the materials, receives the work, and pronounces on its execution, is almost invariably a man, and upon his decision rests the question whether the operative shall be paid her full wages, or whether any portion of her miserable earnings shall be deducted because the work is not done to his satisfaction. In many cases he wields a power the determinations of which amount to this: "Shall I have any food to-day, or shall I starve?"[43]

To what extent did this system of capitalist control rely on its female subject? That is, to what extent did it depend on a gendered definition of sewing and home manufacturing, on the relative powerlessness of women in any confrontation with men (whether employers or husbands), and on the cheaper rates axiomatically paid for female labor? The fact is that men also worked primarily off the premises and, in so doing, also helped subsidize their employers' production expenses. Thousands of wage-earning tailors were no less vulnerable than women to the structural disadvantages of putting-out, to business cycles and seasonal unemployment, and to the continual growth of the city's labor pool and the wide availability of sewing skills. Tailors were also divided into those who had relatively more or less access to better-paying jobs, the latter an amorphous mass who shared a denigrated status similar to that of women in the production hierarchy. George P. Fox, for instance, not only made sure to publicize his refusal to hire women but just as ostentatiously announced that he employed no "slop-shop tailors" as well. Moreover, men's sewing wages were, on the whole, well below the average earned by city craftsmen in 1850, which was consistent with tradition, inasmuch as tailors, together with shoemakers and candlemakers, had always been at the bottom of the artisanal pecking order. No tailors, tellingly, numbered among the members of New York's General Society of Mechanics and Tradesmen that was founded after the War of Independence.[44]

Nevertheless, tailors had one important recourse from industrial pressures that women did not. They had tailoresses. The "family home shop" not only served the large firms, but it opened up possibilities for the heads of households as well.[45] This is because the sexual prerogative of men—which long predated industrial society but which also proved highly adaptable to the system of waged labor—provided a way for tailors to reclaim proprietary interest in their wives' and daughters' labor and thus make the best of their own growing dependence on waged work. This did not turn every piece-work tailor who had a wife into a market entrepreneur. He continued to operate within the unpredictable terms of waged employment, remaining beholden to the capitalist rather than the customer. At the same time, the wage-earning tailor participated in the same industrializing patriarchy that now effected a wholesale exploitation of the female class of laborers. He functioned on a continuum of production relations in which the boundaries between employer and employee, between exploiter and exploited, were obscure. It was not always possible to determine just where one stood in this food chain, the waged tailor often filling both roles at once.[46]

These relations began in the family but did not stop there. Journeymen paying an extra thirteen cents a week for a chair "for a girl" in one of the city's sewing lofts were participating in the same system. So, too, was the tailor who received more work than he alone could handle and hired perhaps three to five (or even more) "outside hands . . . for the most part female," whom he then personally supervised. In fact, many tailors were able to take advantage of the proletarianization of their craft. As the clothing industry grew in volume and variety, and its appetite for labor likewise exploded, new employment opportunities presented themselves, particularly those that involved coordinating manufacturers' labor requirements and laborers' basic need for work. Thus, for example, the *Herald* was able to insinuate that the giant 1850 strike was launched by "sub-bosses" who filled orders for the large houses. The *Herald* was, of course, only too happy to cast aspersions on the virtuous rhetoric of the strikers ("To prevent the growth of an unwholesome aristocracy whose only aim is to acquire wealth by the robbery of the toiling masses," as the Journeymen's Society described their mission at the height of the summer's protests). But the *Herald*'s suggestion was not implausible. The *Tribune* had reported a few years earlier that the city's journeymen tailors were initiating "farming operations" by passing their jobs on to women or other "inferior workmen." A journeyman who received, for instance, $6.25 for each custom dress coat or frock he made up would instead pay a wage of three or four dollars a week to others for actually doing the work. Sometimes the tailor simply gave the job to the highest—or, in this case, lowest—bidder. "By this means," the *Herald* noted in 1857, "the persons who employ such hands are generally enabled to make a very handsome profit." Tailors who had failed to reverse or at least to control the commercialization of their craft, and who had been left with few prospects for a proprietorship, could become brokers in labor themselves and so claim a share of the surplus labor they had lost.[47]

The strike in 1850 was a part of this ongoing negotiation: an attempt by wage earners to secure a position in the market. Thus, John Donnelly remarked at a Congress of Trades meeting devoted to the tailors' strike that "the only thing they could be rallied on, was the prices." The tailors were clearly anxious to find a practical foundation on which to base their relations with employers. "Never was the demand for a rise of wages more moral, moderate and just," one of them insisted. "Even many of our most esteemed employers acknowledge this, and not only adhere to the new bill of prices, but also favor this movement in other ways—inasmuch as it serves the interest of the employer as well as the employed." In contrast to 1819 and 1836, there were no demands in 1850 for reasserting labor's control of the work process. In fact, memories of 1836 seemed to cast a long shadow. "Never . . . has any piece of cloth been taken away by a member of the Tailors Society with the intention of depriving any person of his property," the strikers declared in affirming their allegiance to the market's fundamental axiom. There was no dispute, in other words, over the property rights of the capitalist, only a tug-of-war over each sides' share of the marginal value. The strike was a bargaining tool used by the supply side to attempt to gain an advantage in the labor market. The strikers thus subscribed to Edwin Freedley's distinction between fair-paying employers and exploitative ones. Daniel Devlin, who immediately accepted the bill of prices proposed by the Journeymen's Society, was a good employer. C. T. Longstreet, who would not raise wages, was a bad employer, and subsequently became the target of protests, street demonstrations, and bad press. But, significantly, not even the violence ultimately directed against his establishment (by the German branch of the Journeymen's Society) apparently hurt Longstreet's business, or that of the other houses whose workers walked out over the summer. The credit reports supplied by Dun & Co. did not consider labor disputes detrimental to the business standing and creditworthiness of these companies. Such early experts in venture capital were keenly aware of the structural asymmetry of power between capital and labor.[48]

It was extremely difficult for labor to control the volume of supply in any way that resembled the strategic ability of capitalists to respond to market pressures. All three thousand of Longstreet's employees, for instance, had to eat. And, unlike Longstreet himself, they needed their weekly wage from him in order to do so. The only chance labor had of leveling the playing field was to unite and act as a single body, too. By 1850 the clothing industry's employees had accordingly organized themselves into groups of salesmen, cutters, journeymen, journeymen who "worked for customers," and shirt sewers. The fact that their organization also rested on basic categories of national, religious, linguistic, and sexual difference would only seem to enhance their ability to act in concert. The truth is, however, that such a scheme played into the production logic of the capitalist, who organized labor exactly on the basis of these social categories, while it obscured the common position of all wage earners in the labor market. But the alternative was to embrace industrial reality and recognize that the commodity was now the common denominator of their work life, and increasingly of their social identity as well. What relationship did the farm wife in Connecticut sewing work shirts during the winter months have with the German journeyman in the metropolis making up frock coats? Who would admit that they were now effectively interchangeable? Certainly neither of them. Who among these workers would want to identify themselves as a universal commodity, especially when intuition told them that the fundamental problem the supply side faced in the labor market was exactly this surfeit and homogenization of labor? So when the 1850 strike ended in a general acceptance by the city's clothing houses of the Journeyman Society's bill of prices, with its careful division of tasks into convenient production categories, it was in fact a great victory for capitalism. [49]

- - - - -

Skilled work was not a highly valuable property in industrial life. *Hunt's* acknowledged that basic condition when it observed that "abundant harvests, barns bursting with grain, herds of fat cattle and fatter hogs, will not make a farmer prosperous." The best-selling sentimentalist, T. S. Arthur, similarly acknowledged the plight of skilled labor in his story "The Tailor's Apprentice," in which the master tailor, Stoat, who is being squeezed from above and below, struggles to extract a respectable living from his proprietorship. The story includes an ode to Stoat's artistry as he goes about repairing a torn seam:

> He carefully ripped the welt off in the first place, and with a wet sponge-rag and hot iron, succeeded in making it, under the process of stretching, an inch longer. This would extend down at least one-half of the ugly rent. He next trimmed the ragged edges of the torn cloth, and closed it with a seam as small as it was possible to make. Then biting open the seam, he concealed it in a great measure, by sewing it backwards and forward on the right side with a fine needle and split silk,—finally, he scratched the nap over the seam, with the point of a needle, which so completely concealed it, after it had been pressed, that none but the most practiced eye could have detected it. [50]

The fictional Stoat was representative of thousands of city tailors whose stoves heated both their "goose" and their family's meals, and who depended on modest repair work for their living: replacing the seating on a pair of pants, attaching a new set of buttons to a vest, or sewing a new velvet collar onto a coat. A. L. Sayre, who purchased ready-mades at Brooks Brothers and new vests from a custom tailor, also brought garments to be mended on a regular basis, repairs that cost him a total of $1.03 over fourteen months. In light of such meager sums, the prospect of receiving bulk orders from the city's clothing houses, for which he would then hire extra hands, must have been alluring indeed, affording these tailors a welcome opportunity to make up a bill larger than a dollar or two. Thus, the industry created a subcontracting niche for masters whose proprietary independence was simultaneously being compromised by the same industrial market.[51]

Subcontracting, of course, was not new. It was in use in the 1830s when the country entrepreneur advertised in the *Journal of Commerce* for piecework to distribute to village women. It was adopted by master tailors in Philadelphia after the War of Independence, when the clothier general transferred responsibility for outfitting the U.S. Army from the voluntary efforts of patriotic wives and daughters into the hands of artisans, who then did their own hiring from the city's pool of tailors and tailoresses. It was in evidence earlier still, in the eighteenth century, when an English ready-made clothing manufacturer was unable to estimate the exact size of his labor force because he sent so much of the work out to various parishes. Now, however, in the mid-nineteenth century, such practices became a focus of unprecedented public attention. They were even accorded a new name. These "sweaters," said George Foster, barely able to contain his repulsion, "carry competition to its lowest and most wretched extent. . . . Sometimes the sweater himself employs undersweaters . . . and so, in the end, the at first inadequate payment given for the work is taxed, first by the master-workman for his profits and the support of his splendid shop and his elegant and fashionable family up town; next, for the greedy profit of the remorseless shaver and sharper; and then again, for one or two, and sometimes three, of his underlings."[52]

Sweating had obvious advantages for the clothier, relieving him of "the necessity of registering the name of, and looking after the, in some cases, incredible large number of hands which he would otherwise be obliged to do." The "assembly line" of off-season merchant-tailor shops, inside journeymen, "back shop" men, subcontractors, and outworkers did not immediately, or even necessarily, lower a clothier's labor costs. But it allowed him to avoid risks by passing on production responsibilities to others. As such, sweating was an elaboration of previous methods of putting-out—a direct extension of the ongoing attempts to create the most flexible production system possible for a highly mixed market. At the same time, the system also offered those with relatively less capital an opportunity to make a profit in the industrial age. Notices in the mass-circulating dailies for sewing labor, so prevalent in the mid-1830s, were gone by the next decade, apparently replaced by tiers of subcontractors who drew on their own social networks of neighborhood and ethnicity in the atomizing city. The industry increasingly relied on an interlocking network of mutual dependencies reaching down to the lowliest, most antiquated tailor's shop, such as Stoat's, not to mention to the newly arrived immigrant working at home with his wife and children. It was not unusual for saloon and boardinghouse keepers to become active subcontractors of sewing labor as well. In the 1850s, sewing-machine agents also got in on the action, not only selling and renting machines but including machine operators in the deal as well. A machine together with an operator cost two dollars a day (less if they were hired by the week). It was also possible to hire only the sewing operator at $1.25 to $1.50 a day.[53]

The continued development of subcontracting was responsible for the drop in the average size of clothing businesses in New York, from 137 employees in 1850 to 71 in 1860. Indeed, as clothing manufacturing reached its industrial apogee, its production practices began to resemble the more decentralized operations of earlier times. A firm's size and its direct control over much of the production process were no longer measures of industrial progress in the trade. Cutting might remain under close supervision at the firm, for example, but sponging—shrinking the cloth in preparation for cutting—would now be sent out to specialty firms. The same was true of starching the finished goods. Or the owner of "a number of sewing machines" could advertise for "regular work" from tailors, who then pressed and finished the garments he had sewn up.[54] Sweating thus served the marketing ambitions of clothiers who sought to satisfy a myriad of regions, tastes, and generations but who couldn't possibly themselves make up such a huge range of goods. Sweating allowed them to produce all these goods without any new machinery. They instead used an older technology—the subdivision of work—now made more powerful by the birth of a mass market in labor.

Of course, an important mechanical breakthrough in the production of clothing did occur: a machine was invented for sewing, to be "seen in practical operation" on the Bowery as early as 1851 at Smith & Conant's clothing warehouse. Virginia Penny reported that the machine allowed "a woman [to] do all the stitching of twelve pairs of cloth pantaloons in a day." Not only that, but "a coat that formerly required 2 days by hand, can be made in a sixth of a day." According to a more pedantic study published in 1861, frock coats that took 16 hours and 35 minutes to stitch by hand could be made up by a machine in 2 hours and 38 minutes. The time needed to produce a satin vest was reduced from over 7 hours to a little more than an hour. Shirts, whose light fabrics made them an early candidate for mechanical sewing, dropped from 14 hours and 26 minutes apiece to an hour and a quarter. The sewing machine thus satisfied the popular teleologies of industrial progress. As the *Tribune* put it: "The needle is sure soon to be consigned to the lumber-room where our grandmothers' 'great wheel,' 'little wheel,' loom and 'swifts' are now silently mouldering." In the same spirit, Wheeler & Wilson, manufacturers of sewing machines, wondered "how [the woman] has endured the drudgery of hand-sewing, just as the rail traveler marvels at the slow coaches of former days."[55]

But the sewing machine was no railroad: the latter, in fact, was far more crucial to the rise of the clothing industry. In marked contrast to the radical changes brought about by the nineteenth century's mechanization of so many other production processes—first and foremost among them spinning and weaving—the sewing machine actually reinforced many of the preexisting methods of clothing production. Machine technology, for instance, was far less significant for the clothing revolution than was the new measuring and drafting technology that made the lot system possible. Nor did the sewing machine have a particularly novel affect on the nature of sewing. Both its affordability and its portability matched the traditional flexibility required by clothing production, whereas most other industrial machines tended to limit flexibility. Rather than necessitating a centralized factory reorganization of the labor process, the sewing machine strengthened the almost ad hoc nature of production in an industry zealously minimizing its fixed costs. The machine also made it practical for an enterprising journeyman or family head who had access to a loan (and hire-purchase plans now proliferated, offered by sewing-machine loan companies responding to the intense competition among machine manufacturers) to set himself up as a subcontractor, hire his own sewers, and promise the clothing houses reliably standardized production.[56] Thus, the sewing machine became part of the shrinking of the size of clothing businesses themselves and their growing reliance on subcontracted, or sweated, labor.

Specialization continued apace. Mackin & Brother, for instance, bought their cloth on the accounts of jobbers who placed production orders with them. A. K. Ingraham made up garments on commission for Southern houses. The safest way to enter the highly volatile California market was also through such "wholesale manufacturing." Morrison Levy & Co.'s creditors breathed a sigh of relief when the firm decided not to open its own store in San Francisco but to sell its goods to local retailers instead. Baker, Nelson & Co. made up assortments of garments "expressly" for the California market, though they also refrained from marketing them directly. Some firms continued to send a partner to New York to oversee manufacturing. Abraham Hirschberg moved from Charleston, South Carolina, to Carsonville, Georgia, and then on to Atlanta, at which point he began to manufacture his own clothing in New York. Others used their provincial retail experience as a springboard to wholesale manufacturing, as, for example, did William Seligman when he moved from San Francisco to New York in 1852. Griessman and Hoffman actually closed their stores in Mississippi and Tennessee in 1858 to devote themselves exclusively to manufacturing, in this case for the South. Trowbridge Dwight & Co. closed their house in New Orleans in 1850 and became jobbers in the Southern market, using the services of such firms as Mackin & Brother to have the goods made up.[57]

Specialization was demographic as well as geographic. The segmentation of the market into price categories was nothing new. Henry Brooks founded his business on just such a niche, namely, the retail of relatively inexpensive goods. But in the 1850s these divisions became far more standard: the clothing market was sufficiently large and well established that production could be divided into permanent segments. This changed the relationship between cost and price. In the 1830s Francis Cooke would write from Augusta to order "$1.62 vests" or "$4.87 pants." James Edney would then shop for the appropriately priced cloth and have the items made up accordingly. In this instance, the retail price dictated how much could be spent on production. The creation of manufacturing niches signaled a reverse in that relationship. Permanent price lines now became practical, allowing manufacturers to specialize in goods within a particular price range, and modern mass consumption began to take shape. Indeed, this was the economic underpinning of "one-price" shopping.[58]

In the 1830s James Edney not only made up drawers and shirts but was responsible for a full price range of outer garments for "the highly variable market" in Augusta. Ten years later there were any number of firms specializing in this price category or another. Patrick Hogan and John Harris, for example, each had a thousand dollars invested in their West Street tailoring businesses in 1850, but each produced for markedly different markets. Hogan spent $500 on 500 yards of cloth. Harris bought 6,000 yards of fabrics for $1,000, thus spending six times less per yard than Hogan. In making up his far cheaper cloths, John Harris also hired far cheaper labor. His thirteen employees, twelve of whom were women, produced three hundred pairs of pantaloons, a thousand pairs of overalls, and a thousand shirts per year. Patrick Hogan instead employed two men and two women to produce one hundred coats and four hundred pairs of pants each year, garments that were obviously intended for a different class of customers. But the annual earnings of these two firms pursuing two such distinct business strategies were roughly the same. When the St. Louis clothing jobbers J. and W. Van Deventer advertised the arrival of "fine winter clothing from New York" in the fall of 1849, they simultaneously announced that a second shipment of "a large addition to our wholesale stock for the country trade" was also on hand. The two shipments could have been purchased from Hogan and Harris, respectively.[59]

The sweater was integral to this "devolution" of the industry into a myriad of production and marketing niches. He promised to meet deadlines, juggled orders, paid deposits on the cloth, delivered the goods on time, hired from a labor pool he knew firsthand, kept more hands in employment than he usually had work for in anticipation of rush jobs—he assumed, in short, most of the risks of manufacturing.[60] Small wonder, then, that most clothing houses quickly agreed to the wage demands of the striking journeymen in 1850. Since they directly employed fewer and fewer of their sewers, they wouldn't be obligated always to pay "journeyman's" rates anyway. The sweater established his own modest circulation of goods, cash, and credit—a business rhythm—specifically designed to fill a particular need. But he avoided most fixed costs of doing business, as he assembled and disbanded his workforce in accordance with orders. This allowed him to get by on the smallest of profit margins. The simple tools and portable materials, the tedious hours and unhealthy surroundings, and the low piece-rates that ensured work discipline in a buyer's labor market—none of these were the sweater's invention, however. Instead, he synthesized all the familiar elements of commerce—family relationships, manufacturing techniques, rented workspace, the putting-out of labor, and the fact that "garments can be made just about anywhere."[61]

None were novel aspects of a novel labor system. Even the economic exploitation of women's dependent position in society was no innovation, although emerging middle-class ideas about a specifically feminine nature that was, among other things, incompatible with industrial effort now seemed to make sweating especially abhorrent. It was rather sweating's apparent primitiveness, precisely its reliance on past practices rather than on any new forms of labor, that made it a new production category, and a problematic one at that. Contemporaries were still unused to thinking that unprecedented levels of mass production and distribution could rest on the decentralized, small-scale, labor-intensive practices of the past, just as many still clung to the notion that industrial progress was antithetical to impoverishment and pauperization.

6

The Seamstress

The growing vulnerability of working women in industrial society provoked a forceful response. In 1825 hundreds of them went out on strike against New York City clothing houses. In 1831 these same women organized themselves into a mass-membership United Tailoresses' Society. At a time when journeymen were still devoting their political efforts to a defense of artisanal prerogatives in the master's shop, these "tailoresses" (the appellation itself testified to an advanced degree of industrial consciousness, excluding as it did the more traditional dressmaking of the "sempstress") already understood that in a capitalist economy no aspect of the work relationship remained nonnegotiable. What's more, this insight was born of their very womanhood, that which was supposed to be the most transcendent, immutable quality of their lives but which actually now revolutionized their situation and turned working women into a distinct industrial class.

No one can help us but ourselves, Sarah Monroe, a leader of the United Tailoresses' Society, declared. Tailoresses should consequently organize a trade union with a constitution, a plan of action, and a strike fund. Only then could we "come before the public in defense of our rights." The Wollstonecraftian rhetoric was conscious. Lavinia Wright, the society's secretary, argued that the tailoresses' low wages and hard-pressed circumstances were a direct result of the way power was organized throughout society to ensure women's subordination in all social relations. The tailoresses' society now saw a chance to overturn that patriarchy by redefining woman's nature in accordance with the changing conditions of industrial production. In so doing they called into question any notion of a transcendent female passivity or even domesticity. Sarah Monroe: "It needs no small share of courage for us, who have been used to impositions and oppression from our youth up to the present day, to come before the public in defense of our rights; but, my friends, if it is unfashionable for the men to bear oppression in silence, why should it not also become unfashionable with the women? Or do they deem us more able to endure hardship than them themselves?" The United Tailoresses' Society challenged both their employer's haughty manipulation of their labor power and the axiom of female submissiveness and thereby revealed a powerful truth: not only was the homespun synthesis of domesticity and industry being sundered by capitalism, but neither of its constituent parts—neither domesticity nor industry—could be transplanted intact into the new reality. Such perspicacity provoked a visceral response, however. The Quakers threw the tailoresses out of their regular meeting hall. And the *Boston Evening Transcript* denounced the society's "unfeminine" ways, advising the New York tailoresses to desist from such politicking and be content with their scissors and pincushions.[1]

The advice was ignored. "If we are true to ourselves and each other, they cannot harm us," Monroe obstinately, and rather hopefully, declared. These women well understood that the *Evening Transcript*'s paternalism offered no real protection in the competitive economy that emptied a woman's traditional industry of any of its traditional meaning. In June 1831, taking advantage of the temporary development of a seller's labor market, the society proceeded to draw up a list of prices to be presented to employers, declaring that its members would refuse to work for less. Within a week, close to two thousand tailoresses went out on strike in New York. Their cause attracted considerable attention as well as the enthusiastic support of the labor press. Proposals were made by male trade unionists for a boycott of the city's tailors. A campaign against prison labor, which undercut sewing wages, was suggested. There was also talk of raising a subscription for establishing a cooperative store that would offer liberal remuneration, sick pay, and retirement benefits. Nothing came of any of these ideas, however. Within a fortnight the tailoresses returned to work, having to content themselves with an "Address to the Public" expounding on their hardships.[2]

Those hardships now emerged as a general topic of conversation in America. This was already evident in 1829 when Mathew Carey compared a tailoress's income against her expenses and derived a stark arithmetical deficit, or when the appallingly low wages and consequent sufferings of sewing women in Baltimore, Pittsburgh, Philadelphia, Boston, and New York became a pressing subject of discussion in the press during the 1830s. It was also evident when parties on both sides of the tariff question enlisted needleworkers— "who, of all the descriptions of laborers in our country, were the most poorly paid," as Senator Benton declaimed in congressional debate in 1842—to buttress the moral authority of their respective visions of economic development. And it was evident in 1851, when George Templeton Strong worried in his diary about "our swarms of seamstresses to whom their utmost toil in monotonous daily drudgery gives only bare subsistence, a life barren of hope and of enjoyment." Strong's observation was part of a general recital of contemporary tragedies that included the slum at Five Points, immigrant ghettos, "hordes of dock thieves," troops of girls "brutalized . . . beyond redemption by premature vice," and that other most archetypal victim of modernity, the ragpicker. The seamstress was first on his list because she represented better than any of the others precisely what had changed, and what was now becoming a central dynamic of capitalist democracy: not only the passing of the household era of production but with it a social order in which women, and most men, had been safely ensconced under the aegis of the household's patriarch.[3]

Strong's seamstress became a permanent station on the physiognomical tour of the corrupted metropolis. Espied on a still-deserted Broadway each morning at 7:30 on her way to the downtown stores, she was known to toil pathetically "in starvation and filthy rags." For Virginia Penny, she embodied the age's social deformities: "The habits of the sempstress are indicated by the neck suddenly bending forward, and the arms being, even in walking, considerably bent forward, or folded more or less upward from the elbows." Even *Hunt's Merchant's Magazine*—responding to yet another newspaper series on the labor conditions of New York's working class, this one published in the *Herald* and its first installment devoted to the city's seamstresses—saw fit to reprint a stanza from the notorious doggerel of English class protest, the "Song of the Shirt." It was implicit acknowledgment that European degradation had crossed the ocean. As *Hunt's* declared: "There is no class of workwomen who are more entitled to our sympathy and encouragement than the [seamstresses], for there are none who are more poorly paid for their work, or who suffer more privation and hardship."[4]

The seamstress, or tailoress—the etymological distinction soon lost its political significance—thus represented two principal effects of the industrial revolution: waged independence and waged exploitation. This was not as paradoxical as it might at first seem. Both conditions were unmistakably modern, and both stood in opposition to patriarchal ideas of woman's role and status, not to mention patriarchal notions of civic order in general. At the same time, each now pointed to a distinct future. On the one hand, the United Tailoresses' Society was ready to embrace the social possibilities of

Two 1849 illustrations of the suffering seamstress, one from George Foster's
muckraking *New York in Slices* (*above*) and the other from *Godey's Lady's
Book* (*facing*). The seamstress—a victim of the ruthless labor market—was a
favorite symbol of the social costs of industrial progress. As such, she made a
vital contribution to the creation of a democratic patriarchy.

an industrial system that turned women into free economic agents, at least
in principle. The propertied classes, on the other hand, were most emphatic
in decrying the nefarious effects of the wage system. Such rhetoric suited
their attempts to resurrect female domesticity for a capitalist age, for it allowed them to view the victimization of the seamstress by the wage as proof of
women's unsuitability to the labor market. That same market was, of course,
teeming with cheap female labor, which had proven so salutary to the profit
margin. However, this was no case of bourgeois hypocrisy. It was a sign, rather,
of a serious historical dilemma of the kind often faced by revolutionary classes:
how to control the very social forces that they have unleashed.

In replacing land with labor as the economy's most important form of
property, capitalism made each person responsible for negotiating his, or her,
own terms of employment. That system swept aside the static, corporate organization of household labor. But what would then keep social life from be-

coming as temporary, conditional, negotiable, fluid, and ultimately vulnerable to destruction as any other exchange in the market? The danger was
personified by Lize, the wage-earning everywoman, who could be seen without escort at the Apollo Ball-Room, on the east side of Broadway at Canal
Street, consorting with a mix of urban types during her evening leisure, or
spending her cash earnings, to the consternation of Sarah Hale, editor of
Godey's Lady's Book, on fashionable garments that she then provocatively
wore at ankle length. Hers was a culture where "a general free and easy kind of
semi-morality prevails," a visitor to the city reported in the 1850s, "the result
of freedom from restraint, and the presence of contaminating influences."[5]
Nevertheless, as threatening as it was deemed to be, that same freedom from
restraint was an essential element in industrial progress. In seeking to resolve
this conundrum, the employer class actually ended up embracing its source,
that is, the market's tendency to ruin women.

At first glance, they should have avoided doing any such thing. The seamstress's sufferings seemed to repudiate industrial conceits about the better
world now under construction. Armies of women sewing cut-rate seasonal
piecework in all the country's major cities constituted a scandalously iniqui-
tous example of one person's sacrifice exchanged for another's gain. As such,
the seamstress exposed the purported inclusiveness of a "middle landscape"

of industrial progress as so much fancy. And, in fact, that was exactly what radical critics such as George Lippard charged. "Now, gentle and comfortable people, who smack your lips as you say—'Any one that is not idle and improvident can get along; the idle, the improvident, the criminal only are poor'—will you tell us the particular sin of this girl-woman, who is now digging her grave with her needle?"[6]

There were some, of course, who attempted to deny responsibility for her condition. Edwin Freedley claimed that respectable clothiers in New York and Philadelphia paid women well, "notwithstanding the competition in the trade." He instead placed the blame for the seamstress's condition on the Chatham Street shops. "Chatham Street Clo' Dealers," as everyone knew, were a distinctly foreign element, indifferent to if not entirely ignorant of the nation's social traditions. By assigning responsibility to them, true Americans could be exonerated. But the seamstress's deplorable situation was too deeply implicated in the industrial system to simply be blamed on "extortionists, Jews, and Germans," as Virginia Penny less politely identified the exploiters of female labor. Instead of assigning a scapegoat, in fact, most middle class ideologues preferred to face the issue head on. As proponents of the industrial market system themselves, they had no recourse to agrarian household solutions. They required new means of domestication. Only by proving her unsuitability to industrial-age freedom—by emphasizing the distress caused her by the labor market—could waged women be redomesticated and their threat to authority be contained.[7] Thus it was that the suffering seamstress became a symbol of the times and that the inequities of the marketplace proved vital to the bourgeoisie's ideological as well as material needs.[8]

- - - - -

The capitalist ideal of the fallen seamstress was already in evidence in the Reverend Ezra Stiles Ely's visit to a "certain poor widow" in 1811. Ely recorded in his diary that she sewed nankeen pantaloons and common shirts for the eighth of a dollar while the consumer paid many shillings for the same goods. He also recognized that the resulting poverty was no fault of her own. By the late twenties, when Ely actually published his journal of visits to the poor, these concerns had become widespread. In a series of essays and public appearances, Mathew Carey made the straitened circumstances of the seamstress's existence—one implausibly lived "in the most prosperous country in the world!"—a special cause. He "applied in Philadelphia and New-York personally, or by letter, to above fifty ladies in each city" to come to the seamstresses' aid. He bought advertising space in the newspapers, in which he published denunciations concerning her situation. He sponsored a national essay contest on the subject of the seamstress and saw to it that his "appalling" statistics circulated widely. They were, for instance, picked up, though unaccredited, by the *Working Man's Advocate* for use in its own attacks against the "overgrown system of competition." Still celebrated for her contribution to industrial progress in Tench Coxe's introductory remarks to the third federal census in 1814, the seamstress now suffered hideous distress in the terms of Carey's political economy. She labored in her own apartments for "wages . . . utterly inadequate to [her] support," and in jobs "so precarious" that she was "often unemployed." Forced to survive on 3½ cents a day, the seamstress effectively had five choices in her life, according to Carey. She could beg. She could rely on the good offices of the overseers of the poor, which was a form of begging. She could steal. She could starve. Or she could "sell herself into pollution." Carey enlisted the testimony of the Reverend Ezra Stiles Ely, whose "eighteen years of intimate acquaintance with many of the industrious poor" now qualified him as an expert on the matter, to argue that even a common slave was better compensated for his labor than was the seamstress.[9]

Carey's victims of industrialization were not exclusively sewing women. He was also concerned about the starvation wages paid the builders of canals and turnpikes. He understood that the industrial economy was pauperizing a large segment of the industrious classes and that it could no longer be assumed that economic progress brought universal benefits. Not everyone who wanted to work, Carey contended, could find employment, and those who worked did not necessarily earn enough to support themselves and their families. The suffering of the poor, it followed, was not always the result of their own failings. "Idleness" and "dissipation" were terms that needed to be redefined. But of all the new victims of industrial revolution, the seamstress was unique. "By the law of her being, [she] is excluded from paths in which coarser man may make a livelihood," as Carey observed in the epigraph he chose for his well-known essay "Public Charities in Philadelphia" (1828). In other words, women's industry was unsuited to the competitive rigors of the new economy because women were necessarily restricted to those few trades appropriate to their natural skills. Natural female domesticity—women's tendency toward "sedentary occupations," which Tench Coxe considered to have made them so well suited for work in the nascent clothing industry—was now mobilized to stake the opposite claim, that women were unsuitable for such work. Their suffering was all the more unacceptable because they were also by nature orderly, regular, and industrious, while most working-class men were deserving of the epithets of idleness, dissipation, and intemperance so often applied to them.[10]

Carey's solution was no less modern than the problem itself: pity.[11] The deserving poor would be saved by an "Appeal to the Wealthy of the Land," as Carey titled an 1833 collection of essays summarizing his previous several years of writings and speeches. He turned to those "ladies" of New York and Philadelphia who, after "pondering deeply, and frequently, and lastingly on the deplorable conditions" of female exploitation, would devote themselves to alleviating the seamstresses' misery. He appealed to "every principle of honour, justice, and generosity" of upright men to convince them to pay adequate wages. Such a spirit of benevolence would constitute "a delightful oasis in the midst of the arid deserts of sordid selfishness" so characteristic of market society.[12]

One such oasis was the Tailoresses' and Seamstresses' Benevolent Society, which convened at the Mott Street Chapel the day after twenty New York journeymen tailors were convicted of conspiracy for their part in the 1836 strike, with the aim of ameliorating the hardship of thousands of "females, widows, and orphans." Like the journeymen tailors, New York's seamstresses had also actively protested throughout the tumultuous winter and spring of labor unrest in 1836. But when the mass-circulating *Sun* protested their exploitation and demanded an increase in their wages (albeit with few illusions that such a thing would happen), it did so in moral rather than political terms, discussing the need to "defend" the seamstresses "against low temptations," a euphemism for what Carey had already euphemistically called choosing to "sell themselves into pollution." Likewise, when the Tailoresses & Seamstresses Clothing Establishment opened on Broadway in 1837, it anchored its appeal in "savings of 25 per cent" and in the compassion of potential patrons, reminding the male public that their custom would make the employment of large numbers of industrious females possible and would provide charitable aid to sick and ailing women. The cooperative, in other words, was a benevolence project, not an alternative political economy. While the Tailoresses' and Seamstresses' Benevolent Society deliberately excluded men from its May meeting—save those with special invitations—the pathos manifested in the meeting's repeated references to "our present suffering condition," together with the marked absence of the political insolence characteristic of the United Tailoresses' Society earlier in the decade, seemed designed to best appeal to a public without feminist leanings. The Benevolent Society turned to "every friend to justice and humanity," an almost verbatim echo of Carey's earlier call to "the humanity and the sense of justice" of the privileged classes. The very inclusion of "benevolence" in the society's name signaled a depoliticization of the subject. And, indeed, by the end of the year the organization was firmly under middle-class male sponsorship. The mayor presided at a December meeting convened at the Broadway Tabernacle, and John Jacob Astor commended its aims to the favorable attention of the public at large.[13]

Such pity proved to be a pan-class sentiment. This was already clear during the tailoresses' strike of 1831, when a supporter spoke in terms distinct from the women's own Wollstonecraftian creed: "It will be seen who are and who are not friends of the widows and orphans, and of suffering, unprotected females." Within a few years it had become obvious that the revolt of the United Tailoresses' Society against the capitalist version of patriarchal license had no place in male-led working-class resistance to industrialization, resistance that also preferred a rhetoric of female victimhood. Thus, a letter from "a tailoress" was read to striking tailors in 1836 that "produced a flood of sympathy for the cause of the wretched females." "I believe, fully," the anonymous needleworker wrote, "that if we could enlist the gentlemen in the cause, something could be done for us. . . . My only motive in addressing these imperfect lines for your consideration, is to find out if there is not sympathy enough in noble man yet to do something for suffering females." Self-abnegation had replaced self-assertion as the seamstresses' principal class expression, if not as their principal political strategy. Was this the lesson they had drawn from the failure of their more radical measures in 1831? Or was their abnegation the terms of alliance with their own working-class husbands, fathers, and other ostensible supporters who sought to mobilize their own patriarchal authority to reinforce an eroding position in the face of market forces?[14]

In fact, female waged independence was no less problematic for male proletarians than it was for the bourgeoisie. In discussions on female labor held between 1834 and 1836 by the National Trades' Union of affiliates from northeastern cities, women were accordingly denied the right to organize themselves. Working-class men, no less than their bosses, also aspired to establish a home supported by their own earnings, in which women were free "to perform the duties of the household," whether such a home was intended to preserve a preindustrial corporate ethos or to provide a refuge from the meaner world of commerce. In any event, these aspirations were not necessarily a cultural capitulation to middle-class propriety. They were certainly a defense against capitalist power. Working-class opponents of the industrial order in the city understood that losing control of their wives' and daughters' labor to employers—and we have seen how important a wife's unpaid labor was to a young journeyman tailor—was the avenue by which the whole wage-earning population would ultimately lose any modicum of independence. The household, in other words, would be the basis of an attempt by men and women alike to use the market to their own advantage and thereby avoid complete domination by the world of capital. And since male wage earners could no longer rest their authority in the family on the agrarian property rights of yore, they turned to the new democratic patriarchy, which so matched bourgeois versions of respectability, to prop up their position. Thus the *Working Man's Advocate* embraced both domestic privacy and political economy in its advice to "the working women of New York" at the outbreak of a new wave of labor activism in 1845: "First, the evils under which you are suffering are similar to those complained of by the mechanics and other working men, and that your cause is one and same. If your fathers, husbands, and brothers were doing well, as a general rule you would be doing well too . . . because so many of you would then be out of the occupations, which you now follow, that the rest would necessarily be much better compensated."[15]

The similarity between working-class perceptions of women's labor and the pity championed by the employer class received its clearest expression in the attempt on the part of the Industrial Congress to organize shirt sewers in New York in 1851, a campaign led by Mr. E. W. Paul, secretary of the Carpenters' Association, and a handful of other congress activists. Their purpose was familiar. The Shirt Sewers' Union, it was announced, would come to the aid of "the defenseless girl" who "often wrestles with poverty, hunger, [and] temptation." A stanza from the "Song of the Shirt" was included in newspaper notices:

> Oh, men, with sisters dear,
> Oh, men with mothers and wives;
> It is not *linen* you're wearing out,
> *It's human creatures' lives.*[16]

Like the United Tailoresses' Society's earlier eschewal of the appellation "seamstress," there was lexical significance in the congress's choice of shirt sewers as the standard-bearers in the fight against the exploitation of waged women. Whyshould shirt sewers be representative of the seamstresses' plight, given that needleworkers, as a rule, toiled at a whole range of products? Most obviously, shirts paid less than any other garment, making them exclusively women's work and uniquely identified with women. More importantly, men's shirts were still widely made up at home. They were still perceived as properly existing outside the labor market, the product of household rather than waged industry. That women were being so dreadfully exploited by shirt manufacturers thus underlined how capitalism intruded into all realms of home life, eventually subverting women's very domesticity.[17] At a meeting of the Shirt Sewers' Union held at the headquarters of the Carpenters' Association, speaker after speaker rose to condemn the ruthless exploitation of "these greatly oppressed female Industrialists." Mr. J. D. Hennessy defined the goals of the new union, and Messrs. Heath, Hennessy, and Smith were appointed secretaries. Charles Castle, Edward Boots, Benjamin Price, Captain Turner, and various other activists, reformers, and association types all rose to address the rally, offer resolutions, draft a constitution, and plan the next meeting. At one point, toward the end of the evening, the chairman considered it time to call on the "suffering Shirt Sewers" themselves, to hear first-hand testimony of their condition. They did not disappoint.

> A lady, whose appearance showed strong symptoms of poverty, stated that she had quit working this morning when she heard of the call for this meeting, as it was *an ease to her long sufferings*. . . . She stated she made California Shirts for Mr. Wilson of Maiden-Lane and William St. at 6d. and 9d. a piece per dozen; they were to be well stitched in every way, and all she could make was two dozen weekly, and to work day and night. She further stated that she had not eaten any kind of meat in three weeks but once. . . . At the instance of Capt. Turner, a collection was taken up for her and a snug sum realized.[18]

– – – – –

The same benevolence animated middle-class activism, although in this case the protest was led by women. They were practicing the private politics of pity as envisioned by Mathew Carey who, in his paeans to the suffering seamstress, had identified domestic women as particularly adept at benevolence, "feeling her cheek mantle with shame over the unpitied and unrelieved woes of hundreds and thousands of her own sex." Hers was an explicitly disinterested project, as suited both its virtuous and its female nature. In 1837, in the wake of the panic, such women founded the Tailoresses and Seamstresses Charitable Society, which was devoted to the already hackneyed mission of relieving "the wants and distress of those who are sick and unable to work, or to obtain employment," and used funds raised by the husbands of the new society's officers to mitigate the seamstress's suffering.[19]

The middle-class woman's assumption of responsibility for the seamstress made the two of them simultaneously allies and antagonists, mirror images gazing at each other across a no-man's-land separating virtue and corruption. This happened because the bourgeoisie insisted on dividing women's work into two: unfeminine waged labor was arrayed against a true woman's unwaged devotion to her domestic vocations. The contrast seemed obvious enough but was actually difficult to maintain in the face of women's massive presence in the labor market, a presence that issued precisely from their womanhood, which was the reason for the lower cost of their labor. Tens of thousands of waged females in the city threatened to expose axioms concerning the "true" nature of female domesticity as no more than a self-interested ideology, for that class whose members most strenuously subscribed to the view of women as naturally unsuited to waged labor was also the one that most profited from her waged presence in the market. The concern for the seamstress's condition expressed by her domestic, middle-class "sisters" was no cynical manipulation, however. The latter knew that they, too, were equally threatened by an industrial revolution that had dissolved women's traditional household position. Indeed, the seamstress's suffering personified the vulnerability of all women in the new market-driven, fraternal democracy. It also pointed to the dire need to reestablish a home that would offer them social standing and support. In finding the seamstress living "in the upper story of some poor, ill-constructed unventilated house in a filthy street [where] . . . all the processes of cooking, eating, sleeping, washing, working and *living* are indiscriminately performed," and by subsequently making the seamstress an anti-ideal of hygienic and moral disorder, the true woman sought to define a new female domesticity that could protect both of them from the ravages of capitalist revolution. As such, resurrecting patriarchy for a democratic age— a patriarchy that reinforced female submission while also creating a new class hierarchy, just as patriarchy had always done—may have been the most important women's work of all in the nineteenth century.[20]

The character of this new domesticity was worked out in one of the era's favorite images of female helplessness, the widow. Widows, of course, were not a new object of concern. Their anomalous status as heads of households in a patriarchal world had been the focus of discussion and legislation long before the age of capital. However, the figure of the widow now acquired a new significance, already evident in 1831, when the United Tailoresses' Society had anchored their wage demands in a woman's need to support her own family. The response to this female demand for a breadwinner's wage was countered by turning the widow, that most independent of women, into a special object of charity. Accordingly, the Society for the Relief of Poor Widows with Small Children cited the testimony of an applicant for relief: "During my married life, I never knew what it was to want. My husband was kind, and made us all comfortable. I tried to keep the children and my rooms clean, and to be ready for him when he returned from his work. But when he was taken sick, I soon spent all he had earned, and was obliged to bind shoes . . . to buy medicine and food. He died, and I was left alone with my little babes. . . . My *mind was gone*." Just beneath the self-pity and hysteria lay the critical inference that, had she a man, this widow would not be wanting. As it was, the society deemed her and her small children "a poor but most exemplary family." Her lack of a husband justified their charity. The seamstress-widows who populated sentimental fiction all likewise bespoke the helplessness of women forced to live outside of the protective male aegis.[21]

But while confirming women's dependence on men, the widow also showed how women suffered the sins of men. Earlier in the century these were the offenses of insufficiently frugal mechanics. As Isabella Graham explained to the Society for the Relief of Poor Widows with Small Children in 1800, the mechanic class often failed to put aside enough for their families. A few decades later, however, the culprit was the businessman. "The husband died suddenly; his estate was insolvent: and now the story is clear." So went the condensed version of male delinquency, as narrated by George Lippard, who became the chairman of a subscription campaign on behalf of Philadelphia's seamstresses in 1850. The widow reduced to sewing for a meager livelihood as a result of the failures of an irresponsible husband seduced by get-rich schemes was a symbol of the moral bankrupty of market society. In a story entitled "The Seamstress" that appeared in *Godey's Lady's Book* in 1848, Catharine Beecher wrote how Mrs. A. and her daughter became "dependent entirely on the labors of the needle" after her prosperous merchant-husband suffered a heavy run of losses that left him broke and soon dead. The same sudden reduction "from comparative comfort to a bare subsistence" befell the Elliott widow and her daughters in Charles Burdett's novel, *The Elliott Family* (1845), although in their case it was unclear whether the husband passed from the scene before or after the family's fall from grace. Even the headstrong seamstress whose fictional diary was serialized in the feminist journal *The Una*, and who steadfastly remained unbroken by temptation and poverty, had been reduced to a desperate waged existence by her family's downward mobility. These sundry widows and orphans—orphans being a variation on the theme of women unable to manage on their own—paid the cruel price for the commercial caprice of their men and laid bare the industrial threat to their lives: how capitalism first impoverished women and then took advantage of their impoverishment by hiring them at a cut rate.[22]

Bourgeois women who protested the seamstresses' recurrent fall from domestic comfort thus became critics of capitalist power. As such they gave voice to middle class apprehensions regarding market society. "Our men are sufficiently money-making. Let us keep our women and children from the contagion as long as possible," wrote Sarah Hale, whose *Godey's Lady's Book* published a series of scathing lithographs in 1849 depicting the foibles of male politesse, ranging from "the first cigar" to the partisan hypocrisies of electioneering.[23] This protest did not mean, however, that all women shared a common lot. Quite the opposite. Her poverty actually denied the widow full feminine status. In his mournful story, "Lizzie Glenn; or, The Trials of a Seamstress," T. S. Arthur described the day his heroine was forced to put her ten-year-old out to work. "How could she part with her boy? How could she see him put out among strangers? How could she bear to let him go away from her side, and be henceforth treated with no regard to his tender years? . . . The very thought made her sick." In this case, there was no distinguishing fact from sentimental fiction. As the bylaws of the Society for the Relief of Poor Widows directed: "No widow shall be assisted, who, having a child fit for service, will not consent to its being put out to trade or service . . . unless satisfactory reasons can be given to the contrary." They continued: "It shall be the duty of the Manager to report to the Board, from time to time, such widows under her care as have children of age to be bound to trades, or put out to service." The widow, in short, was trapped in a closed system of recrimination. Those maternal instincts that made her a worthy object of pity ("a poor but most exemplary family") were at once the source of her damnation, her incapacity to take proper care of her children. This betrayal by the widow of her own womanhood helped her middle-class "sisters" rebuild patriarchy, for their own domesticity simultaneously embraced fraternity, by acknowledging the female home's separation from democratic public life, and hierarchy, by restricting that ideal home to members of a specific class. Indeed, these "true" women enjoyed the best of both worlds. They used the widow-seamstress to protest against the vulnerability of women, including themselves, in market society. At the same time, that protest allowed them to separate themselves from the seamstress and claim an authority of their own distinct from both the male exploiter and the female victim. In this way, these practitioners of middle-class pity became responsible for a disinterested sphere of life free of commercial corruptions, giving them exclusive access to virtue and making them an essential counterbalance to the failings of industrial revolution.[24]

This program was served even more effectively by another ubiquitous symbol of the seamstress's plight, the prostitute, who emerged as a distinct social problem at the same time that wage labor did in the 1820s. These were the years when *McDowall's Journal* and *Magdalen Facts* began to count the number of "loose women" walking the streets, when the Female Benevolent Society and Female Moral Reform Society began to intercede on their behalf, and when the police began escalating public efforts to control what was now defined as a menacing crime. No one better represented the dangerous antisocial effects of the commercializing city than the prostitute. She personified the conflict between virtuous home and self-interested economy, and the latter's threat to the family, morality, and love, now all separately ensconced in the former. Indeed, the prostitute was the logical outcome of women's engagement in the market. She emerged as the catastrophic underside of progress in these years, "a perfect image of the savagery that lurks in the midst of civilization," as Baudelaire recognized her significance to the age, a particularly personal example of the "creative destruction" inherent in capitalist revolution. [25]

The impoverished widow's ostensible opposite, the prostitute was no less the victim of capitalism. She no less constituted a flesh-and-blood indictment of men's misuse of power. The very fact that "no station is secure" and that even middle-class girls could sink into whoredom opened another front in domesticity's rhetorical attack on the industrial market. The prostitute became a modern problem when female nature was redefined to be moral rather than sexual, when the view of women as inherently lusty gave way to an emphasis on their modesty and innocence. Prostitutes were no longer seen as driven by their own sexual desire but rather were victims of uncontrolled male desire. Capitalist prostitution accordingly became a problem of demand rather than supply. When the New York state legislature debated the particularities of sexual regulation in the 1830s and 1840s, women reformers demanded that they enact punishments for male clients, adulterers, and impregnators of unmarried females, that is, that they delimit male hegemony over "defenseless" women. The sexual politics of benevolence sought to raise the fallen woman by overturning that double standard by which, as the novelist George Thompson wrote in 1854, "a woman who once loses her virtue can never recover her position in society—while the man who sins a thousand times, is a thousand times applauded." Sarah Hale made it clear where true virtue lay: "Though human nature in both sexes is rendered sinful or prone to sin by the 'fall,' yet women's nature has never sunk to the brute sensuality of man's; this comparative purity has kept her mind, as regards morality, above the standard which even the most Christian men fix for their own sex." [26]

The seamstress was the practical link between capitalism and whoredom, since she seemed inevitably to "sell herself into pollution." Like the prostitute, the seamstress was also interchangeable, commodified, and exploited. By the time William Sanger proved the connection between waged poverty and prostitution in the bevy of statistics and social taxonomies he published in 1859 under the title *The History of Prostitution*, he only confirmed what Mathew Carey had claimed thirty years earlier and that had informed the seamstress trope ever since: that the pitiful wage paid for women's work was what drove them into prostitution.[27]

This identification of selling one's labor and selling one's self was, of course, a favorite equation of radical protest. That did not, however, prevent middle-class women from embracing the same logic, although with one crucial revision: the figure of the prostitute made it clear that the problem issued less from waged labor itself than it did from female waged labor. This directed protest away from class to gender—or, as Nancy Armstrong has observed, the political problems inherent in industrial relations were turned into a sex scandal. And so, in linking female poverty to female vice, Sanger's sociology provided ideal support for the new capitalist patriarchy. It put waged men in their place for failing to protect their women. Meanwhile, it promoted the virtue of the bourgeois home. By equating the seamstress's work with that of the prostitute it also devalued women's waged industry in a way that clearly disqualified it from serving as the origin of value and thus the basis of civic equality for women, which would have elevated working-class women over the boss's wife and would have buttressed the independence of working-class families in general.[28]

Thus we can begin to understand the political importance of the feminization of poverty. The New York Association for Improving the Condition of the Poor, for instance, which was not originally founded specifically to help women, had by the 1840s defined three classes of the poor most worthy of aid: indigent widows and abandoned women with young children, educated and "even accomplished females" reduced from comfortable circumstances and left with no ability to support themselves, and females of comfortable circumstances suddenly impoverished by the death of a husband or other family. Women had become those most deserving of charity, in short, because their very dependent nature as females made them incapable of surviving in the rough and tumble of the market. This, in turn, made it possible to lay the debased seamstress's transgressions against femininity and domesticity at the feet of an industrial system best left to men. But there was another important implication. If a woman's innate dependence made her deservingly poor, then poor men were distinctly less deserving. Such reasoning informed Carey's divison of the pauperized class into industrious women and idle men. This then made it easier to explain the frequent exclusion of unpropertied men from civic power, which otherwise contradicted the democratic promises of fraternity. Thus, the gendering of poverty turned exploitation itself into a matter of sexual rather than class relations. By making the seamstress's victimization a uniquely female event, the general issue of waged dependence—which was especially acute among needleworkers (who were, as the *New York Tribune* observed, especially "bound to their employers by a vital relationship, by chords whose slightest vibrations touch their hearts")—could be emptied of any overt political content.[29]

The widow and the prostitute filled another important role in the making of democracy: they helped transform virtue from a political value into a private trait. Entrapped in the mundane and material details of survival, each day betraying their conjugal and maternal duties, to the point of practicing a market-driven promiscuity, widows and prostitutes were the definitive counterpoints to true womanly virtue, which was still located, as it had always been, in the home.[30] As in republican thought, industrial-age virtue remained an ethic of disinterest and self-sacrifice. It continued to be the antipode of personal desire and corruption and the enemy of enslavement to material necessity. It still rested on the cohesion of the household and on the civic sanctity of marriage. But domesticity was no longer the arena of that other most important of republican values—industry. Rather than informing public industry, virtue now pertained to intimate behavior. That is why the virtueless prostitute became known as a "public woman." In fact, by guiding the intercourse of private persons, far from the corrupted world of class relations, virtue could actually now be said to have increased in importance, to have become the most tangible test of selfhood, of moral intent, and, of course, of physical chastity.[31]

- - - - -

The trope of the suffering seamstress was summarized in an 1852 travelogue of a recent sojourn in New York written by William Bobo, a South Carolinian interested in exposing the corruptions of northern industrial life. An hour after a notice appeared calling for five hundred girls to work on making up pantaloons, Bobo recounted, hundreds were to be seen flocking to the address, a second-storey warehouse. He described the subsequent events:

> "You advertised for hands on pantaloons this morning?" she tremblingly asks of the man with the quill behind his ear.
> "Yes, we want some hands this week; do you want a job?" he replies.

"Yes, sir; I would like to have something to do this week," answers the girl.

"How many pair can you make?"

"I will try to get six pair done."

"You are a stranger to us, and before we can let you have the work, you must give some security for the return of it."

Eight shillings will do. She gives it if she has it. If not, she hurries back home, and takes her bonnet or dress to the pawnbrokers.

Having to sell her own clothes for a chance to work on a surplus inventory of ready-mades was not the end of the sewing girl's humiliations, however. A week later she returns with the bundle of finished pantaloons, handing them to the overseer. You have ruined the job, he accuses her after examining the goods. He tosses the whole lot under the counter, refusing to pay her, let alone return her dollar deposit: "It is all we shall ever get for our goods, which you have spoilt." Meanwhile, Bobo informs us, the pantaloons fall through a trapdoor leading to the pressing room, where they are ironed, sorted, and packed up. Not only does the clothier thus get his work done for nothing, but he even raises a few hundred extra dollars in unreturned deposits to finance shipping costs. The girl is left on the street. "'I have lived honestly,'" she reasons to herself, "'worked hard for my first employers, done all I could to satisfy their demands, and I am now left without a place to lay my head, a cent in my pocket, or a friend to ask for assistance. I see I cannot live by honest means, and will by dishonest ones, rather than go to the poor-house.' She deliberately walks out and sells herself for gold. This is not surprising at all. And from the brothel to the grave."[32]

There were numerous variations on this scene. In *New York: Its Upper Ten and Lower Million*, for instance, George Lippard's seamstress-heroine succeeds in fending off her employer's attempts to leverage his bargaining position into sexual favors. She even eventually overcomes her poverty, an achievement foreshadowed in her impeccable diction, which discloses a lost patrician pedigree, a favorite device of sentimental fiction. Ned Buntline, however, writing in a less ironic style than Lippard, presented a more credible denouement to this new urban morality tale: "'A shilling for a shirt!' she muttered, half unconscious of the great truth she was uttering, 'a shilling for the making of a shirt—a shilling that bribes one to throw down her needle and her soul, and pick up the wanton's wiles that lead only to dark ruin and eternal night! Oh! ye sharp, shrewd men of business . . . your low, MEAN rates of wages are nothing more than premiums to incite them to abandon industry, honesty and virtue, and become lawless, criminal and vile.'"[33]

Buntline's nostalgic incantation of "industry, honesty, and virtue" was revealing of how the seamstress's victimization was narrated in a republican idiom that contrasted city and country, ostentation and simplicity, corruption and industry. Typically, advertising copy for *The Orphan Seamstress* promised a story about "the snares which are laid in the Great City, to take every country girl from the path of virtue and happiness and plunge her into shame and misery." Likewise, in a chapter devoted to New York's "needlewomen," George Foster begged the "real Woman" to "stay calmly where you are, beneath your own pure skies, and amid the virtuous freshness of your home." In Allen Hampden's 1859 novel, *Hartley Norman*, the employers who refuse to raise Hartley's pious mother's pitiful sewing wages, the Shavers, are suitably "purse-proud parvenus" who live for display. In Charles Burdett's *The Elliott Family*, Clara Elliott is unable to collect the twelve shillings owed her for two dresses ordered by the spoiled daughters of the nouveau riche Mr. Simmons, the Simmonses having already left the city for the summer. Clara, together with her sister Laura, who sews coarse pants for two-and-a-half shillings apiece, are left to care for their sickly mother without having enough money for food, let alone medicines. As in the less commercial past, here, too, the values of hard work and simplicity are arrayed against extravagance and luxury. But with a telling difference: in contrast to the "homespun dress of honesty" in Benjamin Franklin's ode from a century before, the seamstress's faded gown and tattered shawl are no longer the proud signs of civic virtue. They are, instead, the mark of suffering and victimhood. "Necessity impels me to the practice of industry—without it, I should starve," Laura Elliott explains in an empty echo of the female contribution to industry during the days of the Revolution, when necessity and industry were allied in women's spinning as a demonstration of patriotic verve directed against the corruptions of empire. Even when the capitalist suffers for his sins—and Simmons, the wholesale clothier who pays Laura a pittance for sewing pants, eventually suffers bankruptcy and disgrace—there is no redemption. The Elliott women suffer a far worse fate.[34]

A late-eighteenth-century account of women's industry provides a telling measure of what subsequently changed: "Suffer me . . . to express to the contributors of the American Manufactory the exquisite pleasure I felt some time ago in being at the factory at the time a great number of the poor women attended to return the flax, etc. which they had spun, and to receive others. I observed they all received their pay, though small, with great pleasure; their smiling countenances bespoke a degree of happiness, in which I felt my very soul to participate."[35] These eighteenth-century spinners overcame their poverty through diligent work, which also contributed to the public happiness since it supported the national effort to replace English imports with "American cloths." Nor was their contribution a temporary one, a unique function of the political emergency. Women's work filled a central role in the new republic, resolving the structural tension between agricultural and manufacturing priorities. Washington was openly optimistic, for instance, that "much might be done" by women (and children) working in industry. Their efforts meant that fewer men would have to abandon their rightful place behind the plow. Women's labor, in other words—carried out under the secure aegis of the patriarchal household and resting on women's civic inferiority—was a key to both material development and political virtue. It similarly figured as such in Hamilton's seminal *Report on Manufacturers* in 1792 and in Tench Coxe's embrace of "female aid in manufactures" a decade after that.[36]

But as the household system of manufacturers passed into history, this female "portion of the national labor" became a problematic category. "National labor" was now part of an economy of waged individuals rather than of corporate families, organized by the anonymous market rather than by the paterfamilias, promoting work and life outside of male—or, indeed, anyone's—full control. The response was to transform the traditional gendered division of labor (spinning, for instance, had always been a female activity) into a gendered definition of labor in general by which women could no longer participate in industry without sacrificing their womanhood. True, her contribution to the household remained important, but in an increasingly ready-made world such domestic requirements as keeping the "household decently clad" relied far less on women's own productive efforts.[37] And so, the nineteenth-century seamstress was at once the successor and the antithesis of the proud spinner. Sewing replaced spinning as the defining female domestic activity in the nineteenth century. But such industry no longer signaled the woman's potential for assuming her place in the pantheon of public virtue. Instead, the sewer of mass consumables represented the resignation of the subordinate sex to the worst of all possible fates. Invariably driven to prostitution by loneliness and poverty the seamstress in fact became the ultimate repudiation of virtue.

In contrast to the public nature of the homespun, promoting the common good was now best "exercised in the shade, and in silence." Such modesty was manifest in the efforts of an anonymous philanthropist who established an asylum for women and "whose most honorable distinction it is to do good by stealth and blush to find it fame." "Contending for your rights," women were told on another occasion, would only "stir . . . up the selfish feelings of others." Virtue's hues, T. S. Arthur declared, in yet another morality tale

The spinning wheel had become the object of sentimental fiction by the time
the *Ladies' Companion* published this illustration in 1840, to accompany a
story entitled "The Spinning Wheel." (Courtesy of the Collection of the
New-York Historical Society, neg. 75525)

of polite living published in *Godey's*, "are brighter by the aid of a favourable
obscurity, than when they are exposed to the rays of a burning sun." And
while industry, prudence, and economy might still be considered by some to
be components of virtue, they paled in importance next to "weightier things,"
those moral imperatives that actually had no physical manifestation at all. In
fact, virtue now seemed to become entirely ethereal: not only an antidote to
lust but the antithesis of the material world in general.[38]

This divorce of virtue from economics and politics was a significant moment in the capitalist revolution, for it allowed Americans to continue to balance private wants and public needs while also practicing an ethic of *caveat*

emptor and founding contractual obligations on free will. In a society in which homespun values of self-sacrifice were in fact inconceivable for both capitalists and proletarians, locked as they were in the newly democratized contest for power, the new, private virtue could still provide the basis for proper self-government without having disastrous effects on industrial progress. Indeed, virtue was ostensibly now separated from property altogether, to which republicanism had joined it two centuries earlier.[39]

Of course, it was much harder for poor women to be virtuous. "We must have the name and place of residence of every man, woman and child who works for us. It is our rule, and we never depart from it," the foreman-clerk informs T. S. Arthur's seamstress, who desperately needs the work. But she is loathe to divulge her address, or even tell him her name, for fear that he will use his control over her employment to apply sexual pressure. But what practical choice did she have? It did little good to sanctify her poverty, as Freeman Hunt had tried to do when he admonished fashionable young ladies in the city to adopt the modest and honest habits of "the poor seamstresses." Ned Buntline, for one, suffered no such hypocrisy. "*Empty praise—*A NAME for *Honesty and Virtue*," he spat out in his *G'hals of New York*. Buntline understood that, despite its private appearance, virtue was bound up with political prerogative. So did Lippard: "And so you blame the White Slave, that she listens to the voice of Sin, when it comes clad in gold, while Virtue by the custom of the large city, only bears injustice, starvation, and cankered lungs?"[40]

The polite classes, however, were unconvinced by such jeremiads. Proletarian confessions of vice only confirmed their own sense of superiority. What's more, they put radicals like Buntline and Lippard in the position of denouncing virtue, which proved that the bourgeoisie were indeed the inheritors of republicanism's modesty and self-restraint. William English's *Gertrude Howard* brought the point home. Gertrude is a poor seamstress of virtuous character, one who averts her eyes from the "impertinent gaze" of dandies in the street. She lives in a neighborhood of "misery and wretchedness" but keeps her own room a site of "order and neatness." She tends her ailing parents and thus realizes a semblance of proper family life. True, her family has suffered a precipitous fall that has brought them from a little cottage in a green valley to a city tenement, from "bright summer" to "cold winter." But "what's past cannot be helped," and, as Gertrude acknowledges, "we must submit to the decrees of Providence." The vicissitudes of fate could not negate Gertrude's innate virtue, however, which was neither an act of will or a conscious ethic but an instinct, the most private trait of all. Gertrude becomes the object of the seductions of Frederick Clarance, a rich profligate, the only son of an eminent merchant, "petted and indulged in every whim," who spares no expense in gratifying his appetites and desires. Frederick offers to pay Gertrude's family's rent and other expenses if she agrees to become his mistress, but she obviously, and effortlessly, repulses his insistent offers of gold. Nor does she have any cause for regret, for the same native propriety that resists Frederick Clarance's corruption draws her into marriage with George Templeton, a young dry-goods clerk at the start of his career who barely has enough money to support himself (which explains his willingness to enter into matrimony with a poor seamstress). Templeton is a man of integrity, which eventually draws the notice of a patron who, impressed by his "good character and prompt business habits," decides to bankroll Templeton. Before long, he and his bride acquire wealth and standing. His hard-earned riches, the antithesis of Frederick Clarance's inherited fortune, are the fitting reward—and ultimate manifestation—of Gertrude Howard's virtue.[41]

The story's distinction between inherited wealth and earned wealth was an important detail, for it connected virtue to industry while idleness remained a vice. The best way to help the newly indigent, as the Society for the Prevention of Pauperism in New-York proclaimed, was thus to teach them industriousness and put them to work producing things (the proceeds from which would then fund the operations of benevolence). Such an approach was not new. Spinning schools had emerged in the second half of the eighteenth century as solutions to the newly recognized problem of female poverty and idleness. In the nineteenth century, however, inculcating the habits of industry meant a practicum in waged labor, which is what the objects of the Society for the Prevention of Pauperism's charitable largesse received. So did the cases treated by the Ladies Depository, whose second annual report, undersigned by such notables as Mrs. King and Mrs. Aspinwall, excitedly recounted the many articles made up by its charges that had met with ready sale in the organization's store. "Encouraged by such increased patronage, the Managers of the Depository have determined to extend the object of their Society, and instead of confining their permits to a particular class, to give them to all respectable females who sew neatly, and who have no other means of support." The depository then proceeded to hire an extra agent whose job it was to give out and receive work, to cut patterns, and to examine each finished article.[42]

Benevolence, in other words, organized itself by the same industrial logic that guided ostensibly more interested entrepreneurs. The Society for the Promotion of Industry, the Orphan Asylum Society, the city Alms House, the Society for the Employment and Relief of the Poor, the Female Guardian

Society, the Five Points House of Industry—all marketed the products of the sewing labor of those who received their charity. When a do-gooder set up a mission in Five Points in the early 1850s and needed to ensure that the project would both support itself and provide corrective discipline to the neighborhood's fallen denizens, he started a clothing manufactory. The reasons were the same as those that motivated aspiring businessmen: clothing was a simple enterprise to organize, it required only a modest capital expenditure, and it rested on a labor force already in place. Sometimes these charity manufactories retailed their own products, as the Ladies Depository did. Usually, however, they appended themselves to the capitalists. The *Tribune* published a detailed account of one such project, that of a benevolent woman who had opened an asylum in a large house, located "in a convenient situation for business," where women worthy of relief could live and work together with their younger children (those "not yet of an age to earn their own independence"). She supplied them with sewing jobs "at the usual prices." In those cases when the cloths came from the city's " 'starvation' houses," the anonymous patroness paid the difference. She thus ensured her charges if not a liberal, then at least a living wage. She also advanced the full amount due for work already delivered so they would not be dependent on the employer's often dilatory pay schedule. In addition, her establishment employed a man to carry the goods back and forth to clothiers, saving the seamstresses a delay "which, in the usual cases, reduced their small earnings so disastrously." What all this in effect meant, however, was a subsidy for the city's industries. City charities subcontracted production, organized a workforce, delivered goods, and streamlined operations. Because they were important large-scale employers of labor, there were also instances, Carey charged, when the activities of benevolence organizations actually forced wages down. Whether he knew it or not, Cornelius Mathews thus spoke right to the point in his 1853 *Pen and Ink Panorama of New-York City*, when he sarcastically accused the city's charity types of "reforming the world by wholesale."[43]

Idleness, however, was no more appropriate to the propertied woman than to the poor one. "No excellence of mind or soul can be hoped from an idle woman," as *Godey's Lady's Book* declared, a self-evident maxim to anyone who took her virtue seriously.[44] Work—her own work—and not just motherhood proved essential to woman's place in the new patriarchy. Thus, Horace Bushnell opened his celebration of "The Age of Homespun" by quoting from Proverbs: "She looketh well to the ways of her household, And eateth not the bread of idleness." The hard-working mother and wife became a centerpiece of Bushnell's mid-nineteenth-century efforts to recreate a republican culture befitting the industrial middle classes. He conjured spindle and distaff and nostalgically recalled that labor had once been the mark of "a lady of the highest accomplishment." Bushnell often referred, in private as well as in public, to his own mother's uncompromising devotion to house and farm. She had been an equal partner in her family's material struggles and frugalities, and was fully implicated in their success or failure. What's more, she had carried out her innumerable responsibilities with "scarcely . . . a look of damage." By "spen[ding] their nervous impulse on their muscles" the spinners of yore had less need to "keep . . . down the excess, or calm . . . the unspent lightning, by doses of anodyne" than did the frail specimens of femininity in the age of the ready-made.[45]

Bushnell's prescriptions for female industry in the industrial age were given graphic expression in the *Lady's Self-Instructor in Millinery, Mantua Making and All Branches of Plain Sewing*, written by an "American Lady" in 1844. The manual's frontispiece pictured a woman sitting at work in pastoral repose, ensconced on a sunlit, vine-covered portico, framed by handsome marble columns, gazing intently at the sewing in her hands. The utopian setting and rich drapery recalled the neoclassical goddesses who were the mythic representatives of republican industry and modesty in post-Independence America.[46]

The picture was no abstract parable. Students at New York's Female Academy were told that, from the earliest times, work with the needle was "the fitting occupation of Women." Plain sewing and marking—embroidering letters in counted cross-stitch—were part of the standard curriculum of girls' schools, such as Miss Forbes's school, which served New York City's elite. The daughter of one Gramercy Park family conscientiously documented her daily sewing in her journal: "Sewed industriously all evening preparing skirts for walking through muddy road. . . . Spent afternoon in sewing room with Mama . . . ripped lace off old blue satin evening gown . . . inserted two new whalebones in corset as old ones were bent and uncomfortable . . . sewed new tapes in Hoop . . . ran fresh ribbons in chemises & corset covers."[47] The prevalence of women's work was also evident in the fact that sewing machines, originally built for commercial purposes, were almost immediately targeted at middle-class homes. Responding to popular demand, Wheeler & Wilson, Singer, Grover & Baker, and Willcox & Biggs began producing decorative "family machines" and promoting them in elaborate city showrooms or in advertising copy featuring additional accouterments of gentility. Within just a few years sales of these family machines equaled those of industry machines.[48]

Virtuous sewing as depicted in 1844 on the frontispiece of *A Lady's
Self-Instructor in Millinery, Mantua Making and All Branches of Plain Sewing*.
Middle-class women were certainly not idle. However, they did not prostitute
their labor for anyone's pecuniary gain. (Courtesy of the Collection of the
New-York Historical Society, neg. 75674)

True women, it turns out, sewed incessantly. In so doing, *Godey's* explained, they contributed to the household economy:

Two mothers had each a good black satin dress; in the course of time they
became, as unfortunately all dresses will, too shabby, or too old-fashioned for
their wearers' use. One mother picked hers to pieces, washed and ironed it,
and made from it two handsome-looking mantles for her daughters. The other
adapted hers for a petticoat, and spent five dollars in the purchase of new mantles for her two daughters. The mantles made of the old material were far the
better looking, and the more serviceable. Now one dollar would have bought
a petticoat; and thus the saving of four dollars might have been made for the
pocket of the husband.[49]

Regardless of who actually realized the greater savings, both women were certainly busy applying their own labors to such an end. That was the point. Accordingly, a woman who refused to sew her husband's buttons became a caricature of the selfish wife who gave her leisure over to fashionable concerns rather than domestic ones. A commitment to sewing, in fact, distinguished the middle class from an indolent aristocracy. Catharine Beecher complained in "The Seamstress" that nouveau riche women tended to neglect their daily sewing once "they had moved into a large house and set up a carriage and addressed themselves to being genteel." This soon led to their betrayal of the maternal obligation to pass along womanly skills to their daughters. As another *Godey's* archetype of womanhood explained: "There are some things which I prefer doing myself . . . although I am enabled to hire servants. My husband enjoys home-made luxuries far more than he could the inventions of a French confectioner, and this alone would be a sufficient inducement for me to continue my old fashioned system of housekeeping." The *Ladies' Wreath* also endorsed such "old fashioned systems" and remembered approvingly a time when "not only the wives and daughters of the stout yeomanry of our country were inured to habits of useful industry, but those noble matrons, whose names will go down to the latest posterity with honor, were patterns of frugality and domestic economy." And so the nonwaged productivity of domestic women could only enhance their standing, tying them as it did to the nation's foundation myths and contrasting them to the corruptions of both the the the faux-European aristocrat and the seamstress toiling in a system of exploitative waged labor.[50]

In such a spirit of disinterested industry, *Godey's* introduced a new monthly feature in 1847 that it called the "Ladies' Work Department." This regular column published instructions for making purses, scarves, cuffs, mats, stockings, muffatees, opera caps, artificial flowers, and countless other "little love gifts of exquisite beauty and taste." "And then, how dearly these will be valued by the receiver! Not the most costly present bought with money would be so highly prized as the delicate trifle made by the fair hand that presents it."[51] Virtuous because it was selfless, "ladies' work" was undertaken in order to balance the family's budget or to create "highly prized" gifts for others. It looked back to the days of "The Spinning-Wheel," when "we were taught . . . that we must not live only or mainly to enjoy ourselves" but "that our first earthly duties were to make ourselves useful to our fathers' family." Untainted by commercial exchange, the homemade efforts of true women offered an obvious contrast to a world of ready-made commodities and interchangeable labor. They also defined gentility. Starting around 1830, "choice specimens of Needlework, Drawings, Paintings and other *useful* articles" (my emphasis) replaced the cloth, carpeting, and hose of yore at New England agricultural fairs. This "fancywork" was a clear function of the new industrial cornucopia. In fact, its popularity stemmed from its ability to bridge women's ethereal virtue and the more solid, and enticing, world of things. At the same time, being selfless, such domestic production ostentatiously distanced the virtuous woman from the market's corruptions.[52]

Homages to female labor thus did not contradict the new patriarchal separation of women and industry. Indeed, they strengthened it. Horace Bushnell tellingly ignored the commercial aspects of the eighteenth century's homespun economy in his celebration of the lost tradition of women's work. This then allowed him to divorce virtuous women from capitalist production without sacrificing the republican equivalence of industry and virtue. Moreover, with virtue now firmly ensconced in the home, he could turn it into a bourgeois value. The "little love gifts of exquisite beauty and taste" created by true women thus became part of a tradition born a hundred years earlier when the Daughters of Liberty had enlisted in public spinning demonstrations previously confined to the poor. That tradition was continued after Independence by patriotic knitting clubs founded to assist widows and orphans. Now it was pursued by ladies sewing circles, such as the New York Clothing Society, an auxiliary of the Female Assistance Society, whose members made clothing for the poor, many of whom, of course, made clothing for a living. It was a self-flattering contrast whose farcical aspects escaped the notice of the virtuous. In willful obliviousness to the political reality they had created, in fact, the members of the Ladies' Sewing Society of Baltimore convened once a week in the evening to sew for charity on the premises of Myer Wiesenfeld's clothing manufactory, which Wiesenfeld had so generously contributed to their benevolent project. Such benevolence had proven to be good for both home and business.[53]

A Fashion Regime

The comedy hit of the 1845 dramatic season at the Park Theater in New York was a play entitled *Fashion*, written by Anna Mowatt, who enjoyed a minor reputation as a public reader and poet. The play's hero, Adam Trueman, has come to the city to visit his old friend Tiffany, whom he knew before the latter's rise from country peddler to metropolitan dry-goods wholesaler. Trueman is an original tiller of the soil and a veteran of the Revolutionary era whose landed wealth has not corrupted his native simplicity. This is clear from the moment he first appears onstage in a rough overcoat, coarse trousers, and heavy boots covered in dirt. His country style appalls the urban sophisticates, but it allows Trueman to see through the carefully rehearsed pretensions of a gallery of idle hangers-on to Tiffany's new wealth, starting with Mrs. Tiffany herself, who zealously conceals her lowly Canal Street origins by filling her conversation with mangled French aphorisms. Other members of the retinue include Mr. Frogg, an impoverished patrician, Mr. Twinkle, a literatus of dubious talents who seeks to secure the Tiffanys' patronage by marrying their daughter, Seraphina, and is tolerated only because of Mrs. Tiffany's need to adorn herself not only in feathers and mantle but in a cultural savoir faire no less available for purchase ("It is all the rage to patronize poets"), and Count Jolimaitre, a would-be European royal bedecked in jewelry and colored vest and scarf (Trueman: "I should have thought he was a tailor's walking advertisement") whose purported lineage—actually a sham—promises to the arriviste Mrs. Tiffany the very acme of status and whom she consequently favors as a future husband for Seraphina. The family's city mansion, which Trueman refers to as a "show-box" rather than a home, is further inhabited by a liveried Negro servant, a foreign-born lady's maid, and Gertrude, the innocent music teacher draped in identifiably virtuous white muslin who rebuffs the count's lascivious attentions and who, it turns out—surprising no one, to be sure—is Trueman's long-lost niece, and heiress. [1]

Before virtue can pay off, however, Trueman must rescue his old friend Tiffany from the soulless existence of his counting house: from imminent bankruptcy, from possible imprisonment for forging a number of promissory notes, and from his own clerk, Snobson, who, in exchange for his silence about the forgeries, also demands Seraphina's hand. While Mrs. Tiffany is thus conniving to marry her daughter off to the specious count, Mr. Tiffany is no less anxious to prostitute her for his needs to the greedy Snobson. Only Trueman saves this collection of fools from themselves.

"Seventy-two last August! strong as a hickory and every whit as sound!" Trueman is proud of how little he has changed since the time of the nation's great rebellion against imperial insolence. Indeed, he is still fighting homespun virtue's war against luxury and corruption. "This *fashion*-worship has made heathens and hypocrites of you all! *Deception* is your household God! A man laughs as if he were crying, and cries as if he were laughing in his sleeve. Everything is something else from what it seems to be." The rhetoric was entirely familiar, and yet something no longer rang true about Trueman. In this respect, *Fashion* was an antebellum reprise of Royall Tyler's *The Contrast*, the New York stage hit, produced fifty years earlier, about a Yankee rustic's protest against fashionable caprice. In satirizing the world of fashion, *The Contrast* had mobilized the familiar cant of republican virtue to raise serious questions about simplicity's actual relevance to a world of material progress. *Fashion* now went an extra step. Though her audiences doubtless laughed hardest at the supercilious exertions of Mrs. Tiffany, Jolimaitre, and Twinkle to fashion a suitable persona for themselves, the real object of Mowatt's satire was Trueman. As Poe observed in his review of the play for the *Broadway Journal*, Mowatt's achievement lay not in writing a satire of fashion—another in a long, mediocre history of the same—but in writing the first satire of a satire of fashion. [2]

Her success in doing so rested on the public's desire to measure the distance between their own lives and an earlier age of breeches and buckles. "We are effected with a painful sense of the antique," Poe wrote of watching the play. This was Mowatt's ultimate wink to the audience. Dressing up in colonial costume became a popular activity at fairs and festivals in these years. The practice conflated the whole preindustrial history of American life into a single image of an antiquated past—a costumed pilgrim farmer—that paid homage to the nation's modest origins while simultaneously mocking a more primitive time. [3] Who could now take Trueman's homespun rhetoric seriously anyway? His jeremiads against the corruptions of fashion were the real contrivances: the coarse overcoat and muddy boots were affectations in a ready-made world whose "wonderful alchemy of nature," as Horace Mann explained a few years later, allowed man to create rich gossamers and silks and in the process leave his idleness and ignorance behind. After a visit to America in the mid-1850s Adam de Gurowski accordingly reported that "homespun has . . . disappeared, and the consumption of various articles by twenty odd million Americans surpasses that of one hundred millions of Europeans. . . . The love of show and of shining, of keeping up external appearances, and of thus winning consideration, is carried by the Americans to a degree unusual in Europe." The *Mirror of Fashion* similarly bragged that in Paris, the world's capital of fashion, most of the population still dressed in blouses and caps, whereas in New York a far greater ratio appeared in genteel styles. Was it any wonder, then, that the *Columbian Magazine* pointed to fashion's current "unlimited power" as a sign of the times? "The coat makes the man, is proverbial here," de Gurowski concluded.[4]

In fact, this apotheosis of fashion helped to integrate the homespun vision of civic virtue into the ready-made revolution. Continuing its celebration of American superiority to Europe the *Mirror of Fashion* noted that because so many persons dressed well in the New World, "*here*, the difference between a millionaire and a mechanic is not observable in personal appearance." Once everyone had become a participant in the fashion system, in other words, that system would lose its power to corrupt; dress would no longer divide citizens from one another. Fashion's nefariousness was thus effectively defused by its very universality. This inversion of traditional evils into their own solution was analogous to Madison's epiphany, famously expounded in the *Federalist*, that only a multiplicity of political interests could neutralize the influence of interest in politics. And so, Lady Emmeline Stuart-Wortley was able to make an observation directly opposed to that of Adam de Gurowski without contradicting him: "The tailor has less to do with manufacturing a gentleman here, than in perhaps any other part of the world. For in all other countries you are a little assisted to the conclusion, unwittingly, by the dress; but here not in the least."[5]

The tendency of fashion to cancel itself out suited a democracy of self-invented individuals in which nature's plasticity, traditionally a grave threat to the sumptuary order, would have to be the key to order. In fact, in an industrial age devoted to artifice and material abundance and to the consequent weakening of fixed hierarchies, fashion presented a unique opportunity to create a common ground. Its ability to elicit voluntary compliance—to bring an individual to eagerly forfeit some of his hallowed independence in order to join the reigning mode—made fashion a form of governance: a system of majority rule for a polity that located sovereignty in the free will of every citizen. According to the logic of fashionable emulation, the autonomous citizen found self-expression in the very embrace of public standards of taste. If the tape measure integrated his unique body into a universal market of anonymous customers, fashion made this integration a wholly conscious, indeed enthusiastic, experience. Subjectivity thus became a mass phenomenon. What's more, fashion's reliance on self-rule rather than rule by coercion both recognized and resolved the problem of desire in a liberal age. If all individuals wanted the same things, then fashionable competition would result in more social harmony rather than less, ameliorating the atomizing tendencies of the same market in which fashion now so briskly circulated. That is what led the *Mirror of Fashion* to perhaps surprisingly declare that "every novelty is dangerous." It is also why Tocqueville's observation that "the man you left in New York you find again in almost impenetrable solitudes . . . [the] same clothes, same attitude, same language, same habits, same pleasures" was so politically significant, as was his contention that, in the age of the individual, similarities between persons were far more important than that which distinguished them.[6]

- - - - -

The democratic character of the American regime of bon ton was the subject of an apocryphal battle that took place between "Beauty" and "Fashion" in 1833 in the pages of *Godey's Lady's Book*. "If I give a charm you are certain to spoil it," Beauty accuses Fashion in their contest over moral ascendancy. The evangelical insinuation, of course, was that man's profane ambitions would always remain inferior to the work of God and that fashion could only be an "effacement of Divine Nature," as John Adams once complained, even in an age of man-made progress. But Fashion was quick to counter in rhyming cadence: "A complexion, a shape, you confer now and then / But to One that you give, you refuse it to Ten." As such, Fashion nominated itself as the remedy to Beauty's despotic rule, precisely because of the former's powers of artifice. The resulting democracy of fashion was a decidedly secular order, one that the *Ladies' Companion*, writing a few years later, was not ready to accept. "The disposition for looking well is ruining half the young people in the world," it lamented in 1837, identifying the source of the problem in a generation of transplanted sons and daughters who, having abandoned the countryside and its agrarian ethos, now spent their time gazing in the mirror

A daguerreotype of Edward Knight Collins, businessman,
produced by Mathew Brady's Studio, circa 1840s.
(Courtesy of the Library of Congress)

rather than pursuing "that which is lasting or solid." Thus, "fashion should
not be allowed to bear upon that which cannot be changed except by deception," the *Ladies' Companion* concluded, thereby promulgating natural truth
as the only viable common basis for the subjectivity of a self-made age. Otherwise, everyone would constantly be reinventing themselves. Indeed, what else
but a putative nature could maintain social order once the whip of necessity
had been taken out of the hands of traditional patriarchal authority? Or, as
Horace Bushnell formulated the problem: "The principal danger is, that, in
removing the rough necessities of the homespun age, it may take away, also,
the severe virtues and the homely but deep and true piety by which . . . that
age is so honorably distinguished."[7]

Modernists were not intimidated by fashion's ability to eliminate rough-
ness and severity. There was the obvious response, delivered by the *Mirror of*

Fashion: "Dress is common to all; and it is a consolation to those not naturally gifted, that there is a point at which nature yields to art, and that the ingenuity of man is potent to supply the adornment not vouchsafed by nature." But this was no more than the political philosophy of a trade journal. A more profound reply to neo-homespun proponents of natural truth came a few years after the confrontation between Beauty and Fashion, when *Godey's Lady's Book* explained that, in fact, the nature of nature was change. In other words, fashion's restless variation and its plasticity—what opponents still insisted on calling "deception"—was rooted in none other than the natural world. What was considered beautiful last year, *Godey's* explained, loses its power in the same way that the fall colors fade in the winter. Mutability was the essence of the human condition. "If the very nature of the earth is changed by its own convulsions; if the form of human government, and the monuments of human power and skill cannot endure—if even the religions that predominate in one age are exploded in another; if nothing on the 'earth beneath, or the water under the earth,' preserves its form unchanged, what is there that remains for ever the same?"[8]

The homespun movement had also expected fashion to be an important social force. Organizers of the anti-British protests knew that their success depended on enlisting a large enough number of "Leading Ladies" in the cities and towns who would be able to make coarseness "the fashion." Mathew Carey likewise understood that the successful adoption of his proposal for a national dress would rely on "a few respectable citizens in every state," whose costume would then be universally emulated.[9] But these sartorial politics were nevertheless informed by an impulse that sought a transcendent truth, that is, a social life resting on a permanent order. And so, just as Thomas More envisioned all citizens of his Utopia dressed in locally produced capes "of one color . . . and that the natural color," Mathew Carey called on all federal officers to "dress principally in the manufactures of the united states" and on wealthy women to forgo their costly ornaments. A fashion regime, in contrast, embraced the permanently shifting, multivalent nature of authority. It recognized that private behavior could no longer be mandated by public decree since fashioning one's self had since become a natural right, not to mention a condition of the "free" market. The post-utopian commonwealth had consequently to be constructed on the principle of popular emulation. This provoked opponents of ready-made democracy into denouncing the superficiality of public life and its confusion with an ephemeral universe of commodity exchange, "whole miles of plateglass . . . palaces and carriages and hostelries—fountains and shady walks, splendor, refinement, luxury, and ease!"[10]

Such antagonism toward fashion seemed to echo earlier homespun condemnations of luxury. But there were other ways of updating republican virtue. They found expression, for instance, in the ongoing debate over the tariff, whose details not infrequently focused on the significance of a well-dressed republic. And so proponents of protection often justified their demand to raise duties on imports by arguing that the poor would subsequently be able to afford better clothing. A high tariff on woolens, Tristam Burges contended in a speech to the House of Representatives in 1830, would lower the cost of a coat from eight dollars to three. "A man is, and so a nation is, rich or poor," Burges declared, quoting Adam Smith, in obvious reference to homespun notions of civic virtue by which private property was the key to public happiness. He recalled that a laborer working on the Providence wharves in 1815 was able to purchase four yards of cotton shirting with his daily wage of one dollar. In 1830 that same laborer still earned a dollar. But now, Burges pointed out, thanks to the increased tariff, he could afford ten yards of shirting, and even sixteen if he (inexplicably) purchased them at the wholesale price. "In the one case, the laborer is 150 per cent and in the other he is 300 per cent richer." There was no better vindication of the American System than this success in dressing up the popular classes. [11]

In fact, the same purpose inspired opponents of the tariff. When journeymen tailors petitioned Congress in 1832 for a reduction of the duties on woolens, they argued that the absence of such protection would "greatly increase the demand for the labor of journeymen tailors and tailoresses." Moreover, it would, "at the same time, benefit all classes, by diminishing the price of clothing." George McDuffie, a congressman from South Carolina, likewise described his battle against the Tariff of Abominations as driven by the fear that duties on broadcloth would not increase at as high a rate as duties on coarser woolens, thus favoring the fashions of the rich. [12]

The opposing sides of the tariff divide thus shared a conviction regarding the political importance of a regime of fashion. [13] Their consensus on the material essence of a decent civic life was summed up in a neologism adopted by Edwin Freedley in the late 1850s: a "standard of living." Freedley referred specifically to the need to pay clerks an income "sufficient to insure contentment in the[ir] situation." However, "standard of living" had a far more general application, underlining as it did the centrality of measurable equivalences in a market society and turning them into a test of democratic community. A standard of living, in other words, conflated market equivalences and social equalities. Public happiness, already defined by homespun ideology in skeins and yards, would now be measured by family budgets and the cash price of basic commodities. [14]

Such a quantifiable theory of justice led Mathew Carey to document the injuries done the seamstress by printing budgets that itemized her family's minimal monthly quotient of rent and fuel, shoes and clothing, soap, candles, bread, meat, and vegetables. It was the most effective way to substantiate the lowly condition of her life and the need to bring it up to standard. Raising the standard of living made the general spread of refinement a general logic. No one embraced the Yankee Doodle dandy's proud sartorial failure anymore, as propertied "disinterest" gave way to propertied "self-interest" as the basis not only of social improvement but of human rationality. Wendell Phillips described this American system in an essay that appeared in the *Mirror of Fashion*: "Here everything contributes to progress, and every man, is striving to rise. And he has a motive; for he knows that if he succeeds in accumulating, he will have more influence and a higher social position. But abroad, the poor man has no motive to strive—the mainspring is taken away. Property will not change his condition."[15]

For all its "striving," ready-made fashion nevertheless continued to subscribe to a familiarly modest aesthetic impulse. "Dress so that it may never be said of you, 'What a well-dressed man!'" the *New-York Mirror* advised. "Avoid all excess in your costume," *Burton's Gentleman's Magazine* echoed. Or, as the *New York Aurora* remarked on Boz's realization of the fashionable ideal at the society fête in his honor in 1842: "Mr. Dickens was dressed very neatly—so well, indeed, that we cannot remember how." Quoting Dr. Johnson, Henry Lunettes approvingly noted in the *American Gentleman's Guide* that "the best dressed persons are those in whose attire nothing in particular attracts attention." Likewise, Samuel Wells's 1856 *How to Behave: A Pocket Manual of Republican Etiquette* declared that "a man's vest or cravat must not seem a too important part of him." "When you are once well dressed, for the day, think no more of it afterwards," advised George Fox in his suitably entitled *Fashion: The Power That Influences the World*. And the *Mirror of Fashion* declared that "as long as a man is externally distinguished by anything like a *made-up* appearance—as long as there is any trace of art or study, any symptom of consciousness about him—he is altogether in the wrong."[16] This male modesty was the outcome of "the march of the race from barbarism to the highest degree of present civilization." Savages, Horace Greeley continued, wore few clothes. But they were elaborately arrayed in feathers, paints, and tatooes. Modern man presented the opposite picture. He had forsaken trinkets and other accoutrements—self-advertising "gaudiness and finery" that undermined "the dignity of *manhood*," as the *New-York Mirror* contended— and adorned his person instead with the stuff of "mechanical philosophy, general physical comfort, and productive industry." This final stage of the civilizing process as manifested in men's three-piece sobriety was tellingly underscored in the nineteenth century's best-selling testament to bourgeois sensibility, *Uncle Tom's Cabin*, which overdressed the slave trader on its opening page "in a gaudy vest of many colors, a blue neckerchief, bedropped gayly with yellow spots, and arranged with a flaunting tie."[17]

Although virtuous citizens were prohibited from adopting a "*made-up* appearance," the underlying principle of their dress was not invisibility. A proper male appearance was insistently public: confidently designed to be seen and judged. Rather, fashionable attire avoided calling undue attention to itself by corresponding seamlessly to the standard. "Few will dispute the practical utility of conforming to the general requisitions of Fashion," Henry Lunettes wrote in the *American Gentleman's Guide*. "But while care is taken to avoid the display of undue attention to the adornment of the outer man, everything approaching to indifference or neglect, in that regard, should be considered equally reprehensible." As such, taste was a self-conscious search for the golden middle of social equilibrium. George Fox described the man of sense, who "dresses as well, and in the same manner, as the people of sense and fashion of the place where he is. If he dresses better, as he thinks, that is, more than they, he is a fop; but if he dresses worse, he is unpardonably negligent." The *Mirror of Fashion* transposed Fox's adage into a classical republican triad: "There is no grade out of fashion that civilized man can be happy in; for those above it are tyrants, and those beneath it, dependents." Democratic fashion was firmly ensconced in between. "Part the extremes," Nathaniel Willis wrote in the *New Mirror* in 1843, "widen the distance between wealth and poverty—and you make room for a *middle class* . . . everybody who is not absolutely poor, striving to seem absolutely rich." This striving class, as Wendell Phillips already intimated, was the industrial incarnation of the "middling" sort whose shopping habits were identified as the source of progress by Adam Smith, who, a century earlier, had favorably contrasted them with the prodigality of aristocrats and the asceticism of puritans. Fashion's intermediate position between tyrants and dependents, or aristocrats and puritans, marked off a virtuous middle, virtuous not in the least for its inclusivity. "The wise will ne'er embrace him first, Nor be the last to leave him," the *Ladies' Companion* pedantically observed, perspicaciously referring to fashion by the masculine pronoun.[18]

Fashion's consensual nature was reinforced by the identity of its two most notorious male opponents in New York, the dandy and the b'hoy. The dandy dressed "in some way, markedly unlike everybody else," George Foster explained. He wore coats with small, low collars and exceedingly low stocks. "The sleeves, at the wrist, [were] pinchingly close, and soiled white gloves [were] too short to reach them, leaving a ring of tortured red flesh between them." The pantaloons were likewise fitted so tightly that "they seem capable of standing alone," and his boots—"the neatest of French boots"—were designed to erase the calf altogether. The dandy made "fashion the business and study of his life." He assigned premier status to his outer self, and invested in it accordingly. "The clothing of an exquisite is a work of time and science," *Graham's Magazine* ironically observed. The irony was manifest in the very system the dandy applied to an appearance that, for industrial contemporaries, contradicted the same, for white calfskin gloves, like his "small and smooth" aesthetic in general, made it most impractical to work. Indeed, the dandy ultimately "produced nothing but himself." [19]

The b'hoy was the dandy's ostensible class rival, a rabble-rousing prol who flaunted his contempt for reigning Broadway fashions. "He rolls down the Bowery a perfect meteor," Cornelius Mathews observed of the b'hoy, in "stark staring blue for coat, brick-red for waistcoat, breeches with a portentous green stripe, hat brushed to the highest gloss, shiny as a new kettle." In comparison, "a Broadway exquisite would dwindle to undistinguishable nothingness." The Broadway-Bowery opposition was an important axiom of the day, and the b'hoy's fustian fastidiousness had a distinctly taunting, satiric quality: it was a self-conscious proletarian style designed to affront more rarified sensibilities. However, like the dandy, the b'hoy—tightly fitted into his high-heeled calfskin boots—also established himself as an object of everyone's gaze. Both, moreover, were to be found on the same side of the barricade in challenging bourgeois conventions, social as well as sartorial. [20]

The transgressions of the dandy and b'hoy were not a function of the importance they assigned to their dress. After all, no one invested more meaning in clothing than did advocates of homespun and ready-made ideologues. The particular eccentricities of the dandy's or b'hoy's appearance were far less offensive than was the undisguised interest each of them took in themselves as sartorial subjects. That dilettantism is what violated the fashion maxim by which "we do not allow that to be fashion which goes before the mode, any more than that which lags behind it." Fashion excludes all eccentricity, its ready-made champions defensively insisted. It "especially condemns and repudiates, as vulgar, every species of excess which seeks applause, merely because it is extravagant or striking." The dandy and b'hoy, in other words, took self-fashioning to its logical, antipolitical extreme. Unwilling to acknowledge that the self was not a unique, private phenomenon but a public one, they

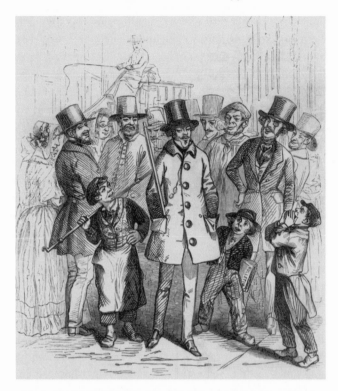

The dandy violated the democratic spirit of the republic's fashion regime by
cultivating a unique appearance. Rather than finding a place in the virtuous
middle, he became the singular object of everyone's gaze. This illustration
accompanied an essay entitled "The Physiology of Dandyism," which
appeared in the February 1852 issue of *Graham's Magazine*. (Courtesy
of the Collection of the New-York Historical Society, neg. 75523)

ended up turning the rhetoric of individualism upon itself, thereby upsetting
the fashionable balance between self and society. That is why their singularly
systematic presentation seemed to be the opposite—a capricious loss of self-
control. They were not tolerated precisely because they threatened to expose
the sober gentleman's studied indifference to the sartorial as no less of a performance, declaring not that the new bourgeois emperor had no clothes, but
that he was dressed to the nines.[21]

The fact is that civic-minded men wore dress coats in the evening and
surtouts in the morning. They owned riding coats, greatcoats, and something
called a duster, which was "the most desirable possible for wearing in railroad

cars." There was a proper time and occasion for gloves, collars, cravats, hats, demi-toilette, morning pantaloons and vests, single-breasted frocks, a business coat, breakfast dress, and shooting and fishing costume. Lunettes's *Gentleman's Guide to Politeness* insisted that a dark claret dress coat together with a white ribbed-silk vest be worn to a wedding, further propounding the general rule that "all . . . should be regulated by the laws of *harmony of color*, and *adaptation of color to complexion*." William Alcott, an important publicist for the emerging cultural consensus, wrote in his *Young Man's Guide* that "it is certainly true that the impressions which a person's first appearance makes upon the minds of those around him are deep and permanent." As Luke Shortfield reported in the *Western Merchant*, "the well-dressed gentleman receives first attentions of servants at hotels, and best accomodations, without paying more; sometimes paying less for the landlord is interested in him becoming a regular customer." Conversely, the meanly dressed "is a mark for the assaults of the low and degraded, who suppose his intellects are on a par with his clothes." Thus, when James Talcott arrived in New York City he took himself shopping for a plug hat and a closely buttoned broadcloth frock coat to facilitate his search for a position as a dry-goods jobber. (He also hired a Negro to push his goods around—apparently no less of a fashionable accoutrement.) "A finished dress indicates a man of the world, one . . . who is at all times ready to mingle in intercourse with those whom he meets with," the *Canons of Good Breeding* explained. Melville described how important male dress was to the social order in his best-selling account of South Sea primitives, *Typee*: "Stripped of the cunning artifices of the tailor, and standing forth in the garb of Eden,—what a sorry set of round-shouldered, spindle-shanked, crane-necked varlets would civilized men appear! Stuffed calves, padded breasts, and scientifically cut pantaloons would then avail them nothing, and the effect would be truly deplorable."[22]

How, then, could anyone pretend that the most effective attire was that in which "nothing in particular attracts attention"? In a story called "Following the Fashions," T. S. Arthur seemed to have exposed the hypocrisy underlying male modesty:

> "You follow the fashions."
> "No, Mary, I do not."
> "Your looks very much belie you, then."
> "Mary!"
> "Nonsense! Don't look so grave. What I say is true. You follow the fashions as much as I do."

"I am sure I never examined a plate of fashions in my life."
"If you have not, your tailor has for you, many a time."[23]

Mary was no doubt right about her brother's fashionability. But he had a point as well. Fashion plates depicting men's styles were not in fact designed for general consumption. They circulated instead in trade journals such as *Le Mirroir de Beau Monde*, the *Quarterly Reports of London and Paris Fashions*, *Taylor's Magazine and Quarterly Reports of Fashion*, the *American Report of the Fashions*, and the *Mirror of Fashion*, which published their illustrations in tandem with the technical details needed to make up the garments. Certainly, men had no intention of cutting and sewing the suits themselves: the illustrations, like the instructions, were intended for tailors. This practice diverged decidedly from that of women's fashion magazines, whose plates, like the magazines themselves, were intended for a general readership. In fact, there was no female counterpart to a trade journal like the *Mirror of Fashion* since women's fashions, unlike men's, were not mass-tailored.[24]

The tailor, in fact, presided over the male "renunciation" of fashion, for by achieving sartorial propriety through his mediation men could ignore "the fashions" without risking the wrong appearance. George Fox stated the point quite explicitly: "While a fop is the slave of fashion, a philosopher surrenders himself to his tailor, whose duty lies in dressing him becomingly." Thus one could embrace the cause of fashion while avoiding any dandyish devotion to individual whim. The *Dry Goods Reporter* celebrated the rationality of such a system in which the garments of "the sterner sex are simply ordered of the tailor, measure taken, and the office is ended." This efficiency suited an age in which idleness was no longer gentlemanly. Was it any wonder, then, that in the nineteenth century a fashionable male could dress in good taste in ten minutes while his female counterpart, according to the *Home Journal*, toiled for hours? That didn't mean that men were less dependent on stiffeners, interfacings, padding, canvas, and wadding. The opposite, in fact, was the case: while women principally relied on undergarments to achieve a fashionable silhouette, tailors, whose drafting systems bragged of their success in overcoming any obstacles that impinged on the proper countenance of the "whole man," built the desired male shape into the clothes themselves.[25]

Virginia Penny, who sought a place for women in this industrial reality by compiling an encyclopedic employment guide for them in the early 1860s, could not understand why "the plan used by tailors, of fitting by measure, is not more generally applied to dress fitting." She knew that the requisite drafting technology existed for women's garments. But the fact remained that

A fashion plate from Joseph Couts's *Practical Guide for the Tailor's
Cutting-Room*, 1848. The tailor presided over the male renunciation of
fashion by allowing men to ignore the fashions without risking the wrong
appearance. (Courtesy of The Winterthur Library, Printed Book and
Periodical Collection)

only men's clothing was mass produced, while the lady's mantua-maker was
notorious for the "endless cuttings, fittings, alterings, and reconstructions"
associated with dressing women. Such a process stood in definitive contrast
to tailoring's acme of standardization and system that could produce a full
suit "on twelve hours' notice," constructed through a mechanical principle
of overlapping sections of arms, trunks, and legs suitable to all.[26] As far as
women's clothing was concerned, the problem was not a technical but a political one. Sartorial rationality had no ideological relevance to female bodies,
which were associated, as we have seen, with excess, instability, and irregu-
larity. So unsuited was their dress to modern life, in fact, that women could

even have a problem doing their shopping: "Stewart's was so crowded when we started to leave [that I] could scarce press my way through the crowds. Oh, what a disadvantage the Hoop is in a crowded aisle."[27]

The hoopskirt embodied the encumbrances of artifice much in the same way that wigs had in the eyes of homespun patriots a century earlier. The difference, of course, was that whereas both men and women had worn wigs, only women wore skirts. The "bug bear—fashion," in other words, no longer divided aristocrat and republican as it had in homespun times, but instead women and men. This made fashion a foundation of the new democratic patriarchy that so insistently gendered all social relations, far more than had its preindustrial predecessor. In 1828 Sarah Hale actually pledged to keep fashion plates out of the pages of *Godey's Lady's Book*. Fashion was a European blight, *Godey's* declared, and hence unsuited to American life. Hale apparently aspired to tie female politesse to national virtue, in the same way that bourgeois men were developing a sartorial aesthetic of "republican simplicity" to consolidate their civic status. But she failed. Within two years Hale's magazine was regularly featuring the latest styles from London and Paris, and women's dress was becoming a negative reflection of male citizenship.[28]

In an attempt to challenge some of this male hubris, Mary continued to admonish her brother:

> "Of course,—you trust to [your tailor] to make your clothes according to the fashion, while I choose to see if the fashions are just such as suit my stature, shape, and complexion, that I may adopt them fully, or deviate from them, in a just and rational manner. So there is this difference between us; you follow the fashions blindly, and I with judgment and discrimination!"

Such male "indiscrimination" pointed to an advanced degree of system and predictability in fashion that was the essence of the ready-made ethos. Men thus proved to be the first mass consumers of clothing. In fact, that same consumption helped to disembody the male, since he did not then have to bother with endless cuttings, fittings, alterings, and reconstructions. This safe distance from corporeal manipulation in turn made men's abstract universal status that much more natural. By not personally having to match his wardrobe to "suit [his] stature, shape, and complexion," the citizen seemed to keep his person aloof from commodity fetishisms. That is to say, while men's dress may have been far more implicated in the commercial and industrial system, women's bodies were in greater danger of contamination from market exchange. The bourgeoisie would have it no other way, for this danger is what pushed the seamstress into whoredom, or allowed everyone to marry off Tiffany's daughter to his or her advantage, and gave Mary no reason to deny her most feminine interest in modifying styles to suit her best. Ready-made fashion, in contrast, protected the (male) civic body from such caprice, thereby demonstrating that capitalism did not actually turn everyone into an ephemeral object of exchange.[29]

"Let all your motions be as easy and natural as if you had no clothes on at all," George Fox advised in a nod to the classical nude and in acknowledgment of the male ambition to create a natural fashion that would not become a separate object of scrutiny in itself. The *Scientific American* explained: "The fine arts flourish best amidst a luxurious people, where wealth is concentrated in the hands of the few. . . . Objects of utility rather than objects of ornate ability, are the characteristics of American genius." Male appearance sought to base itself, as Anne Hollander has observed, on an aesthetic of singular coherence that explained itself. That aesthetic reflected an industrial reality in which extraneous or impractical garments, designed to constrict or extend the body, were replaced by garments cut to fit by means of engineering principles applied to the torso. "*Every garment should leave the wearer perfectly free and uncontrolled in every motion*," the *Mirror of Fashion* italicized. "Any garment which pinches, or incommodes the wearer, will strongly militate against the easy deportment of even the most graceful, and tend to give a contracted and constrained appearance."[30]

The axiomatic divide between male utility and female ornament was popularly symbolized by the trousers, "a form at once typical of and indispensable to the most complex and elaborate civilization." This equation of pants with progress was the background of a scandal provoked by a feminist attempt to address female irrationality through dress reform. The reform campaign promoted a garment named in 1851 for the activist Amelia Bloomer. The new costume heightened the skirt to avoid dragging in the filth of the street (which, like tight lacing, was an old subject of reform protest). More to the point, it replaced the voluminous underskirts with pantaloons gathered at the ankle, or a little above, that were to be made of the same material as the skirt. The "Bloomer," which appeared at the end of a decade of escalating physical constriction in woman's fashions, was designed to forge a new, truer relationship between a woman and her dress and, as a consequence, a more rational relationship to the world at large. Elizabeth Cady Stanton embraced the innovation, for instance, after having witnessed her Bloomer-clad cousin, "with a lamp in one hand, a baby in the other, walk upstairs, with ease and grace, while, with flowing robes, I pulled myself up with difficulty, lamp and baby out of the question."[31]

Like Amelia Bloomer, Stanton and her cousin, Elizabeth Miller, were active campaigners for women's equal rights, and the new costume was an explicit expression of their feminism. As Susan B. Anthony asserted, "I can see no business avocation, in which woman in her present dress *can possibly* earn *equal wages* with man." Amelia Bloomer wrote in *The Lily*, which she edited, that the new outfit was ideally suited for women who were active and did their own housework. "We wash and iron, bake and brew, cook and wash dishes, make beds and sweep the house, etc. etc., and we find the short dress much more *convenient* than the long one." Flowing robes, Bloomer continued, could only appear graceful on women who had nothing other to do than strike poses. The argument had a distinctly homespun inflection. Indeed, the nonfeminist *Ladies' Wreath* described the Bloomer as "a dress altogether American and unique in its character, distinguished from any of those imported from abroad by its surpassing neatness and simplicity." And certainly the cultural perfectionism that motivated these reformers could be compared, if not actually traced, to the ascetic self-sacrifice of the nonimportation crusades of the previous century, when daughters of the genteel classes foreswore their English tea and silks. Proponents of the Bloomer were engaged in a similar sartorial politics directed against the corruptions of fashion. Their dress reform, it was accordingly declared, would obviate "distinctions of physical force, birth and rank . . . and [things] fashionable, aristocratic, and European."[32]

But that was precisely the problem. For, in telling contrast to the homespun era, attempts by women in the industrial age to adopt a dress of virtuous protest required them to don male attire. And wearing trousers—the sole right of men, as contemporaries now repeatedly proclaimed—bordered on the "pantaloonery."[33] Thus, the *Ladies' Wreath*, despite its enthusiasm for such a uniquely virtuous American dress, still refused to endorse the Bloomer. A costume that made it easier for women to walk would also allow them to walk away from their duties. *Peterson's Magazine* observed that women lost all their natural grace when dressed in attire designed for a man's straightforward gait. *Harper's Monthly Magazine* conjured a dystopian future in which women proposed marriage to men. Others warned that Wellingtons, canes, and even cigars couldn't be far behind.

Women, in other words, had no way to participate in sartorial virtue without betraying their nature. That is not to say they did not have a virtuous nature, only that it was a private one, now disconnected from the political economy and civic life represented in democratic dress. Appropriately enough,

A "BLOOMER" (in *Leap Year*).—" Say! oh, say, Dearest, will you be mine?"

STRONG-MINDED "BLOOMER."—" Now, do, Alfred, put down that foolish Novel, and do something rational, and play something. You never practice, now you're married."

Harper's Monthly Magazine responds to the Bloomer in 1852. Here, one Bloomer-clad woman proposes marriage, while another upbraids her novel-reading spouse for neglecting his music lessons. Such "pantaloonery" would mean the end of the natural order.

then, there was no mass production of ready-made clothing for women, just as there were no patented drafting systems designed for women, before the Civil War. In fact, *Godey's Lady's Book*, the leading proponent of the notion that women should use dress to define a separate sphere for themselves, paid only scant attention to the whole Bloomer issue, hoping it would go away, which it soon did. [34]

- - - - -

Men had been shedding extraneous decoration for years, as if in coordination with the growth of democratic sentiment. First to go were the doublet with slashed sleeves, ornaments such as silk roses and knots, and wide lace collars; these were replaced with a white linen shirt, breeches, stockings, coat, waist-coat, and cravat. By the middle of the eighteenth century the three-piece ensemble of breeches, coat, and waistcoat was often made en suite. Full-bodied wigs, huge baggy sleeves, and coats with voluminous full skirts gave way to a slimmer ideal at the end of the century. Coat proportions continued to shrink, the newer designs requiring less material, and better tailoring. Sleeves now outlined the arms; pocket flaps and cuffs disappeared. The skirts of frock coats receded to the sides of the body, and waistcoat skirts also disappeared. By this time the two most "extraneous" ornaments of gentlemanly status—the wig and sword—had been entirely forgotten. [35] The colonial silhouette received its death blow, appropriately enough, soon after the fall of the Bastille, when Thomas Jefferson adopted the sans-culottes style (of "folly, extravagance, and French disbelief" in the words of his enemies). His pantaloons were not the loose trousers traditionally worn by the lower classes, however, but closely fitted, highly tailored leggings. These were then replaced around 1815 by a looser style of trouser. White cravats, or neckcloths, disappeared a decade later. In 1843 the *New Mirror* entitled a series of nostalgic reminiscences of old New York ("steam presses, spinning jenneys, labor-saving machines and the invention and ingenuity of mankind are turning the world topsy-turvy") "The Last of the White Cravats." James Monroe was the last national leader to look at all like an eighteenth-century gentleman. By the time of the bitter 1834 mayoral contest in New York, "silk stocking" had become a Democratic pejorative used for an older generation of neo-Federalist opponents. [36]

The passing of ornament gave way to fit, which progressively loosened up. Emerson dubbed the frock coat one of the utilitarian features of the generation, and Nathaniel Hawthorne described it as "the most comfortable garment that ever man invented." The "comfortable surtout" became something

Cover from the program for the Crystal Palace Exhibition in New York City,
1853. The only acceptable way for women to participate in a ready-made
democracy was to don the mythic garb of a classical goddess. (Courtesy of the
Collection of the New-York Historical Society, neg. 75675)

of a cliché. Such garments were of lighter weight than more traditional coats
and made of softer material. They often lacked a waist seam, and by mid-
century the sleeves had become distinctly baggy at the elbows as well as looser
at the wrists. The shoulders were also boxier. Tight waists, padded chests,
full coat-skirts, and narrow sleeves disappeared as the male silhouette generally became squarer, less elongated, and otherwise more distinct from the
female (as moustaches and sideburns also proliferated in mid-century fash-

ion plates). Designed for both gracefulness and ease, the surtout was daytime wear, intended, that is, "for business and open air recreations." It was often made of linen or a cotton blend, in natural colors, and was relatively easy and inexpensive to produce, which meant that it lent itself that much more easily to mass production. The surtout was what men now wore to the "counting-room and office." In fact, contemporaries began to call this less-fitted style, known for its convenience and comfort as well as its lack of pretension, "business dress." It was indicative of a growing distinction between dressing for (daytime) work and for (evening) ceremony, and it has proven largely impervious to change since the mid-nineteenth century. The best that tailors could hope for was to "beautify the edges" and close them with "ornamental tabs." Thus we find an 1855 business directory describing the era's "self-made" man in terms distinctively reminiscent of Franklin's "homespun Dress of Honesty": "They need no golden helmet or other blazon of wealth to win them the public gaze; in the shock of the conflict, fierce though friendly, the unknown knight, with his plain unostentatious black armor, without page or esquire, proved himself the victorious champion."[37]

It was not a victory of frugality, however. As the aging federalist John Pintard wrote in 1821, "the rapid accumulation of wealth" of recent years had made it "difficult to retrace and fall back to habits of early simplicity."[38] And in the 1860 census account of the rise of the clothing industry, modern conditions were compared to a time "when the straitened pecuniary means and the undeveloped state of all the domestic arts imposed upon all classes a compulsory frugality in regard to apparel." If the welter of production statistics available at mid-century proved anything, it was that such simplicity was no longer compulsory: there was now enough surplus value for everyone. Thomas Ford recalled the transformations that Illinois was undergoing in the 1820s: "With the pride of dress came ambition, industry, the desire of knowledge, and a love of decency." Similarly, James Guild, a Vermont peddler with both business and cultural ambitions, reported how he felt "rather large when he walked through the streets in his new suit."[39] The universal ability to "dress well" was a testament to the democratic cultural achievements of plenty. In an age of "general physical comfort," as *Hunt's* identified the times, fashion could no longer be anyone's monopoly. The tables had, in fact, been turned. As *Putnam's* bluntly remarked in 1857, "We reject the Spartan theory of republican life which simply leads us back to the barbarities of Spartan or Puritan despotism." Or, as *Hunt's* asked, "What would be the condition of workers in silver, if no silver was used?" William Sanger predicted that the ranks of the city's prostitutes would shrink if men would only spend more on their purchases.[40]

Indeed, it made much sense for the bourgeoisie to encourage emulation of its fashions since class autarchy was not a practical method of exercising power in a democracy. If the propertied sought to promote their version of respectability to a universal principle, they had to ensure that their rules of behavior were followed by all. "We have by degrees fallen into a style of dress so inornate and so uncostly, that it is attainable by men of all classes above the very poor." This was welcome news for the *Mirror of Fashion*, inasmuch as it enlarged the market for tailors. But universal access to fashion was not just good for business. Once luxury was no longer a vice, the social disarray resulting when the demos became zealous consumers of goods would no longer constitute a social threat.[41]

In the railway stations of Europe, George Fox wrote in *Fashion: The Power That Influences the World*, the classes were physically segregated. In fact, such barriers were what made it possible for the propertied classes to tolerate the mob's existence. In America there was no such separation, Fox continued, and consequently there was no mob. Thus did this merchant tailor offer an important insight into the liberal episteme. "The rough and dirty are quite out of place," in America, he wrote, since, if they were to exist, they would be "sure to be close at your side." As a result, propriety was as general in the United States "as it is exclusive in most countries," which is why the *Mirror of Fashion* had to keep apologizing for including white liveried servants in their fashion plates. Livery was a costume of service, a most demeaning badge of servility fit only for "Long Island niggers" or for the "two Ethiopians" dressed in scarlet coats, cocked hats, plush breeches, and white stockings who were put on guard as a publicity stunt outside a new bazaar at the corner of Liberty and Broadway in January 1844.[42]

The makers of European fashion had, of course, little concern for the un-liveried status of the "eight millions of white men and boys over the age of fifteen" living in the republic. At the same time, the American sumptuary regime—the republic's political ability to dress up its citizens—was a recurring subject of interest on the part of Europeans traveling to the New World to observe democracy firsthand and then reporting back on the great experiment to their countrymen (in accounts avidly followed in the American press, as Europe remained integral to Americans' self-definition). All depicted sartorial equality as a uniquely American phenomenon. James Boardman wrote during a visit in the late 1820s that those New Yorkers "who earn their bread by the sweat of their brow" were all extremely well turned out. Michael Chevalier supported that impression when he reported that "the United States are certainly the land of promise for the labouring class," a conclusion he reached after landing in New York in 1834, where every day seemed like Sunday. "Every man was warmly clad in an outer garment; every woman had her cloak and bonnet of the latest Paris fashion. . . . What a contrast between our Europe and America!" he declared. "All classes were well dressed," William Chambers likewise noted. "When operatives had finished the labours of the day, they generally changed their garments, and were as neatly attired as those in higher stations." Francis Wyse could identify a foreign tourist by the "style and mediocre cut of his entire vesture," while Henry Fearon was struck by the fact that, watching a military field day in Pittsfield in 1818, he could not distinguish between officers and enlisted men. Tocqueville and Richard Cobden both noted how government officers in the United States were on an equal footing with the citizenry, to the extent that they even dressed the same. A Swede wrote of New York's immigrant working class in 1841 that were "dressed in a way we are accustomed to see only among the gentry." A decade later Adam de Gurowski made the same observation: "Peasants, villagers, almost all the laboring populations in Europe are generally poorly and cheaply clad; suits of clothes among them are hereditary, and women often principally wear those of their grandmothers. If America is deprived of the picturesque costumes to be found among European nations, she has far less tatters." Or, as an Englishman wryly remarked in 1847: "Fustian is little known in America. Canvass-back ducks they have in abundance, but no canvass-backed people." But Lady Emmeline Stuart-Wortley was the most succinct: "A mob in the United States is a mob in broad-cloth. If we may talk of a rabble in a republic, it is a rabble in black silk waistcoats."[43]

"Silk waistcoats," "tailor-made men," and even a certain "love of show" were not at odds with "republican equality." Mobs in broadcloth proved rather that democracy was not inherently coarse or unrestrained. Since political progress was measured by material affluence, as Americans were increasingly wont to measure it, then poverty was a far more suitable fate for the European masses. It was thus a notable victory for virtue that "Americans . . . are always neatly and well dressed; their clothes far better and more fashionably made (after the latest London and Paris style) than of the same classes in England."[44]

If Americans still defined their greatness "by the comparative lack of elevation of any one man above the rest," as Emerson claimed they did, this leveling now took place not in the coarse, homemade terms of homespun but in those of a fine suit of factory-manufactured (and usually imported) broadcloth, cut in a modern style, invariably one originating in London or Paris, and distributed to the market by a network of clothing wholesalers and merchant tailors spanning the continent. In "the age of mechanical philosophy, of general physical comfort, and productive industry," sartorial virtue was no longer a paean to scarcity and self-sacrifice but to industrial plenty and cultural refinement, and to that refinement's availability to all citizens. Thus, in "The Moral Significance of the Crystal Palace," an oration delivered at the opening of the Exhibition of the Industry of All Nations in New York City in 1853, the Reverend Henry W. Bellows affirmed the virtue of material abundance: "Luxury is debilitating and demoralizing only when it is exclusive. . . . The peculiarity of the luxury of our time, and especially of our country, is its diffusive nature; it is the opportunity and the aim of large masses of our people; and this happily unites it with industry, equality, and justice." Public happiness was attained not through frugality but through its opposite, mass consumption made possible by mass production. This was an "industrial luxury," a middle landscape for the new century, which, no less than the homespun before it, was supposed to include all citizens. "Now the interests of everyone are all intertwined together," *Hunt's* declared in 1840, celebrating the end of household manufacturing.[45]

There was nothing strange, therefore, when George P. Fox stated his ambition "to adorn the Doric simplicity of American principles by the inimitable grace and elegance of an appropriate cosmopolitan costume," or when *Putnam's* equated Spartan republicanism with "Spartan . . . despotism," or when the 1860 census described homespun as a temporary imposition.[46] "Without fashion," the *Mirror of Fashion* insisted, echoing Franklin's sentiments during the Sans Souci controversy, "commerce would be reduced from a wealthy giant to a sickly lilliputian." Reviewing the 1853 Exhibition of the Industry of All Nations at the Crystal Palace, Horace Greeley concluded that "every sober mechanic has his one or two suits of broadcloth, and, so far as mere clothes go, can make as good a display, when he chooses, as what are called the upper classes." And the *United States Magazine and Democratic Review*, Greeley's partisan rivals, called that achievement no less than "revolutionary," given that "articles of clothing are now at the command of the lowest members of society, which, but a century since, were scarcely within the reach of crowned heads." The first thing that attracted one's attention upon arriving in New York, a Welsh immigrant wrote in 1844, was the city's people, "all so neatly and comfortably clad." "The stranger is involuntarily led to enquire," he continued, as to "where are the working classes—the tattered and half-fed, miserable-looking starvelings . . . of his native land." The contrast between Europe and America was no less severe— or flattering to the latter—as it had been a century before. Now, however, the republic offered plenty while aristocracy and absolutism were identified with scarcity.[47]

All this democratic abundance did not mean, of course, that everyone on the street looked to be of equal station. The *New-York Illustrated News*, in an 1860 "Photograph of Broadway," made that explicit in contrasting the 7:30 A.M. rush of "laborers, shop boys and factory girls" to the 9:00 A.M. vision of "merchants and clerks hurrying to their place of business," the first as recognizable by their rough, patched, and stained garb as the latter by their refined outerwear. Ready-made democracy, in other words, was anything but a classless society. George Templeton Strong, with an eye for the defining detail of modernity, understood that the ideal of a "finished model of the Anglo-Saxon" was at best a theoretical postulation. "There is poetry enough," he wrote,

> latent in the South Street merchant and the Wall Street financier; in Stewart's snobby clerk chaffering over ribbons and laces; in the omnibus driver that conveys them all from the day's work to the night's relaxation and repose; in the brutified denizens of the Points and the Hook; in the sumptuous star courtesan of Mercer Street thinking sadly of her village home; in the Fifth Avenue ballroom; in the Grace Church contrast of eternal vanity and new bonnets; in the dancers at Lewis Jones's and Mr. Schiff's, and in the future of each and all.[48]

Indeed, there was no shortage of persons who had been bypassed by the clothing revolution altogether. In Schoharie County, New York, Henry Conklin later recalled that in these years he and his brothers stayed in bed on wash day since they each had only one set of garments. James Moran got married in a homespun jacket in Milledgeville, Georgia, in 1825, and in Iowa Margaret Murray's mother was still fleecing and cleaning wool, and then coloring the yarn herself, in 1853.[49]

But American democracy did not have to be a classless society. As Samuel Wells explained: "True republicanism requires that every man shall have an equal chance—that every man shall be free to become as unequal as he can." Likewise, George Opdyke, clothier turned cloth importer turned banker turned mayor of New York, wrote in his self-published *Treatise on Political Economy*: "If there are those who fail to partake of the proffered advantages the fault must be their own, since the policy presents no features of exclusiveness or inequality." The proof of the pudding, in other words, was not in how many did not belong, but in how many did.[50] And in the prevailing democratic conditions no one had an excuse for not looking their best—in

"The Daguerreotypist," from the May 1849 issue of *Godey's Lady's Book*.
By mid-century, three million daguerreotypes were being made a year. The
personal portrait was now no less mass-produced than was the clothing.

not achieving a "standard of living." Thus, during the visit of the Prince of
Wales to New York in the fall of 1860, the *New York Tribune* was incredulous
at the refusal of the city's carriage drivers who participated in his cortege to
don "sober and neat" suits.[51]

However, while the "masses" did not exactly divide their appearance between morning sack and evening frock, they did at least distinguish between
a work smock and Sunday going-out clothes. And this provided a strong basis
for optimism: the demos would strive to invent itself as a satisfied bourgeois.
As Walt Whitman observed of the working class at market: "So marvelous
an influence hath money in making a man feel valiant and as good as his
neighbor." And William Chambers explained to his English readers that in
America, "when operatives had finished the labours of the day, they generally
changed their garments, and were as neatly attired as those in higher stations."
Such a self-image found a most conscious expression when those operatives
sat for their portrait, which, by the 1850s, no longer entailed the application

of oil to canvas. In 1853 the *Tribune* estimated that three million daguerreotypes were being made a year, and for as little as 25 cents one could pose at
any number of studios located in cities or towns throughout the country (or,
if need be, wait for an itinerant daguerreotypist to arrive in the village). The
mass production of these images seems, at first glance, to be a measure of
just how much things had changed in the hundred years since John Singleton Copley created his portraits of the colonial gentry by capturing in paint
the lush velvets and silks of their overtly refined appearance. However, just
like Copley's subjects, almost no one in a ready-made democracy posed for a
portrait in their work clothes either.[52]

Nathaniel Willis, a leading purveyor of style for New York's propertied classes, complained in the 1840s that he lived in a "nation of black coats." It was little wonder, he lamented, that his fastidious British friends characterized Broadway as "a procession of undertakers." Willis, who built his magazine career on the democratization of fashion without ever really coming to terms with the idea, recognized that if fashion was no longer being dictated by an elite, that did not mean there was no dictatorial control over appearance. If, as Thomas Gratton claimed, each American was "as might be said, 'his own gentleman,'" and "there is no standard for them, from the want of a permanent class in society to be looked up to and imitated," then why did they look so much alike?[1]

A clue can be found in the instructions Andrew Jackson issued to American diplomats in 1829 governing their proper appearance in foreign capitals. The president prescribed a black coat, either a black or white vest, a three-cornered *chapeau de bras*, and a sword to be worn in a white scabbard. Although the costume was defined by its "comparative cheapness" and by its "adaptation to the simplicity of our institutions," it struck a polite, even dignified, appearance. To the extent that it proved ideologically provocative, this rested on the fact that foreign governments required the diplomatic corps to dress at court not merely in a dignified manner but in the martial regalia favored by the monarchical aesthetic. The only ornamentation Jackson now allowed was a single gold star affixed to the bottom of each coat collar.[2]

The adoption of such a civic costume was not directed solely at European ostentation. It was no less a remonstration against what the Jacksonians considered the aristocratic predilections of previous administrations, which had approved a diplomatic uniform consistent with foreign manners: a blue coat lined with white silk, a gold-embroidered cape with cuffs to match, white cassimere breeches, gold knee buckles, white silk stockings, and gold or gilt shoe buckles. Far from being a curiosity, in other words, the new directive on dress was an element of Jackson's wide-ranging democratic program for American politics. Indeed, the issue had arisen during the fierce presidential campaign of the year before, when a young congressman, James Buchanan, delivered a diatribe in the House of Representatives aimed at the sartorial habits of American diplomats posted abroad. He berated the ridiculous spectacle of American ministers "bedizened in all the colors of the rainbow." American manners, Buchanan insisted, in rhetoric reminiscent of revolutionary proclamations of the 1760s, "ought to be congenial to the simplicity and dignity of our institutions. In every attempt to ape the splendor of the representatives of monarchical Governments, we must fail."[3]

Buchanan was himself the American ambassador to the court of St. James twenty-five years later, when the diplomatic dress code reemerged as the subject of ideological polemic. In 1853 William Marcy, the secretary of state in Franklin Pierce's new administration, issued a circular ordering American ministers in foreign capitals to appear at court in "the simple dress of an American citizen." Such a presentation was thought to best express their "devotion to republican institutions." Again, the pronouncements were intended principally for domestic consumption. In response to Marcy's circular letters of support poured into the State Department from all over the country, or so it was reported. The *New York Herald*, contemptuous of a foreign policy carried out by symbols and gestures, nevertheless recognized the measure of public approbation "from Cape Cod to California" that Marcy's sartorial patriotism was sure to elicit. In fact, one such expression of support could be read the same day in the pages of the *New York Post*, which applauded Marcy's contribution to the creation of a "national individuality." An American minister abroad, the *Post* elaborated, "should be an American; he should look like an American, talk like an American, and be an American example." The nativism was palpable, but so was the familiar grammar of homespun virtue, for the *Post* defined such an American national identity as resting, first and foremost, on the rejection of livery and all other badges of "servility," "barbarity," and personal dependence so characteristic of despotism and so markedly absent from the American style of governance.[4]

In London, James Buchanan was given the opportunity to practice the sartorial fidelity to republican principles he had so fervently preached a generation earlier. He did not disappoint. "A minister of the United States should . . . wear something more in character with our democratic institutions than a coat covered with embroidery and gold lace," he wrote to Marcy in February 1854, after his absence at the opening of Parliament—necessitated by his refusal to wear court costume—was reported in all the London papers and provoked the threat of an official inquiry in the House of Commons. In fact, Buchanan had been negotiating with Sir Edward Cust, the master of ceremonies, since the previous October in search of a compromise that would satisfy his government's instructions while respecting the exalted character of the queen, "both as a sovereign and a lady." One tentative solution allowed Buchanan to appear at court in the same formal attire he wore to the president's levees in Washington, with the single addition of a black-handled, black-hilted dress sword whose monochrome plainness made it "more manly and less gaudy." Victoria, however, took umbrage at Buchanan's pantaloons, and a different arrangement had to be found. Someone suggested to Buchanan that he adopt for the purpose the civilian dress worn by President Washington. After all, no one could question its republican authenticity. At the same time, such an anachronistic appearance would satisfy the court's sumptuary bias toward the mock heroic. Buchanan considered the idea. "But," he wrote, "after examining Stewart's portrait [of Washington], at the house of a friend, I came to the conclusion that it would not be proper for me to adopt this costume. I observed, 'Fashions had so changed since the days of Washington, that if I were to put on his dress and appear in it before the chief magistrate of my own country, at one of his receptions, I should render myself a subject of ridicule for life.'"[5]

It was a telling observation. The fact is, Marcy's tribute to "the simple dress of an American citizen," for all its obvious symbolism, touched upon fundamental questions concerning political life in an industrial age. It was not enough to flatter the United States by comparing it to a decadent Europe, or even by comparing democracy to monarchy. American democratic identity had to rest on the country's own political inheritance, that "simple and unostentatious course which was deemed so proper, and was so much approved in the earliest days of the republic," as Marcy described it in his circular. Franklin—"our first and most distinguished representative at a royal court"—was promoted to archetype: he had appeared at Versailles in plain dress, devoid of embroidery, and had even abandoned the traditional wig in favor of his own hair. But just as no one in 1853 could suitably don Franklin's high-waisted coat and knee breeches, so the "simple and unostentatious" politics of homespun virtue had to be adapted to a new social and material reality.[6]

The industrial century did not lack for sartorial images of civic virtue. Reviewing the "Great Dress Question" in 1868, when the issue yet again erupted into political controversy, the *Nation* correctly observed that "the 'simple dress of an American citizen' is, of course, a very vague term inasmuch as it includes all varieties of costume from full evening dress down to shirt sleeves and homespun pantaloons." In fact, every such variation was in evidence. An 1835 statue of Alexander Hamilton erected at the exchange on Wall Street depicted him in contemporary eighteenth-century garb and then wrapped him in an outer layer of classical drapery, a medley that made Hamilton a founding father of 1776 while according his revolutionary achievements a transcendent status of classical Roman provenance.[7] The same iconographical strategy was evident in the engraved frontispiece of J. Franklin Reigart's *United States Album*, an image-laden homage to national identity published in 1844. It featured Washington on a steeply elevated pedestal standing before a craggy wilderness. He was dressed in a hunting shirt (which had its own virtuous associations to the War of Independence, not to mention an obvious pertinence to nineteenth-century continental expansion) over which, again, classical robes were draped.[8] There was, perhaps, no more telling metaphor for the revolutionary transition from an agrarian to an industrial world than the incongruity of these separate layers. Still, this was a style of dress better suited to statuary than to citizens going about their daily business. In the rest of Reigart's *United States Album* a more practical range of sartorial symbols was on display. The peruser could find inspiration in Maine's state seal, which depicted a sailor and a farmer standing side by side, attired in their respective working denims and linsey-woolseys; or in Indiana's pioneer, stripped to his waist while felling trees to clear the prairie; or in Kentucky's two fastidiously groomed gentlemen dressed in morning coats and meticulously tailored pantaloons, clasping each other's hands in civic affection against a well-appointed interior of books, Doric columns, and plush sofas; or in Massachusetts's half-naked Indian warrior, his state of undress not the result of strenuous labor, as in the case of the Indiana pioneer, but a testament to his antediluvian innocence.[9]

What the Indian, the working man, the pioneer, and the civilized bourgeois shared was a formative role in the nation's material history. Each represented a distinct stage in America's march to industrial greatness, much as New York's procession in honor of the Constitution had first dramatized that narrative on Broadway sixty years earlier. That procession seemed to reach its culmination on a November afternoon in 1849 when the young dry-goods clerk Edward Tailer walked up Manhattan's Tenth Avenue to check on the progress of the

"The 'simple dress of an American citizen' is, of course, a very vague term inasmuch as it includes all varieties of costume from full evening dress down to shirt sleeves and homespun pantaloons," the *Nation* observed in 1867. Indeed, the full range of sartorial virtue was already on display in 1844, in these four state seals from J. Franklin Reigart's *United States Album*. (Courtesy of The Winterthur Library, Printed Book and Periodical Collection)

INDIANA.

KENTUCKY.

Hudson River Railroad, then under construction. "I was much pleased with what I saw," he wrote later that day in his diary. The great railroad was destined "to convey . . . the exhaustless riches of the western states into our very midst at all seasons of the year."[10]

Tailer's observation on America's success in "subduing the material world," as Michael Chevalier described the national ethos after a tour of the country in 1834, was not only an industrial slogan. It was a fashion statement as well. "We do not—with the painter or sculptor—imitate nature," the *Mirror of Fashion* proclaimed; "we create anew or change her appearance."[11] Whereas the homespun era still subscribed to the ancient relationship between dress and scarcity that dated back to the biblical expulsion from the garden, the ready-made turned the tables on the age-old claim that virtue lay in making do with less. "Even in Paris—'the city of taste,'—*par excellence*, there are not more persons that wear coats, than in [New York]." And that, in fact, was the point Marcy wanted to make in clothing the country's diplomats in the "simple dress of an American citizen." In America fashion was not handed down from social elites to a sycophantic public. Rather, the common man was king, and popular taste ruled. In contrast to the "freaks and follies of foreign fancy," democratic dress would be "strictly consonant with American feelings and predilections," which issued from the bottom up, like social power in general.[12]

Clearly, then, democracy had found its apposite expression in the properly fitted suit. The history of that suit—a tale of wholesale credit and fixed retail prices, of standardized body measurements and armies of interchangeable needlewomen, of in-house cutters and putting-out sweaters, of convenient business frocks and the dandy's pinched cuffs—is a history of the birth of a society of unprecedented flux, size, and variation. It is also an account of the ways that society was made governable. The challenge of governability was considerable, if only because the democracy that ultimately proved to be the basis of industrial stability was originally perceived to be no less than a threat to the social order. A great transformation had indeed taken place in the transition from homespun to ready-made, both in the nature of politics and in the relationship of persons to "goods." The result was a republic constituted not by the workingman's artisanal pride in his productive independence but by the clerk's ever-so conscious sycophancy, not by the protests of sweated seamstresses against wage exploitation but by the charity type's new-found pity for their condition, not by the b'hoy's self-styled proletarianism but by his employer's monotonous new "office dress." This democracy was not the consummation of any grand social vision—not Robert Owen's or Samuel

Slater's—but was rather the accumulated effect of the petty entrepreneur's peripatetic search for quick profits. This is not, in short, a heroic story but a banal one. In fact, there is nothing less heroic than the mutual embrace of capitalism and democracy.

Notes

Introduction

1. "Great transformation" is borrowed from Karl Polanyi, *The Great Transformation: The Political and Economic Origins of Our Time* (Boston: Beacon Press, 1944). For Gandhi's conviction that *khadi* would bring "economic freedom and equality of all," see Mahatma Gandhi, *Hind Swaraj and Other Writings*, ed. Anthony J. Pavel (Cambridge: Cambridge University Press, 1997), pp. 173–74. See also Norbert Elias, "Etiquette and Ceremony: Conduct and Sentiment of Human Beings as Functions of the Power Structure of Their Society," in *The Court Society*, trans. Edmund Jephcott (Oxford: Basil Blackwell, 1983), pp. 78–116; and Daniel Purdy, *The Tyranny of Elegance: Consumer Cosmopolitanism in the Era of Goethe* (Baltimore: Johns Hopkins University Press, 1998), pp. 147–79.

2. The "simple dress of an American citizen" appears in a circular issued in 1853 by William Marcy, Franklin Pierce's secretary of state, on the subject of the appropriate attire for American diplomats abroad. See 36th Congress, 1st sess., Exec. Doc. no. 31 ("Extract from circular, dated Department of State, June 1, 1853"), p. 4.

3. John Locke, *The Second Treatise of Government*, ed. Thomas P. Peardon (Indianapolis: Bobbs-Merrill, 1952 [1690]), p. 79.

4. The quote is from Daniel J. Boorstin, *The Americans: The Colonial Experience* (New York: Vintage Books, 1958), p. 20. Boorstin is a prolific representative of the consensus tradition. However, Louis Hartz's *The Liberal Tradition in America: An Interpretation of American Political Thought since the Revolution* (New York: Harcourt Brace Jovanovich, 1955), although nearly unreadable today, is considered to be the standard-bearer of this school. See, too, Richard Hofstadter, *American Political Tradition and the Men Who Made It* (New York: Vintage Books, 1948), for a more interesting, because more conflicted, variety of consensus history.

5. The common denominator of what I call here "republican history" is the axiomatic opposition between capitalism and democracy. This shared premise still allows for sharp differences over the actual nature of that opposition, however. Charles Sellers, for instance, unmistakably acknowledges capitalism's emerging domination of politics and society over the first half of the nineteenth century (making him something of a kindred spirit of Richard

Hofstadter). Nevertheless, he insists that these new market relations destroyed a prior, if not an a priori, democratic culture. See Charles Sellers, *The Market Revolution: Jacksonian America, 1815–1846* (New York: Oxford University Press, 1991). Others insist on democracy's (somehow identified with republicanism's) success in resisting the forces of capital. A good example of this Thompsonian version of American class war is Sean Wilentz, *Chants Democratic: New York City and the Rise of the American Working Class, 1788–1850* (New York: Oxford University Press, 1984). Wilentz's account of the 1850 clothing strike in New York City as an American version of the Paris June Days can be contrasted to the different depiction of the same events to follow in chapter 5. For a recent critique of the "primal scene of proletarianization" so essential to republican historiography, see James Livingston, "Modern Subjectivity and Consumer Culture," in *Getting and Spending: European and American Consumer Societies in the Twentieth Century*, ed. Susan Strasser et al. (New York: Cambridge University Press, 1998), pp. 413–29.

6. The historiographical underpinnings of this view of capitalism's central and troubled place in the American democratic tradition can be found in Gordon S. Wood, *The Creation of the American Republic, 1776–1787* (New York: W. W. Norton, 1969); Joyce Appleby, *Capitalism and a New Social Order: The Republican Vision of the 1790s* (New York: New York University Press, 1984); Morton J. Horwitz, *The Transformation of American Law, 1780–1860* (Cambridge, Mass.: Harvard University Press, 1977); William Appelman Williams, *The Contours of American History* (New York: W. W. Norton, 1988); and Elizabeth Blackmar, *Manhattan for Rent, 1785–1850* (Ithaca, N.Y.: Cornell University Press, 1989).

7. Alexis de Tocqueville, *Democracy in America*, ed. J. P. Mayer (Garden City, N.Y.: Doubleday, 1969). For a passionate lament about the rise of this "social" meaning of the political, see Hannah Arendt, *On Revolution* (New York: Penguin Books, 1963).

8. Tocqueville, *Democracy in America*, p. 531; Horace Greeley et al., *The Great Industries of the United States* (Hartford, Conn.: J. B. Burr & Hyde, 1872), pp. 587–92 (the quotes are from pp. 589 and 590).

9. I consistently avoid the term *market revolution*, a currently popular rubric under which the early decades of American industrialization are subsumed. Doubtless a neat phrase, adopted from Charles Sellers's jeremiad of the same name, this systematic distinction between a market and an industrial revolution is also historically misleading, tying *industrial* change to the machine technology and size of enterprises of the late nineteenth century rather than to the transformations in social relations born of the wage and commodity. What's more, industrial society continues to this day to (re)organize itself through the market. Indeed, a history of late-twentieth-century political economy could equally well be entitled *Market Revolution*. See Melvin Stokes and Stephen Conway, eds., *The Market Revolution in America: Social, Political, and Religious Expressions, 1800–1880* (Charlottesville: University Press of Virginia, 1996).

10. On the "release of energy," see Willard Hurst, *Law and the Conditions of Freedom in the Nineteenth-Century United States* (Madison: University of Wisconsin Press, 1956); on "creative destruction," see Joseph A. Schumpeter, *Capitalism, Socialism, and Democracy* (New York: Harper & Brothers, 1950).

11. Horace Greeley, *Art and Industry as Represented in the Exhibition at the Crystal Palace* (New York: Redfield, 1853), p. 231.

12. Jackson and the *American Review* quoted in Robert V. Remini, ed., *The Age of Jackson* (New York: Harper & Row, 1972), pp. 116–17 and 184–85, respectively; Alexander Hamilton, John Jay, and James Madison, *The Federalist* (New York: Modern Library, 1788), p. 58.

13. On the newly gendered nature of modern democracy, see the essays in Carole Pateman, *The Disorder of Women: Democracy, Feminism, and Political Theory* (Stanford, Calif.: Stanford University Press, 1989). On the political significance of gender in industrializing America in the spheres of urban space, partisan culture, and marriage, respectively, see David Scobey, "Anatomy of the Promenade: The Politics of Bourgeois Sociability in Nineteenth-Century New York," *Social History* 17, no. 2 (May 1992): 203–27; Paula Baker, "The Domestication of Politics: Women and American Political Society, 1780–1920," *American Historical Review* 89 (June 1984): 620–47; and T. Walter Herbert, *Dearest Beloved: The Hawthornes and the Making of the Middle-Class Family* (Berkeley: University of California Press, 1993). "Peace and order and prosperity" is quoted in Joyce Appleby, "The Social Consequences of American Revolutionary Ideals in the Early Republic," in *The Middling Sorts: Explorations in the History of the American Middle Class*, ed. Burton J. Bledstein and Robert D. Johnston (New York: Routledge, 2001), p. 36.

14. The nineteenth-century seamstress has been the subject of numerous studies, which have invariably presented her as a heroine of anticapitalist protest rather than as a vehicle for the growing capitalist hegemony, as I argue in chapter 6. See, for instance, Philip S. Foner, *Women and the American Labor Movement: From the First Trade Unions to the Present* (New York: Free Press, 1982); Christine Stansell, "The Origins of the Sweatshop: Women and Early Industrialization in New York City," in *Working-Class America: Essays on Labor, Community, and American Society*, ed. Michael H. Frisch And Daniel J. Walkowitz (Urbana: University of Illinois Press, 1983), pp. 78–103; and Mari Jo Buhle, "Needlewomen and the Vicissitudes of Modern Life: A Study of Middle-Class Construction in the Antebellum Northeast," in *Visible Women: New Essays on American Activism*, ed. Nancy A. Hewitt and Suzanne Lebsock (Urbana: University of Illinois Press, 1993), pp. 145–65. Comparisons to the European seamstress—who was no less politicized than her American sister—would be a good place to begin a study of the differences in radical politics between the Old World and the New. See, for instance, Joan Wallach Scott, "Work Identities for Men and Women: The Politics of Work and Family in the Parisian Garment Trades in 1848," in *Gender and the Politics of History* (New York: Columbia University Press, 1988), pp. 93–112; Judith G. Coffin, *The Politics of Women's Work: The Paris Garment Trades, 1750–1915* (Princeton, N.J.: Princeton University Press, 1996); Sheila Rowbotham, "A New Vision of Society: Women Clothing Workers and the Revolution of 1848 in France," in *Chic Thrills: A Fashion Reader*, ed. Juliet Ash and Elizabeth Wilson (Berkeley: University of California Press, 1992), pp. 189–99; and Sally Alexander, "Women's Work in Nineteenth-Century London: A Study of the Years 1820–50," in *The Rights and Wrongs of Women*, ed. Juliet Mitchell and Ann Oakley (London: Penguin Books, 1976), pp. 59–111.

15. On the present as a reification of the past, see Walter Benjamin, "Paris, the Capital of the Nineteenth Century," in *The Arcades Project*, trans. Howard Eiland and Kevin McLaughlin (Cambridge, Mass.: Harvard University Press, 1999); the quote is from p. 4.

Chapter One

1. Dulany quoted in Edmund Morgan and Helen M. Morgan, *The Stamp Act Crisis: Prologue to Revolution* (Chapel Hill: University of North Carolina Press, 1953), p. 86; William R. Bagnall, *The Textile Industries of the United States* (Cambridge, Mass.: Riverside Press, 1893), 1:37–38; Rush quoted in John F. Kasson, *Civilizing the Machine: Technology and Republican Values in America, 1776–1900* (New York: Penguin Books, 1977), pp. 9–10. See also the *Pennsylvania Chronicle*, Feb. 20, 1769; and the *Boston Chronicle*, March 28 and April 4, 1768.

2. Bagnall, *Textile Industries of the United States*, 1:58–59; *Boston Gazette*, Jan. 18, 1768; Beverly Gordon, "Dressing the Colonial Past: Nineteenth-Century New Englanders Look Back," in *Dress in American Culture*, ed. Patricia A. Cunningham and Susan Voso Lab (Bowling Green, Ohio: Bowling Green State University Popular Press, 1993), p. 101; Gail Gibson, "Costume and Fashion in Charleston, 1769–1782," *South Carolina Historical Magazine* 82, no. 3 (1981): 240; Bruce Allan Ragsdale, "Nonimportation and the Search for Economic Independence in Virginia, 1765–1775" (Ph.D. dissertation, University of Virginia, 1985), p. 137, for the Burgess ball (and see p. 101); a "Virginian" quoted in the *Pennsylvania Gazette*, July 19, 1770; a "Freeborn American" quoted in the *Pennsylvania Gazette*, May 12, 1768. See also Jack P. Greene, ed., *Colonies to Nation, 1763–1789* (New York: McGraw-Hill, 1967), p. 47; Alice Morse Earle, *Two Centuries of Costume in America* (New York: Macmillan Company, 1903), p. 741, and *Colonial Dames and Good Wives* (Boston: Houghton Mifflin, 1900), pp. 240–75; Arthur Harrison Cole, *The American Wool Manufacture* (Cambridge, Mass.: Harvard University Press, 1926), 1:61–62; and Elizabeth W. Smith, "A Reminiscence," *Pennsylvania Magazine of History and Biography* 46, no. 1 (1922): 55–56.

3. The *Virginia Gazette* quoted in Kenneth Silverman, *A Cultural History of the American Revolution* (New York: Columbia University Press, 1987), pp. 505–6; Adams quoted in Gordon S. Wood, *The Radicalism of the American Revolution* (New York: Alfred A. Knopf, 1992), p. 17 (and see p. 16); for "Brutus," see Greene, ed., *Colonies to Nation*, p. 157. See also Ferenz Fedor, *The Birth of the Yankee Doodle* (New York: Vantage Press, 1976), pp. 90–103. On Yankee Doodle's continued popularity as a symbol for all sides during the Revolution, see Marianne Holdzkom, "Parody and Pastiche: Images of the American Revolution in Popular Culture, 1765–1820" (Ph.D. dissertation, Ohio State University, 1995), pp. 218–23.

4. *Pennsylvania Gazette*, May 12, 1768.

5. Washington quoted in Ragsdale, "Nonimportation and the Search for Economic Independence," p. 100; Franklin quoted in the *Gazetteer and New Daily Advertiser*, Jan. 2, 1766; *Boston Gazette*, Jan. 25, 1768; and, for the Cordwainers Fire Company, the *Pennsylvania Chronicle*, Feb. 20, 1769.

6. On the householder's role in political sovereignty see, for instance, Edmund S. Morgan, *Inventing the People: The Rise of Popular Sovereignty in England and America* (New York: W. W. Norton, 1988); J. G. A. Pocock, *Politics, Language, and Time: Essays on Political Thought and History* (Chicago: University of Chicago Press, 1989); Isaac Kramnick, "The 'Great National Discussion': The Discourse of Politics in 1787," *William and Mary Quarterly*, 3d ser., 14, no. 1 (Jan. 1988): 15–22; and Bernard Bailyn, *The Origins of American Politics* (New York: Vintage Books, 1967).

7. *Boston Gazette*, Jan. 18, 1768; Attlee quoted in the *Pennsylvania Gazette*, June 14, 1770. See also J. Leander Bishop, *A History of American Manufactures from 1608 to 1860*

(Philadelphia: Edward Young & Co., 1868), 1:375–77; Arthur Meir Schlesinger, *The Colonial Merchants and the American Revolution, 1763–1776* (New York: Frederick Ungar, 1957), pp. 64–65, 77, 122–23, and 289; Bagnall, *Textile Industries*, 1:57; and *All Sorts of Good Sufficient Cloth: Linen-Making in New England, 1640–1860* (North Andover, Mass.: Merrimack Valley Textile Museum, 1980), p. 21. For a good description of the cloth production process, see Alice Morse Earle, *Home Life in Colonial Days* (New York: Macmillan Company, 1917), pp. 166–76, 192–203; and Adrienne D. Hood, "Organization and Extent of Textile Manufacture in Eighteenth-Century Rural Pennsylvania: A Case Study of Chester County" (Ph.D. dissertation, University of California at San Diego, 1988).

8. Adam Smith, *An Inquiry into the Nature and Causes of the Wealth of Nations*, ed. R. H. Campbell and A. S. Skinner (Oxford: Clarendon Press, 1976 [1776]), 2:661; Bishop, *History of American Manufactures*, 1:328; Cole, *American Wool Manufacture*, 1:5–6; Bagnall, *Textile Industries*, 1:11–16; Victor S. Clark, *History of Manufactures in the United States, 1607–1860* (New York: McGraw-Hill, 1929), 1:9–35, 80–81; Carole Shammas, *The Pre-Industrial Consumer in England and America* (Oxford: Clarendon Press, 1990), pp. 64–65, 98–99, and 269; U.S. Census Office, *Manufactures of the United States in 1860, Compiled from the Original Returns of the Eighth Census* (Washington, D.C.: Government Printing Office, 1865), p. xxix; and Bishop, *History of American Manufactures*, 1:305–6, 325–30, 337–41, and 381–82.

9. *Pennsylvania Gazette*, Oct. 25, 1750. See also T. H. Breen, "An Empire of Goods: The Anglicization of Colonial America, 1690–1776," *Journal of British Studies* 25, no. 4 (Oct. 1986): 477, 485–96, and "'Baubles of Britain': The American and Consumer Revolutions of the Eighteenth Century," in *Of Consuming Interests: The Style of Life in the Eighteenth Century*, ed. Cary Carson, Ronald Hoffman, and Peter J. Albert (Charlottesville: University Press of Virginia, 1994), pp. 468–72; John J. McCusker and Russel R. Menard, *The Economy of British America, 1607–1789* (Chapel Hill: University of North Carolina Press, 1985), pp. 279–86; Wood, *Radicalism of the American Revolution*, pp. 134–38; John J. McCusker, "The Current Value of English Exports, 1697–1800," *William and Mary Quarterly*, 3d ser., 28, no. 4 (Oct. 1971): 623–27; Thomas M. Doerflinger, "Farmers and Dry Goods in the Philadelphia Market Area, 1750–1800," in *The Economy of Early America: The Revolutionary Period, 1763–1790*, ed. Ronald Hoffman et al. (Charlottesville: University Press of Virginia, 1988), pp. 167–72, 177–79; Max George Schumacher, "The Northern Farmer and His Markets During the Late Colonial Period" (Ph.D. dissertation, University of California, 1948), pp. 140–42; and Joseph Ernst, "'Ideology' and an Economic Interpretation of the Revolution," in *The American Revolution: Explorations in the History of American Radicalism*, ed. Alfred F. Young (Dekalb: Northern Illinois University Press, 1976), pp. 161–82.

10. See Richard L. Bushman, "Shopping and Advertising in Colonial America," in *Of Consuming Interests*, ed. Carson, Hoffman, and Albert; Beverly Lemire, *Fashion's Favourite: The Cotton Trade and the Consumer in Britain, 1660–1800* (Oxford: Oxford University Press, 1991), pp. 12–42, 100–114. On Revere, see Claudia Kidwell, "Introduction," in Joan L. Severa, *Dressed for the Photographer: Ordinary Americans and Fashion, 1840–1900* (Kent, Ohio: Kent State University Press, 1995), pp. ix–x. The pictorial brilliance of the fabrics in Copley's portraits was considerably toned down after the anti-imperial protests began, and in 1774 Copley left America for good. See Carrie Rebora et al., eds., *John Singleton Copley in America* (New York: Metropolitan Museum of Art, 1995).

11. On homespun and the trans-Atlantic economy, see Lorena S. Walsh, "Urban Amenities and Rural Sufficiency: Living Standards and Consumer Behavior in the Colonial Chesapeake, 1643–1777," *Journal of Economic History* 43, no. 1 (March 1983): 109–17; Carole Shammas, "How Self-Sufficient Was Early America?" *Journal of Interdisciplinary History* 13, no. 2 (autumn 1982): 247–72, and *Pre-Industrial Consumer*, pp. 52–56, 61–62; Gloria L. Main, "Gender, Work, and Wages in Colonial New England," *William and Mary Quarterly*, 3d ser., 51, no. 1 (Jan. 1994): 63–64; Bettye Hobbs Pruitt, "Self-Sufficiency and the Agricultural Economy of Eighteenth-Century Massachusetts," *William and Mary Quarterly*, 3d ser., 41, no. 3 (July 1984): 333–64; Adrienne D. Hood, "The Material World of Cloth: Production and Use in Eighteenth-Century Rural Pennsylvania," *William and Mary Quarterly*, 3d ser., 53, no. 1 (Jan. 1996): 43–66; and Laurel Thatcher Ulrich, *The Age of Homespun: Objects and Stories in the Creation of an American Myth* (New York: Alfred A. Knopf, 2001), pp. 146, 190–96, 103–5, 202–3, and 218–20.

12. For the text of the "Association" issued by the first Continental Congress, see Greene, ed., *Colonies to Nation*, pp. 247–50.

13. Benjamin Franklin, letter of June 11, 1722, to the *New-England Courant*, Benjamin Franklin Papers, Library of America edition on Wordcruncher CD-ROM. On late-seventeenth-century fashionableness in the American colonies, see William B. Weeden, *Economic and Social History of New England, 1620–1789* (Williamstown, Mass.: Corner House Publishers, 1978 [1890]), pp. 286–90; and Leo Marx, *The Machine in the Garden: Technology and the Pastoral Ideal in America* (New York: Oxford University Press, 1964), pp. 93–94, 98. For a parallel discourse on English fashion and national identity, see Erin Skye Mackie, *Market à la Mode: Fashion, Commodity, and Gender in the "Tatler" and the "Spectator"* (Baltimore: Johns Hopkins University Press, 1997), pp. 94–98.

14. "The Forefather's Song" quoted in Bishop, *History of American Manufactures*, 1:302; Benjamin Franklin, "The Busy-Body," no. 3, *American Weekly Mercury* (Philadelphia), Feb. 18, 1728, and "On Simplicity," *Pennsylvania Gazette*, April 13, 1732 (for "homespun Dress of Honesty" and "the first Ages of the world"). On Davenport, see Carl Bridenbaugh, ed., *Gentleman's Progress: The Itinerarium of Dr. Alexander Hamilton, 1744* (Chapel Hill: University of North Carolina Press, 1948), p. 161. See also Norman S. Fiering, "Benjamin Franklin and the Way to Virtue," *American Quarterly* 30, no. 2 (summer 1978): 199–223; Edmund S. Morgan, *The Puritan Dilemma: The Story of John Winthrop* (Boston: Little, Brown, 1958); Jack P. Greene, "The Concept of Virtue in Late Colonial British America," in *Virtue, Corruption, and Self-Interest: Political Values in the Eighteenth Century*, ed. Richard Matthews (Bethlehem, Pa.: Lehigh University Press, 1994), pp. 39–41; Isaac Kramnick, "Corruption in Eighteenth-Century English and American Political Discourse," in *Virtue, Corruption, and Self-Interest*, ed. Matthews, pp. 55–75; Daniel Walker Howe, *Making the American Self: Jonathan Edwards to Abraham Lincoln* (Cambridge, Mass.: Harvard University Press, 1997), pp. 22–33; and Frank Lambert, " 'Pedlar in Divinity': George Whitefield and the Great Awakening, 1737–1745," *Journal of American History* 77, no. 3 (Dec. 1990): 812–37. On the birth of secular politics in America, see Richard L. Bushman, *From Puritan to Yankee: Character and the Social Order in Connecticut, 1690–1765* (New York: W. W. Norton, 1967); and J. E. Crowley, *This Sheba, Self: The Conceptualization of Economic Life in Eighteenth-Century America* (Baltimore: Johns Hopkins University Press, 1974).

15. See Crowley, *This Sheba, Self*, pp. 6, 16, and 17–33; James T. Kloppenberg, "The Virtues of Liberalism: Christianity, Republicanism, and Ethics in Early American Political Discourse," *Journal of American History* 74, no. 1 (June 1987): 17.

16. "Middle landscape" is borrowed from Marx, *Machine in the Garden*, pp. 35–51, 76–105 ("independent and hardy YEOMANRY" is from p. 105); Crowley, *This Sheba, Self*, pp. 16–33 ("a comfortable subsistence" is from p. 30). See also Irma B. Jaffe, "Ethics and Aesthetics in Eighteenth-Century American Art," in *The American Revolution and Eighteenth-Century Culture*, ed. Paul J. Korshin (New York: AMS Press, 1986), p. 160.

17. On the dual role of commerce as the source of corruption and of civic advance, see M. M. Goldsmith, *Private Vices, Public Benefits: Bernard Mandeville's Social and Political Thought* (Cambridge: Cambridge University Press, 1985); Istvan Hont and Michael Ignatieff, *Wealth and Virtue: The Shaping of Political Economy in the Scottish Enlightenment* (Cambridge: Cambridge University Press, 1983), pp. 1–44; J. G. A. Pocock, *The Machiavellian Moment: Florentine Political Thought and the Atlantic Republican Tradition* (Princeton, N.J.: Princeton University Press, 1975), pp. 469–71, 494–98; John P. Diggins, *The Lost Soul of American Politics: Virtue, Self-Interest, and the Foundations of Liberalism* (Chicago: University of Chicago Press, 1984); Cathy Matson and Peter Onuf, "Toward a Republican Empire: Interest and Ideology in Revolutionary America," *American Quarterly* 32, no. 4 (fall 1985): 496–531; Kramnick, "Corruption in Eighteenth-Century English and American Political Discourse," in *Virtue, Corruption, and Self-Interest*, ed. Matthews, pp. 55–75; and Lance Banning, "Some Second Thoughts on Virtue and the Course of Revolutionary Thinking," in *Conceptual Change and the Constitution*, ed. Terence Ball and J. G. A. Pocock (Lawrence: University Press of Kansas, 1988).

18. *Pennsylvania Gazette*, June 16, 1768 (and see July 21, 1768); Hood, "Organization and Extent of Textile Manufacture," pp. 194–97, 223. As the *New-York Weekly Journal* explained as early as 1734: "We only want Frugality and Industry to make us Opulent" (quoted in Matson and Onuf, "Toward a Republican Empire," p. 516).

19. *Pennsylvania Gazette*, June 16, 1768. See also E. B. O'Callaghan, *The Documentary History of the State of New-York* (Albany, N.Y.: Weed, Parsons & Co., 1850–51), p. 734; *Boston Gazette*, Dec. 7, 1767; and Gibson, "Costume and Fashion in Charleston," p. 240. On the "practicality" of virtue, see Albert H. Wurth, Jr., "The Franklin Persona: The Virtue of Practicality and the Practicality of Virtue," in *Virtue, Corruption, and Self-Interest*, ed. Matthews, pp. 76–102.

20. Cato quoted in Howe, *Making of the American Self*, p. 14; *Boston Gazette* ("Every Man who will take Pains") quoted in Breen, "'Baubles of Britain,'" pp. 466–67; *Boston Gazette*, Dec. 7, 1767; Mause's advertisement quoted in Bagnall, *Textile Industries*, 1:54. See also Rita Susswein Gottesman, *The Arts and Crafts in New York, 1777–99: Advertisements and News Items from New York City Newspapers* (New York: New-York Historical Society, 1938), p. 329; Crowley, *This Sheba, Self*, pp. 72, 116; Ragsdale, "Nonimportation and the Search for Economic Independence," pp. 101–2, 110–11, 123, 127, 135–36, 325–26, and 340; Wood, *Radicalism of the American Revolution*, p. 117; and Ira Berlin, *Many Thousands Gone: The First Two Centuries of Slavery in North America* (Cambridge, Mass.: Harvard University Press, 1998), p. 302.

21. Gilman quoted in Laurel Thatcher Ulrich, "Cloth, Clothing, and Early American

Social History," *Dress* 18 (1991): 41. See also Patricia A. Trautman, "Captain Edward Marrett, a Gentleman Tailor" (Ph.D. dissertation, University of Colorado, 1982), p. 93; Richard B. Morris, *Government and Labor in Early America* (Boston: Northeastern University Press, 1981 [1946]), p. 393; Bridenbaugh, ed., *Gentleman's Progress*, p. 164; Richard L. Bushman, *The Refinement of America: Persons, Houses, Cities* (New York: Vintage Books, 1993), pp. 69–74; Clark, *History of Manufactures*, 2:207–8; and Rolla Milton Tryon, *Household Manufactures in the United States, 1640–1860* (New York: Augustus M. Kelley, 1966 [1917]), pp. 92, 101.

22. See Linda Welters and Judanne Janacek, "The Social Meaning of Homespun Clothing in New England," paper presented at a symposium of the Costume Society of America, May 18, 1991, pp. 1–5; Susan Anderson Hay, "From Husbandman to Gentleman: Costume in Prerevolutionary Providence, Rhode Island," abstract of a paper paper presented at a symposium of the Costume Society of America, May 18, 1991; Bishop, *History of American Manufactures*, 1:331; Bushman, *Refinement of America*, pp. 71–72; Hood, "Organization and Extent of Textile Manufacture," pp. 214–17; Gary B. Nash, *The Urban Crucible: Social Change, Political Consciousness, and the Origins of the American Revolution* (Cambridge, Mass.: Harvard University Press, 1979), pp. 343–48; Wood, *Radicalism of the American Revolution*, pp. 271–78; and "Verse Occasioned by Seeing the North-Spinning, in Boston" (1769), for "Rich and Poor all turn the Spinning Wheel."

23. In the nineteenth century, making a virtue out of economic necessity became known as the "work ethic." See Jonathan A. Glickstein, *Concepts of Free Labor in Antebellum America* (New Haven, Conn.: Yale University Press, 1991).

24. On the Pennsylvania Associators, see "Devices and Mottoes," *Pennsylvania Gazette*, Jan. 12, 1747. See also Wood, *Radicalism of the American Revolution*, pp. 4–30; Sean Wilentz, *Chants Democratic: New York City and the Rise of the American Working Class, 1788–1850* (New York: Oxford University Press, 1984), pp. 65–66, 92–93, and 95; Greene, "The Concept of Virtue" in *Virtue, Corruption, and Self-Interest*, ed. Matthews; and Pocock, *Machiavellian Moment*, pp. 514–15.

25. Kasson, *Civilizing the Machine*, p. 19; the *Philadelphiad* (1784) quoted in Silverman, *Cultural History of the American Revolution*, p. 506; Timothy Dwight, *Greenfield Hill: A Poem* (New York: Childs and Swaine, 1794), part 6, lines 7–10. See also Cole, *American Wool Manufacture*, 1:140–41; McCusker, "The Current Value of English Exports," pp. 621–22; Edmund S. Morgan, "The Puritan Ethic and the American Revolution," in *The Challenge of the American Revolution* (New York: W. W. Norton, 1976), pp. 129–31; and Gibson, "Costume and Fashion in Charleston," pp. 245–46, for scarlet coats in Charleston.

26. *American Museum* 2, no. 2 (Aug. 1787): 165; *New-York Gazette and General Advertiser*, Aug. 9, 1799; Earle, *Home Life in Colonial Days*, pp. 185–86; Bagnall, *Textile Industries*, 1:110–11; Morgan, "The Puritan Ethic and the American Revolution," p. 137 (and see pp. 129–31). See also Kasson, *Civilizing the Machine*, pp. 14–19, 31; and Charles Warren, "Samuel Adams and the Sans Souci Club in 1785," *Proceedings of the Massachusetts Historical Society* 60 (May 1927): 319–20.

27. *American Museum* 3, no. 1 (Jan. 1788): 89, and 2, no. 2 (Aug. 1787): 118–19. See also Kasson, *Civilizing the Machine*, pp. 14–15; Silverman, *Cultural History of the American Revolution*, pp. 506–7; and Jacob E. Cooke, *Tench Coxe and the Early Republic* (Chapel Hill: University of North Carolina Press, 1978), pp. 182–216, 236–37.

28. Paine quoted in Jack P. Greene, *The Intellectual Construction of America: Exceptionalism and Identity from 1492 to 1800* (Chapel Hill: University of North Carolina Press, 1993), pp. 184–85; Silverman, *Cultural History of the American Revolution*, pp. 451, 450, for Washington's "servile adherence" and "new realities" (and see pp. 494–95). See also Garry Wills, "Washington's Citizen Virtue: Greenough and Houdon," *Critical Inquiry* 10, no. 3 (1984): 420–40; Bernard Rudofsky, *Are Clothes Modern? An Essay on Contemporary Apparel* (Chicago: Paul Theobald, 1957), pp. 178–79; Lynn Hunt, "Symbolic Forms of Political Practice," in *Politics, Culture, and Class in the French Revolution* (Berkeley: University of California Press, 1984), pp. 52–86; and Quentin Bell, *On Human Finery*, 2d ed. (New York: Schocken Books, 1976), pp. 72–76.

29. *Gazette of the United States*, quoted in Gottesman, *Arts and Crafts in New York*, p. 328. See also Merideth Wright, *Everyday Dress of Rural America, 1783–1800* (New York: Dover Publications, 1990), p. 9.

30. Bagnall, *Textile Industries*, 1:102–3; Bishop, *American Manufactures*, 1:418; William L. Stone, *History of New York City From the Discovery to the Present Day* (New York: Virtue & Yorston, 1872), pp. 303–4; Clark, *History of Manufactures*, 1:46, 366, and 448.

31. Bagnall, *Textile Industries*, 1:42–44; Bishop, *American Manufactures*, 1:375–77; Alexander Hamilton, *Report of the Secretary of the Treasury of the United States, on the Subject of Manufactures* (Dublin: P. Byrne, 1792), p. 76; Arthur Harrison Cole, ed., *Industrial and Commercial Correspondence of Alexander Hamilton* (New York: Augustus M. Kelley, 1968 [1928]), pp. 43, 76–81. See also Patricia A. Cunningham, "Simplicity of Dress: A Symbol of American Ideals," in *Dress in American Culture*, ed. Cunningham and Lab, p. 189; and Laurel Thatcher Ulrich, "Wheels, Looms, and the Gender Division of Labor in Eighteenth-Century New England," *William and Mary Quarterly*, 3d ser., 55, no. 1 (Jan. 1998): 20–22. On one woman's spinning and weaving in 1791–92, see Margo Culley, ed., *A Day at a Time: The Diary Literature of American Women from 1764 to the Present* (New York: Feminist Press at the City University of New York, 1985), pp. 69–76.

32. On the processions, see Richard L. Bushman, *King and People in Provincial Massachusetts* (Chapel Hill: University of North Carolina Press, 1992), pp. 242–44; Howard B. Rock, ed., *The New York City Artisan, 1789–1825* (Albany: State University of New York Press, 1989), p. 16; Silverman, *Cultural History of the American Revolution*, pp. 580–86; D. T. Valentine, *Manual of the Corporation of the City of New York for 1865* (New York: New York Common Council, 1865), pp. 570–71; and Wilentz, *Chants Democratic*, pp. 70–71. Of relevance to the New York processions is the remark that "the political economists began their historical accounts with a dark age of natural barbarism, not the golden age favored by republican theorists" (Matson and Onuf, "Toward a Republican Empire," p. 518). Both processions—Boston's as well as New York's—can be said to have illustrated Adam Smith's labor theory of value: see Louis Dumont, *From Mandeville to Marx: The Genesis and Triumph of Economic Ideology* (Chicago: University of Chicago Press, 1977), pp. 82–108. On the significance of alphabetization, see Cynthia J. Koepp, "The Alphabetical Order: Work in Diderot's *Encyclopédie*," in *Work in France: Representations, Meaning, Organization, and Practice*, ed. Steven Laurence Kaplan and Cynthia J. Koepp (Ithaca, N.Y.: Cornell University Press, 1986). On progress in America, see Drew R. McCoy, *The Elusive Republic: Political Economy in Jeffersonian America* (New York: W. W. Norton, 1980). On progress in its broader

cultural meaning, see Mary Poovey, *A History of the Modern Fact: Problems of Knowledge in the Sciences of Wealth and Society* (Chicago: University of Chicago Press, 1998), pp. 214–63.

33. See Greene, *Intellectual Construction of America*, pp. 71, 78, 102–4, and 114–16 (Crevecoeur is quoted on p. 104); *Gazette of the United States* quoted in Gottesman, *Arts and Crafts in New York*, p. 328.

34. Cole, ed., *Industrial and Commercial Correspondence of Hamilton*, pp. 3–5; Dennis D. More, *More Letters from the American Farmer: An Edition of the Essays in English Left Unpublished by Crevecoeur* (Athens: University of Georgia Press, 1995), p. 71. For the text of Tyler's *The Contrast*, see Edwin H. Cady, ed., *Literature of the Early Republic* (New York: Rinehard & Co., 1950), pp. 392–449; and see Silverman, *Cultural History of the American Revolution*, pp. 558–63.

35. Benjamin Franklin, "On Simplicity," *Pennsylvania Gazette*, April 13, 1732; Thomas Jefferson, *Notes on the State of Virginia*, ed. William Peden (New York: W. W. Norton, 1982 [1787]), pp. 164–65; Lester J. Cappon, ed., *The Adams-Jefferson Letters* (Chapel Hill: University of North Carolina Press, 1959), 2:190–91. Since the "specimens of homespun" were sent by separate post, Jefferson was not yet aware that Adams's "homespun" gift was actually two volumes of Adams's collected essays and not the cloths of household provenance that Jefferson so enthusiastically now considered of national import. We do not know whether Jefferson appreciated Adams's irony once he realized his mistake.

36. Warren, "Samuel Adams and the Sans Souci Club," pp. 322–30 (the quote is from p. 322). See also Silverman, *Cultural History of the American Revolution*, pp. 558–63; Joyce Appleby, *Liberalism and Republicanism in the Historical Imagination* (Cambridge, Mass.: Harvard University Press, 1992), p. 8; and Tamara Plakins Thornton, *Cultivating Gentlemen: The Meaning of Country Life among the Boston Elite, 1785–1860* (New Haven, Conn.: Yale University Press, 1989), p. 10; as well as Robert Gross's comment in Linda Kerber et al., "Forum: Beyond Roles, Beyond Spheres: Thinking about Gender in the Early Republic," *William and Mary Quarterly*, 3d ser., 46, no. 3 (July 1989): 575.

37. *Boston Observer* quoted in Gordon S. Wood, ed., *The Rising Glory of America, 1760–1820* (New York: George Braziller, 1971), pp. 144–45. See also Matson and Onuf, "Toward a Republican Empire," pp. 517–18; and Jean-Christophe Agnew, *Worlds Apart: The Market and the Theater in Anglo-American Thought, 1550–1750* (Cambridge: Cambridge University Press, 1986), pp. 174–75.

38. Adams quoted in Neil Harris, *The Artist in American Society: The Formative Years, 1790–1860* (Chicago: University of Chicago Press, 1982), p. 31; Smith, *Inquiry into the Nature and Causes of the Wealth of Nations*, 1:96; Gordon S. Wood, *The Creation of the American Republic, 1776–1787* (New York: W. W. Norton, 1969), pp. 478–79 ("every Distinction" is from p. 479). See also Myron F. Wehtje, "The Ideal of Virtue in Post-Revolutionary Boston," *Historical Journal of Massachusetts* 17, no. 1 (winter 1989): 74–75; and Silverman, *Cultural History of the American Revolution*, p. 508. On luxury's elasticity as a tool of political approbation from the sixteenth century onward, see John Sekura, *Luxury: The Concept in Western Thought, Eden to Smollett* (Baltimore: Johns Hopkins University Press, 1977), pp. 60–62, 64–65.

39. Benjamin Franklin, letter of June 11, 1722, to the *New-England Courant*, Benjamin Franklin Papers, Library of America edition on Wordcruncher CD-ROM; Silverman, *Cul-*

tural History of the American Revolution, p. 516 and, for Mason, p. 574. See also Wood, *Radicalism of the American Revolution*, pp. 19–20, 250–59; Richard R. Beeman, "Deference, Republicanism, and the Emergence of Popular Politics in Eighteenth-Century America," *William and Mary Quarterly*, 3d ser., 49, no. 3 (July 1992): 428–30; Pocock, *Politics, Language, and Time*, pp. 145–46; Wehtje, "The Ideal of Virtue," pp. 69–72; Jeffrey Barnouw, "American Independence: Revolution of the Republican Ideal—A Response to Pocock's Construction of the 'Atlantic Republican Tradition,' " in *The American Revolution and Eighteenth-Century Culture*, ed. Paul J. Korshin (New York: AMS Press, 1986), pp. 41, 45; Kloppenberg, "Virtues of Liberalism," pp. 9–33; Franklin A. Kalinowski, "David Hume and James Madison on Defining 'The Public Interest,' " in *Virtue, Corruption, and Self-Interest*, ed. Matthews; and Bell, *On Human Finery*, p. 23.

40. Society for the Promotion of Useful Arts, *Transactions in the State of New York* (New York, 1807), pp. 88–90; Franklin quoted in the *Pennsylvania Gazette*, May 12, 1768. See also Joyce Appleby, "Commercial Farming and the 'Agrarian Myth' in the Early Republic," *Journal of American History* 68, no. 4 (March 1982): 833–49.

41. Horace Bushnell, "The Age of Homespun," speech delivered in 1851 at Litchfield, Connecticut, on the occasion of the centennial celebration, in *Centennial Celebration* (Hartford, Conn.: Edwin Hunt, 1851), pp. 112, 114–16, and 123–24. On the industrial century's nostalgic reinvention of the colonial past, see Gordon, "Dressing the Colonial Past," pp. 109–35. See also the *New Mirror*, April 29, 1843, for an anticipation of Bushnell's rhetoric.

42. "Dependence; or What Made One Woman Meanly Penurious," *The Una*, April 1, 1853. According to the *Ladies' Companion*, spinning belonged to "those [past] days of primitive contentment" (Aug. 1840, p. 20).

43. Brigham Young quoted in Ruth Vickers Clayton, "Clothing and the Temporal Kingdom: Mormon Clothing Practices, 1847 to 1887" (Ph.D. dissertation, Purdue University, 1987), p. 125; the *Subterranean*, June 27, 1846.

44. Bushnell, "The Age of Homespun," p. 126; Stephen N. Elias, *Alexander T. Stewart: The Forgotten Merchant Prince* (Westport, Conn.: Praeger, 1992), p. 30. There were other acknowledgments of the influence of New England's "early thrift and industry" on the country's commercial success. See "The Influence of the Trading Spirit upon the Social and Moral Life in America," published in the Whig-aligned *American Review*, vol. 1 (Jan. 1845), and excerpted in Robert V. Remini, ed., *The Age of Jackson* (New York: Harper & Row, 1972), pp. 183–89. Matthew Hale Smith ascribes Stewart's business success to the same homespun origins in *Sunshine and Shadow in New York* (Hartford: J. B. Burr and Co., 1868), p. 31.

45. *Hunt's Merchant's Magazine*, May 1840, p. 368.

46. Frederick Law Olmsted, *The Cotton Kingdom* (New York: Random House, 1984), pp. 141, 539–41, and 506–7. An earlier version of the same argument is found in Tocqueville's comparison of the two banks of the Ohio River. See Alexis de Tocqueville, *Democracy in America*, ed. J. P. Meyer (Garden City, N.Y.: Doubleday, 1969), pp. 345–48. For a Georgian plantation woman complaining about Northern women's ignorance of household skills, see Ann DuPont, "Textile and Apparel Management in the Nineteenth-Century Plantation South," *Ars Textrina* 18 (Dec. 1992): 54. In an 1846 poem published in the prolabor *Voice of Industry*, John Greenleaf Whittier inverted the Southern condemnation of Northern ready-

made culture, favorably comparing the humble Northern spinner to the haughty Southern planter. But to do so the radically inclined Whittier had to write sentimental lines about the spinner singing by her wheel "at the low cottage door" in a journal that was published in the industrial city of Lowell, Massachusetts. See Alice Kessler-Harris, *Out to Work: A History of Wage-Earning Women in the United States* (New York: Oxford University Press, 1982), p. 42.

47. Myrtie Long Candler, "Reminiscences of Life in Georgia During the 1850s and 1860s," pt. 3, *Georgia Historical Quarterly* 33, no. 3 (Sept. 1949): 227; Mary Elizabeth Massey, *Ersatz in the Confederacy* (Columbia: University of South Carolina Press, 1952), pp. 186–91. See also George C. Rable, *Civil Wars: Women and the Crisis of Southern Nationalism* (Urbana: University of Illinois Press, 1989), pp. 91–95; Margaret Thompson Ordonez, "A Frontier Reflected in Costume: Tallahassee, Leon County, Florida, 1824–1861" (Ph.D. dissertation, Florida State University, 1978), p. 161; Richard Maxwell Brown, "Violence and the American Revolution," in *Essays on the American Revolution*, ed. Stephen C. Kurtz and James H. Huston (New York: W. W. Norton, 1973), pp. 113–14; and Eugene D. Genovese, *The World the Slaveholders Made* (Hanover, N.H.: Wesleyan University Press, 1988), pp. 165–94.

48. For wartime army contracts with New York clothiers, see National Archives, RG 92, Records of the Office of the Quartermaster General, entry no. 1246 (regular supplies contracts). On the homespun uniforms of Southern soldiers, see Judith C. Stewart-Abernathy et al., *Life Threads: Clothing Fashions in Early Arkansas, 1810–1870* (Little Rock: Arkansas Territorial Restoration, 1989), p. 24. On Brooks Brothers, see William R. Bagnall, "Sketches of Manufacturing Establishments in New York City, and of Textile Establishments in the United States" (1977), manuscript, Merrimack Valley Textile Museum, North Andover, Mass., pp. 335–55. See also George Fitzhugh, "The Revolutions of 1776 and 1861 Contrasted," *Southern Literary Messenger* 37 (Nov.–Dec. 1863): 718–26.

Chapter Two

1. *Niles' Weekly Register*, June 28, 1817; Rush quoted in John F. Kasson, *Civilizing the Machine: Technology and Republican Values in America, 1776–1900* (New York: Penguin Books, 1977), pp. 9–10; *Hunt's Merchant's Magazine*, Oct. 1840, pp. 305–10 (the quotes are from p. 308; see also May 1840, pp. 363–64); U.S. Census Office, *Manufactures of the United States in 1860, Compiled from the Original Returns of the Eighth Census* (Washington, D.C.: Government Printing Office, 1865), p. lxii.

2. *The General Description of All Trades* (1747), quoted in Nora Waugh, *The Cut of Men's Clothes, 1600–1900* (New York: Theatre Arts Books, 1964), p. 91; George G. Foster, *New York Naked* (New York: De Witt and Davenport, 1849), pp. 137–38.

3. See "clothiers" in *Wilson's Business Directory of New York City, 1860* (New York, 1860), and "slop sellers" in the *New Trade Directory for New York, 1800* (New York, 1860); Chamber of Commerce of New York, *Annual Report*, 1858, pp. 38–40. See also Joseph Dorfman, *The Economic Mind in American Civilization, 1606–1865* (New York: Viking Press, 1946), 2:593–97; and Maurice Dobb, *Theories of Value and Distribution since Adam Smith: Ideology and Economic Theory* (New York: Cambridge University Press, 1973), pp. 69–73. Arguably the best account of the early decades of national industrialization in the United States remains Robert Greenhalgh Albion, with the collaboration of Jennie Barnes Pope, *The Rise of New York Port, 1815–1860* (New York: Charles Scribner's Sons, 1939). See, in addition, George

Rogers Taylor, *The Transportation Revolution, 1815–1860* (New York: Rinehart & Co., 1951); Douglass C. North, *The Economic Growth of the United States, 1790–1860* (New York: W. W. Norton, 1966); and D. W. Meinig, *The Shaping of America: Continental America, 1800–1867* (New Haven, Conn.: Yale University Press, 1993).

4. Alexander Stuart, "Anniversary Address Before the American Institute of the City of New-York" (New York: [American Institute], 1844), p. 19; Adam Smith, *An Inquiry into the Nature and Causes of the Wealth of Nations*, ed. R. H. Campbell and A. S. Skinner (Oxford: Clarendon Press, 1976 [1776]), 1:22. See also Henry Wansey, *Practical Observations on Wool*, 2d ed. (Salisbury, Eng.: J. Easton, 1800).

5. These categories were machinery, hardware and cutlery, cannon and small arms, precious metals, various metals, granite and marble, bricks and lime, wool, cotton, silk, flax, mixed textile manufactures, tobacco, hats and caps, leather and tanneries, soap and candles, distilled and fermented liquors, powder mills, drugs, medicines, paints and dyes, glass and earthenware, sugar refining, paper, printing and binding, cordage, musical instruments, carriages and wagons, grist, flour, oil and sawmills, ships, furniture, and houses. See Carroll D. Wright, *The History and Growth of the United States Census* (Washington, D.C.: Government Printing Office, 1900), pp. 309–12; Alexander Hamilton, *Report of the Secretary of the Treasury of the United States, on the Subject of Manufactures* (Dublin: P. Byrne, 1792); and Patricia Cline Cohen, *A Calculating People: The Spread of Numeracy in Early America* (Chicago: University of Chicago Press, 1982), pp. 175–204.

6. This definition of manufacturing is taken from Noah Webster, *An American Dictionary of the English Language* (New York: Harper & Brothers, 1845). Edwin Freedley noted in the late 1850s that the meaning of "manufacture" had become "an extremely flexible one." See Freedley, *Philadelphia and Its Manufactures* (Philadelphia: Edward Young, 1858), p. 21. For a general discussion of the economic significance of manufacturing in this era, see Keith Tribe, *Land, Labour and Economic Discourse* (London: Routledge & Kegan Paul, 1978).

7. *Abstract of the Statistics of Manufactures, According to the Returns of the Seventh Census*, Jos. C. G. Kennedy, superintendent, 35th Congress, 2d sess., Senate Exec. Doc. no. 39, p. 35; George P. Fox, *Fashion: The Power That Influences the World*, 3d ed. (New York: Sheldon & Co., 1872), p. 22. See also Thorstein Veblen, *The Theory of Business Enterprise* (New York: Mentor Books, 1932 [1904]), pp. 19, 27.

8. *New York Post*, April 24, 1822, and, for "33⅓ per cent," Jan. 2, 1822. On British dumping, see Arthur Harrison Cole, *The American Wool Manufacture* (Cambridge, Mass.: Harvard University Press, 1926), 1:80–81, 145–47; Ray Bert Westerfield, "Early History of American Auctions—A Chapter in Commercial History," *Transactions of the Connecticut Academy of Arts and Sciences* (May 1920): 168, 186–91, and 202; and Chester Whitney Wright, *Wool-Growing and the Tariff: A Study in the Economic History of the United States* (New York: Russell & Russell, 1910), pp. 41–57. Yearly breakdowns of textile imports after 1821 are to be found in the annual *Commerce and Navigation Reports* of the United States Congress. See also the *New York Post*, Jan. 5, Jan. 10, and Aug. 16, 1822.

9. See the *New York Post*, Aug. 16, 1822 (and see March 27 and Sept. 16, 1822); *Philadelphia Directory and Register, 1816–22* (Philadelphia, 1816–22); David Alexander, *Retailing in England During the Industrial Revolution* (London: Athlone Press, 1970), p. 185; and B. L. Anderson, "Entrepreneurship, Market Process and the Industrial Revolution in England," in

B. L. Anderson and A. J. H. Latham, *The Market in History* (London: Croom Helm, 1986), pp. 172–73, 178, and 181.

10. *New York Post*, May 9, 1825; Jan. 2, 1822; and April 3, 1828. See also the *Post* for April 29, 1824; April 3, 1828; and March 27, 1830; and F. Fitzgerald De Roos, *Personal Narrative of Travels in the United States and Canada in 1826* (London: William Harrison Ainsworth, 1827), pp. 5–6. On Whitmarsh's fashionable reputation, see "Some Incidents in the Life of the 'New-York Loafer,'" *Ladies' Companion*, Sept. 1837.

11. See *Longworth's American Almanac, New-York Register, and City Directory, 1816–19* (New York: David Longworth, 1816–19); *Mercein's City Directory, New-York Register, and Almanac, 1820* (New York, 1820); Henry Bradshaw Fearon, *Sketches of America: A Narrative of a Journey of Five Thousand Miles through the Eastern and Western States* (London: Longman, Hurst, Rees, Orme, and Brown, 1818), pp. 10–11. See also the illustration of a tailor's shop in Carl Bridenbaugh, *Colonial Craftsman* (New York: New York University Press, 1950).

12. D. T. Valentine, *Manual of the Corporation of the City of New York for 1864* (New York: New York Common Council, 1864), pp. 753–54; *New York Post*, July 13, 1819. See also Catharine Street store ledger, 1822, box 03, A.3, book 2A; sales book, 1824–29, box 03, A.3, book 3; and "Report on the Founding," box 01, BB.1, F10, Brooks Brothers Archive, Chantilly, Va.; William R. Bagnall, "Sketches of Manufacturing Establishments in New York City, and of Textile Establishments in the United States" (1977), manuscript, Merrimack Valley Textile Museum, North Andover, Mass., pp. 344–36; and *Longworth's American Almanac, New-York Register, and City Directory, 1806–19* (New York: David Longworth, 1806–19).

13. A. T. Stewart quoted in Stephen N. Elias, *Alexander T. Stewart: The Forgotten Merchant Prince* (Westport, Conn: Praeger, 1992), p. 4. See also Matthew Hale Smith, *Sunshine and Shadow in New York* (Hartford, Conn.: J. B. Burr & Co., 1868), p. 56.

14. See Albion, *Rise of New York Port*, pp. 12–13, 55–61, and 63; Ira Cohen, "The Auction System in the Port of New York, 1817–1837," *Business History Review* 45, no. 4 (winter 1971): 488–89, 493–98; and Fred Mitchell Jones, *Middlemen in the Domestic Trade of the United States, 1800–1860* (Urbana: University of Illinois Press, 1937), pp. 34, 70. See also James E. Vance, Jr., "Transportation and the Geographic Expression of Capitalism," in *Geographic Perspectives in History*, ed. Eugene D. Genovese and Leonard Hochberg (New York: Oxford University Press, 1989), pp. 125–27.

15. Westerfield, "Early History of American Auctions," pp. 197–98 (and see pp. 168, 186–91, and 202); Joseph Scoville, *Old Merchants of New York City* (New York: Carleton, 1863), p. 25; *Nantucket Enquirer*, Jan. 17, 1825; *Niles' Weekly Register*, Sept. 9, 1826 (and see June 21, 1823). See also Cole, *American Wool Manufacture*, 1:80–81, 145–47; and Wright, *Wool-Growing and the Tariff*, pp. 41–57.

16. See the *New York Post*, Aug. 16, April 24, and Jan. 5, 1822; Westerfield, "Early History of American Auctions," pp. 182–84 and 196–98; Elias, *Alexander T. Stewart*, p. 21; Cohen, "The Auction System," pp. 495, 499; Albion, *Rise of New York Port*, p. 276; and Wright, *Wool-Growing and the Tariff*, p. 49. For details on fabrics, see Margaret Thompson Ordonez, "A Frontier Reflected in Costume: Tallahassee, Leon County, Florida, 1824–1861" (Ph.D. dissertation, Florida State University, 1978), pp. 268–76; and Florence M. Montgomery, *Textiles in America, 1650–1870* (New York: W. W. Norton, 1984), pp. 192–93, 238–39, 287–89, 298, and 325.

17. *New York Post*, April 20 and July 13, 1819; Charles H. Haswell, *Reminiscences of an Octogenarian of the City of New York* (New York: Harper & Brothers, 1896), pp. 57, 72, and 77. On the absence of shears and needles from the arms of merchant tailors, see Cecil A. Meadows, *Trade Signs and Their Origin* (London: Routledge & Kegan Paul, 1957), pp. 52–53.

18. Maurice Dobb, "Entrepreneur," in Edwin Seligman, ed., *Encyclopedia of the Social Sciences*, vol. 5 (New York: Macmillan Company, 1931), p. 559; Egal Feldman, "New York's Men's Clothing Trade, 1800–1861" (Ph.D. dissertation, University of Pennsylvania, 1959), p. 77. See also David J. Saposs, "Colonial and Federal Beginnings," in *History of Labour in the United States*, ed. John R. Commons et al. (New York: Macmillan Company, 1918), 1:28–58. On the other, preindustrial, meaning of capitalist, see, for instance, the advertisements in the *New York Times*, "To capitalists" and "Important to capitalists," Sept. 29, 1835.

19. *New York Post*, Jan. 2, 1822 ("Measure Business"); for Burk's separate advertisement to provincial dealers, see the *New York Post*, April 24, 1822.

20. *Western Monthly Review* quoted in Meinig, *Shaping of America*, p. 415. See also Gerry Beth Gilbert, "An Examination of the Influence of Social and Economic Development on East Tennessee Dress from 1790 to 1850" (M.S. thesis, University of Tennessee, 1971), pp. 30–31, 38–39, and 42–43. As the anecdote of the merchant tailor's wagon illustrates, Dickens generally abused Americans' untiring interest in the commercial. Thus the double entendre in the title of his *American Notes for General Circulation* (London: Penguin Books, 1972 [1842]) (for the anecdote, see pp. 220–28).

21. Waddell advertisement, *St. Louis Beacon*, April 13, 1829; New Orleans city boosters quoted in John Adams Paxton, *New Orleans Directory and Register* (New Orleans, 1822). For the other clothing stores, see the *Louisville Public Advertiser*, Feb. 5, 1823; the *Louisville Gazette*, Dec. 20, 1825; S. Jones, *Pittsburgh in the Year Eighteen Hundred and Twenty-Six* (Pittsburgh, 1826); and the *Nashville Republican and State Gazette*, March 11 and Oct. 31, 1828. On clothing in New Orleans, see the *New Orleans Annual Advertiser* (New Orleans: Stephen E. Percy & Co., 1832); Feldman, "New York's Men's Clothing Trade, 1800–1861," pp. 76–78; Taylor, *Transportation Revolution*, pp. 9, 107, and 164; Margaret Myers, *The New York Money Market* (New York: Columbia University Press, 1931), 1:43–44; and Albion, *Rise of New York Port*, pp. 95–96, 118–19. For a good description of the continental credit system and the New York–New Orleans axis, see the *United States Magazine and Democratic Review* 2, no. 6 (May 1838): 116–18; and Albert O. Greef, *The Commercial Paper House in the United States* (Cambridge, Mass.: Harvard University Press, 1938), pp. 15–17.

22. Edwin T. Freedley, *Leading Pursuits and Leading Men: A Treatise on the Principal Trades and Manufactures of the United States* (Philadelphia: Edward Young, 1854), p. 90. See also Jones, *Middlemen in the Domestic Trade*, pp. 10–11, 49; Ralph M. Hower, "Urban Retailing in 1850," in Stanley J. Shapiro and Alton F. Doody, comps., *Readings in the History of American Marketing, Settlement to Civil War* (Homewood, Ill.: Richard Irwin, 1968), p. 296; Glenn Porter and Harold C. Livesay, *Merchants and Manufacturers: Studies in the Changing Structure of Nineteenth-Century Marketing* (Baltimore: Johns Hopkins University Press, 1971), pp. 7, 10, and 21–22; Diane Lindstrom, *Economic Development in the Philadelphia Region, 1810–1850* (New York: Columbia University Press, 1978), p. 3; and Thomas C. Cochran, *Two Hundred Years of American Business* (New York: Basic Books, 1977), pp. 14–15, 29.

23. See Stuart Bruchey, *Cotton and the Growth of the American Economy: Sources and*

Readings (New York: Harcourt, Brace & World, 1967), pp. 241–45; *Augusta Chronicle and Sentinel*, July 15, 1829; March 8, 1833; and April 19, 1834; John A. James, *Money and Capital Markets in Postbellum America* (Princeton, N.J.: Princeton University Press, 1978), pp. 51–54; North, *Economic Growth of the United States*, pp. 66–71; and Meinig, *Shaping of America*, pp. 241, 286, and 324. On the mechanics of financing interregional exchange in the 1820s and 1830s, see Peter Temin, *The Jacksonian Economy* (New York: W. W. Norton, 1969), pp. 44–112.

24. On these Broad Street establishments, see Linda Ellen Peters, "A Study of the Architecture of Augusta, Georgia, 1735–1860" (Ph.D. dissertation, University of Georgia, 1983), pp. 104–5; *Augusta Chronicle and Sentinel*, July 9, Nov. 8, Nov. 22, and Dec. 27, 1834; Feb. 7, March 21, May 30, Aug. 29, and Oct. 17, 1835; May 28, and Sept. 24, 1836; Jan. 26, Feb. 6, Feb. 16, March 27, and Oct. 23, 1837. See also the *Georgian*, May 1, 1829; May 3, 1830; May 3, 1831; and April 14, 1837; and the *Charleston Directory and Register, 1835–36* (Charleston, S.C.: D. J. Dowling, 1835–36).

25. James M. Edney, of New York, N.Y., letter book to Francis H. Cooke, of Augusta, Georgia, 1835–37, letters of Feb. 3, 1836, and Oct. 21, 1835, Special Collections, Rutgers University, New Brunswick, N.J.; *Augusta Chronicle and Sentinel*, Nov. 1, 1823 (for William Hills's advertisement).

26. *Augusta Chronicle and Sentinel*, Jan. 26, 1837. Edney to Cooke, letters of Nov. 11, 1837, and Oct. 31, 1835; *New York As It Is, in 1833, and Citizens' Advertising Directory*, ed. Edwin Williams (New York: J. Disturnell, 1833); Charles C. Jones, *Memorial History of Augusta, Georgia* (Syracuse, N.Y.: D. Mason & Co., 1890), p. 172.

27. See the *Augusta Chronicle and Sentinel*, Jan. 26, 1837; Edney to Cooke, letter of Nov. 21, 1835. See also the *Chronicle and Sentinel* for Jan. 27, March 27, and Oct. 23, 1837. On the growth of the provincial market in these years, see Lindstrom, *Economic Development*, pp. 12–17.

28. See Bernard Bailyn, *Voyagers to the West: A Passage in the Peopling of America on the Eve of the Revolution* (New York: Albert A. Knopf, 1986), p. 14; Meinig, *Shaping of America*, p. 232, 351; John Beaucamp Jones [Luke Shortfield], *The Western Merchant* (Philadelphia: Grigg, Elliot & Co., 1849), p. 80; and H. S. Tanner, *A Description of the Canals and Railroads of the United States* (New York: T. R. Tanner and J. Disturnell, 1840), pp. 173–74. For E. D. Cooke's debtors, see the *Georgia Journal*, Jan. 30, 1831, and June 13, 1833. On general stores, see business records, box 3, item 8, and box 31, item 6, Warshaw Collection of Business Paraphernalia, Smithsonian Institution, Washington, D.C.; James Shorter Papers, collection no. 1091, letter of Aug. 20, 1826, Georgia Historical Society, Savannah, Ga.; Lewis E. Atherton, *The Southern Country Store, 1800–1860* (Baton Rouge: Louisiana State University Press, 1949), pp. 84–85; and Freedley, *Leading Pursuits and Leading Men*, p. 90.

29. Linda Baumgarten, *Eighteenth-Century Clothing at Williamsburg* (Williamsburg, Va.: Colonial Williamsburg Foundation, 1986), p. 204. These unfitted garments are to be distinguished from "Negro" clothing, which could include "suits" of "blue jackets and trowsers, well lined" (*The Georgian*, Nov. 27, 1823). See also Ann DuPont, "Textile and Apparel Management Functions Performed by Women in the Nineteenth-Century Plantation South," *Ars Textrina* 18 (Dec. 1992): 55–56; Gerilyn Tandberg, "Field-Hand Clothing in Louisiana and Mississippi During the Ante-Bellum Period," *Dress* 6 (1980): 89–90; Joan M. Jensen,

"Needlework as Art, Craft, and Livelihood Before 1900," in *A Needle, a Bobbin, a Strike: Women Needleworkers in America*, ed. Joan M. Jensen and Sue Davidson (Philadelphia: Temple University Press, 1984), p. 9; Ordonez, "A Frontier Reflected in Costume," pp. 180–83; and the *New York Herald*, Sept. 3, 1836.

30. See Myron O. Stachine, " 'For the Sake of Commerce': Rhode Island, Slavery, and the Textile Industry," pamphlet accompanying the 1982 exhibit "The Loom and the Lash," Museum of Rhode Island History, Providence, R.I. See also Isaac Lippincott, "A History of Manufactures of the Ohio Valley, to 1860" (Ph.D. dissertation, University of Chicago, 1912), pp. 169–70. On army production, see the National Archives, RG 92, Records of the Office of the Quartermaster General, entry no. 225 (Consolidated Correspondence File, 1794–1915).

31. See Edney to Cooke, letters of March 26, April 30, and Feb. 27, 1836. See also letters of June 28 and July 25, 1835; March 19, 1836; and March 31 and Sept. 26, 1837.

32. See Caroline F. Ware, *The Early New England Cotton Manufacture: A Study in Industrial Beginnings* (Boston: Houghton Mifflin, 1931), p. 31. See also Edney to Cooke, letters of Oct. 3, Oct. 10, Oct. 25, and Dec. 26, 1835; March 19 and Oct. 7, 1836; and Jan. 27, 1837; and the *Augusta Chronicle and Sentinel*, Feb. 16 and March 27, 1837.

33. Hansjorg Siegenthaler, "What Price Style? The Fabric-Advisory Function of the Drygoods Commission Merchant, 1850–1880," *Business History Review* 41, no. 1 (1967): 38. "Capitalist realism" is borrowed from Michael Schudson, as quoted in Arjun Appadurai, "Introduction," in *The Social Life of Things: Commodities in Cultural Perspective* (Cambridge: Cambridge University Press, 1986).

34. Edney to Cooke, letters of June 22, 1835; and and Sept. 17, 1836. See also letters of March 21, March 26, April 30, and Aug. 29, 1836.

35. Cost estimates are based on Patricia A. Trautman, "Captain Edward Marrett, a Gentleman Tailor" (Ph.D. dissertation, University of Colorado, 1982); John Shephard, of New York, N.Y., Merchant Tailoring Accounts, Ac. 861 and Ac. 1721, Special Collections, Rutgers University, New Brunswick, N.J.; Edney to Cooke, letter of Feb. 13, 1836; U.S. Census Office, Seventh Census (1850), Products of Industry, raw data, New York County, N.Y. On fluctuations in cloth prices, see the National Archives, RG 92, Records of the Office of the Quartermaster General, entry no. 2118 (special items, check lists, indexes, etc., 1830–33).

36. Edney to Cooke, letter of Nov. 14, 1837. See also letters of Aug. 11, Sept. 19, and Oct. 21, 1837, and, for more on the cloth supply, letters of Oct. 31, 1835; Jan. 9, Feb. 27, Feb. 29, April 2, April 23, and Aug. 19, 1836; and Jan. 21, March 1, Nov. 24, and Dec. 12, 1837. See, in addition, Cole, *American Wool Manufacture*, 1:289–91; Porter and Livesay, *Merchants and Manufacturers*, p. 27; "Staples and Clarke" in *Classified Mercantile Directory for the Cities of New-York and Brooklyn* (New York: J. Disturnell, 1837); Lewis E. Atherton, "The Problem of Credit Rating in the Ante-Bellum South," *Journal of Southern History* 12, no. 4 (Nov. 1946): 536–37, 550; and the *Augusta Directory, 1841* (Augusta, Ga.: W. B. Kuhlke, 1841). On the personal dynamic of credit arrangements in these years, see Asa Greene, *The Perils of Pearl Street, Including a Taste of the Dangers of Wall Street* (New York: Betts & Anstice, and Peter Hill, 1834), pp. 116–24.

37. George Gifford, *Before the Honorable Philip F. Thomas . . . in the Matter of the Application of Elias Howe, Jr., for an Extension of His Patent for Sewing Machines* (New York: W. W. Rose, 1860), p. 1; Rolla Milton Tryon, *Household Manufactures in the United States,*

1640–1860 (New York: Augustus M. Kelley, 1966 [1917]), pp. 298–300, 370–75; *Hunt's Merchant's Magazine*, Oct. 1840, p. 308; William Cronon, *Nature's Metropolis: Chicago and the Great West* (New York: W. W. Norton, 1991), p. 61.

38. *Hunt's Merchant's Magazine*, Oct. 1840, pp. 305–10 (the quotations are from pp. 307 and 305); Winifred Barr Rothenberg, *From Market-Places to a Market Economy: The Transformation of Rural Massachusetts, 1750–1850* (Chicago: University of Chicago Press), p. 4. See also Jean-Christophe Agnew, *Worlds Apart: The Market and the Theater in Anglo-American Thought, 1550–1750* (Cambridge: Cambridge University Press, 1986), pp. 17–55.

39. Tocqueville quoted in Marvin Meyers, *The Jacksonian Persuasion: Politics and Belief* (New York: Vintage Books, 1957), p. 131; Mary Austin Holley, "The Gentry of Texas," in *The Leaven of Democracy: The Growth of the Democratic Spirit in the Time of Jackson*, ed. Clement Eaton (New York: George Braziller, 1963), pp. 268–69 (for the "great Ball" in Valesco, Texas); *Augusta Chronicle and Sentinel*, Jan. 9 and May 28, 1936; Edney to Cooke, letter of June 28, 1835. See also Cronon, *Nature's Metropolis*, p. 61; Carolyn R. Shine, "Hunting Shirts and Silk Stockings: Clothing Early Cincinnati," *Queen City Heritage* 45, no. 3 (fall 1987): 45–46; Tryon, *Household Manufactures*, pp. 298–300, 370–75; Thomas Ford, *A History of Illinois, from Its Commencement as a State in 1818 to 1847*, ed. Milo Milton Quaife (Chicago: R. R. Donnelley & Sons, 1945), pp. 129–30; Meinig, *Shaping of America*, p. 223; Gilbert, "East Tennessee Dress," pp. 39–42; *United States Economist, and Dry Goods Reporter*, Nov. 6, 1852, and May 7, 1853; Lewis E. Atherton, *The Frontier Merchant in Mid-America* (Columbia: University of Missouri Press, 1971), p. 67, and *The Southern Country Store, 1800–1860* (Baton Rouge: Louisiana State University Press, 1949), p. 133; and the *Iowa News*, July 1, 1837. In addition, see the Samuel Lane advertisement in the *Charleston Directory and Register, 1835–36*; Ordonez, "A Frontier Reflected in Costume," pp. 30–31, 150–52; Christiana Holmes Tillson, *A Woman's Story of Pioneer Illinois*, ed. Milo Milton Quaife (Chicago: R. R. Donnelley & Sons, 1919), p. 85; *Augusta Chronicle and Sentinel*, March 24, 1832; Aug. 2, July 11, and Aug. 29, 1835; and B. Read and H. Bodman, *Description of the Gentlemen's Winter Fashions* (New York: By the authors, 1836).

40. See Eugene D. Genovese, "The Janus Face of Merchant Capital," in *The Fruits of Merchant Capital: Slavery and Bourgeois Property in the Rise and Expansion of Capitalism*, by Eugene D. Genovese and Elizabeth Fox-Genovese (New York: Oxford University Press, 1983), pp. 5–25; Harry L. Watson, "Slavery and Development in a Dual Economy: The South and the Market Revolution," in *The Market Revolution in America: Social, Political, and Religious Expressions, 1800–1880*, ed. Melvin Stokes and Stephen Conway (Charlottesville: University Press of Virgina, 1996), pp. 43–73; and Douglas R. Egerton, "Markets Without a Market Revolution: Southern Planters and Capitalism," *Journal of the Early Republic* 16 (summer 1996): 207–21.

41. *New York Sun*, Sept. 11, 1835. See also Asa Greene, *A Glance at New York* (New York: A. Greene, 1837), pp. 132–34.

42. Advertisements for Young & Van Eps, *New York Herald*, June 7 and July 7, 1836; advertisements for Hobby, Husted & Co., *New York Herald*, May 7 and April 30, 1836; *New York Sun*, Nov. 19, 1835, and *New York Herald*, May 7, 1836 (for "girls . . . to do fancy work in the house"); Helen Sumner, *History of Women in Industry in the United States*, 61st Congress, 2d sess., Senate Doc. no. 645, 94:121. On the production frenzy, see the *New York Transcript*,

Aug. 21 and Sept. 15, 1835; the *New York Herald*, March 4, May 7, June 7, and July 7, 1836; the *New York Sun*, Sept. 11 and Sept. 26, 1835; Jan. 6, April 26, and May 25, 1836; and the *Morning Courier and New-York Enquirer*, May 24, 1836.

43. Edney to Cooke, letters of Feb. 13 and Dec. 31, 1836; Jan. 6 and Jan. 11, 1838.

44. Richard S. Rosenbloom, "A Conjecture about Fashion and Vertical Process Integration," *Business History Review* 37, nos. 1–2 (1963): 94–95; Edney to Cooke, letters of Oct. 7, 1936, and March 1, 1837. On F. J. Conant's buying strategy, see Feldman, "New York's Men's Clothing Trade," p. 25. See also the *New York Herald*, Feb. 18 and July 7, 1836; and the *Morning Courier and New-York Enquirer*, May 24, 1836.

45. *Working Man's Advocate*, June 10, 1831; *Philadelphia Public Ledger*, Sept. 21, 1837.

46. Edney to Cooke, letter of April 22, 1837. See also Davis Rich Dewey, *Financial History of the United States* (New York: Longmans, Green, 1907), p. 225; Atherton, *Southern Country Store*, pp. 21–22. On these commercial stratagems more generally, see Greene, *Perils of Pearl Street*. On the easiness with which neophytes from the South could obtain credit in New York, see Joseph G. Baldwin, *The Flush Times of Alabama and Mississippi* (New York: Sagamore Press, 1957).

47. Channing quoted in David G. Pugh, *Sons of Liberty: The Masculine Mind in Nineteenth-Century America* (Westport, Conn.: Greenwood Press, 1983), p. 4.

48. Cathy Matson and Peter Onuf, "Toward a Republican Empire: Interest and Ideology in Revolutionary America," *American Quarterly* 32, no. 4 (fall 1985): 520; *Hunt's Merchant's Magazine*, Oct. 1840, p. 309–10; Everett quoted in Gordon S. Wood, *The Radicalism of the American Revolution* (New York: Alfred A. Knopf, 1992), p. 359; Robert Remini, ed., *The Age of Jackson* (New York: Harper and Row, 1972), p. 53 (quoting Jackson's Maysville veto of 1830). See also the discussion of "Weber's last theory of capitalism," in Randall Collins, *Weberian Sociological Theory* (Cambridge: Cambridge University Press, 1986), pp. 19–44. One should not overstate the frontier's self-sufficiency with regard to clothing prior to the ready-made era, however. See, for instance, Elizabeth A. Perkins, "The Consumer Frontier: Household Consumption in Early Kentucky," *Journal of American History* 78, no. 2 (Sept. 1991): 486–510.

49. See Linton Wells, "The House of Seligman," typescript, 1931, New-York Historical Society, New York, pp. 1–56; Jesse Seligman, *In Memorium*, 1894 (printed for private circulation), pp. 9–14, 131–32; Leslie Meyers Zomalt, "An Exercise in Caution: The Business Activities of the Joseph Seligman Family in the Nineteenth-Century American West" (Ph.D. dissertation, University of California at Santa Barbara, 1979), pp. 8–9, 21–27, 30–31, and 36–40; *New York County*, vol. 198, pp. 130, 137, and 167; and *Green County, Alabama*, vol. 11, p. 255, in the R. G. Dun & Co. Collection, Baker Library, Harvard University Graduate School of Business Administration, Cambridge, Mass.; and Chauncey M. Depew, ed., *One Hundred Years of American Commerce, 1795–1895* (New York: D. O. Haynes & Co., 1895), p. 562. There were any number of similar stories. See, for instance, Haiman Spitz's experience, as recorded in Jacob Rader Marcus, *Memoirs of American Jews, 1775–1865* (New York: Ktav Publishing House, 1974), pp. 291–99.

50. Complaint of the "country tailor" quoted in the *New York Tribune*, June 16, 1849; Singer advertisement, *Valley Farmer* (Louisville), Sept. 1856; *Mirror of Fashion*, vol. 12, no. 5 (May 1850), pp. 33–34 (and see vol. 11, no. 11 [Nov. 1849]); *Hunt's Merchant's Magazine*,

Jan. 1849, p. 116; *United States Economist, and Dry Goods Reporter*, Nov. 6, 1852. See also Lillian Schlissel, Byrd Gibbens, and Elizabeth Hampsten, eds., *Far from Home: Families of the Westward Journey* (New York: Schocken Books, 1989), p. 39; and Freedley, *Leading Pursuits and Leading Men*, p. 90. Clothing was also a favored item for trade with Indians on the way west. See Maria Barbara McMartin, "Dress of the Oregon Trail Emigrants, 1843 to 1855" (M.S. thesis, Iowa State University, 1977), pp. 24–25.

51. *Hunt's Merchant's Magazine*, Jan. 1849, p. 116; Devlin advertisement in *Wilson's Illustrated Guide to the Hudson River, 1849* (New York, 1849). Biographical facts appear in Devlin's *New York Times* obituary, Feb. 23, 1867. See also "Devlin" in *Sheldon & Co.'s Business or Advertising Directory, 1845* (New York: John F. Trow & Co., 1845); and William E. Devlin, "Shrewd Irishmen: Irish Entrepreneurs and Artisans in New York's Clothing Industry, 1830–1880," in *The New York Irish*, ed. Ronald H. Bayor and Timothy J. Meagher (Baltimore: Johns Hopkins University Press, 1996), p. 184.

52. Freedley, *Leading Pursuits and Leading Men*, pp. 97–98. See also *New York County*, vol. 198, p. 196, and vol. 365, p. 123, in the R. G. Dun & Co. Collection, Baker Library, Harvard University Graduate School of Business Administration, Cambridge, Mass. For a photo of Devlin's store, see Mary Black, *Old New York in Early Photographs* (New York: Dover Publications, 1973), p. 52. A receipt issued by Devlin can be found in men's clothing, box 4, "Devlin," Warshaw Collection of Business Paraphernalia, Smithsonian Institution, Washington, D.C.

53. Freedley, *Leading Pursuits and Leading Men*, pp. 97–98. See also *Hunt's Merchant's Magazine*, Jan. 1849, p. 116; the *New York Herald*, April 18, 1852; and Stanley Chapman, "The Innovative Entrepreneurs in the British Ready-Made Clothing Industry," *Textile History* 24, no. 1 (1993): 20.

54. J. C. Gobright, *The New-York Sketch Book and Merchant's Guide* (New York, 1859), pp. 44–45, for Wilde & Co.; for the two "magnificent" hotels, see William Hancock, *An Emigrant's Five Years in the Free States of America* (London: T. Cautley Newby, 1860), p. 36; advertisements in *Boyd's Pictorial Directory of Broadway, 1859* (New York: Andrew Boyd, 1859). See also illustration of Grand Street store, box 01, BB.1, F6, Brooks Brothers Archive, Chantilly, Va.; Moses Beach, *The Wealthy Citizens of the City of New York*, 13th ed. (New York: Sun Office, 1855), p. 14; "New York Daguerreotyped," *Putnam's Monthly: A Magazine of Literature, Science, and Art*, Feb. 1853, p. 128; and the *United States Economist, and Dry Goods Reporter*, May 7, 1853. During these years Lord and Taylor opened an equally ornate palace at Broadway and Grand (*New-York Illustrated News*, Sept. 1, 1860). Concerts were performed at the City Assembly Room just above Grand Street: see George Templeton Strong, *The Diary of George Templeton Strong, Young Man in New York, 1835–1849*, ed. Allan Nevins (New York: Macmillan Company, 1952), entry for Nov. 9, 1859. On the neighborhood of Grand and Broadway, see Timothy Gilfoyle, *City of Eros: New York City, Prostitution, and the Commercialization of Sex, 1790–1920* (New York: W. W. Norton, 1994), pp. 120–21.

55. "The Clothing Manufacture," *Bulletin of the National Association of Wool Manufacturers* 4, no. 11 (April–June 1873): 124 (and see pp. 126, 130–33). See also *Eighty Years' Progress of the United States* (Hartford, Conn.: L. Stebbins, 1869), p. 309; N. S. B. Gras and Henrietta M. Larson, *Casebook in American Business History* (New York: F. S. Crofts and Co., 1939), pp. 687–68; Fred Mitchell Jones, *Middlemen in the Domestic Trade of the United States, 1800–*

1860 (Urbana: University of Illinois, 1937), pp. 10–11; and Porter and Livesay, *Merchants and Manufacturers*, p. 74.

56. See *New York County*, vol. 198, pp. 114, 149; vol. 199, pp. 208, 263, 280, and 294; and vol. 203, pp. 666, 676; *Charleston, South Carolina*, vol. 6, pp. 174, 175; *St. Louis, Missouri*, vol. 1, pt. 1, pp. 57, 234, and vol. 1, pt. 2, p. 369; *Tennessee (Cocke County)*, vol. 4, pp. 80, 112; and *North Carolina (Buncombe County)*, vol. 4, p. 114, in the R. G. Dun & Co. Collection, Baker Library, Harvard University Graduate School of Business Administration, Cambridge, Mass. See also U.S. Census Office, Seventh Census (1850), Population Schedule, Buncombe County, North Carolina, p. 192; *Morning Courier and New-York Enquirer*, July 20, 1850, for Brooks Brothers; and Feldman, "New York's Men's Clothing Trade," pp. 45–46. In fact, there were a whole variety of ways to move into cloth. The firm of Tweedy, Moulton, and Plimpton, dry-goods importers and jobbers, merged with the business of William Gardner, a ready-made clothing dealer. Another cloth house hired the chronically indebted Davenport & Gardner, a custom-tailoring business, to produce an entire stock of clothing for them on commission. In 1851 the successful dry-goods jobbers Gould Germond & Co. went into clothing manufacturing. In 1850 the clothier Charles Horton became a partner in the dry-goods firm of P. C. Barnum & Co., while Peter Barnum's brother, Joshua, was made a partner in Horton's clothing business. See entries on Pfeiffer, Hirsch, Davenport & Gardner, Gould Germond, and P. C. Barnum in the New York Trade Agency's ledger "for the exclusive use and benefit of Mr.s Bernard, Balmforth & Co.," Feb. 6, 1851, New-York Historical Society, New York.

57. Opdyke also ended up in banking, having been elected the first Republican mayor of New York in 1861 (*Men's Wear*, 60th anniversary issue, Feb. 10, 1950, p. 199). On Opdyke's and Scott's businesses, see *New York County*, vol. 198, p. 195; vol. 200, p. 364; vol. 365, p. 184; and vol. 369, p. 585, in the R. G. Dun & Co. Collection, Baker Library, Harvard University Graduate School of Business Administration, Cambridge, Mass. See also *New York County*, vol. 197, p. 78; vol. 198, p. 129; and vol. 200, p. 364; *Tennessee (Shelby County)*, vol. 29, p. 12; and *Louisiana (New Orleans)*, vol. 10, p. 363, also in the R. G. Dun & Co. Collection; the *New-York Illustrated News*, Dec. 10, 1859; Opdyke's obituary in the *New York Times*, June 13, 1880; and George Wilson, *Portrait Gallery of the Chamber of Commerce of the State of New York* (New York: Press of the Chamber of Commerce, 1890), pp. 60–61.

58. *United States Economist, and Dry Goods Reporter*, Nov. 6, 1852. See also U.S. Census Office, *Manufactures of the United States in 1860*, p. xiv; Jones, *Middlemen in the Domestic Trade*, p. 13; men's clothing, box 11, "Reed, Brothers & Company," Warshaw Collection of Business Paraphernalia, Smithsonian Institution, Washington, D.C.; Samuel Terry, *How to Keep a Store* (New York: Fowler & Wells, 1891), p. 75; Freedley, *Leading Pursuits and Leading Men*, p. 90; and Joseph H. Appel, *The Business Biography of John Wanamaker, Founder and Builder* (New York: Macmillan Company, 1939), pp. 45–46. In addition, see the *United States Economist, and Dry Goods Reporter* for May 8, June 12, July 31, and Aug. 14, 1852; Feb. 26, May 7, and May 28, 1853; and Jan. 7, Jan. 14, Aug. 12, and Sept. 2, 1854; the *New York Herald*, Oct. 21, 1857; and Cole, *American Woolen Industry*, 1:272, 286, and 294–95.

Chapter Three

1. On the nineteenth century's clothing revolution, see William C. Browning, "The Clothing and Furnishing Trade," in *One Hundred Years of American Commerce, 1795–1895*,

ed. Chauncey M. Depew (New York: D. O. Haynes & Co., 1895), pp. 561–65. Thomas P. Kettel, "Cothing Trade," in *Eighty Years' Progress of the United States* (Hartford, Conn.: L. Stebbins, 1869), pp. 309–11; Horace Greeley et al., *The Great Industries of the United States* (Hartford, Conn., J. B. Burr & Hyde, 1872), pp. 587–92. For similar perspectives, see "The Clothing Trade," *Hunt's Merchant's Magazine*, March 1864, p. 233; U.S. Census Office, *Manufactures of the United States in 1860, Compiled from the Original Returns of the Eighth Census* (Washington, D.C.: Government Printing Office, 1865), pp. lix–lxv; Isaac Walker, *Dress: As It Has Been, Is, and Will Be* (New York: Isaac Walker, 1885), pp. 78–79; Jesse Eliphant Pope, *The Clothing Industry in New York* (Columbia: University of Missouri Press, 1905); Egal Feldman, *Fit for Men* (Washington, D.C.: Public Affairs Press, 1961); and Claudia B. Kidwell and Margaret C. Christman, *Suiting Everyone: The Democratization of Clothing in America* (Washington, D.C.: Smithsonian Institution Press, 1974).

2. On preindustrial dressing, see, for instance, Jonathan Prude, "To Look upon the 'Lower Sort': Runaway Ads and the Appearance of Unfree Laborers in America, 1750–1800," *Journal of American History* 78, no. 1 (June 1991): 124–59; Carole Shammas, *The Pre-Industrial Consumer in England and America* (Oxford: Clarendon Press, 1990).

3. Nathaniel Whittock, *The Complete Book of Trades* (London: John Bennett, 1837), p. 430. On the reputation of ready-made clothing, see Beverly Lemire, "Redressing the History of the Clothing Trade in England: Ready-Made Clothing, Guilds, and Women Workers, 1650–1800," *Dress* 21 (1994): 62–64.

4. See John Pintard, *Letters from John Pintard to His Daughter* (New York: New-York Historical Society, 1940), 2:112 (letter of Dec. 7, 1821); Joseph Couts, *A Practical Guide for the Tailor's Cutting-Room* (London: Blackie and Son, 1848), p. 60.

5. See "tailors" and "clothiers" in *Doggett's New York Business Directory for 1841–42* (New York: John Doggett, 1841–42); *Doggett's New York Business Directory for 1844–45* (New York: John Doggett, 1844–45); and *Sheldon & Co.'s Business or Advertising Directory, 1845* (New York: John F. Trow & Co., 1845). The division of men's clothing stores into "clothiers" and "tailors" was less strict in the business directories of the 1830s. See, for instance, *New York As It Is, in 1833, and Citizens' Advertising Directory*, ed. Edwin Williams (New York: J. Disturnell, 1833).

6. *Brooks Brothers Centenary, 1818–1918* (New York: Brooks Brothers, 1918); Feldman, *Fit for Men*, pp. 31–32; advertisement, box 01, BB.1, F10, Brooks Brothers Archive, Chantilly, Va. Henry's transformation from a grocer into a clothier can be followed in his personal listing in the annual editions of *Longworth's American Almanac, New-York Register, and City Directory, 1805–19* (New York: David Longworth, 1805–19). Equally revealing was Brooks Brothers' celebration of its 175th anniversary in 1993, which again featured a company history, albeit now in the form of a video produced by the History Factory, Chantilly, Virginia. Revising the earlier version of events, the video, which was shown in all the company's stores, reinstated Henry Brooks's commercial, as opposed to artisanal, pedigree. Apparently in the 1990s there was no longer any reason to conceal the founder's canny entrepreneurialism.

7. Thus the industrial taxonomy used in the manufacturing schedule of the 1850 census perspicaciously assigned clothiers and tailors to the same production category.

8. See Edgar Allan Poe, "The Business Man," in Poe, *Comedies and Satires* (New York:

Penguin Books, 1987), pp. 100–108. Charles Baudelaire described Poe as a man "who regarded Progress, that great idea of modern times, as an idiot's delight." See "Edgar Allan Poe," in Charles Baudelaire, *The Painter of Modern Life and Other Essays*, trans. Jonathan Mayne (New York: De Capo, 1986), pp. 69–110 (the quote is from p. 73). See also Kenneth Silverman, *Edgar A. Poe: Mournful and Never-Ending Remembrance* (New York: Harper Perennial, 1991), pp. 219–30.

9. Poe, "The Business Man," pp. 102–3. On the early provenance of tailors' tricks, see *Character of a Pilfering Tailor, or a True Anatomy of Monsieur Stitch, in All His Tricks and Qualities* (London, 1675). See also *Hunt's Merchant's Magazine*, July 1854, p. 138.

10. *New York Tribune*, Nov. 15, 1845.

11. *New York Herald*, Sept. 14, 1841 (and see May 7, 1841; and June 2, 1844).

12. *New York Tribune*, Oct. 3, 1845 (and see July 22, 1844). For Booth's $30,000, see *New York County*, vol. 365, p. 102, and vol. 198, p. 127, in the R. G. Dun & Co. Collection, Baker Library, Harvard University Graduate School of Business Administration, Cambridge, Mass.

13. *New Mirror*, Jan. 27, 1844 ("opposite the Fountain"); *New York Tribune*, March 7, 1845. See also William Jennings's advertisement in *Sheldon & Co.'s Business or Advertising Directory, 1845*; Nathaniel Parker Willis, "Ephemera," in *Dashes at Life with a Free Pencil* (New York: J. S. Redfield, 1847), pp. 56–57. Jennings is also mentioned in Edgar Allen Poe's story "Some Words with a Mummy," *American Review*, April 1845. On the commercialization of Broadway in the 1830s and 1840s, see Eleanor Ewart Southworth, "Mirrors for a Growing Metropolis: Printed Views of Broadway, 1830–1850" (M.A. thesis, University of Delaware, 1985), p. 76.

14. Jennings advertisement, *New York Tribune*, Oct. 3, 1845. On the growth of demand in these years, even during the deflation of the early 1840s, see Peter Temin, *The Jacksonian Economy* (New York: W. W. Norton, 1969). As an English retailer wrote a few years later: "The same amount of capital is made to do a greater quantity of work than before. In fact, the substitution of quick for slow sales is precisely like an improvement in machinery which cheapens the cost of production." Quoted in Dorothy Davis, *A History of Shopping* (London: Routledge & Kegan Paul, 1966), p. 259.

15. *New York Tribune* quoted in Asa Greene, *A Glance at New York* (New York: A. Greene, 1837), pp. 132–34; Nathaniel Parker Willis, "Walk in Broadway," *New Mirror*, Oct. 21, 1843; *Aurora*, "Extra" edition, Feb. 1842; advertisements for Martin's tailoring shop, *New York Herald*, Aug. 2, 1841, and May 22, 1842. On George Foster, see Peter Buckley, "To the Opera House: Culture and Society in New York City, 1820–1860" (Ph.D. dissertation, State University of New York at Stony Brook, 1984), pp. 145–46.

16. Advertisement for Martin's tailoring shop, *New York Herald*, May 22, 1842; Samuel Terry, *How to Keep a Store* (New York: Fowler & Wells, 1891), pp. 71–72, 149–50 ("As he parts with these goods" is from p. 150). See also Diane Lindstrom, *Economic Development in the Philadelphia Region, 1810–1850* (New York: Columbia University Press, 1978), p. 12; Stephen N. Elias, *Alexander T. Stewart: The Forgotten Merchant Prince* (Westport, Conn: Praeger, 1992), p. 21; David Alexander, *Retailing in England During the Industrial Revolution* (London: Athlone Press, 1970), pp. 161–65, 173–85; Ralph Hower, *History of Macy's of New York, 1858–1919* (Cambridge, Mass.: Harvard University Press, 1943), pp. 18–21; Carol Halpert Schwartz, "Retail Trade Development in New York State in the Nineteenth Cen-

tury, with Special Reference to the Country Store" (Ph.D. dissertation, Columbia University, 1963), pp. 79–80, 86; and Davis, *History of Shopping*, pp. 187–89.

17. Advertisement for Arthur Levy's Broadway Cash Tailoring Establishment, *New York Herald*, March 23, 1841; *Hunt's Merchant's Magazine*, Dec. 1839, p. 547; William P. M. Ross, *The Accountant's Own Book and Business Man's Manual* (Philadelphia: G. B. Zieber & Co., 1848), p. 17 (and see p. 15); *Hunt's Merchant's Magazine*, Dec. 1853, p. 776.

18. *Niles' Weekly Register*, Oct. 26, 1822.

19. T. S. Arthur, *The Seamstress: A Tale of the Times* (Philadelphia: R. G. Berford, 1843), pp. 26–27.

20. *New York Post*, May 9, 1825. See also George Templeton Strong, *The Diary of George Templeton Strong, Young Man in New York, 1835–1849*, ed. Allan Nevins (New York: Macmillan Company, 1952), entry for Sept. 26, 1836; *Sheldon & Co.'s Business or Advertising Directory, 1845*; *New York Tribune*, Sept. 3, 1850; March 18 and March 29, 1854; Egal Feldman, "New York's Men's Clothing Trade, 1800 to 1861" (Ph.D. dissertation, University of Pennsylvania, 1959), p. 24; and *New York County*, vol. 365, p. 104, in the R. G. Dun & Co. Collection, Baker Library, Harvard University Graduate School of Business Administration, Cambridge, Mass.

21. Cost estimates of tailors' production expenses are based on Patricia A. Trautman, "Captain Edward Marrett, a Gentleman Tailor" (Ph.D. dissertation, University of Colorado, 1982); John Shephard, of New York, N.Y. Merchant Tailoring Accounts, Ac. 861 and Ac. 1721, Special Collections, Rutgers University, New Brunswick, N.J.; James M. Edney, of New York, N.Y., letter book to Francis H. Cooke, of Augusta, Georgia, 1835–37, letter of Feb. 13, 1836, Special Collections, Rutgers University, New Brunswick, N.J.; U.S. Census Office, Seventh Census (1850), Manufactures Schedule, raw data, New York County, N.Y.

22. "In Favor of Increase of Duties on Ready-Made Clothing," April 28, 1828, 20th Congress, 1st sess., Doc. no. 914; "Petition of the Journeymen Tailors of Philadelphia," Jan. 30, 1832, 22d Congress, 1st sess., Doc. no. 39. See also related petitions from 1828: 20th Congress, 1st sess., Doc. no. 918; 20th Congress, 1st sess., Sen. Docs. nos. 181, 182, 188, and 191. On cloths and duties, see the *New York Post*, March 27, 1830; Robert Greenhalgh Albion, with the collaboration of Jennie Barnes Pope, *The Rise of New York Port, 1815–1860* (New York: Charles Scribner's Sons, 1939), p. 64; and F. W. Galton, *Select Documents Illustrating the History of Trade Unionism*, vol. 1, *The Tailoring Trade* (London: Longmans, Green, 1896).

23. T. S. Arthur, "The Trials of a Needlewoman," *Godey's Lady's Book*, April 1854, p. 330.

24. John R. Commons et al., *A Documentary History of American Industrial Society* (Cleveland: Arthur H. Clark, 1910), 4:143 (for a full transcript of the trial, see 4:99–264). See also Galton, *Select Documents*, 1:128; and the *New York Post*, Jan. 2, Feb. 18, and Oct. 21, 1822, and April 29 and May 4, 1824. The strike has also received attention from historians, most recently, and perceptively, Christopher L. Tomlins, *Law, Labor, and Ideology in the Early American Republic* (New York: Cambridge University Press, 1993), pp. 128–79.

25. Edney to Cooke, letter of Sept. 20, 1835. See also the *New-York Daily Sentinel*, Sept. 7, 1831; and the *New York Post*, Oct. 12, 1833.

26. Commons et al., *Documentary History*, 4:315–33; *New York Sun*, May 26, May 28,

and May 30, 1836; Edney to Cooke, letter of June 5, 1835; Tomlins, *Law, Labor, and Ideology*, pp. 128–79.

27. Edney to Cooke, letter of Oct. 21, 1835; *New York Herald*, July 15, 1841.

28. See Commons et al., *Documentary History*, 4:327–33, which reproduces Judge Edwards's ruling. See also the *New York Sun*, May 26, 28, and 30, 1836; *New-York American*, Feb. 9, 1836; *Morning Courier and New-York Enquirer*, May 31, 1836. On the slate rule, see Galton, *Select Documents*, 1:lix, lxxxi, and 89–90; Barbara Taylor, " 'The Men Are as Bad as Their Masters . . .': Socialism, Feminism and Sexual Antagonism in the London Tailoring Trade in the 1830s," in *Sex and Class in Women's History*, ed. Judith L. Newton, Mary P. Ryan, and Judith R. Walkowitz (London: Routledge & Kegan Paul, 1983), pp. 206–14.

29. *New York Herald*, July 23, 1844; see also Feb. 25, 1836. On the tailors' strikes of 1844, see the *Working Man's Advocate*, July 27 and Aug. 3, 1844. On a shift in the capital-labor paradigm that could explain the *Herald*'s changed point of view, see Tomlins, *Law, Labor, and Ideology*, pp. 128–79.

30. *Mirror of Fashion*, n.s., vol. 3, no. 1 (Jan. 1855), pp. 1–2; and n.s., vol. 1, no. 10 (Oct. 1853), p. 1. See also the *Mirror of Fashion*, vol. 12, no. 5 (May 1850), p. 33; Anne Hollander, *Sex and Suits* (New York: Alfred A. Knopf, 1994), pp. 5–9, 88–92; and George P. Fox, *Fashion: The Power That Influences the World*, 3d ed. (New York: Sheldon & Co., 1872), pp. 120–22.

31. Willis, "Ephemera," in *Dashes at Life with a Free Pencil*, pp. 10, 19.

32. *New York Tribune*, July 22, 1844; *Sheldon & Co.'s Business or Advertising Directory, 1845*; Edney to Cooke, Oct. 3, 1835. See also Edwin T. Freedley, *Philadelphia and Its Manufactures* (Philadelphia: Edward Young, 1858), p. 221; Francis Wyse, *America, Its Realities and Resources* (London: T. C. Newby, 1846), 3:20. In 1835, Edney paid his cutter $1,000 (Edney to Cooke, letters of Oct. 3, Oct. 25, and Oct. 26, 1835). By the end of the next decade, cutters' salaries had reached $2,000 (*Mirror of Fashion*, vol. 11, no. 11 [Nov. 1849], p. 1). On the importance of a cutter's reputation, see the Ryder Brothers' advertisement in the *New York Herald*, June 25, 1844, and also that of "a cutter" in the *New York Herald*, March 21, 1855. See also the *Mirror of Fashion*, n.s., vol. 3, no. 3 (March 1855), pp. 21–22.

33. Couts, *Practical Guide for the Tailor's Cutting-Room*, pp. 62–63.

34. J. M. Bostian, *Directions for Measuring and Drafting Garments* (Sunbury: By the author, 1850), p. 3.

35. *Mirror of Fashion*, n.s., vol. 1 (1853), p. 30; Linda Morton, "American Pattern Drafting Systems for Men in the Nineteenth Century" (M.A. thesis, Colorado State University, 1981), p. 34; W. H. Stinemets, *A Complete and Permanent System of Cutting* (New York: Narine & Co., 1844), n.p.; Stinemets advertisement, *New York Herald*, May 1, 1846 (and see May 31, 1844, and May 2, 1845); U.S. Patent Office, letters patent no. 415, Sept. 28, 1837; Francis Mahan, *Mahan's Protractor and Proof Systems of Garment Cutting*, Spring and Summer Report for 1839, no. 8 (Philadelphia), p. 10.

36. Claudia B. Kidwell, *Cutting a Fashionable Fit: Dressmakers' Draftmaking Systems in the United States* (Washington, D.C.: Smithsonian Institution Press, 1979), pp. 129–33. See also Morton, "American Pattern Drafting Systems," pp. 34–35.

37. Fitzmaurice advertisement, *New York Herald*, Aug. 21, 1841; "List of Premiums Awarded by the Managers of the Fifteenth Annual Fair," American Institute Papers, case no. 4, New-York Historical Society, New York. See also T. Oliver's and H. Levett's adver-

tisements to New York tailors, *New York Herald*, Aug. 27 and Sept. 9, 1841, and April 13, 1848; Feldman, "New York's Men's Clothing Trade," p. 190. In addition, see George Gifford, *Before the Honorable Philip F. Thomas . . . in the Matter of the Application of Elias Howe, Jr., for an Extension of His Patent for Sewing Machines* (New York: W. W. Rose, 1860), p. 15; B. Read and H. Bodman, *New Superlative System of Cutting* (London and New York, 1837); *J. S. Bonham's Improved Garment Cutter for 1853* (Knoxville, Tenn., 1853), quoted in Morton, "American Pattern Drafting Systems," p. 34; *New York Herald*, May 1, 1846; and B. T. Pierson, *Directory of Newark* (Newark, N.J.: Price & Lee Co., 1846–47).

38. Stinemets advertisement, *New York Herald*, May 1, 1846; Sanford & Knowles advertisement, *Carroll's New York City Directory, 1859* (New York: Carroll & Co., 1859), p. 80. See also the *Mirror of Fashion*, vol. 11, no. 1 (Jan. 1849), p. 1; *The Gem, or Fashionable Business Directory* (New York, 1844), p. 82; Charles Stokes and Edward T. Taylor, *Charles Stokes & Co.'s Illustrated Almanac of Fashion* (Philadelphia, 1864), p. 28; and the H. A. Pierson advertisement in the *Floridian*, Oct. 25, 1834, reproduced in Margaret Thompson Ordonez, "A Frontier Reflected in Costume: Tallahassee, Leon County, Florida, 1824–1861" (Ph.D. dissertation, Florida State University, 1978), p. 154.

39. Samuel A. Ward and Asahel F. Ward, *The Philadelphia Fashions and Tailors' Archetypes* (Philadelphia, 1849), n.p.; *Mirror of Fashion*, vol. 10, no. 7 (July 1848), p. 8; Genio Scott and James Wilson, *A Treatise on Cutting Garments to Fit the Human Form . . . Accompanied by a Periodical Report of Fashions* (New York, 1841) (for the "Super Rule System"); *Mirror of Fashion*, n.s., vol. 1, no. 3 (March 1853), p. 63. See also Kidwell, *Cutting a Fashionable Fit*, pp. 129–33; Mary L. Davis-Meyers, "The Development of American Menswear Pattern Technology, 1822 to 1860," *Clothing and Textiles Research Journal* 10, no. 3 (spring 1992): 12–20.

40. *Cleveland Herald*, Sept. 2, 1825 (and see Oct. 12, 1827); *Georgia Journal*, Nov. 15, 1827; *Mirror of Fashion*, vol. 11, no. 1 (Jan. 1849), p. 1; *National Banner and Nashville Whig*, Jan. 3, 1831; Tocqueville quoted in Marvin Meyers, *The Jacksonian Persuasion: Politics and Belief* (New York: Vintage Books, 1957), p. 131. See also Davis-Meyers, "Development of American Menswear Pattern Technology," pp. 14–15; *New York Herald*, May 1, 1846; *Mirror of Fashion*, vol. 10, no. 7 (July 1848), p. 8; Ward and Ward, *Philadelphia Fashions and Tailors' Archetypes*; Morton, "American Pattern Drafting Systems," p. 68; *New York Herald*, Aug. 27, 1841; and Scott and Wilson, *Treatise on Cutting Garments*.

41. Gabriel Henry Chabot, *The Tailors' Compasses; or, An Abridged and Accurate Method of Measurement* (Baltimore: J. Matchett, 1829), title page; Read and Bodman, *New Superlative System of Cutting*, p. 3. See also Kidwell, *Cutting a Fashionable Fit*, pp. 4–6; Scott and Perkins, *The Tailor's Master-Piece, Being the Tailor's Complete Guide, for Instruction in the Whole Art of Measuring and Cutting, According to the Variety of Fashion and Form, with Plates, Illustrative of the Same* (New York, 1837); Alison Adburgham, *Shops and Shopping, 1800–1914: Where, and in What Manner, the Well-Dressed Englishwoman Bought Her Clothes* (London: George Allen and Unwin, 1964), p. 41; *Mirror of Fashion*, n.s., vol. 3 (1855), p. 49; and Neil Harris, *Humbug: The Art of P. T. Barnum* (Chicago: University of Chicago Press, 1973). On the new entrepreneurial definition of art, see Paul Johnson, " 'Art' and the Language of Progress in Early-Industrial Paterson: Sam Patch at Clinton Bridge," *American Quarterly* 40, no. 4 (Dec. 1988): 433–49.

42. See Kidwell, *Cutting a Fashionable Fit.*

43. Nora Waugh, *The Cut of Men's Clothes, 1600–1900* (New York: Theatre Arts Books, 1964), p. 130; Kidwell, *Cutting a Fashionable Fit,* pp. 7–9.

44. Kidwell and Christman, *Suiting Everyone,* p. 41; Scott and Perkins, *The Tailor's Master-Piece, Being the Tailor's Complete Guide, for Instruction in the Whole Art of Measuring and Cutting,* n.p.; *New York Herald,* Sept. 1, 1841. See also Kidwell, *Cutting a Fashionable Fit,* pp. 4–6; Trautman, "Captain Edward Marrett," pp. 49–52; Ward and Ward, *Philadelphia Fashions and Tailors' Archetypes.*

45. On proportionality, see Davis-Meyers, "Development of American Menswear Pattern Technology," pp. 12–18; New York City Tailor, measurement book, 1828–31, New-York Historical Society, New York; Morton, "American Pattern Drafting Systems," pp. 2, 24.

46. J. O. Madison, *Elements of Garment Cutting* (Hartford, Conn.: Case, Lockwood & Brainard Company, 1878), pp. 5–6, 112, and 160 (and see pp. 6–7, 162). "Knowledge of the human shape" is from *The Tailor's Director, Containing an Important Discovery for Fitting the Human Shape, by Anatomical Principles* (New York, 1833), quoted in Morton, "American Pattern Drafting Systems," pp. 23–24. See also Kidwell, *Cutting a Fashionable Fit,* p. 9.

47. William McWiswell, "Mode of Cutting the Bodies of Coats in One Piece," U.S. Patent Office, letters patent no. 1119, April 10, 1839; Madison, *Elements of Garment Cutting,* pp. 127–28 (also see also pp. 9–17); Henry C. Carey quoted in Angela Miller, *The Empire of the Eye: Landscape Representation and American Cultural Politics, 1825–1875* (Ithaca, N.Y.: Cornell University Press, 1993), p. 69. See also Mark Seltzer, *Bodies and Machines* (New York: Routledge, 1992), pp. 49–64.

Chapter Four

1. *Mirror of Fashion,* n.s., vol. 3 (1855), p. 1; *Mirror of Fashion,* n.s., vol. 1, no. 10 (Oct. 1853), p. 1; "to expansion [and] diffusion" is William Ellery Channing quoted in David G. Pugh, *Sons of Liberty: The Masculine Mind in Nineteenth-Century America* (Westport, Conn.: Greenwood Press, 1983), p. 4; *New-York Illustrated News,* Sept. 1, 1860.

2. Edgar Allan Poe, "The Man of the Crowd," in *The Norton Anthology of American Literature,* 2d ed., ed. Nina Baym et al. (New York: W. W. Norton, 1985), 1:1383; Benjamin Franklin, letter of June 11, 1722, to the *New-England Courant,* Benjamin Franklin Papers, Library of America edition on Wordcruncher CD-ROM; Alexis de Tocqueville, *Democracy in America,* ed. J. P. Mayer (Garden City, N.Y.: Doubleday, 1969), p. 537. See also George P. Fox, *Fashion: The Power That Influences the World,* 3d ed. (New York: Sheldon & Co., 1872), pp. 120–22.

3. *New-York Mirror,* Aug. 13, 1836 (for "the majority of our readers" and "recherché dressed persons"; see also Sept. 27, 1828, and Sept. 25, 1831); Egal Feldman, "New York's Men's Clothing Trade, 1800–1861" (Ph.D. dissertation, University of Pennsylvania, 1959), pp. 174–76; *New Mirror,* Oct. 7, 1843, p. 8; "Glimpses at Gotham," *Ladies' Companion,* Feb. 1839; Peter Buckley, "To the Opera House: Culture and Society in New York City, 1820–1860" (Ph.D. dissertation, State University of New York at Stony Brook, 1984), pp. 192–93. See also Richard Cobden, *The American Diaries of Richard Cobden,* ed. Elizabeth Hoon Cawley (Princeton, N.J.: Princeton University Press, 1952), p. 120; Charles Dickens, *American Notes for General Circulation* (London: Penguin Books, 1972), p. 76; F. Fitzgerald De Roos, *Personal*

Narrative of Travels in the United States and Canada in 1826 (London: William Harrison Ainsworth, 1827), p. 7; and D. T. Valentine, *Manual of the Corporation of the City of New York for 1865* (New York: New York Common Council, 1865), p. 596. For more on New York's retail commercialization, see Mrs. Felton, *American Life: A Narrative of Two Years' City and Country Residence* (London: Simpkin, Marshall and Co., 1842), p. 35; Abram C. Dayton, *Last Days of Knickerbocker Life in New York* (New York: G. P. Putnam's Sons, 1897), pp. 11–12; and William Hurd Hillyer, *James Talcott, Merchant and His Times* (New York: Charles Scribner's Sons, 1937), pp. 20–23.

The "spirit of the age" had turned the entire lower half of the city into a hub of commerce. In 1830 half of the properties on Broadway below Canal Street were still residences. By 1850 not even 10 percent were, and two-thirds of the addresses on Broadway were those of retail stores. Neighboring streets, such as Liberty between Broadway and Greenwich, were "completely metamorphosed." On this urban transformation, see Eleanor Ewart Southworth, "Mirrors for a Growing Metropolis: Printed Views of Broadway, 1830–1850" (M.A. thesis, University of Delaware, 1985), p. 76. See also Valentine, *Manual of the Corporation of the City of New York for 1865*, pp. 509–655.

4. By the start of the 1830s, however, the vision of New York as stable and monumental already clashed with reality. As Fay himself remarked in his commentary on an engraving of Pearl Street: "We must say for our artist, that however admirably he represented the street itself, he has not . . . furnished an adequate idea of the pressure and confusion, to be found generally in this and similar parts of the city—boxes, barrels, bales, carts, and barrows; men running hither and thither . . . so that it would be by no means impossible, should a timid girl . . . be jostled off the walk with a most unceremonious disregard of decency. . . . [But] business is business." See Theodore S. Fay, *Views of New-York and Its Environs* (New York: Peabody & Co., 1831), p. 46. See also Southworth, "Mirrors for a Growing Metropolis," pp. 19, 22, and 76.

5. Horner's illustration of Broadway can be found in I. N. Phelps Stokes, *The Iconography of Manhattan Island* (New York: Robert H. Dodd, 1926), vol. 3, plate 113, and also pp. 616–17. For an analogous view of lower Manhattan, see vol. 6, plate 98a.

6. *Putnam's Monthly: A Magazine of Literature, Science, and Art*, April 1853, pp. 353–68 ("Half the city" is from p. 357); "Diary of Henry Southworth, 1850–51" (manuscript), entry for Jan. 13, 1851, New-York Historical Society, New York; Fay, *Views of New-York*, p. 8; Curtis quoted in Lois W. Banner, *American Beauty* (New York: Alfred A. Knopf, 1983), p. 34; "Stewart and the Dry-Goods Trade of New York," *Continental Monthly*, Nov. 1862, p. 530; Philip Hone, *The Diary of Philip Hone, 1828–1851*, ed. Allan Nevins (New York: Kraus Reprint Co., 1969), entries for May 31, 1850, and April 26, 1847. See also *Putnam's Monthly*, Feb. 1853, pp. 124–35; Gunthar Barth, *City People: The Rise of Modern City Culture in Nineteenth-Century America* (New York: Oxford University Press, 1980), p. 124; *New York Tribune*, March 18, 1854; and James Robertson, *A Few Months in America, Containing Remarks on Some of Its Industrial and Commercial Interests* (London: Longman and Co., 1854), p. 6. In addition, see the discussion of "Haussmanization" in T. J. Clark, *The Painting of Modern Life: Paris in the Art of Manet and His Followers* (London: Thames and Hudson, 1985), pp. 30–60.

7. George Templeton Strong, *The Diary of George Templeton Strong, Young Man in New York, 1835–1849*, ed. Allan Nevins (New York: Macmillan Company, 1952), entry for Feb.

21, 1840; Karl Marx, "Manifesto of the Communist Party," in Robert C. Tucker, ed., *The Marx-Engels Reader*, 2d ed. (New York: W. W. Norton, 1978), p. 476; *Mirror of Fashion*, n.s., vol. 1, no. 9 (Sept. 1853), p. 113. See also J. C. Gobright, *The New-York Sketch Book and Merchant's Guide* (New York, 1859), pp. 44–45; William R. Bagnall, "Sketches of Manufacturing Establishments in New York City, and of Textile Establishments in the United States" (1977), manuscript, Merrimack Valley Textile Museum, North Andover, Mass., pp. 351–52; "Phial of Dread," *Harper's New Monthly Magazine*, Nov. 1, 1859; "New York Daguerreotyped," *Putnam's Monthly*, Feb. 1853, pp. 126–29. In addition, see Marshall Bermann, *All That Is Solid Melts into Air: The Experience of Modernity* (New York: Simon and Schuster, 1982), pp. 87–171; William Hancock, *An Emigrant's Five Years in the Free States of America* (London: T. Cautley Newby, 1860), pp. 27–29; and the *United States Economist, and Dry Goods Reporter*, May 7, 1853.

8. "Thoroughness," *Putnam's Monthly*, quoted in Barth, *City People*, p. 122; Brooks Brothers advertisement, *Boyd's Pictorial Directory of Broadway*, 1859.

9. "Those noble mirrors . . . doubling all this wealth by a brightly burnished vista of unrealities": Nathaniel Hawthorne, *House of the Seven Gables: A Romance* (New York: New American Library, 1961), p. 48.

10. For Olds's "coat-forms," see U.S. Patent Office, letters patent no. 8858, April 6, 1852. See also Gobright, *New-York Sketch Book*, p. 45; *United States Economist, and Dry Goods Reporter*, May 7, 1853; Alison Adburgham, *Shops and Shopping, 1800–1914: Where, and in What Manner, the Well-Dressed Englishwoman Bought Her Clothes* (London: George Allen and Unwin, 1964), pp. 96–97; *Hunt's Merchant's Magazine*, March 1849, p. 348; illustration of Grand Street store, box 01, BB.1, F6, Brooks Brothers Archive, Chantilly, Va.; and George Lippard, *New York: Its Upper Ten and Lower Million* (Cincinnati, Ohio: H. M. Rulison, 1853), p. 50. Illustrations of the interiors of clothing stores can be found in Charles Stokes and Edward T. Taylor, *Charles Stokes & Co.'s Illustrated Almanac of Fashion* (Philadelphia, 1864); George W. Simmons, *Oak Hall Pictorial* (Boston: Oak Hall, 1854), p. 5; and the *New-York Illustrated News*, July 28, 1860.

11. The term *phantasmagoria* appears in the *Ladies' Companion*, Sept. 1837 (and also in Strong, *Diary of George Templeton Strong*, entry for Sept. 1, 1856); Daniel Devlin advertisement, *Carroll's New York City Directory, 1859* (New York: Carroll & Co., 1859); James Wilde, Jr., advertisement, Gobright, *New-York Sketch Book*, pp. 44–45. Information about Sally Shephard's visit to Brooks Brothers can be found in the diary of Sally Inman Kast Shephard, box 01, BB.1, F5, Brooks Brothers Archive, Chantilly, Va. See also the Payan & Carhart ad in *Twitt's Directory of Prominent Business Men* (New York, 1858), p. 106.

12. Alfred Munroe & Co. advertisement, *New York Herald*, April 18, 1852; Silvers & Armitrage advertisement, *Sheldon & Co.'s Business or Advertising Directory, 1845* (New York: John F. Trow & Co., 1845). See also Harry E. Resseguie, "Alexander Turney Stewart and the Development of the Department Store, 1823–1876," *Business History Review* 39 (autumn 1965): 310; Stephen N. Elias, *Alexander T. Stewart: The Forgotten Merchant Prince* (Westport, Conn.: Praeger, 1992), p. 74; Robert Hendrickson, *The Grand Emporiums: The Illustrated History of America's Great Department Stores* (New York: Stein and Day, 1979), p. 27; Elizabeth Wilson, *Adorned in Dreams: Fashion and Modernity* (London: Virago Press, 1985), p. 146; Ralph Hower, *History of Macy's of New York, 1858–1919: Chapters in the Evolution of the*

Department Store (Cambridge, Mass.: Harvard University Press, 1943), p. 5; and Philippe Perrot, *Fashioning the Bourgeoisie: A History of Clothing in the Nineteenth Century*, trans. Richard Bienvenu (Princeton, N.J.: Princeton University Press, 1994), pp. 58–79.

13. Edwin T. Freedley, *A Practical Treatise on Business, or How to Get, Save, Spend, Give, Lend, and Bequeath Money* (Philadelphia: Lippincott, Grambo & Co., 1855), p. 126; Fox, *Fashion*, pp. 102–3; *Lippincott's Magazine*, 1871 (referring to the reassurances of shopping of A. T. Stewart's store), quoted in Elias, *Alexander T. Stewart*, pp. 18–19. See also *Citizen and Stranger's Pictorial and Business Directory for the City of New York* (1853), ed. Solyman Brown (New York: Charles Slalding & Co., 1853); *Twitt's Directory of Prominent Business Men*, p. 35; David Alexander, *Retailing in England During the Industrial Revolution* (London: Athlone Press, 1970), pp. 161–65, 173–74; Robert James Myers, *The Economic Aspects of the Production of Men's Clothing* (Chicago: University of Chicago Libraries, 1937), pp. 208–9; Ben Fine and Ellen Leopold, *The World of Consumption* (London: Routledge, 1993), p. 77; Raymond de Roover, "The Concept of the Just Price: Theory and Economic Policy," *Journal of Economic History* 18, no. 4 (Dec. 1958): 418–38; and Rosalind Williams, *Dream Worlds: Mass Consumption in Late Nineteenth-Century France* (Berkeley: University of California Press, 1982), p. 67. On one-price policies in the countryside, see Christopher Clark, *The Roots of Rural Capitalism: Western Massachusetts, 1780–1860* (Ithaca, N.Y.: Cornell University Press, 1990), pp. 223–24.

14. P. L. Rogers advertisement, *Irish American*, Sept. 9, 1854; Stokes and Taylor, *Charles Stokes & Co.'s Illustrated Almanac of Fashion*, p. 4; Alfred Munroe & Co. advertisement, *Citizen & Stranger's Pictorial and Business Directory* (1853); Smith Brothers' advertisement, *New York Herald*, April 18, 1852. On fitting rooms, see the description of George Fox's store in the *New York Morning Express*, Aug. 12, 1850; and see the photograph of Jacob Reed's Clothing Store in Philadelphia, with its large signs advertising "One Price" shopping, in Jacob Reed's Sons, *One Hundred Years Ago: Jacob Reed's Sons, Founded 1824* (Philadelphia: Jacob Reed's Sons, 1924). See also Resseguie, "Alexander Turney Stewart," pp. 309–10; men's clothing, box 4, "Dorr," Warshaw Collection of Business Paraphernalia, Smithsonian Institution, Washington, D.C.; Wayland A. Tonning, "The Beginnings of the Money-Back Guarantee and the One-Price Policy in Champaign-Urbana, Illinois, 1833–1880," *Business History Review* 30, no. 2 (June 1956): 197; *Twitt's Directory of Prominent Business Men*, p. 35; *Carroll's New York City Directory, 1859*; and U. S. Census Office, Seventh Census (1850), Products of Industry, raw data, New York County, N.Y.

15. Smith Brothers' advertisement, *Carroll's New York City Directory, 1859*; P. L. Rogers advertisement, *Irish American*, Sept. 9, 1854 (and see his ad in the *New York Tribune*, Oct. 19, 1850); *Irish American*, Jan. 22, 1850. See also U.S. Census Office, Eighth Census (1860), Products of Industry, raw data, New York County, N.Y.

16. Cornelius Mathews, *A Pen and Ink Panorama of New-York City* (New York: John S. Taylor, 1853), pp. 126–33 ("stacked high to the very ceiling" and "with more of an eye to comfort" are from p. 127); F. B. Baldwin advertisement, *Twitt's Directory of Prominent Business Men*, p. 94 (for "equals, if not surpasses" and "gorgeous jewelers' shops"); Nathaniel Willis quoted in the *New Mirror*, Oct. 21, 1843. See also the entry for "Bowery," *New York City Street Directory, 1851*; Allan Stanley Horlick, *Country Boys and Merchant Princes: The Social Control of Young Men in New York* (Lewisburg, Pa.: Bucknell University Press, 1975),

p. 55; "Glimpses at Gotham," *Ladies' Companion*, April 1839, p. 291; William Bobo, *Glimpses of New-York City* (Charleston, S.C.: J. J. McCarter, 1852), pp. 18–19, 161–63; Fitz-Hugh Ludlow, "American Metropolis," *Atlantic Monthly*, Jan. 1865; and Marie Louise Hankins, *Women of New York* (New York: Marie Louise Hankins & Co., 1861), p. 36.

17. *New Mirror*, Oct. 21, 1843. On the geography of men's clothing stores, see George G. Foster, *New York in Slices, by an Experienced Carver* (New York: W. F. Burgess, 1849), pp. 12–16.

18. Henry Lunettes [Margaret Cockburn Conkling], *The American Gentleman's Guide to Politeness* (New York: Derby & Jacobson, 1857), pp. 35–36 (for "shabby-genteel look" and also "The observers point him out"); Dayton, *Last Days of Knickerbocker Life*, p. 168; *New Mirror*, Oct. 21, 1843 (for "bulged and strained" and "frayed and brownish"); Isaac S. Lyon, *Recollections of an Old Cartman* (New York: New York Bound, 1984 [1872]), p. 123; *New-York Mirror*, Aug. 2, 1823 (vol. 1, no. 1); "New York, Twenty-Five Years Ago," *Ladies' Companion*, Aug. 1841. See also Myers, *Economic Aspects of the Production of Men's Clothing*, p. 14; and David Holman and Billie Persons, *Buckskin and Homespun: Frontier Texas Clothing, 1820–1870* (Austin, Tex.: Wind River Press, 1979), p. 48.

19. "The Misfortunes of a New Coat," *Ladies' Companion*, Sept. 1834. See also the *New-York Mirror*, Oct. 24, 1829.

20. Lunettes, *American Gentleman's Guide to Politeness*, p. 35. See also the *Ladies' Companion*, Aug. 1841, p. 196; the *New-York Mirror*, Aug. 2, 1823; and Nathaniel Parker Willis, "Ephemera," in *Dashes at Life with a Free Pencil* (New York: J. S. Redfield, 1847), p. 153.

21. *Godey's Lady's Book*, May 1854, p. 422; Lunettes, *American Gentleman's Guide to Politeness*, pp. 29–30. See, too, the description of Goldwaite's tired garments in Nathaniel Hawthorne's "Peter Goldwaite's Treasure," in *Twice-Told Tales* (Boston: Houghton Mifflin, 1907), pp. 430–31.

22. Samuel Robert Wells, *How to Behave: A Pocket Manual of Republican Etiquette* (New York: Fowler and Wells, 1856), p. 35; *Mirror of Fashion*, vol. 11, no. 3 (March 1849), p. 17 (for "Pantaloons for full dress"); *Mirror of Fashion*, n.s., vol. 1 (1853), pp. 83, 102, 122, 133, 143, and 152 (the quotes are from p. 102). See also "Diary of Henry Southworth, 1850–51," entry for July 1, 1851; and the *Mirror of Fashion*, n.s., vol. 3 (1855), pp. 3, 70. For Degroot's prices, see his advertisement in the *New York City Mercantile Register*, 1848–49; for Rogers's, see the *New York Tribune*, May 1, 1850; on Mann & McKimm, see the *Working Man's Advocate*, Dec. 14, 1844. J. C. Booth's ads can be found in men's clothing, box 2, "Booth," Warshaw Collection of Business Paraphernalia, Smithsonian Institution, Washington, D.C. For Mulligan's ad, see the *Irish American*, Feb. 17, 1850; and, for James Lacy's, the *New York Herald*, May 31, 1844.

23. Henry Bradshaw Fearon, *Sketches of America: A Narrative of a Journey of Five Thousand Miles through the Eastern and Western States* (London: Longman, Hurst, Rees, Orme, and Brown, 1818), pp. 27; *New York Post*, May 10, 1828; *New York Herald* quoted in Amy Gilman Srebnick, *The Mysterious Death of Mary Rogers: Sex and Culture in Nineteenth-Century New York* (New York: Oxford University Press, 1995), p. 61; *New York Tribune*, Sept. 4, 1841; Asa Greene, *The Perils of Pearl Street, Including a Taste of the Dangers of Wall Street* (New York: Betts & Anstice, and Peter Hill, 1834), p. 27. See also Mary Ryan, *Cradle of the Middle Class: The Family in Oneida County, New York, 1790–1865* (New York: Cambridge Uni-

versity Press, 1981), p. 108; Elias, *Alexander T. Stewart*, pp. 12–13, 60–66; Joseph F. Kett, *Rites of Passage: Adolescence in America, 1790 to the Present* (New York: Basic Books, 1977), pp. 96–102; and Stuart Blumin, *The Emergence of the Middle Class: Social Experience in the American City, 1760–1900* (Cambridge: Cambridge University Press, 1989), pp. 73, 89–91. For other sightings of the clerk as an identifiable public, see the *United States Economist, and Dry Goods Reporter*, June 18, 1853; "Diary of Samuel Edgerly" (manuscript), entries for Feb. 8 and March 9, 1859, Manuscripts and Archives Division, New York Public Library, New York; "Diary of Henry Southworth, 1850–51," entries for Feb. 3, Feb. 26, March 20, and June 17, 1851; "New York Daguerreotyped," *Putnam's Monthly*, Feb. 1853; Bobo, *Glimpses of New-York City*, pp. 15–16; and Willis, "Ephemera," p. 9.

24. Richard L. Bushman, *The Refinement of America: Persons, Houses, Cities* (New York: Vintage Books, 1993), p. 71; J. W. Hayes, *The Draper and Haberdasher*, 4th ed. (London: Houlston and Son, 1878), p. 13. See also Foster, *New York in Slices*, pp. 65–66; Ralph M. Hower, "Urban Retailing in 1850," in Stanley J. Shapiro and Alton F. Doody, comps., *Readings in the History of American Marketing, Settlement to Civil War* (Homewood, Ill.: Richard Irwin, 1968), p. 298; James M. Edney, of New York, N.Y., letter book to Francis H. Cooke, of Augusta, Georgia, 1835–37, letter of March 26, 1836, Special Collections, Rutgers University, New Brunswick, N.J.; "Diary of Henry Southworth, 1850–51," entry for June 17, 1851; Gerald Carson, *The Old Country Store* (New York: Oxford University Press, 1954), p. 65; receipt for Mr. H. E. Laurence, July 20, 1858, BB.2, DF9, Brooks Brothers Archive, Chantilly, Va.; Cobden, *American Diaries of Richard Cobden*, ed. Cawley, p. 93; Charles H. Haswell, *Reminiscences of an Octogenarian of the City of New York* (New York: Harper & Brothers, 1896), p. 148; Henry Collins Brown, ed., *Valentine's Manual of Old New York*, new series (New York: Valentine's Manual Inc., 1916–28), 1:134; Helen Sumner, *History of Women in Industry in the United States*, 61st Congress, 2d sess., Senate Doc. no. 645, 94:164–65; J. Leander Bishop, *A History of American Manufactures from 1608 to 1860* (Philadelphia: Edward Young & Co., 1868), 2:468, and 3:61–64; Freedley, *Philadelphia and Its Manufactures* (Philadelphia: Edward Young, 1858), pp. 224–25; and *Ninth U.S. Census: The Statistics of the Wealth and Industry of the United States* (Elmsford, N.Y.: Maxwell Reprint Company, 1971), vol. 7 of *American Industry and Manufactures in the Nineteenth Century: A Basic Source Collection*.

25. Edney to Cooke, letter of March 26, 1836; see also the letter of April 13, 1837; Greene, *Perils of Pearl Street*, p. 36 (and see pp. 25–26); Hillyer, *James Talcott*, pp. 42–43.

26. "Diary of Edward N. Tailer" (manuscript), entry for Nov. 16, 1850, New-York Historical Society, New York; J. C. Booth advertisement, *New York Tribune*, July 22, 1844 (for "Cheapness" and "in every respect equal"); George Simmons quoted in Jesse Eliphant Pope, *The Clothing Industry in New York* (Columbia: University of Missouri Press, 1905), p. 3; *Mirror of Fashion*, vol. 11, no. 11 (Nov. 1849); Alfred Munroe & Co. advertisement, *Industry of All Nations*, nos. 3–4 (double issue) (New York, 1853); Jacobs brothers' advertisement, *New York Mercantile Union Business Directory* (New York: French, Pratt, & Henshaw, 1850), pp. 47–48; W. H. Degroot advertisement, *Irish American*, Sept. 9, 1854. See also the *Mirror of Fashion*, vol. 12, no. 5 (May 1850) and no. 9 (Sept. 1850); Claudia B. Kidwell and Margaret C. Christman, *Suiting Everyone: The Democratization of Clothing in America* (Washington, D.C.: Smithsonian Institution Press, 1974), p. 59.

27. For Sayre's purchases, see A. L. Sayre, ledger of personal expenses, 1848, box 03, A.3,

books 5, 6, and 7, Brooks Brothers Archive, Chantilly, Va. See also assorted personal receipts, BB.1, DF4; BB.1, F101; BB.2, DF4; and BB.2, DF5, Brooks Brothers Archive, Chantilly, Va.; *Hunt's Merchant's Magazine*, Jan. 1849, p. 116; *Irish American*, Sept. 9, 1854; *Bulletin of the National Association of Wool Manufacturers* 4, no. 11 (April–June 1873), p. 124; *New York Tribune*, July 22, 1844; *New York Mercantile Union Business Directory*, 1850, pp. 47–48; and "Diary of Edward N. Tailer," entry for May 12, 1849.

28. Carson, *Old Country Store*, p. 65; Walt Whitman, "Broadway," in *New York Dissected* (New York: Rufus Rockwell Wilson, 1936), p. 120. See also Matthews, *Pen and Ink Panorama*, p. 134.

29. *New-York Illustrated News*, Sept. 1, 1860; Thoreau quoted in Richard F. Teichgraeber, " 'A Yankee Diogenes': Thoreau and the Market," in *The Culture of the Market: Historical Essays*, ed. Thomas L. Haskell and Richard F. Teichgraeber III (New York: Cambridge University Press, 1993), p. 294; *Burton's Gentlemen's Magazine*, July 1838, pp. 69–70; *New York Herald*, Sept. 1, 1841. See also Francis Wyse, *America, Its Realities and Resources* (London: T. C. Newby, 1846), 2:376–77; *New York Sun*, Oct. 12, 1835; "Diary of Edward N. Tailer," entry for Nov. 8, 1850; Thomas Cochran, *Business in American Life: A History* (New York: McGraw-Hill, 1972), p. 97; David Lockwood, *The Blackcoated Worker: A Study in Class Consciousness*, 2d ed. (Oxford: Clarendon Press, 1989), p. 21; *New York Herald*, Aug. 20, Aug. 23, Sept. 2, Sept. 3, and Sept. 6, 1841; and Greene, *Perils of Pearl Street*, pp. 25–26.

30. Robert Crowe, *The Reminiscences of Robert Crowe, the Octogenerian Tailor* (New York, n.p., n.d.), pp. 22–23. For more on Whitman's dress as a "seafaring man," see Charles Townsend Harris, *Memories of Manhattan in the Sixties and Seventies* (New York: Derrydale Press, 1928), p. 6. See also the engraving of the "down and out" Whitman that appeared as the frontispiece in the 1855 edition of *Leaves of Grass*, reproduced in Raymond Jackson Wilson, *Figures of Speech: American Writers and the Literary Marketplace, from Benjamin Franklin to Emily Dickinson* (New York: Alfred A. Knopf, 1989; repr. Baltimore: Johns Hopkins University Press, 1990), p. 276. In a piece entitled "Clerk from the Country," dated March 24, 1842, Whitman wrote: "He had been fitted out from home—his parents no doubt under the influence of that mischievous idea which makes country people think it better for their sons to be counter jumpers than American farmers." See *Walt Whitman of the New York Aurora, Editor at Twenty-Two*, ed. Joseph Jay Rubin and Charles H. Brown (Westport, Conn.: Greenwood Press, 1950), p. 29. Whitman's antagonism toward "counter jumpers" apparently became a trademark of his, as is evident in a 1860 parody of *Leaves of Grass* published in *Vanity Fair*: "I am the Counter-jumper, weak and effeminate. / I love to loaf and lie about dry-goods" (quoted in Wilson, *Figures of Speech*, p. 278).

31. *United States Economist, and Dry Goods Reporter*, June 18, 1853 (and see Aug. 28, 1852); *New Mirror*, May 11, 1844; Boardman quoted in Carl Bode, ed., *Midcentury America: Life in the 1850s* (Carbondale: Southern Illinois University Press, 1972), pp. 43–46 (the quote is from p. 43); *Hunt's Merchant's Magazine*, June 1849, p. 686 (and see Aug. 1853, p. 264). For Stewart's arrangements, see Mary Ann Smith, "John Snook and the Design for A. T. Stewart's Store," *New-York Historical Society Quarterly*, 58, no. 1 (1974).

32. C. H. Butler, "The Merchant Clerks," *Columbian Magazine*, July 1847, pp. 63–70 (the quote is from p. 63); *Hunt's Merchant's Magazine*, May 1849, pp. 570; Emerson quoted in John G. Cawelti, *Apostles of the Self-Made Man* (Chicago: University of Chicago Press,

1965), p. 86; a young clerk's "I am alone" quoted in Carroll Smith-Rosenberg, "Sex as Symbol in Victorian Purity: An Ethnohistorical Analysis of Jacksonian America," in *Turning Points: Historical and Sociological Essays on the Family*, ed. John Demos and Sarane Spence Boocock, *American Journal of Sociology* 84 (supplement, 1978), p. 234; Poe, "The Man of the Crowd," p. 1382; "large and miscellaneous" and "theaters, gambling houses," from the *New-York Mirror*, Jan. 15, 1832, quoted in Elizabeth Blackmar, *Manhattan for Rent* (Ithaca, N.Y.: Cornell University Press, 1989), p. 137; Richard Robinson quoted in Timothy J. Gilfoyle, *City of Eros: New York City, Prostitution, and the Commercialization of Sex, 1790–1920* (New York: W. W. Norton, 1994), pp. 97–98. See also Horlick, *Country Boys and Merchant Princes*, p. 11; Joyce Appleby, "New Cultural Heroes in the Early National Period," in *Culture of the Market*, ed. Haskell and Teichgraeber, p. 166; Jean-Christophe Agnew, *Worlds Apart: The Market and the Theater in Anglo-American Thought, 1550–1750* (Cambridge: Cambridge University Press, 1986), p. 202; Srebnick, *Mysterious Death of Mary Rogers*, pp. 53–54; Ryan, *Cradle of the Middle Class*, pp. 125–27; Carroll Smith-Rosenberg, "Bourgeois Discourse and the Age of Jackson: An Introduction," in Smith-Rosenberg, *Disorderly Conduct: Visions of Gender in Victorian America* (New York: Alfred A. Knopf, 1985), pp. 79–89; Horace Bushnell, "The Age of Homespun," speech delivered in 1851 at Litchfield, Connecticut, on the occasion of the centennial celebration, in *Centennial Celebration* (Hartford, Conn.: Edwin Hunt, 1851), p. 123; Willis, "Ephemera," p. 154; and Clark, *Painting of Modern Life*, pp. 235–37.

33. *New York Tribune*, May 13, 1850; Karl Marx, *Capital* (Moscow: International Publishers, 1959), 3:289–301 (the quote is from p. 289); Freedley, *Leading Pursuits and Leading Men*, p. 158; *Hunt's Merchant's Magazine*, May 1849, p. 570. For the labor movements, see, for instance, the *New York Tribune*, June 17, 1850. See also Carl N. Degler, "Labor in the Economy and Politics of New York City, 1850–1860" (Ph.D. dissertation, Columbia University, 1952), p. 58.

34. "A Day in New-York," *New-York Mirror*, Aug. 33, 1840. "Epistemological instability" is borrowed from Thomas L. Haskell and Richard F. Teichgraeber III, "Introduction," in *Culture of the Market*, ed. Haskell and Teichgraeber, p. 29. "Every one *employed* in the store," Edwin Freedley insisted, "should be made to stand on the support nature gave him" (*Practical Treatise on Business*, p. 119).

35. Sylvester Judd, *Richard Edney and the Governor's Family* (1850), quoted in Cawelti, *Apostles of the Self-Made Man*, p. 48; Freedley, *Leading Pursuits and Leading Men*, p. 155.

36. John Trumbull, "The Progress of Dulness" (1773), part 2, in *Poetical Works* (Hartford, Conn.: Samuel Goodrich, 1820); Philip Freneau and Charles Brockden Brown's *Arthur Mervyn* are quoted in Steven Watts, "Masks, Morals, and the Market: American Literature and Early Capitalist Culture, 1790–1820," *Journal of the Early Republic* 6, no. 6 (summer 1986): 132, 138, respectively.

37. *Boston Observer*, quoted in Gordon S. Wood, ed., *The Rising Glory of America, 1760–1820* (New York: George Braziller, 1971), pp. 144–45; Greene, *Perils of Pearl Street*, p. 10; Carson, *Old Country Store*, p. 65; "Diary of Henry Southworth, 1850–51," entry for Feb. 5, 1851; Edward Everett quoted in Everett Michael Newbury, "Healthful Employment: Hawthorne, Thoreau, and Middle-Class Fitness," *American Quarterly* 47, no. 4 (Dec. 1995): 686. See also Barbara M. Cross, *Horace Bushnell: Minister to a Changing America* (Chicago: University of Chicago Press, 1958), pp. 1–12. Barnum also questioned the nostalgic renditions of rural idylls

of Bushnell's homespun kind and proclaimed his preference for living "in a more charitable and enlightened age." See Neil Harris, *Humbug: The Art of P. T. Barnum* (Chicago: University of Chicago Press, 1973), p. 209.

38. "Diary of Edward N. Tailer," entries for Jan. 22–25, 1849 (and see July 1, 1853). See also William E. Dodge, *Old New York* (New York: Dodd, Mead & Company, 1880), p. 7; Freedley, *Leading Pursuits and Leading Men*, p. 155.

39. Greene, *Perils of Pearl Street*, pp. 25–26; Foster, *New York in Slices*, pp. 8–9. See also Paul Johnson, "'Art' and the Language of Progress in Early-Industrial Paterson: Sam Patch at Clinton Bridge," *American Quarterly* 40, no. 4 (Dec. 1988): 433–39; Dorothy Davis, *A History of Shopping* (London: Routledge & Kegan Paul, 1966), p. 260; and Stuart Bruchey, *Enterprise: The Dynamic Economy of a Free People* (Cambridge, Mass.: Harvard University Press, 1990), p. 131.

40. George G. Foster, *New York Naked* (New York: De Witt and Davenport, 1849), p. 28. See also the *New-York Mirror*, Nov. 3, 1838; Strong, *Diary of George Templeton Strong*; Michael Moon, *Disseminating Whitman: Revision and Corporeality in Leaves of Grass* (Cambridge, Mass.: Harvard University Press, 1991), p. 58; and Joel H. Ross, *What I Saw in New-York* (Auburn, N.Y.: Derby & Miller, 1852), pp. 136–42.

41. Robertson, *A Few Months in America*, p. 17; Jacob Rader Marcus, *Memoirs of American Jews, 1775–1865* (New York: Ktav Publishing House, 1974), 2:103; *New-York Mirror*, Nov. 3, 1838; Strong, *Diary of George Templeton Strong*, entry for Nov. 13, 1850.

42. Agnew, *Worlds Apart*, p. 68; "Got-him" from Joseph G. Baldwin, *The Flush Times of Alabama and Mississippi* (New York: Sagamore Press, 1957), p. 83; *Nantucket Enquirer*, Jan. 17, 1825; Herman Melville, *White-Jacket* (New York: Oxford University Press, 1990 [1850]), p. 40. See also Lawrence D. Breenan, "The Concept of Business Ethics Reflected in America's Literary Awakening, 1820–1835" (Ph.D. dissertation, New York University, 1950), p. 345.

43. *Burton's Gentleman's Magazine*, July 1838, p. 69; *Mirror of Fashion*, vol. 11, no. 11 (Nov. 1849), cover; vol. 10, no. 8 (Aug. 1848), p. 6; vol. 11, no. 4 (April 1849), p. 25; and, for "freaks and follies" and "strictly consonant with," the *Mirror of Fashion* quoted in the *New Mirror*, Jan. 13, 1844. See also the *Mirror of Fashion*, vol. 10. no. 7 (July 1848), p. 5; and the *New Mirror*, Jan. 27, 1844. On liveried servants, see the *Mirror of Fashion*, n.s., vol. 1, no. 11 (Nov. 1853), p. 3; and n.s., vol. 3, no. 6 (June 1855), p. 40.

On the question of whether America "is ready for liveries," see Willis, "Ephemera," pp. 185, 187. According to the *New Mirror* (Jan. 6, 1844), a store opened in 1844 at Broadway and Liberty Street whose doormen were "two Ethiopians in scarlet coats, cocked hats, plush small-clothes, and white stockings." See also the treatment of the liveried negro servant in Anna Cora Mowatt, *Fashion; or, Life in New York* (New York: Samuel French, 1964); as well as Nathalie Dana, "Farm to City—A New York Romance," *New-York Historical Society Quarterly* 49, no. 3 (July 1965): 233; and Bobo, *Glimpses of New-York City*, p. 192.

44. *Mirror of Fashion*, vol. 12, no. 2 (Feb. 1850), p. 13 (for "conservative"); Agnew, *Worlds Apart*, p. 188 (and see pp. 171, 174–75); *Mirror of Fashion*, quoting the *New York Herald*, vol. 11, no. 6 (June 1849), p. 43; *Mirror of Fashion*, vol. 11, no. 4 (April 1849), p. 25. See also Thomas Carlyle, *Selected Writings*, ed. Alan Shelston (London: Penguin Books, 1971), pp. 89–112; and the *Mirror of Fashion*, vol. 11, no. 1 (Jan. 1849), p. 6; no. 2 (Feb. 1849), p. 9; and no. 9 (Sept. 1849), p. 68; vol. 12, no. 5 (May 1850), pp. 33–34; and n.s., vol. 3, no. 1 (Jan.

1855), p. 8. On low-cost custom tailoring typically advertised in working-class newspapers, see, for example, the *Aurora*, July 17, 1843; the *Subterranean*, June 27, 1846; and the *Working Man's Advocate*, Feb. 1, 1845.

45. Alexander Bryan Johnson quoted in Haskell and Teichgraeber, "Introduction," in *Culture of the Market*, ed. Haskell and Teichgraeber, pp. 28–29. See also Cawelti, *Apostles of the Self-Made Man*, pp. 40–43. Franklin would probably not have been shocked by Johnson's advice, since he had endorsed conscious efforts to acquire virtue, and he also changed the style of his coat to suit events and circumstances. See Wilson, *Figures of Speech*, pp. 20–65. Baudelaire made the connection between Franklin's self-making and capitalist ethics in an 1856 essay on Edgar Allan Poe: "the noble land of Franklin, the inventor of the ethics of the shop-counter." See Charles Baudelaire, "Further Notes on Edgar Poe," in *The Painter of Modern Life and Other Essays*, ed. and trans. Jonathan Mayne (New York: De Capo, 1964), p. 101.

46. *New-York Mirror*, April, 11, 1835; *Ladies' Companion*, May 1836. Poe seemed uncharacteristically optimistic in "The Man of the Crowd," contending that it is "difficult to imagine how they ["individuals of dashing appearance"] should ever be mistaken for gentlemen by gentlemen themselves" (p. 1383).

47. *New York Tribune* quoted in Srebnick, *Mysterious Death of Mary Rogers*, p. 23; Bobo, *Glimpses of New-York City*, p. 36; *New-York Mirror*, March 19, 1842; Willis, "Ephemera," p. 19; Thomas Colley Grattan, *Civilized America* (New York: Johnson Reprint Corporation, 1969 [1859]), 1:188–89. See also the well-dressed murderers of Mary Rogers as pictured in an 1843 pamphlet about the murder in Srebnick, *Mysterious Death of Mary Rogers*, p. 26.

48. Joseph Scoville quoted in Horlick, *Country Boys and Merchant Princes*, p. 93; *New-York Mirror*, Oct. 17, 1829 (for "all things to all men"); Herman Melville, *The Confidence Man: His Masquerade* (New York: Penguin Books, 1990 [1857]), p. 109 (although the theme of the death of truth emerges most explicitly in *Billy Budd, Sailor*). P. T. Barnum tried to salvage something of this epistemological crisis when he wrote that a man without confidence doesn't realize "that every sham shows that there is a reality, and that hypocrisy is the homage that vice pays to virtue" (Harris, *Humbug*, p. 217). See also Karen Halttunen, *Confidence Men and Painted Women: A Study of Middle-Class Culture in America, 1830–1870* (New Haven, Conn.: Yale University Press, 1982); and the *New York Herald*, July 8 and July 11, 1845.

49. Edney to Cooke, letter of April 13, 1837. See also Clark, *Painting of Modern Life*, pp. 47–50. Robert Owen began his working life as a clerk, eventually leaving because "the slavery every day of the week seemed more than my constitution could support" (quoted in Davis, *History of Shopping*, p. 189).

50. Horace Mann, *A Few Thoughts for a Young Man: A Lecture* (Boston: Ticknor, Reed, and Fields, 1850), pp. 13–14; Emerson quoted in Jean V. Mathews, *Toward a New Society: American Thought and Culture, 1800–1830* (Boston: Twayne Publishers, 1991), p. 71; Noah Webster, *An American Dictionary of the English Language Containing the Whole Vocabulary of the First Edition . . . the Entire Correction and Improvements of the Second Edition . . . to Which Is Prefixed an Introductory Dissertation* (Springfield, Mass.: George and Charles Merriam, 1849).

51. Freedley, *Practical Treatise on Business*, p. 119; Hoffman quoted in Horlick, *Country Boys and Merchant Princes*, p. 111. See also Martin J. Wiener, "Market Culture, Reckless Pas-

sion, and the Victorian Reconstruction of Punishment," in *Culture of the Market*, ed. Haskell and Teichgraeber, p. 140; Mary Ryan, "Empire of the Mother: American Writing about Domesticity, 1830–1860," *Women and History*, nos. 2–3 (summer–fall 1982): 62; Norma Clarke, "Strenuous Idleness: Thomas Carlyle and the Man of Letters as Hero," in *Manful Assertions: Masculinities in Britain since 1800*, ed. Michael Roper and John Tosh (London: Routledge, 1991), pp. 35–36; and Appleby, "New Cultural Heroes," in *Culture of the Market*, ed. Haskell and Teichgraeber, pp. 170–77.

52. Hone, *Diary of Philip Hone*, entry for Sept. 10, 1846. See also Daniel Walker Howe, *Making the American Self: Jonathan Edwards to Abraham Lincoln* (Cambridge, Mass.: Harvard University Press, 1997), pp. 8–9; and Merrill D. Peterson, ed., *Democracy, Liberty, and Property: The State Constitutional Conventions of the 1820s* (Indianapolis: Bobbs-Merrill, 1966), pp. 187–214.

53. *New Mirror*, June 22, 1844. See also *Hunt's Merchant's Magazine*, Jan. 1849, p. 119; Horlick, *Country Boys and Merchant Princes*, p. 111 (and also pp. 118–19); Freedley, *Practical Treatise on Business*, p. 119; Smith-Rosenberg, *Disorderly Conduct*, pp. 46, 90; and John F. Kasson, *Rudeness and Civility: Manners in Nineteenth-Century America* (New York: Hill & Wang, 1990), p. 150.

54. Follen quoted in John R. Betts, "Mind and Body in Early American Thought," *Journal of American History*, 54, no. 4 (March 1968): 794 (and see pp. 801, 803); *American Review* quoted in Robert V. Remini, ed., *The Age of Jackson* (New York: Harper & Row, 1972), p. 185; *Manual of Self-Education* excerpted in David Brion Davis, *Antebellum American Culture: An Interpretive Anthology* (Lexington, Mass.: D. C. Heath and Company, 1979), p. 71; Harold Aspiz, *Walt Whitman and the Body Beautiful* (Urbana: University of Illinois Press), pp. 183–96 (the quote is from p. 186). "Strenuously idle" is borrowed from Clarke, "Strenuous Idleness." See also Johnson, "'Art' and the Language of Progress," p. 440; T. J. Jackson Lears, *Fables of Abundance: A Cultural History of Advertising in America* (New York: Basic Books, 1994), pp. 29–30; Richard L. Bushman, *The Refinement of America: Persons, Houses, Cities* (New York: Vintage Books, 1993), p. xiv; Newbury, "Healthful Employment," pp. 681–710; Blumin, *Emergence of the Middle Class*, pp. 66–107; and "Diary of Henry Southworth, 1850–51," and "Diary of Edward N. Tailer." The *American Review* also noted that "our virtues are the virtues of merchants and not of men" (quoted in Remini, ed., *Age of Jackson*, p. 187).

55. W. H. Stinemets, *A Complete and Permanent System of Cutting* (New York: Narine & Co., 1844), n.p.; *Mirror of Fashion*, n.s., vol. 1, no. 9 (Sept. 1853), p. 113. "Disciplinary economy" is obviously borrowed from Michel Foucault, *Discipline and Punish: The Birth of the Prison*, trans. Alan Sheridan (New York: Vintage Books, 1995). New efforts to forbid masturbation were probably the most notorious expression of this new-found public interest in bodily discipline. See Stephen Nissenbaum, *Sex, Diet, and Debility in Jacksonian America: Sylvester Graham and Health Reform* (Chicago: Dorsey Press, 1980), pp. 28–29; Michael Sappol, "The Cultural Politics of Anatomy in Nineteenth-Century America: Death, Dissection, and Embodied Social Identity" (Ph.D. dissertation, Columbia University, 1997), pp. 271, 298; Mark Seltzer, *Bodies and Machines* (New York: Routledge, 1992), pp. 60–61, 76–77; and Daniel Purdy, "The Veil of Masculinity: Clothing and Identity via Goethe's *Die Leiden des jungen Werthers*," *Lessing Yearbook* 27 (1995): 106–9.

56. *Mirror of Fashion*, n.s., vol. 1 (1853), p. 30.

57. Foster, *New York in Slices*, p. 11. See also the *Ladies' Companion*, Jan. 1836; Hone, *Diary of Philip Hone*, entry for March, 29, 1845; Claudia Brush Kidwell and Valerie Steele, *Men and Women: Dressing the Part* (Washington, D.C.: Smithsonian Institution Press, 1989), p. 129; Clark, *Painting of Modern Life*, pp. 63–73; Anne Hollander, *Sex and Suits* (New York: Alfred A. Knopf, 1994); and Seltzer, *Bodies and Machines*, pp. 75, 123–25.

58. *New Mirror*, April 27, 1844, p. 56; *New-York Mirror*, Dec. 28, 1833, quoted in Buckley, "To the Opera House," pp. 22, 257. See also the *Ladies' Companion*, Jan. 1836; Hone, *Diary of Philip Hone*, entry for March, 29, 1845; and Foster, *New York in Slices*, p. 11.

Chapter Five

1. *New York Tribune*, Aug. 6, 1850. See also the *Tribune* for July 19, July 23, July 26, July 31, Aug. 2, and Aug. 6, 1850; the *New York Herald*, July 25, July 26, July 31, Aug. 5, and Aug. 6, 1850; the *New York Post*, July 25, 1850; the *New York Morning Express*, July 21, July 22, and July 25, 1850; the *New Yorker Staats Zeitung*, July 27, Aug. 10, and Aug. 17, 1850; and Carl N. Degler, "Labor in the Economy and Politics of New York City, 1850–1860: A Study of the Impact of Early Industrialism" (Ph.D. dissertation, Columbia University, 1952), p. 81.

2. Bruce Levine, *The Spirit of 1848: German Immigrants, Labor Conflict, and the Coming of the Civil War* (Urbana: University of Illinois Press, 1992), p. 132; Philip Hone, *The Diary of Philip Hone, 1828–1851*, ed. Allan Nevins (New York: Kraus Reprint Co., 1969), entry for June 6, 1836. See also the *New York Herald*, July 25, July 26, and Aug. 5, 1850; and the *New Yorker Staats Zeitung*, July 27, 1850.

3. Robert Greenhalgh Albion, with the collaboration of Jennie Barnes Pope, *The Rise of New York Port, 1815–1860* (New York: Charles Scribner's Sons, 1939), pp. 336; Charles Dickens, *American Notes for General Circulation* (London: Penguin Books, 1972 [1842]), pp. 12 9; Robert James Myers, *The Economic Aspects of the Production of Men's Clothing* (Chicago: University of Chicago Libraries, 1937), p. 32. See also the *New York Tribune*, July 29, 1850; the *New Yorker Staats Zeitung*, Aug. 10, 1850; William E. Devlin, "Shrewd Irishmen: Irish Entrepreneurs and Artisans in New York's Clothing Industry, 1830–1880," in *The New York Irish*, ed. Ronald H. Bayor and Timothy J. Meagher (Baltimore: Johns Hopkins University Press, 1996), pp. 171, 175; Richard B. Stott, *Workers in the Metropolis: Class, Ethnicity, and Youth in Antebellum New York City* (Ithaca, N.Y.: Cornell University Press, 1990), pp. 35–38, 73, 86, 89, and 94; Robert Ernst, *Immigrant Life in New York City, 1825–1863* (New York: Octagon Books, 1979), pp. 27, 76–7 7, 102, and 214–17; and Edwin T. Freedley, *Leading Pursuits and Leading Men: A Treatise on the Principal Trades and Manufactures of the United States* (Philadelphia: Edward Young, 1854), p. 91.

4. Sean Wilentz, *Chants Democratic: New York City and the Rise of the American Working Class, 1788–1850* (New York: Oxford University Press, 1984), p. 56; Walter Licht, *Industrializing America: The Nineteenth Century* (Baltimore: Johns Hopkins University Press, 1995), p. 50; *Abstract of the Statistics of Manufactures, According to the Returns of the Seventh Census*, Jos. C. G. Kennedy, superintendent, 35th Congress, 2d sess., Senate Exec. Doc. no. 39.

5. *Abstract of the Statistics of Manufactures, According to the Returns of the Seventh Census*; *New York Tribune*, June 16, 1849. The total city workforce in crafts and manufacturing, according to the 1855 New York City census, was 91,947 (Ernst, *Immigrant Life in New York City*, pp. 214–17). See also U. S. Census Office, Seventh Census (1850), Products of Industry,

raw data, New York County, N.Y.; U.S. Census Office, *Manufactures of the United States in 1860, Compiled from the Original Returns of the Eighth Census* (Washington, D.C.: Government Printing Office, 1865), pp. lviii–lxv; and Stott, *Workers in the Metropolis*, p. 37. For an example of how 1850 census aggregates for labor became the basis for what was popularly regarded as fact, see James Robertson, *A Few Months in America, Containing Remarks on Some of Its Industrial and Commercial Interests* (London: Longman and Co., 1854), p. 15.

6. *New York Herald*, Oct. 21, 1857.

7. See Mary Ellen Roach and Joanne Bubolz Eicher, *Dress, Adornment, and the Social Order* (New York: John Wiley & Sons, 1965), pp. 32–33; Grace Rogers Cooper, *The Sewing Machine: Its Invention and Development* (Washington, D.C.: Smithsonian Institution Press, 1976). When the U.S. Army had to be expanded from a modest Jeffersonian muster of several thousand to ten times that number at the outbreak of war in 1812, the clothier general set up the same production system that would form the basis of the commercial industry in the following decade, although the army's system was driven by technical needs rather than by the profit motive. A building was rented in the center of Philadelphia, cutters were hired, and bundles of precut cloth, along with the requisite trimmings, were distributed directly to local needleworkers to sew up into uniforms. Records were kept in large alphabetized volumes of all the jobs put out, of the names of the tailors and tailoresses taking the work, and of the goods for which each was responsible. (The number of employees sewing for the army's Clothing Department reached nearly 5,000 during the war.) The system proved far more efficient than the army's previous approach, which had been to rely on Philadelphia master tailors, who would then subcontract the jobs to local sewers with whom they worked. The new system also ensured a greater uniformity of cut and sizing. By the end of the fighting the army was capable of manufacturing 2,000 to 3,000 suits a week and 85,000 assorted other garments a month. See Erna Risch, *Quartermaster Support of the Army: A History of the Corps, 1775–1939* (Washington, D. C.: Office of the Quartermaster General, 1962), pp. 145–4 7, 253. See also the letter of January 15, 1809, written by Capt. William P. Bennet, about the problems he was having with the army's contracting system: National Archives, RG 92, Records of the Office of the Quartermaster General, entry no. 225 (Consolidated Correspondence File, 1794–1915). On the direct commercial applications of the army's mass-production system, despite the fact that it was designed for efficiency, not profit, see David A. Hounshell, *From the American System to Mass Production, 1800–1932: The Development of Manufacturing Technology in the United States* (Baltimore: Johns Hopkins University Press, 1984), pp. 15–65. And see D. J. Smith, "Army Clothing Contractors and the Textile Industries in the Eighteenth Century," *Textile History* 14, no. 2 (1983): 153–63.

8. Margaret Stewart and Leslie Hunter, *The Needle Is Threaded: The History of an Industry* (London: Heinemann/Newman Neame, 1964), p. 2; John Shephard of New York, N.Y., Merchant Tailoring Accounts, vol. 2 daybook (or "Waste Book"), April 20, 1786, Special Collections, Rutgers University, New Brunswick, N.J. See also Linda Morton, "The Training of a Tailor," *Dress* 8 (1982): 22; Catherine L. Roy, "The Tailoring Trade, 1800–1920, Including an Analysis of Pattern Drafting Systems and an Examination of the Trade in Canada" (M.S. thesis, University of Alberta, 1990), p. 83; and T. S. Arthur, *The Tailor's Apprentice: A Story of Cruelty and Oppression* (Philadelphia: Godey & McMichael, 1843), pp. 4–5.

9. *New York Herald*, Sept. 2, 1855; J. O. Madison, *Elements of Garment Cutting* (Hartford,

Conn.: Case, Lockwood & Brainard Company, 1878), p. 152. For "cutters" listed as a separate occupation, see the New York State Census (1855), New York County, raw data. See also Egal Feldman, "New York's Men's Clothing Trade, 1800 to 1861" (Ph.D. dissertation, University of Pennsylvania, 1959), pp. 102, 191; Devlin, "Shrewd Irishmen," in *New York Irish*, ed. Bayor and Meagher, pp. 175, 179; and the *New York Herald*, May 1, 1846. For more on cutting as a distinct profession, see the *New York Herald*, March 21, 1855, and the *New York Tribune*, June 21, 1850, as well as Stinemets's advertisements in the May 31, 1844, and May 2, 1845, editions of the *Herald*, and T. Oliver's and H. Levett's advertisements to New York tailors in the *Herald* for Aug. 27 and Sept. 9, 1841; Sept. 18, 1846; and April 13, 1848.

10. James M. Edney, of New York, N.Y., letter book to Francis H. Cooke, of Augusta, Georgia, 1835–37, letter of Oct. 26, 1835, Special Collections, Rutgers University, New Brunswick, N.J.; *Mirror of Fashion*, vol. 11, no. 11 (Nov. 1849). See also Edney to Cooke, letter of Oct. 3, 1835; and the *Mirror of Fashion*, vol. 11, no. 7 (July 1849), p. 50, and n.s., vol. 3, no. 3 (March 1855), pp. 21–22. On C. A. Hughes, see *New York County*, vol. 364, p. 69, and vol. 365, p. 102 (and see vol. 211, p. 274; vol. 212, p. 377; and vol. 365, p. 105), in the R. G. Dun & Co. Collection, Baker Library, Harvard University Graduate School of Business Administration, Cambridge, Mass. On R. B. Valentine, see Freedley, *Leading Pursuits and Leading Men*, p. 91.

11. Hobby, Husted & Co. advertisement, *New York Herald*, May 7, 1836. See also Nathaniel Whittock, *The Complete Book of Trades* (London: John Bennett, 1837), p. 432; Sarah Levitt, "Cheap Mass-Produced Men's Clothing in the Nineteenth and Early Twentieth Centuries," *Textile History* 22, no. 2 (1991): 183–84; Ava Baron and Susan E. Klepp, " 'If I Didn't Have My Sewing Machine . . .': Women and Sewing Machine Technology," in *A Needle, a Bobbin, a Strike: Women Needleworkers in America*, ed. Joan M. Jensen and Sue Davidson (Philadelphia: Temple University Press, 1984), p. 29; H. L. Eades, "Instruction Book, 1847–48," Manuscript Collection, Library of Congress, Washington, D.C.; Alison Beazeley, "The 'Heavy' and 'Light' Clothing Industries, 1850–1920," *Costume*, no. 7 (1973): 55; Jesse Eliphant Pope, *The Clothing Industry in New York* (Columbia: University of Missouri Press, 1905), pp. 22–23; and *Clothier and Hatter*, Aug. 15, 1873.

12. Edwin T. Freedley, *Philadelphia and Its Manufactures* (Philadelphia: Edward Young, 1858), p. 22 2; *Hunt's Merchant's Magazine*, March 1849, pp. 347–48 (and see Jan. 1849, p. 116); Arnoux advertisement in Feldman, "New York's Men's Clothing Trade," p. 24; *Bulletin of the National Association of Wool Manufacturers* 4, no. 11 (April–June 1873): 124, 126, and 130–33 ("lot system" is from p. 132); Freedley, *Leading Pursuits and Leading Men*, p. 155 (and see p. 96). See also Martin E. Popkin, *Organization, Management and Technology in the Manufacture of Men's Clothing* (London: Sir Isaac Pittman & Sons, 1939), pp. 91–99, 101–5, 109, 112–13, and 120–21; *New York Herald*, Oct. 21, 1857; Madison, *Elements of Garment Cutting*, p. 112; and Egal Feldman, *Fit for Men* (Washington, D.C.: Public Affairs Press, 1961), p. 100.

13. *New York Tribune*, June 16, 1849; Caroline Cowles Richards, *Village Life in America, 1852–1872* (London: T. Fisher Unwin, 1912), pp. 73–74; *Niles' Weekly Register*, Aug. 30, 1817; Joseph Couts, *A Practical Guide for the Tailor's Cutting-Room* (London: Blackie and Son, 1848), p. 25; Nora Waugh, *The Cut of Men's Clothes, 1600–1900* (New York: Theatre Arts Books, 1964), p. 131. The same counting (of stitches) became fashionable again with the

invention of the sewing machine. See Ruth Brandon, *A Capitalist Romance: Singer and the Sewing Machine* (Philadelphia: J. B. Lippincott, 1977), p. 67. See also Edney to Cooke, letters of July 25, Oct. 21, and Oct. 31, 1835; April 2, 1836; and Jan. 21, 1837.

14. *Hunt's Merchant's Magazine*, March 1849, p. 348 (and see Jan. 1849, p. 116). See also the *New York Tribune*, June 16, 1849; Boston Board of Trade, *Report of Committee on Bureau of Clothing and Equipments, March 7, 1862* (Boston, 1862), p. 4; Thomas Dublin, *Transforming Women's Work: New England Lives in the Industrial Revolution* (Ithaca, N.Y.: Cornell University Press, 1994), pp. 158, 187; Stott, *Workers in the Metropolis*, pp. 108–20; and Wilentz, *Chants Democratic*, pp. 122–24.

15. Men's clothing, Lewis and Hanford, Spring Catalogue (1849), Warshaw Collection of Business Paraphernalia, Smithsonian Institution, Washington, D.C. See also Joan M. Jensen, "Needlework as Art, Craft and Livelihood Before 1900," in *A Needle, a Bobbin, a Strike*, ed. Jensen and Davidson, p. 5; Eileen Collard, "Canadian Trousers in Transition," *Cutters Research Journal* (winter 1990), p. 8; Laurie Casey Crawford, "The Analysis of Mid-Nineteenth-Century Men's Outer-Garments from a Deep Ocean Site" (Ph.D. dissertation, Ohio State University, 1994), pp. 73, 145, 147, and 204; New York City Tailor, measurement book, 1828–31, New-York Historical Society, New York; *Citizen and Stranger's Pictorial and Business Directory for the City of New York* (1853), ed. Solyman Brown (New York: Charles Slalding & Co., 1853), p. 109; and Ellen Leopold, "The Manufacture of the Fashion System," in *Chic Thrills: A Fashion Reader*, ed. Juliet Ash and Elizabeth Wilson (Berkeley: University of California Press, 1992), p. 112. On Lewis and Hanford, see also U.S. Census Office, Seventh Census (1850), Products of Industry, raw data, New York County, N.Y.

16. *Journal of Commerce*, Aug. 29, 1834; Boston Board of Trade, *Report of Committee on Bureau of Clothing and Equipments, March 7, 1862*, p. 4. See also Helen Sumner, *History of Women in Industry in the United States*, 61st Congress, 2d sess., Senate Doc. no. 645, 94: 121, 140–41; Edith Abbott, *Women in Industry: A Study in American Economic History* (New York: Appleton and Company, 1924), p. 220; *New York Tribune*, June 16, 1849, and June 8, 1853; and Stott, *Workers in the Metropolis*, p. 31. On the broad geographical base of clothing production, see also Freedley, *Leading Pursuits and Leading Men*, p. 91; *New York Herald*, Oct. 21, 1857; Virginia Penny, *The Employments of Women: A Cyclopaedia of Woman's Work* (Boston: Walker, Wise & Co., 1863), pp. 110–310; William C. Browning, "The Clothing and Furnishing Trade," in *One Hundred Years of American Commerce, 1795–1895*, ed. Chauncey M. Depew (New York: D. O. Haynes & Co., 1895), p. 563; Percy W. Bidwell and John I. Falconer, *History of Agriculture in the Northern United States, 1620–1860* (New York: Peter Smith, 1941), p. 253; *Working Man's Advocate*, June 10, 1831; *Godey's Lady's Book*, May 1845, p. 206; and Victor S. Clark, *History of Manufactures in the United States, 1607–1860* (New York: McGraw-Hill, 1929), 1: 73, 96–97, 144, and 175–76.

17. *Working Man's Advocate*, July 13, 1844. See also *Hunt's Merchant's Magazine*, March 1849, p. 348; Edney to Cooke, letters of June 22, Nov. 28 and Dec. 26, 1835; and April 2 and Nov. 19, 1836; Penny, *Employments of Women*, pp. 111–14, 356; *New York Herald*, Oct. 21, 1857; Duncan Bythell, *The Sweated Trades: Outwork in Nineteenth-Century Britain* (New York: St. Martin's Press, 1978), p. 76; Eileen Yeo and E. P. Thompson, *The Unknown Mayhew: Selections from the "Morning Chronicle," 1849–1850* (New York: Schocken Books, 1971), p.

192; and Mabel Hurd Willett, *The Employment of Women in the Clothing Trade* (New York: Columbia University Press, 1902), p. 33.

18. See *Hunt's Merchant's Magazine*, March 1849, p. 348; Bythell, *Sweated Trades*, pp. 158, 182, 192, and 194; and Stott, *Workers in the Metropolis*, p. 23.

19. For the advertisement, see the *New York Transcript*, Oct. 24, 1835. See also the *New York Sun*, May 25, 1836; Penny, *Employments of Women*.

20. See R. I. Davis, *Men's Garments, 1830–1900: A Guide to Pattern Cutting* (London: B. T. Batsford, 1989), p. 12; T. S. Arthur, *The Seamstress: A Tale of the Times* (Philadelphia: R. G. Berford, 1843), pp. 9–13; Morton, "The Training of a Tailor," p. 22; Roy, "The Tailoring Trade," p. 83; and *Hunt's Merchant's Magazine*, Aug. 1853.

21. See the *New York Tribune*, July 18 and July 19, 1850.

22. See David Brody, "Time and Work During Early American Industrialism," *Labor History* 30, no. 1 (winter 1989): 27; Yeo and Thompson, *Unknown Mayhew*, p. 207; Charles Jacob Stowell, *Studies in Trade Unionism in the Custom Tailoring Trade* (Bloomington, Ill.: Journeymen Tailors Union of America, 1913), p. 18; Stewart and Hunter, *The Needle Is Threaded*, pp. 43–44; and John R. Commons et al., *A Documentary History of American Industrial Society* (Cleveland, Ohio: Arthur H. Clark Company, 1910), 4:113, 137, 143, and 152. On the practice of tailors in London, see F. W. Galton, *Select Documents Illustrating the History of Trade Unionism*, vol. 1, *The Tailoring Trade* (London: Longmans, Green, and Co., 1896), p. 128.

23. *New York Tribune*, Aug. 14, 1845, and Aug. 1, 1851. See also Charles Burdett, *The Elliott Family; or, The Trials of New-York Seamstresses* (New York: Baker & Scribner, 1845), p. 75; U.S. Bureau of Labor (Chas. P. Neill), *Woman and Child Wage-Earners in the United States*, vol. 2, *Men's Ready-Made Clothing* (Washington, D.C.: Government Printing Office, 1911), pp. 226, 242; and the Society for the Relief of Poor Widows with Small Children, *Annual Report*, 1859.

24. Arthur, *The Seamstress*, p. 4; Penny, *Employments of Women*, pp. 308–9 (and see pp. 111–12, 350); Society for the Relief of Poor Widows with Small Children, *Annual Report*, 1859. See also Freedley, *Leading Pursuits and Leading Men*, p. 92; Amy Gilman Srebnick, "True Womanhood and Hard Times: Women and Early New York Industrialization, 1840–1860" (Ph.D. dissertation, State University of New York at Stony Brook, 1979), pp. 84, 93, and 123; and Stott, *Workers in the Metropolis*, pp. 106–7.

25. See Feldman, *Fit for Men*, p. 103; Penny, *Employments of Women*, pp. 111–15; Christine Stansell, *City of Women: Sex and Class in New York, 1789–1860* (Urbana: University of Illinois Press, 1982), pp. 111–12, 114; and Melanie Tebbutt, *Making Ends Meet: Pawnbroking and Working-Class Credit* (London: Methuen, 1983), pp. 6–31.

26. John Dix, *Sketch of the Resources of the City of New-York* (New York: G. & C. Carvill, 1827), quoted in Alan Pred, "Manufacturing in the Mercantile City, 1880–1840," in *Cities in American History*, ed. Kenneth T. Jackson and Stanley K. Schultz (New York: Alfred A. Knopf, 1971), p. 118; T. J. Clark, *The Painting of Modern Life: Paris in the Art of Manet and His Followers* (London: Thames and Hudson, 1985), p. 59.

27. *New York Tribune*, Aug. 14, 1845. See also Elizabeth Blackmar, *Manhattan for Rent* (Ithaca, N.Y.: Cornell University Press, 1989), pp. 72–112; Wilentz, *Chants Democratic*, p. 404; and Stott, *Workers in the Metropolis*, pp. 195–201. On the real estate investments made

by clothiers, see, for example, the entries for McGrath & Thorn, Wm. H. Degroot, Hadden, Taylor & Co., and Jonas Conkling & Co., all in the New-York Trade Agency, credit ledger, Feb. 6, 1851, New-York Historical Society, New York. See also Arthur, *The Seamstress*, p. 7; Brian Danforth, "The Influence of Socioeconomic Factors upon Political Behavior: A Quantitative Look at New York City Merchants, 1828–1844" (Ph.D. dissertation, New York University, 1974), p. 105; Joseph Scoville, *Old Merchants of New York City* (New York: Carleton, 1863, first series), p. 138; and Moses Beach, *The Wealth and Biography of the Wealthy Citizens of the City of New York City*, 6th ed. (New York: Sun Office, 1845), p. 27, and 13th ed. (New York: Sun Office, 1855), p. 19.

28. See Stanley Nadel, "Kleindeutschland: New York City's Germans, 1845–1880" (Ph.D. dissertation, Columbia University, 1981), p. 141; *British Mechanic's and Labourer's Hand Book* (London: C. Knight, 1840), pp. 217–29; and the *New York Tribune*, March 31, 1854.

29. See the Five Points House of Industry, *Annual Report* (New York, 1856), p. 17; Wilentz, *Chants Democratic*, p. 124; Nadel, "Kleindeutschland," p. 141 (for Griesinger's letter). See also Penny, *Employments of Women*, p. 310; *New York Herald*, July 8, 1844; and Stansell, *City of Women*, p. 117. Young children could be a hindrance, of course, although a weekly income of ten dollars made it possible to hire a servant to look after them. Older children, meanwhile, could be integrated into home production, carrying out the same less skilled tasks once given to apprentices. See Ernst, *Immigrant Life in New York City*, pp. 27, 76–77, 27; Nadel, "Kleindeutschland," pp. 141–42; Stott, *Workers in the Metropolis*, p. 97; and Abbott, *Women in Industry*, pp. 221–23.

30. Larcom quoted in Marguerite A. Connolly, "The Transformation of Home Sewing and the Sewing Machine in America, 1850–1929" (Ph.D. dissertation, University of Delaware, 1994), p. 1; John Pintard, *Letters from John Pintard to His Daughter* (New York: New-York Historical Society, 1940), 1:212 (letter of Aug. 13, 1819); "Diary of Samuel Edgerly" (manuscript), entry for Jan. 7, 1859, Manuscripts and Archives Division, New York Public Library, New York; Catharine Beecher, *A Treatise on Domestic Economy, for the Use of Young Ladies at Home, and at School* (New York: Harper & Brothers, 1848), p. 301. For more on women sewing, see Richard B. Morris, *Government and Labor in Early America* (Boston: Northeastern University Press, 1981 [1946]), pp. 386–87; Jane C. Nylander, *Our Own Snug Fireside: Images of the New England Home, 1760–1860* (New York: Alfred A. Knopf, 1993), pp. 150–51; Anna Green Winslow, *Diary of a Boston School Girl of 1771*, ed. Alice Morse Earle (Detroit: Singing Tree Press, 1970 [repr. of 1894 ed.]), p. 40–41; Richards, *Village Life in America*, pp. 27, 49; Jeanne Boydston, *Home and Work: Housework, Wages, and the Ideology of Labor in the Early Republic* (New York: Oxford University Press, 1990), p. 41; and Beverly Gordon, "Meanings in Mid-Nineteenth Century Dress: Images from New England Women's Writings," *Clothing and Textiles Research Journal* 10, no. 3 (spring 1992): 50–51.

31. Catharine Street store ledger, 1818, box 03, A.3, book 2, Brooks Brothers Archive, Chantilly, Va.

32. *New York Sentinel*, July 19, 1831; Edney to Cooke, letters of Oct. 21, Oct. 25, and Oct. 26, 1835. See also the *Working Man's Advocate*, Aug. 6, 1831; Sumner, *History of Women in Industry*, pp. 120–21; and the *New York Herald*, July 15, 1841.

33. See Dublin, *Transforming Women's Work*, p. 157; Sally Alexander, "Women's Work in

Nineteenth-Century London: A Study of the Years 1820-1850," in *The Rights and Wrongs of Women*, ed. Juliet Mitchell and Ann Oakley (New York: Penguin Books, 1976), p. 97; Elizabeth Wayland Barber, *Women's Work, the First Twenty Thousand Years: Women, Cloth, and Society in Early Times* (New York: W. W. Norton, 1994), pp. 33, 71, 76, 78, 83, and 85; Boydston, *Home and Work*, pp. 88-89, 125, and 134-35; Mary P. Ryan, *Cradle of the Middle Class: The Family in Oneida County, New York, 1790-1865* (New York: Cambridge University Press, 1981); Alice Kessler-Harris, *Out to Work: A History of Wage-Earning Women in the United States* (New York: Oxford University Press, 1982), pp. 27, 39; Carol Groneman Pernicone, "The 'Bloody Ould Sixth': A Social Analysis of a New York City Working-Class Community in the Mid-Nineteenth Century" (Ph.D. dissertation, University of Rochester, 1973), pp. 145-46, 164; Stott, *Workers in the Metropolis*, pp. 102-4; Hasia R. Diner, *Erin's Daughters in America: Irish Immigrant Women in the Nineteenth Century* (Baltimore: Johns Hopkins University Press, 1983), p. 59; Bythell, *Sweated Trades*, pp. 166-67; and Stansell, *City of Women*, p. 115.

34. The *Emigrant's Dictionary* and the table of average weekly wages, from the Tenth Annual Report of the Massachusetts Bureau of Labor (1879), quoted in Abbott, *Women in Industry*, pp. 218 and 224, respectively. See also Henry Bradshaw Fearon, *Sketches of America: A Narrative of a Journey of Five Thousand Miles through the Eastern and Western States* (London: Longman, Hurst, Rees, Orme, and Brown, 1818), pp. 33-34; as well as the *New York Tribune*, June 8, 1853, and *New York Herald*, June 11, 1853. Virginia Penny recorded several comparisons between women's and men's wages. For example, one clothier, who paid a "girl" $4.00 as an operator with steady work, paid workmen $8.00 to $10.00 a week for work by the piece (i.e., outwork). Brooks Brothers paid indoor work by the week: $5.00 for women, $7.00 for men (for ten-hour days). At Devlin's, too, shop work was paid by the week, outwork by the piece. As a representative of the firm remarked, "we pay men better, because they are stronger and more capable, and have more experience. Men receive [$]9-12. It requires four years for [a] man to learn [the] business; two years for women so as to earn $4." See Penny, *Employments of Women*, pp. 111-14, 310 (the quote is from p. 114). See also Joan Scott, " 'L'ouvrière! Mot impie . . .': Women Workers in the Discourse of French Political Economy, 1840-1860," in *The Historical Meanings of Work*, ed. Patrick Joyce (New York: Cambridge University Press, 1987), pp. 124-25.

35. Penny, *Employments of Women*, pp. 352-55 (the quotes are from pp. 354 and 355).

36. *New York Tribune*, March 7 and Aug. 14, 1845. The number of employees of each clothing business is broken down by gender in the U.S. Census Office, Seventh Census (1850), Products of Industry, raw data, New York County, N.Y. See also Amy Gilman Srebnick, *The Mysterious Death of Mary Rogers: Sex and Culture in Nineteenth-Century New York* (New York: Oxford University Press, 1995), pp. 7-8; Maria Maxwell, *Ernest Grey; or, The Sins of Society* (New York: T. W. Strong, 1855), p. 23; *New York Tribune*, March 27 and Nov. 15, 1845; Degler, "Labor in the Economy and Politics of New York City," pp. 100, 109; Srebnick, "True Womanhood and Hard Times," pp. 53, 160-64; Dublin, *Transforming Women's Work*, p. 157; Nancy Grey Osterud, *Bonds of Community: The Lives of Farm Women in Nineteenth-Century New York* (Ithaca, N.Y.: Cornell University Press, 1991), p. 150; Pernicone, "The 'Bloody Ould Sixth,' " p. 30; Christine Stansell, "The Origins of the Sweatshop: Women and Early Industrialization in New York City," in *Working-Class America: Essays on Labor, Community,*

and American Society, ed. Michael H. Frisch And Daniel J. Walkowitz (Urbana: University of Illinois Press, 1983), p. 82; and Diane Lindstrom, "The Economy of Antebellum New York City" (manuscript), pp. 16–20.

37. The *Lady's Book*, vol. 1 (1830), p. 276; *New York Post*, April 20, 1819 (and see July 13, 1819). See also Meredith Wright, *Everyday Dress of Rural America, 1783–1800* (New York: Dover Publications, 1990), p. 107; and Howard B. Rock, "A Woman's Place in Jeffersonian New York: The View from the *Independent Mechanic*," *New York History* 63, no. 4 (Oct. 1982): 266. When journeymen from Philadelphia and Boston (but not from New York) petitioned Congress to amend the tariff on woolens in 1828 and again in 1832, they expressed their concern for a "very extensive and worthy class" of tailoresses for whom work had to be found. Their employers adopted their language verbatim. But such paternalism could not be maintained in light of the growing importance of female waged labor. See "Petition of the Journeymen Tailors of Philadelphia," Jan. 30, 1832, 22d Congress, 1st sess., Doc. no. 39; "In Favor of Increase of Duties on Ready-Made Clothing," April 28, 1828, 20th Congress, 1st sess., Doc. no. 914. See also the related petitions from 1828 of the merchant tailors of Philadelphia, the master tailors of Philadelphia, the journeymen tailors of Philadelphia, and the merchant tailors of New York: 20th Congress, 1st sess., Sen Docs. nos. 181, 182, 188, and 191, respectively.

38. See Beverly Lemire, "Redressing the History of the Clothing Trade in England: Ready-Made Clothing, Guilds, and Women Workers, 1650–1800," *Dress* 21 (1994): 63; John Styles, "Clothing the North: The Supply of Non-Elite Clothing in the Eighteenth-Century North of England," *Textile History* 25, no. 2 (1994): 152–54; and Claudia Kidwell, *Cutting a Fashionable Fit: Dressmakers' Draftmaking Systems in the United States* (Washington, D.C.: Smithsonian Institution Press, 1979), p. 9. See also "Men Mantua Makers," in Frazar Kirkland, *Cyclopaedia of Commercial and Business Anecdotes* (New York: D. Appleton and Co., 1865), p. 611; and Lois W. Banner, *American Beauty* (New York: Alfred A. Knopf, 1983), pp. 74–75.

39. Fox quoted in the *New York Morning Express*, Feb 1, 1850. See also U.S. Census Office, Seventh Census (1850), Manufactures Schedule, raw data, New York County, N.Y.; Penny, *Employments of Women*, p. 345.

40. George Gifford, *Before the Honorable Philip F. Thomas . . . in the Matter of the Application of Elias Howe, Jr., for an Extension of His Patent for Sewing Machines* (New York: W. W. Rose, 1860), pp. 9–10; *New York Tribune*, March 27, 1851.

41. *New York Herald*, June 7, 1853. See also the *New York Herald*, June 11, 1853; and the *New York Tribune*, June 8, 1853. On the promiscuous nature of sewing in the city, see Penny, *Employments of Women*.

42. Quoted in Srebnick, "True Womanhood and Hard Times," p. 32.

43. William W. Sanger, *The History of Prostitution: Its Extent, Causes, and Effects throughout the World* (New York: Harper & Brothers, 1859), p. 533. See also Michael Burawoy, *The Politics of Production: Factory Regimes under Capitalism and Socialism* (London: Verso, 1985), p. 54.

44. Fox advertisement, *New York Morning Express*, Feb. 1, 1850. For a list of members in the General Society of Merchants and Tradesmen, see the *New York Directory for 1786, Illustrated with a Plan of the City* (repr. New York: Trow City Directory Co., 1889). See also

Stott, *Workers in the Metropolis*, p. 40; W. J. Rorabaugh, *The Craft Apprentice: From Franklin to the Machine Age in America* (New York: Oxford University Press, 1986), p. 6; and Adam Smith, *An Inquiry into the Nature and Causes of the Wealth of Nations*, ed. R. H. Campbell and A. S. Skinner (Oxford: Clarendon Press, 1976), 1:116–35. For more on the low status of tailors as artisans, see the *Broadway Journal*, March 15, 1845; Kirkland, *Cyclopaedia of Commercial and Business Anecdotes*, p. 405; George Templeton Strong, *The Diary of George Templeton Strong, Young Man in New York, 1835–1849*, ed. Allan Nevins (New York: Macmillan Company, 1952), entry for Dec. 19, 1839; Wright, *Everyday Dress of Rural America*, p. 107; and the *New-York Mirror*, May 12, 1838.

45. See Abbott, *Women in Industry*, pp. 221–23; Philadelphia Sewing Machine Loan Company, *Constitution and By-Laws* (Philadelphia, 1857); and Ben Fine and Ellen Leopold, *The World of Consumption* (London: Routledge, 1993), p. 104. Not only in connection with tailoring work did the family prove to be a means for facilitating the transition to capitalism; this could also be the case in textile factories. See Anthony F. C. Wallace, *Rockdale: The Growth of an American Village in the Early Industrial Revolution* (New York: W. W. Norton, 1972), pp. 164–83.

46. In 1836 the French invented a new term—*apiéceur*—to denote someone who functioned simultaneously as a boss and a worker in the garment trade. See Nancy L. Green, *Ready-to-Wear and Ready-to-Work: A Century of Industry and Immigrants in Paris and New York* (Durham, N.C.: Duke University Press, 1997), p. 147. See also Blackmar, *Manhattan for Rent*, pp. 67, 124–25; *New York Tribune*, Nov. 15, 1845; Stansell, "Origins of the Sweatshop," pp. 84, 94–95; and Penny, *Employments of Women*, pp. 111–12.

47. Penny, *Employments of Women*, pp. 113–14 (and see p. 355); *New York Tribune*, July 29, 1850 (for "outside hands" and "To prevent the growth"), and Nov. 15, 1845 ("farming operations" and "inferior workmen"); *New York Herald*, July 26, 1850 ("sub-bosses"), and Oct. 21, 1857 ("By this means"). For more on "farming" out work in the city, see the *Mirror of Fashion*, vol. 12, no. 9 (Sept. 1850), p. 65; Mark Seltzer, *Bodies and Machines* (New York: Routledge, 1992), p. 26; James A. Schmiechen, *Sweated Industries and Sweated Labor: The London Clothing Trades, 1860–1914* (Urbana: University of Illinois Press, 1984), p. 17; and Stansell, "Origins of the Sweatshop," pp. 84–85.

48. *New York Tribune*, July 26, 1850 (for Donnelly and the Congress of Trades meeting), and July 27, 1850 ("Never . . . has any piece of cloth"). See also the *New York Herald*, July 26, 1850. On Dun & Co., see Roy A. Foulke, *The Sinews of American Commerce* (New York: Dun & Bradstreet, 1941). For a different interpretation of the 1850 strike, see Wilentz, *Chants Democratic*, pp. 377–83.

49. See Claus Offe, "The Political Economy of the Labour Market" and "Two Logics of Collective Action," in Offe, *Disorganized Capitalism: Contemporary Transformations of Work and Politics* (Cambridge, Mass.: MIT Press, 1985); Robert Gray, "The Languages of Factory Reform in Britain, c. 1830–1860," in *Historical Meanings of Work*, ed. Joyce, pp. 158–59.

50. *Hunt's Merchant's Magazine*, Oct. 1840, pp. 305–10 (the quote is from p. 307); Arthur, *The Tailor's Apprentice*, p. 5.

51. See A. L. Sayre, ledger of personal expenses, 1848, box 03, A.3, books 5, 6, and 7, Brooks Brothers Archive, Chantilly, Va. See also the *Working Man's Advocate*, Dec. 14, 1844; Arthur, *The Tailor's Apprentice*, pp. 4–5, 20; *New York Transcript*, Sept. 15, 1835; Pope,

Clothing Industry in New York, p. 20; Wilentz, *Chants Democratic*, pp. 45–47; Maxine Berg, "Small Producer Capitalism in Eighteenth-Century England," *Business History* 35, no. 1 (Jan. 1993): 19–20, 25; Leopold, "Manufacture of the Fashion System," in *Chic Thrills*, ed. Ash and Wilson, p. 108; Feldman, "New York's Men's Clothing Trade," p. 42; and John Rule, "The Property of Skill in the Period of Manufacture," in *Historical Meanings of Work*, ed. Joyce, pp. 110–13.

52. George G. Foster, *New York Naked* (New York: De Witt and Davenport, 1849), pp. 137–38. See also the *Journal of Commerce*, Aug. 29, 1834; Risch, *Quartermaster Support of the Army*, pp. 49–52; Alice Morse Earle, *Home Life in Colonial Days* (New York: Macmillan Company, 1917), pp. 247–48; and the National Archives, RG 92, Records of the Office of the Quartermaster General, entry no. 225 (Consolidated Correspondence File, 1794–1915: letter of Feb. 1804). For Tench Coxe's letter to the secretary of war, see entry no. 2117 ("letters sent, Office of Purveyor of Public Supplies, 1800–1812") (Masterson List no. 15). In addition, see the contracts of John Curry, Sarah Phillips, and Martha Sweeny with the army's clothier general, also in entry no. 225 (Consolidated Correspondence File, 1794–1915); and Lemire, "Redressing the History of the Clothing Trade," p. 69. On the practice of putting-out in the seventeenth and eighteenth centuries, see Beverly Lemire, *Dress, Culture and Commerce: The English Clothing Trade Before the Factory, 1660–1800* (London: Macmillan Press, 1997), pp. 55–64.

53. *New York Herald*, Oct. 21, 1857. See also Bythell, *Sweated Trades*, pp. 184–85; Jesse Thomas Carpenter, *Competition and Collective Bargaining in the Needle Trades, 1910–1967* (New York: New York State School of Industrial and Labor Relations, Cornell University, 1972), pp. 107–8; Berg, "Small Producer Capitalism," pp. 22–23; Fine and Leopold, *World of Consumption*, p. 94; Steven Fraser, "Combined and Uneven Development in the Men's Clothing Industry," *Business History Review* 57 (winter 1983): 522–47; Pernicone, "The 'Bloody Ould Sixth,' " p. 105; and Penny, *Employments of Women*, pp. 310–11.

54. *New York Herald*, Oct. 21, 1857. See also Stott, *Workers in the Metropolis*, p. 41; Fraser, "Combined and Uneven Development in the Men's Clothing Industry"; *Bulletin of the National Association of Wool Manufacturers* 4, no. 11 (April–June 1873): 131; *New York Herald*, March 21, 1855, and Oct. 21, 1857; Popkin, *Organization, Management and Technology*, pp. 101–5; Madison, *Elements of Garment Cutting*, p. 112; Feldman, *Fit for Men*, pp. 43–44, 100; and Freedley, *Leading Pursuits and Leading Men*, p. 93.

55. Singer advertisement, *New York Herald*, Feb. 21, 1851; Penny, *Employments of Women*, p. 311; *New York Tribune*, June 18, 1853; *Armitage & Moseley's Annual Circular (Wheeler & Wilson's Celebrated Family Sewing Machines)* (Albany, N.Y.: C. Van Benthuysen, 1859), p. 5. See also Cooper, *Sewing Machine*, p. 58.

56. See Penny, *Employments of Women*, pp. 111, 310–12, 342–45, and 351–52; William R. Bagnall, "Sketches of Manufacturing Establishments in New York City, and of Textile Establishments in the United States" (1977), manuscript, Merrimack Valley Textile Museum, North Andover, Mass., pp. 32–33, 47–48; *Hunt's Merchant's Magazine*, Sept. 1859, p. 380; Fine and Leopold, *World of Consumption*, pp. 103–6; *New-York Illustrated News*, Nov. 19, 1859; *Scientific American*, Jan. 29, 1859; Cooper, *Sewing Machine*, p. 58; Brandon, *A Capitalist Romance*, pp. 117–18; Gifford, *Before the Honorable Philip R. Thomas*, pp. 11, 14–21; *New York Tribune*, Jan. 1, 1851; Baron and Klepp, " 'If I Didn't Have My Sewing Machine . . . ,' "

p. 32; *Men's Wear*, 60th anniversary issue, Feb. 10, 1950, p. 203; Philadelphia Sewing Machine Loan Company, *Constitution and By-Laws*; and Nancy Page Fernandez, " 'If a woman had taste . . .': Home Sewing and the Making of Fashion, 1850–1910" (Ph.D. dissertation, University of California at Irvine, 1987), pp. 228–30.

57. For Mackin & Brother, Abraham Hirschberg, and Griessman & Hoffman, see *New York County*, vol. 200, pp. 357, 360, and 362, respectively, in the R. G. Dun & Co. Collection, Baker Library, Harvard University Graduate School of Business Administration, Cambridge, Mass. For A. K. Ingraham's commission work and for information on Morrison Levy & Co., William Seligman, and Trowbridge Dwight & Co., see the New-York Trade Agency, credit ledger, Feb. 6, 1851, New-York Historical Society, New York. For Baker, Nelson & Co., see the *Morning Courier and New-York Enquirer*, May 1, 1850.

58. See Edney to Cooke, letter of Sept. 30, 1835 (and see letter of March 19, 1836); Leopold, "Manufacture of the Fashion System," in *Chic Thrills*, ed. Ash and Wilson, p. 112.

59. Feldman, "New York's Men's Clothing Trade," p. 105. See also U.S. Census Office, Seventh Census (1850), Products of Industry, raw data, First Ward, New York County, N.Y.; men's clothing, box 8, "Lewis & Co.," Warshaw Collection of Business Paraphernalia, Smithsonian Institution, Washington, D.C.

60. See Yeo and Thompson, *Unknown Mayhew*, pp. 133, 220; Fraser, "Combined and Uneven Development in the Men's Clothing Industry."

61. Green, *Ready-to-Wear and Ready-to-Work*, p. 144.

Chapter Six

1. Philip S. Foner, *Women and the American Labor Movement: From the First Trade Unions to the Present* (New York: Free Press, 1982), pp. 1–6 (the quotes are from pp. 5 and 6). See also the *New-York Daily Sentinel*, Feb. 17 and March 5, 1831; Christine Stansell, *City of Women: Sex and Class in New York, 1789–1860* (Urbana: University of Illinois Press, 1982), pp. 133–34; and Helen Sumner, *History of Women in Industry in the United States*, 61st Congress, 2d sess., Senate Doc. no. 645, 94:36.

2. Foner, *Women and the American Labor Movement*, pp. 5–7 ("If we are true to ourselves" from p. 5). On the strike, see Alice Kessler-Harris, *Out to Work: A History of Wage-Earning Women in the United States* (New York: Oxford University Press, 1982), pp. 40–41; Stansell, *City of Women*, pp. 134–36; *Working Man's Advocate*, June 10, July 23, Aug. 6, and Aug. 13, 1831; *New-York Daily Sentinel*, July 19, 1831; and Sumner, *History of Women in Industry*, pp. 36–40. The tailoresses' protests, in 1825 and 1831, predated actions by women working under the new factory system. The first strike by female operatives in Lowell, Massachusetts, for instance, broke out in 1834. More significantly, the women in Lowell based their resistance to capitalism on the integrity of their fathers' patriarchal households, in contrast to the tailoresses' decidedly unnostalgic, modern perspective. See Thomas Dublin, *Women at Work: The Transformation of Work and Community in Lowell, Massachusetts, 1826–1860* (New York: Columbia University Press, 1979), pp. 86–107.

3. Senator Benton quoted in U.S. Congress, 62d Congress, 1st sess., Senate Doc. no. 21, p. 178; George Templeton Strong, *The Diary of George Templeton Strong, Young Man in New York, 1835–1849*, ed. Allan Nevins (New York: Macmillan Company, 1952), entry for July 7, 1851. For Mathew Carey, see the *New-York Mirror*, May 14, 1831. See also John B.

Andrews and W. D. P. Bliss, *History of Women in Trade Unions*, 61st Congress, 2d sess., Senate Doc. no. 645, 95:126–27; Guion Griffis Johnson, *Ante-Bellum North Carolina: A Social History* (Chapel Hill: University of North Carolina Press, 1937), pp. 245–48; *New York Tribune*, March 27, 1845; *Working Man's Advocate*, Aug. 23, 1845; and Sumner, *History of Women in Industry*, pp. 138–39. While Virginia Penny adopted an unusually sarcastic tone in cataloguing the employments of seamstresses, she resorted uniquely to subterfuge when describing the desperation of the ragpicker. See Virginia Penny, *The Employments of Women: A Cyclopaedia of Woman's Work* (Boston: Walker, Wise & Co., 1863), pp. 465–68.

4. Maria Maxwell, *Ernest Grey; or, The Sins of Society* (New York: T. W. Strong, 1855), p. 23; Penny, *Employments of Women*, p. 310; *Hunt's Merchant's Magazine*, Aug. 1853, pp. 253–54 (the quote is from p. 253). See also the *New York Herald*, June 11, 1853. Thomas Hood's "The Song of the Shirt" was first published in December 1843, in *Punch*, and became an overnight sensation. See T. J. Edelstein, "They Sang 'The Song of the Shirt': The Visual Iconology of the Streamstress," *Victorian Studies* 23, no. 4 (winter 1980): 183–210.

5. William Hancock, *An Emigrant's Five Years in the Free States of America* (London: T. Cautley Newby, 1860), p. 83. On the freedom of restraint for women in the city, see Adrienne Siegel, *The Image of the American City in Popular Literature, 1820–1870* (Port Washington, N.Y.: Kennikat Press, 1981), p. 118; Peter Buckley, "To the Opera House: Culture and Society in New York City, 1820–1860" (Ph.D. dissertation, State University of New York at Stony Brook, 1984), p. 21; Abram C. Dayton, *Last Days of Knickerbocker Life in New York* (New York: G. P. Putnam's Sons, 1897), pp. 225–26; Joan L. Severa, *Dressed for the Photographer: Ordinary Americans and Fashion, 1840–1900* (Kent, Ohio: Kent State University Press, 1995), p. 4; and Lois W. Banner, *American Beauty* (New York: Alfred A. Knopf, 1983), pp. 74–75, 84.

6. George Lippard, *The Midnight Queen; or, Leaves from New York Life* (1853), excerpted in *George Lippard, Prophet of Protest: Writings of an American Radical, 1822–1854*, ed. David S. Reynolds (New York: Peter Lang, 1986), p. 53. "Middle landscape" is, of course, Leo Marx's term in *The Machine in the Garden: Technology and the Pastoral Ideal in America* (New York: Oxford University Press, 1964).

7. Edwin T. Freedley, *Leading Pursuits and Leading Men: A Treatise on the Principal Trades and Manufactures of the United States* (Philadelphia: Edward Young, 1854), p. 92; Penny, *Employments of Women*, p. 111 (and see p. 309). On the Chatham Street clothiers, see Frazar Kirkland, *Cyclopaedia of Commercial and Business Anecdotes* (New York: D. Appleton and Co., 1865), p. 618; Cornelius Mathews, *A Pen and Ink Panorama of New-York City* (New York: John S. Taylor, 1853), pp. 164–66; William Bobo, *Glimpses of New-York City* (Charleston, S.C.: J. J. McCarter, 1852), p. 115; George G. Foster, *New York in Slices, by an Experienced Carver* (New York: W. F. Burgess, 1849), p. 13; Charles Townsend Harris, *Memories of Manhattan in the Sixties and Seventies* (New York: Derrydale Press, 1928), p. 41; and Michael Walsh, *Sketches of the Speeches and Writings of Michael Walsh, Including His Poems and Correspondence* (New York: Thomas McSpedon, 1843), p. 78.

8. On the creation of democratic patriarchy, see Carole Pateman, *The Disorder of Women: Democracy, Feminism, and Political Theory* (Stanford, Calif.: Stanford University Press, 1989); Amy Dru Stanley, *From Bondage to Contract: Wage Labor, Marriage, and the Market in the Age of Slave Emancipation* (New York: Cambridge University Press, 1998); Elizabeth Blackmar,

Manhattan for Rent, 1785–1850 (Ithaca, N.Y.: Cornell University Press, 1989); Jan Lewis, "The Republican Wife: Virtue and Seduction in the Early Republic," reprinted in Nancy F. Cott, ed., *History of Women in the United States*, vol. 18, pt. 1 (Munich: K. G. Saur, 1994); Linda K. Kerber, "The Paradox of Women's Citizenship in the Early Republic: The Case of *Martin vs. Massachusetts*, 1805," *American Historical Review* 97, no. 2 (April 1992): 349–78; Joyce Appleby, *Liberalism and Republicanism in the Historical Imagination* (Cambridge, Mass.: Harvard University Press, 1992); Paula Baker, "The Domestication of Politics: Women and American Political Society, 1780–1920," *American Historical Review* 89, no. 3 (June 1984): 620–47; David Scobey, "Anatomy of the Promenade: The Politics of Bourgeois Sociability in Nineteenth-Century New York," *Social History* 17, no. 2 (May 1992): 203–27; Nancy Armstrong, *Desire and Domestic Fiction: A Political History of the Novel* (New York: Oxford University Press, 1987); and Thomas Laqueur, *Making Sex: Body and Gender from the Greeks to Freud* (Cambridge, Mass.: Harvard University Press, 1990).

9. The Reverend Ezra Stiles Ely, *Visits of Mercy* (Philadelphia: Samuel F. Bradford, 1829), entry for Jan. 19, 1811, pp. 39–40 (and see the entry for March 13, 1811, p. 83); Mathew Carey, *Appeal to the Wealthy of the Land, Ladies as Well as Gentlemen* (Philadelphia: Stereotyped by L. Johnson, 1833), Essay 12, p. 34; *New-York Mirror*, April 30, 1831; *Working Man's Advocate*, Sept. 11, 1830; Carey, *Appeal to the Wealthy of the Land*, Essay 4, pp. 13–14; Mathew Carey, "Public Charities in Philadelphia" (1828), in Carey, *Miscellaneous Essays* (Philadelphia, 1830), p. 154. See also Mathew Carey, "Remarks on the Character, Conduct, Situation, and Prospects of Those Who Live by the Labor of Their Hands," in the *New-York Mirror*, April 30, May 7, and May 14, 1831; Sumner, *History of Women in Industry*, pp. 131–33; and U.S. Treasury Department, *A Statement of the Arts and Manufactures of the United States of America, for the Year 1810, Digested and Prepared by Tench Coxe* (Philadelphia: A. Cornman, Jr., 1814), p. xxv.

10. Carey, "Public Charities in Philadelphia," p. 153; *New-York Mirror*, May 7, 1831.

11. *New-York Mirror*, April 30, 1831. On the invention of pity and its political import, see, for instance, Thomas L. Haskell, "Capitalism and the Origins of the Humanitarian Sensibility," pts. 1 and 2, *American Historical Review* 90, no. 2 (April 1985): 339–61, and no. 3 (June 1985): 547–66; and Karen Haltunnen, "Humanitarianism and the Pornography of Pain in Anglo-American Culture," *American Historical Review* 100, no. 2 (April 1995): 303–34.

12. Carey, *Appeal to the Wealthy of the Land*, Preface, p. 4, and Essay 1, p. 6 (and see Essay 9, p. 27). See also Mathew Carey, "Report on Female Wages" (1829), in Carey, *Miscellaneous Essays*, pp. 266–72, and "Public Charities in Philadelphia," also in *Miscellaneous Essays*, pp. 153–203 (see especially p. 193); and the *New-York Mirror*, April 30, 1831.

13. *New York Sun*, May 25, 1836; *New York Herald*, July 29, 1837 (for "savings of 25 per cent"); and Sumner, *History of Women in Industry*, p. 123 (quoting Carey, "the humanity and the sense of justice"). See also the *New York Herald*, Feb. 25, March 1, and March 26, 1836; and June 5, 1837; and see the advertisements for the Tailoresses & Seamstresses Clothing Establishment, June 1 and July 29, 1837. In addition, see Stansell, *City of Women*, p. 147, Egal Feldman, *Fit for Men* (Washington, D.C.: Public Affairs Press, 1961), p. 118; and Andrews and Bliss, *History of Women in Trade Unions*, pp. 123–24, 137–38.

14. Foner, *Women and the American Labor Movement*, pp. 6–7; *New York Herald*, Feb. 25, 1836.

15. Stansell, *City of Women*, pp. 4, 81, 88, and 137–39 ("to perform the duties of the household" is from p. 138); *Working Man's Advocate*, March 15, 1845. On the struggle between employers and male wage earners for control over women's labor, see Jeanne Boydston, *Home and Work: Housework, Wages, and the Ideology of Labor in the Early Republic* (New York: Oxford University Press, 1990), pp. 135, 141; Blackmar, *Manhattan for Rent*, pp. 124–25; Annette Kuhn, "Structures of Patriarchy and Capital in the Family," in *Feminism and Materialism: Women and Modes of Production*, ed. Annette Kuhn and AnnMarie Wolpe (London: Routledge and Kegan Paul, 1978), p. 56; *New York Herald*, June 7, 1853; Stanley, *From Bondage to Contract*, pp. 175–98; and Foner, *Women and the American Labor Movement*, pp. 13–34.

16. *New York Tribune*, July 31, 1851.

17. Tellingly, Hood's "Song of the Shirt" was based on the arrest of a woman for pawning trousers, not shirts. See Edelstein, "They Sang 'The Song of the Shirt,'" pp. 186, 204–5. The female monopoly on shirt production is plain from the Catharine Street store ledger, 1818, box 03, A.3, book 2, Brooks Brothers Archive, Chantilly, Va. Shirts and fronts are also the only men's garments for which directions are provided in an "American Lady," *The Lady's Self-Instructor in Millinery, Mantua Making and All Branches of Plain Sewing* (New York: Burgess, Stringer & Co., 1844), pp. 21–22. On the domestic image of shirtmaking, see the *Working Man's Advocate*, June 10, 1831; Laurel Thatcher Ulrich, *Good Wives: Image and Reality in the Lives of Women in Northern New England, 1650–1750* (New York: Alfred A. Knopf, 1982), p. 29; Ellen J. Gehret, *Rural Pennsylvania Clothing* (York, Pa.: Liberty Cap Books, 1976), p. 125; and Jane C. Nylander, *Our Own Snug Fireside: Images of the New England Home, 1760–1860* (New York: Alfred A. Knopf, 1993), p. 162.

18. *New York Tribune*, Feb. 5, 1851 (emphasis in the original). See also the *Tribune* for March 27, July 31, and Aug. 1, 1851; Sumner, *History of Women in Industry*, pp. 59–60; and Stansell, *City of Women*, pp. 150–52.

19. *New-York Mirror*, Aug. 21, 1830; *New York Herald*, June 5, 1837. See also the *Herald* for Feb. 25, March 1, and March 26, 1836; and June 1 and July 29, 1837; Stansell, *City of Women*, p. 147; Feldman, *Fit for Men*, p. 118; and Mary Ryan, *Cradle of the Middle Class: The Family in Oneida County, New York, 1790–1865* (New York: Cambridge University Press, 1981), p. 53.

20. *New York Tribune*, March 8, 1845. On woman's economic role in the eighteenth-century household, see Laurel Thatcher Ulrich, "Wheels, Looms, and the Gender Division of Labor in Eighteenth-Century New England," *William and Mary Quarterly*, 3d ser., 55, no. 1 (Jan. 1998): 3–38. On her continued importance to economic policy after Independence, see Alexander Hamilton, *Report of the Secretary of the Treasury of the United States, on the Subject of Manufactures* (Dublin: P. Byrne, 1792). On her problematic place in the industrial labor market, see Boydston, *Home and Work*; Mary H. Blewett, *Men, Women, and Work: Class, Gender, and Protest in the New England Shoe Industry, 1780–1910* (Urbana: University of Illinois Press, 1988); and Penny, *Employments of Women*. On "domesticity," see Nancy F. Cott, *The Bonds of Womanhood: 'Woman's Sphere' in New England, 1780–1835* (New Haven, Conn.: Yale University Press, 1977), pp. 63–100.

21. Society for the Relief of Poor Widows with Small Children, *Annual Report*, 1840, pp. 4–5. See also Kessler-Harris, *Out to Work*, pp. 17, 24. The remarriage rate of widows began to

drop from the late eighteenth century onward, while the percentage of women who never wed rose. See Nancy F. Cott, "Passionlessness: An Interpretation of Victorian Sexual Ideology, 1790–1850," in *A Heritage of Her Own: Toward a New Social History of American Women*, ed. Nancy F. Cott and Elizabeth H. Pleck (New York: Simon and Schuster, 1979), p. 169. In addition, see Anne M. Boylan, "Women in Groups: An Analysis of Women's Benevolent Organizations in New York and Boston, 1797–1840," reprinted in Cott, ed., *History of Women in the United States*, vol. 16 (Munich: K. G. Saur, 1994), p. 44; and Foner, *Women and the American Labor Movement*, p. 6.

22. Isabella Graham quoted in Paul A. Gilje and Howard B. Rock, *Keepers of the Revolution: New Yorkers at Work in the Early Republic* (Ithaca, N.Y.: Cornell University Press, 1992), p. 278; Catharine Beecher, "The Seamstress," in *Godey's Lady's Book*, Dec. 1848, p. 363; Charles Burdett, *The Elliott Family; or, The Trials of New-York Seamstresses* (New York: Baker & Scribner, 1845), p. 23. See also "Stray Leaves from a Seamstresses [*sic*] Journal," *The Una*, June 1, 1853, p. 68; and William Burns, "The Vest Maker," in Burns, *Life in New York, In Doors and Out of Doors* (New York: Bunce & Brother, 1851).

23. Sarah Hale quoted in Cott, *Bonds of Womanhood*, p. 68. Women's protests against their own tenuous position in the democratic fraternity reached a rhetorical apotheosis when the abandoned heroine in Ann S. Stephens's popular novel *Fashion and Famine* (New York: Bunce and Brother, 1854) murdered her husband as retribution for his exploitation of her womanly affections. For illustrations of less violent protests, see the male foibles depicted in *Godey's Lady's Book*, April, May, June, Aug., Nov., and Dec. 1849; see also Dec. 1848, pp. 363–36; David M. Lubin, *Picturing a Nation: Art and Social Change in Nineteenth-Century America* (New Haven, Conn.: Yale University Press, 1994), pp. 159–203; Armstrong, *Desire and Domestic Fiction*, pp. 3–27; and Mary Ryan, "The Empire of the Mother: American Writing about Domesticity, 1830–1860," *Women and History*, nos. 2 and 3 (summer–fall 1982): 125–26. On women as antimarket crusaders, see Stephanie Coontz, *The Social Origins of Private Life: A History of American Families, 1600–1900* (London: Verso, 1988), pp. 161–250. On the guerrilla warfare between husband and wife in antebellum America, see T. Walter Herbert, *Dearest Beloved: The Hawthornes and the Making of the Middle-Class Family* (Berkeley: University of California Press, 1993), pp. 3–30.

24. T. S. Arthur, *The Seamstress: A Tale of the Times* (Philadelphia: R. G. Berford, 1843), p. 11; Society for the Relief of Poor Widows with Small Children, *Annual Report*, 1838, pp. 8–10. See also T. S. Arthur, "The Trials of a Needlewoman," *Godey's Lady's Book*, Feb.–July, 1854. Another sentimental expression of this closed system of recrimination can be found in C. T. Hinckley, "Making Shirts for a Shilling," *Godey's Lady's Book*, Dec. 1853, p. 530. See also Stansell, *City of Women*, p. 110; Horace Mann, *A Few Thoughts for a Young Man: A Lecture* (Boston: Ticknor, Reed, and Fields, 1850), p. 27; *New York Herald*, June 11, 1853; and the *New-York Mirror*, Feb. 13, 1841.

25. Charles Baudelaire, *The Painter of Modern Life and Other Essays*, ed. and trans. Jonathan Mayne (New York: De Capo, 1964), p. 36. On "creative destruction" in this era, see Stanley I. Kutler, *Privilege and Creative Destruction: The Charles River Bridge Case* (Baltimore: Johns Hopkins University Press, 1971). See also Barbara Meil Hobson, *Uneasy Virtue: The Politics of Prostitution and the American Reform Tradition* (New York: Basic Books, 1987), pp. 32–34; Keith Melder, "Ladies Bountiful: Organized Women's Benevolence in Early Nineteenth-Century America," reprinted in Cott, ed., *History of Women in the United States*,

vol. 16, p. 30; Marilynn Wood Hill, *Their Sisters' Keepers: Prostitution in New York City, 1830-1870* (Berkeley: University of California Press, 1993), pp. 116-35; Anne M. Boylan, "Timid Girls, Venerable Widows, and Dignified Matrons: Life Cycle Patterns among Organized Women in New York and Boston, 1797-1840," *American Quarterly* 38, no. 5 (winter 1986): 795; Caroll Smith-Rosenberg, "Beauty, the Beast, and the Militant Woman: A Case Study in Sex Roles and Social Stress in Jacksonian America," in *A Heritage of Her Own*, ed. Cott and Pleck, pp. 197-99; Christine Buci-Gluckmann, "Catastrophic Utopia: The Feminine as Allegory of the Modern," *Representations* 14 (spring 1986): 223, 227-28; Thomas Laqueur, "Bodies, Details, and the Humanitarian Narrative," in *The New Cultural History*, ed. Lynn Hunt (Berkeley: University of California Press, 1989), p. 182; Mark Seltzer, *Bodies and Machines* (New York: Routledge, 1992), pp. 65-66; and T. J. Clark, *The Painting of Modern Life: Paris in the Art of Manet and His Followers* (London: Thames and Hudson, 1984), pp. 102, 108.

26. Lori D. Ginzberg, *Women and the Work of Benevolence: Morality, Politics, and Class in the Nineteenth-Century United States* (New Haven, Conn.: Yale University Press, 1990), p. 22 and (quoting Sarah Hale) p. 12; George Thompson quoted in Timothy J. Gilfoyle, *City of Eros: New York City, Prostitution, and the Commercialization of Sex, 1790-1920* (New York: W. W. Norton, 1994), p. 148. On combatting the double standard, see Hill, *Their Sisters' Keepers*, pp. 140-41; Amy Gilman Srebnick, *The Mysterious Death of Mary Rogers: Sex and Culture in Nineteenth-Century New York* (New York: Oxford University Press, 1995), pp. 85, 95-99; Hobson, *Uneasy Virtue*, p. 50; Smith-Rosenberg, "Beauty, the Beast, and the Militant Woman," in *A Heritage of Her Own*, ed. Cott and Pleck, pp. 198, 200, 205; Lewis, "The Republican Wife," in Cott, ed., *History of Women in the United States*, vol. 18, pt. 1, pp. 32, 37, and 50-53; and Mary Poovey, "Speaking of the Body: Mid-Victorian Constructions of Female Desire," in *Body/Politics: Women and the Discourses of Science*, ed. Mary Jacobus, Evelyn Fox Keller, and Sally Shuttleworth (New York: Routledge, 1990), pp. 32-33. A modern prohibition against male masturbation can be dated to these same years. See Stephen Nissenbaum, *Sex, Diet, and Debility in Jacksonian America: Sylvester Graham and Health Reform* (Chicago: Dorsey Press, 1980), pp. 25-36, 112-13.

27. William W. Sanger, *The History of Prostitution: Its Extent, Causes, and Effects throughout the World* (New York: Harper & Brothers, 1859).

28. See Armstrong, *Desire and Domestic Fiction*, p. 20; Gilfoyle, *City of Eros*, p. 59; and Hobson, *Uneasy Virtue*, p. 64. On the importance of the prostitute's powerlessness, see Hobson, *Uneasy Virtue*, pp. 74-75; and Srebnick, *Mysterious Death of Mary Rogers*, pp. 80-82. On another culture using prostitution to disqualify a person from civic status, see David M. Halperin, "The Democratic Body: Prostitution and Citizenship in Classical Athens," *Differences* 2, no. 1 (1990): 1-28.

29. Amy Gilman Srebnick, "True Womanhood and Hard Times: Women and Early New York Industrialization, 1840-1860" (Ph.D. dissertation, State University of New York at Stony Brook, 1979), p. 93; *New York Tribune*, June 16, 1849. Likewise, charity was regarded as an effeminizing act. Reporting on its activities in 1856, the Five Points House of Industry described the reaction of one man to the care he received: "When he removed his rags, and clad himself with the warm and comfortable clothes we furnished him, the stout feelings of the man gave way, and he bowed his head and wept like a child" (Five Points House of Industry, *Annual Report* [New York, 1856], p. 15).

30. On the equation of womanly virtue and the home, see Cott, "Passionlessness," pp. 167–68, 172–73, and 175; Pateman, *Disorder of Women*, pp. 25–26, 45–46.

31. See Armstrong, *Desire and Domestic Fiction*, p. 6; Steven Seidman, "The Power of Desire and the Danger of Pleasure: Victorian Sexuality Reconsidered," *Journal of Social History* 24, no. 1 (fall 1990): 47–55; and Lewis, "The Republican Wife," in Cott, ed., *History of Women in the United States*, vol. 18, pt. 1, pp. 44–45. On the eighteenth-century origins of private virtue, albeit as a masculine trait, see Jack P. Greene, "The Concept of Virtue in Late Colonial British America," in *Virtue, Corruption, and Self-Interest: Political Values in the Eighteenth Century*, ed. Richard Matthews (Bethlehem, Pa.: Lehigh University Press, 1994), pp. 27–49; Jean V. Matthews, *Toward a New Society: American Thought and Culture, 1800–1830* (Boston: Twayne Publishers, 1991), p. 152; and Kerber, "Paradox of Women's Citizenship," p. 378.

32. Bobo, *Glimpses of New-York City*, pp. 107–10.

33. Ned Buntline [Edward Judson], *The G'hals of New York* (New York: Robert M. De Witt, 1850), pp. 101–2; George Lippard, *New York: Its Upper Ten and Lower Million* (Cincinnati, Ohio: H. M. Rulison, 1853), pp. 50–51. On Lippard, see, for instance, David S. Reynolds, *Under the American Renaissance: The Subversive Imagination in the Age of Emerson and Melville* (Cambridge, Mass.: Harvard University Press, 1988). On Ned Buntline, see Buckley, "To the Opera House," pp. 240–44. For a nonfictionalized account of the seamstress's utter dependence on the foreman, see the *New York Daily Times*, Feb. 24, Feb. 27, and March 1, 1855.

34. Advertisement for *The Orphan Seamstress* published by Garrett & Co., New York, n.d.; Foster, *New York in Slices*, p. 53; Allen Hampden's *Hartley Norman: A Tale of the Times* quoted in Siegel, *Image of the American City in Popular Literature*, p. 66.; Burdett, *The Elliott Family*, p. 56 (and see pp. 36–39). See also Bobo, *Glimpses of New-York City*, pp. 107–14; Benjamin Franklin, "The Busy-Body," no. 3, *American Weekly Mercury* (Philadelphia), Feb. 18, 1728, and "On Simplicity," *Pennsylvania Gazette*, April 13, 1732. A similar plot animates C. T. Hinckley, "Making Shirts for a Shilling; or, Misery and Magnificence," *Godey's Lady's Book*, Dec. 1853, pp. 422, 528–35.

On spinners in the days of the Revolution, see the *Pennsylvania Chronicle*, Feb. 20, 1769; the *Boston Gazette*, Jan. 18, 1768; the *Pennsylvania Gazette*, May 12, 1768, and July 19, 1770; Rolla Milton Tryon, *Household Manufactures in the United States, 1640–1860* (New York: Augustus M. Kelley, 1966 [1917]), pp. 86–87; Faye E. Dudden, *Serving Women: Household Service in Nineteenth-Century America* (Middletown, Conn.: Wesleyan University Press, 1983), p. 130; Linda K. Kerber, *Women of the Republic: Intellect and Ideology in Revolutionary America* (New York: W. W. Norton, 1986), pp. 105–11; J. Leander Bishop, *A History of American Manufactures from 1608 to 1860* (Philadelphia: Edward Young & Co., 1868), 1:333–41, 345–47; and Laurel Thatcher Ulrich, *The Age of Homespun: Objects and Stories in the Creation of an American Myth* (New York: Alfred A. Knopf, 2001), pp. 76–102.

35. From *Dunlap's Pennsylvania Packet and General Advertizer*, quoted in William R. Bagnall, *The Textile Industries of the United States* (Cambridge, Mass.: Riverside Press, 1893), 1:69–70.

36. John F. Kasson, *Civilizing the Machine: Technology and Republican Values in America, 1776–1900* (New York: Penguin Books, 1977), p. 27 and pp. 9–10. See also Kessler-Harris, *Out to Work*, p. 24.

37. Tryon, *Household Manufactures in the United States*, p. 284 (quoting *Niles'* from 1821) and p. 60. See also Boydston, *Home and Work*, pp. 5, 143.

38. *New York Tribune*, June 8, 1853; John F. Kasson, *Rudeness and Civility: Manners in Nineteenth-Century Urban America* (New York: Hill & Wang, 1990), pp. 160–61; T. S. Arthur, "A Story of the Upper Ten," *Godey's Lady's Book*, Aug. 1848, p. 80. See also Carey, *Appeal to the Wealthy of the Land*, Essay 4, p. 15.

39. See Linda K. Kerber, "The Republican Ideology of the Revolutionary Generation," *American Quarterly* 32, no. 4 (fall 1985): 483–84; Armstrong, *Desire and Domestic Fiction*, p. 15; J. G. A. Pocock, *The Machiavellian Moment: Florentine Political Thought and the Atlantic Republican Tradition* (Princeton, N.J.: Princeton University Press, 1975), pp. 463–64; Drew R. McCoy, *The Elusive Republic: Political Economy in Jeffersonian America* (New York: W. W. Norton, 1980), pp. 48–104; and Kerber, "Paradox of Women's Citizenship," p. 378.

40. Arthur, *The Seamstress*, p. 4; Freeman Hunt, *Worth and Wealth* (New York: Stringer & Townsend, 1856), p. 436; Buntline, *G'hals of New York*, p. 97; George Lippard, *The Man with the Mask* (1849), in *George Lippard, Prophet of Protest*, ed. Reynolds, p. 68. The import of chastity is clear in the disembodied purity of *The Una*'s feminist seamstress: see, for instance, the June 1, 1853, issue. See also the *New York Tribune*, June 8, 1853; the *New-York Mirror*, Aug. 2, 1823, and June 4, 1842; Kasson, *Rudeness and Civility*, pp. 160–61; and Seltzer, *Bodies and Machines*, pp. 98–99.

41. William B. English, *Gertrude Howard, the Maid of Humble Life; or, Temptations Resisted* (Boston: Redding & Co., 1843), pp. 6–7, 26, and 30–31.

42. Second annual report of the Ladies' Depository quoted in the *New-York American*, Jan. 26, 1836. See also "Report to the Managers of the Society for the Prevention of Pauperism in New-York, by Their Committee on Idleness and Sources of Employment," p. 10; "Twenty-Sixth Annual Report of the Orphan Asylum Society in the City of New-York" (1832); and Board of Aldermen, "Report of Commissioners of the Alms House . . . ," Sept. 29, 1834, all three in the Papers of the American Institute, case 2, New-York Historical Society, New York; Sumner, *History of Women in Industry*, p. 118; Srebnick, "True Womanhood and Hard Times," pp. 121–25; Boylan, "Women in Groups," p. 45; and Ulrich, *Age of Homespun*, pp. 161–66.

43. *New York Tribune*, June 8, 1853; Mathews, *Pen and Ink Panorama of New-York City*, p. 170. See also Solon Robinson, *Hot Corn: Life Scenes in New York Illustrated* (New York: De Witt and Davenport, 1854), pp. 50–51; Cornelius Mathews, "Society for Imposture," in Mathews, *The Motley Book: A Series of Tales and Sketches* (New York: J. & H. G. Langley, 1838); Sumner, *History of Women in Industry*, pp. 118–19, 129; Foner, *Women and the American Labor Movement*, p. 8; and David T. Gilchrist, ed., *The Growth of the Seaport Cities, 1790–1825* (Charlottesville: University Press of Virginia, for the Eleutherian Mills-Hagley Foundation, 1967), p. 101. See also the *Herald*'s investigation of "the shirt sewers of the metropolis," *New York Herald*, June 11, 1853.

44. T. S. Arthur, "Gentility," *Godey's Lady's Book*, May 1841, pp. 267–69. See also the poem "The Needle," in the *Lady's Book*, vol. 1 (1830), p. 328:

> The gay belles of fashion may boast of excelling
> In waltz or cotillion—at whist or quadrille;
> And seek admiration by vauntingly telling
> Of drawing, and painting, and musical skill;

But give me the fair one in country or city,
　Whose home and its duties are dear in her heart,
Who cheerfully warbles some rustical ditty
　While plying the needle with exquisite art.
The bright little needle—the swift flying needle,
　The needle directed by beauty and art.

45. Horace Bushnell, "The Age of Homespun," speech delivered in 1851 at Litchfield, Connecticut, on the occasion of the centennial celebration, in *Centennial Celebration* (Hartford, Conn.: Edwin Hunt, 1851), pp. 108–9 and 124 (and see pp. 112, 113–14, and 117–18); "scarcely . . . a look of damage" is quoted in Ann Douglas, *The Feminization of American Culture* (New York: Anchor Books, 1977), p. 53. See also "The Spinning-Wheel," with accompanying illustration, in the *Ladies' Companion*, Aug. 1840, pp. 20–21; Boydston, *Home and Work*, p. 150.

46. An "American Lady," *The Lady's Self-Instructor*, frontispiece (for the citation in full, see n. 17). The same illustration appeared as the frontispiece of T. S. Arthur's *The Lady at Home* (Philadelphia: W. A. Leary & Co., 1850). For examples of goddess iconography, see, for instance, J. Franklin Reigart, *The United States Album, Embellished with the Arms of Each State . . . , Containing the Autographs of the President and Cabinet, etc.* (Lancaster City, Pa.: P. S. Duval, 1844). See also Eric Hobsbawm, "Man and Woman in Socialist Iconography," *History Workshop* 6 (autumn 1978): 122–23.

47. Hazel Hunton, *Pantaloons and Petticoats (The Diary of a Young American)* (New York: House of Field, 1940), pp. 80–81, 92 (and see p. 106 as well). See also "Diary of Samuel Edgerly" (manuscript), entry for Jan. 7, 1859, Manuscripts and Archives Division, New York Public Library, New York. For other evidence of how prevalent an activity sewing was among middle-class women, see John Pintard, *Letters from John Pintard to His Daughter* (New York: New-York Historical Society, 1940), 1:212 (letter of Aug. 13, 1819); Richard B. Morris, *Government and Labor in Early America* (Boston: Northeastern University Press, 1981 [1946]), pp. 386–87; Nylander, *Our Own Snug Fireside*, pp. 150–51; and Anna Green Winslow, *Diary of a Boston School Girl of 1771*, ed. Alice Morse Earle (Detroit, Mich.: Singing Tree Press, 1970 [repr. of 1894 ed.]), pp. 40–41. See also Caroline Cowles Richards, *Village Life in America, 1852–1872* (London: T. Fisher Unwin, 1912), pp. 27, 49; Boydston, *Home and Work*, p. 41; and Beverly Gordon, "Meanings in Mid-Nineteenth Century Dress: Images from New England Women's Writings," *Clothing and Textiles Research Journal* 10, no. 3 (spring 1992): 50–51. On women and sewing in the eighteenth century, see Ulrich, *Age of Homespun*, pp. 143–73.

48. As Wheeler & Wilson declared in an advertising brochure: "These valuable aids to female industry are becoming quite a familiar thing in private families." See *Armitage & Moseley's Annual Circular (Wheeler & Wilson's Celebrated Family Sewing Machines)* (Albany, N.Y.: C. Van Benthuysen, 1859). See also the *New-York Illustrated News*, July 14 and Aug. 26, 1860; and the ad for Singer's Sewing Machines in *Kennedy's St. Louis City Directory for 1857*. On the sewing machine's place in the home, see William R. Bagnall, "Sketches of Manufacturing Establishments in New York City, and of Textile Establishments in the United States" (1977), manuscript, Merrimack Valley Textile Museum, North Andover, Mass., pp. 47–48; *Godey's Lady's Book*, Aug. 1855, p. 185; J. C. Gobright, *The New-York Sketch Book and*

Merchant's Guide (New York, 1859), pp. 70–71; Nylander, *Our Own Snug Fireside*, pp. 150–51; and Grace Rogers Cooper, *The Sewing Machine: Its Invention and Development* (Washington, D.C.: Smithsonian Institution Press, 1976), pp. 45–47.

49. "The Economics of Clothing and Dress," in *Godey's Lady's Book*, May 1854, p. 421. A quite different perspective was offered in 1851 by Elizabeth Cady Stanton, writing in the feminist journal *The Lily*: "Sewing is a dead loss to the one who does it. As an amusement it is contemptible; as an educator of head or heart, worthless; as a developer of muscle, of no avail; as a support, the most miserable of all trades." See *The Lily*, June 1851, excerpted in *The Radical Women's Press of the 1850s*, ed. Ann Russo and Cheris Kramarae (New York: Routledge, 1991), pp. 114–15 (the quotation is from p. 115).

50. Catharine Beecher, "The Seamstress," *Godey's Lady's Book*, Dec. 1848, p. 365; *Godey's Lady's Book*, May 1841, p. 22; *Ladies' Wreath*, vol. 1 (1846), p. 185. See also *Godey's Lady's Book*, Sept. 1845, p. 129; the *Lady's Book*, vol. 1 (1830), p. 328; Boydston, *Home and Work*, pp. 78, 82, 106, and 110; Thomas Butler Gunn, *The Physiology of New York Boarding-Houses* (New York: Mason Brothers, 1857), pp. 62–63; Marian Gouverneur, *As I Remember: Recollections of American Society During the Nineteenth Century* (New York: D. Appleton and Co., 1911), p. 28; "Female Dissipation in High Life," *New-York Mirror*, Oct. 19, 1833; Gordon, "Meanings in Mid-Nineteenth-Century Dress," pp. 50–51; and Harriet Connor Brown, *Grandmother Brown's Hundred Years, 1827–1927* (Boston: Little, Brown, and Co., 1929), p. 123. Women's work was also an important aspect of Harriet Beecher Stowe's indictment of Southern decadence. Compare the two wives—Mary Bird and Marie St. Clare—in chapters 9 and 16, respectively, of *Uncle Tom's Cabin, or, Life among the Lowly* (New York: Penguin Books, 1981 [1852]).

51. *Godey's Lady's Book*, Jan. 1847, pp. 48–50 (the quotations are from p. 48); and see Feb. 1847, pp. 110–12; March 1847, pp. 170–72; and May 1847, pp. 265–67. The *Illustrated Monthly Courier* likewise encouraged such "ladies' work": see, for instance, the fashions page of the December 1, 1848, issue.

52. *Ladies' Companion*, Aug. 1840, pp. 20–21 (for the title "The Spinning-Wheel"); *Ladies' Wreath*, vol. 1 (1846), p. 81; Catherine Kelly, " 'The Consummation of Rural Prosperity and Happiness': New England Agricultural Fairs and the Construction of Class and Gender, 1810–1860," *American Quarterly*, vol. 49, no. 3 (Sept. 1997): 589. See also Nancy Dunlap Bercaw, "Solid Objects / Mutable Meanings: Fancywork and the Construction of Bourgeois Culture, 1840–1880," *Winterthur Portfolio* 26, no. 4 (1991): 233–43.

53. On the New York Clothing Society, see the list of societies in *New York As It Is, in 1833, and Citizens' Advertising Directory*, ed. Edwin Williams (New York: J. Disturnell, 1833), and in the same for 1834. See also the *Occident and American Jewish Advocate* 1, no. 9 (Dec. 1843): 447–509; 9, no. 1 (April 1851): 48–49; and 19, no. 1 (April 1861): 38–39; *Godey's Lady's Book*, Jan. 1849, p. 25; and Caroll Smith-Rosenberg, *Disorderly Conduct: Visions of Gender in Victorian America* (New York: Alfred A. Knopf, 1985), pp. 69–70.

Chapter Seven

1. Anna Cora Mowatt, *Fashion; or, Life in New York* (New York: Samuel French, 1964), pp. 6, 13, and 12. The play was also produced in Boston, in Mobile, Alabama, and in New Orleans. See Eric Wollencott Barnes, *Anna Cora: The Life and Theatre of Anna Cora Mowatt*

(London: Secker & Warburg, 1954), pp. 195–214; and Philip Hone, *The Diary of Philip Hone, 1828–1851*, ed. Allan Nevins (New York: Kraus Reprint Co., 1969), entry for Nov. 18, 1841.

2. Mowatt, *Fashion*, pp. 18, 17; Edgar Allan Poe, review of Mowatt's *Fashion, Broadway Journal*, April 5, 1845, p. 219. See also the *Illustrated Monthly Courier*, Oct. 2, 1848. On Tyler's *The Contrast*, see Kenneth Silverman, *A Cultural History of the American Revolution* (New York: Columbia University Press, 1987), pp. 558–63.

3. Poe, review of Mowatt's *Fashion, Broadway Journal*, April 5, 1845, p. 219. See also Beverly Gordon, "Dressing the Colonial Past: Nineteenth-Century New Englanders Look Back," in *Dress in American Culture*, ed. Patricia A. Cunningham and Susan Voso Lab (Bowling Green, Ohio: Bowling Green State University Popular Press, 1993), pp. 109–10, 126–33; N. T. Hubbard, *Autobiography, with Personal Reminiscences of New York City, from 1798 to 1875* (New York: John F. Trow & Son, 1875), pp. 43–44, 160; Elizabeth McClellan, *Historic Dress in America, 1800–1870* (Philadelphia: George W. Jacobs & Co., 1910), p. 403; and Erin Skye Mackie, *Market à la Mode: Fashion, Commodity, and Gender in the "Tatler" and the "Spectator"* (Baltimore: Johns Hopkins University Press, 1997), p. 101.

4. Horace Mann, *A Few Thoughts for a Young Man: A Lecture* (Boston: Ticknor, Reed, and Fields, 1850), pp. 12–13; Adam de Gurowski, *America and Europe* (1857), excerpted in Carl Bode, ed., *Midcentury America: Life in the 1850s* (Carbondale: Southern Illinois University Press, 1972), p. 6; "Idle Hours—A Chapter on Fashion," *Columbian Magazine*, April 1844, p. 146.

5. *Mirror of Fashion*, vol. 11, no. 9 (Sept. 1849), p. 9; Lady Emmeline Stuart-Wortley, *Travels in the United States, etc., During 1849 and 1850* (London: Richard Bentley, 1851), 1:268. See also Ben Fine and Ellen Leopold, *The World of Consumption* (London: Routledge, 1993), p. 30.

6. *Mirror of Fashion*, n.s., vol. 1, no. 12 (Dec. 1853), p. 29; Alexis de Tocqueville quoted in Marvin Meyers, *The Jacksonian Persuasion: Politics and Belief* (New York: Vintage Books, 1957), p. 131. On universalizing subjectivity, see Mary Poovey, *A History of the Modern Fact: Problems of Knowledge in the Sciences of Wealth and Society* (Chicago: University of Chicago Press, 1998), pp. 147–56.

7. *Godey's Lady's Book*, Aug. 1833, p. 94; John Adams quoted in Richard L. Bushman, *The Refinement of America: Persons, Houses, Cities* (New York: Vintage Books, 1993), p. 200; "Personal Appearance," *Ladies' Companion*, March 1837; Horace Bushnell, "The Age of Homespun," speech delivered in 1851 at Litchfield, Connecticut, on the occasion of the centennial celebration, in *Centennial Celebration* (Hartford, Conn.: Edwin Hunt, 1851), p. 112. On wasting time in front of the mirror, see William A. Alcott, *A Young Man's Guide*, 16th ed. (Boston: T. R. Marvin, 1846 [1834]), pp. 83–84; Joyce Appleby, "Consumption in Early Modern Social Thought," in *Consumption and the World of Goods*, ed. John Brewer and Roy Porter (London: Routledge, 1993), p. 166; and Gordon S. Wood, "Conspiracy and the Paranoid Style: Causality and Deceit in the Eighteenth Century," *William and Mary Quarterly*, 3d ser., 39, no. 3 (July 1982): 401–41.

8. *Mirror of Fashion*, n.s., vol. 3, no. 9 (Sept. 1855), p. 74; *Godey's Lady's Book*, Jan. 1835, p. 48 (and see the Sept. 1843 issue, p. 137, for a recapitulation of the argument). See also Charles Baudelaire, "In Praise of Cosmetics," in *The Painter of Modern Life and Other Essays*, ed. and trans. Jonathan Mayne (New York: De Capo, 1964), pp. 31–38.

9. *Massachusetts Gazette*, Nov. 19, 1767; Mathew Carey in the *American Museum* 2, no. 2 (Aug. 1787): 119. Allowing that "homespun, they say, is not quite so gay / As brocades," the *Boston Gazette* (Jan. 25, 1768), turned for help to society's tastemakers: "For when once it is known this is much wore in town, / One and all will cry out, 'Tis the fashion.'" See also Edmund S. Morgan and Helen M. Morgan, *The Stamp Crisis: Prologue to Revolution* (Chapel Hill: University of North Carolina Press, 1953), p. 86; William R. Bagnall, *The Textile Industries of the United States* (Cambridge, Mass.: Riverside Press, 1893), 1:57; and Elizabeth Wilson, *Adorned in Dreams: Fashion and Modernity* (London: Virago Press, 1985), pp. 11–12.

10. Sir Thomas More, *Utopia*, ed. Edward Surtz, S. J. (New Haven, Conn.: Yale University Press, 1964), p. 74; Mathew Carey in the *American Museum* 3, no. 1 (Jan. 1788): 89; George Foster, *New York in Slices, by an Experienced Carver* (New York: W. F. Burgess, 1849), p. 4. See also James Eli Adams, *Dandies and Desert Saints: Styles of Victorian Masculinity* (Ithaca, N.Y.: Cornell University Press, 1995), p. 152; William A. Alcott, *Familiar Letters to Young Men on Various Subjects* (Buffalo, N.Y.: Geo. H. Derby and Co., 1850), pp. 89, 125–40; and the *New-York Mirror*, June 19, 1830.

11. Tristam Burges, *Speech in the House of Representatives . . . May 10, 1830* (Providence, R.I.: Marshall and Hammond, 1830), p. 9.

12. "Petition of the Journeymen Tailors of Philadelphia," Jan. 30, 1832, 22d Congress, 1st sess., Doc. no. 39; George McDuffie, *Speech in the House of Representatives on the Woollens' Bill, February 7, 1827* (Washington, D.C.: Gales & Seaton, 1827), pp. 4, 7–8.

13. On economic development as the common denominator of political community, see L. Ray Gunn, *The Decline of Authority: Public Economic Policy and Political Development in New York, 1800–1860* (Ithaca, N.Y.: Cornell University Press, 1988), pp. 73–81, 148–51; and Jonathan Prude, *The Coming of Industrial Order: Town and Factory Life in Rural Massachusetts, 1810–1860* (New York: Cambridge University Press, 1983), pp. 240–45. John Ashworth describes the ideological provenance of a new "equality of opportunity" in *"Agrarians" and "Aristocrats": Party Political Ideology in the United States, 1837–1846* (New York: Cambridge University Press, 1987).

14. Edwin T. Freedley, *A Practical Treatise on Business, or How to Get, Save, Spend, Give, Lend, and Bequeath Money* (Philadelphia: Lippincott, Grambo & Co., 1855), p. 121. See also James L. Huston, "The American Revolutionaries, the Political Economy of Aristocracy, and the American Concept of the Distribution of Wealth, 1765–1900," *American Historical Review* 98, no. 4 (Oct. 1993): 1087–88, 1092–94; "A Gentleman," *The Perfect Gentleman; or, Etiquette and Elegance* (New York: Dick & Fitzgerald, 1860), p. 112; and Jean-Christophe Agnew, "The Threshold of Exchange: Speculations on the Market," *Radical History Review* 21 (fall 1979): 99–114.

15. Wendell Phillips, "European and Yankee Life Contrasted," *Mirror of Fashion*, n.s., vol. 1 (1853), p. 55. For an example of Mathew Carey's approach, see *Appeal to the Wealthy of the Land, Ladies as Well as Gentlemen* (Philadelphia: Stereotyped by L. Johnson, 1833), Essay 4, pp. 15–19.

16. *New-York Mirror*, March 21, 1829; "A Modern Philosopher, Lesson the Second," *Burton's Gentleman's Magazine*, Aug. 1837; *New York Aurora*, "Extra" edition, Feb. 1842; Henry Lunettes [Margaret Cockburn Conkling], *The American Gentleman's Guide to Politeness* (New York: Derby & Jacobson, 1857), p. 30; Samuel Robert Wells, *How to Behave: A*

Pocket Manual of Republican Etiquette (New York: Fowler and Wells, 1856), p. 32; George P. Fox, *Fashion: The Power That Influences the World*, 3d ed. (New York: Sheldon & Co., 1872), p. 172; *Mirror of Fashion*, n.s., vol. 3 (1855), p. 56.

17. Horace Greeley et al., *The Great Industries of the United States* (Hartford: J. B. Burr & Hyde, 1872), p. 921; *New-York Mirror*, Dec. 20, 1823; *Hunt's Merchant's Magazine*, May 1840, p. 363; Harriet Beecher Stowe, *Uncle Tom's Cabin, or Life among the Lowly* (New York: Penguin Books, 1981), p. 1. See also the "Idle Hours—A Chapter on Fashion," *Columbian Magazine*, April 1844, p. 146; Anne Hollander, *Sex and Suits* (New York: Alfred A. Knopf, 1994), pp. 84–97; Mark Seltzer, *Bodies and Machines* (New York: Routledge, 1992), pp. 60, 63; and Philippe Perrot, *Fashioning the Bourgeoisie: A History of Clothing in the Nineteenth Century*, trans. Richard Bienvenu (Princeton, N.J.: Princeton University Press, 1994), pp. 32–33.

18. Lunettes, *American Gentleman's Guide to Politeness*, pp. 26–27; Fox, *Fashion*, p. 171; *Mirror of Fashion*, n.s., vol. 3 (1855), p. 25; *New Mirror*, June 10, 1843, p. 160 (and see Sept. 2, 1843); "Fashion," *Ladies' Companion*, March 1835. See also Bushman, *Refinement of America*, p. xv; Karen Halttunen, *Confidence Men and Painted Women: A Study of Middle-Class Culture in America, 1830–1870* (New Haven, Conn.: Yale University Press, 1982), p. 29; G. J. Barker-Benfield, *The Culture of Sensibility: Sex and Society in Eighteenth-Century Britain* (Chicago: University of Chicago Press, 1992), pp. 132–39; and Mackie, *Market à la Mode*, p. 212.

19. See Foster, *New York in Slices*, p. 78; Thompson Westcott, "The Physiology of Dandyism," *Graham's Magazine*, Feb. 1852, p. 122; Jessica R. Feldman, *Gender on the Divide: The Dandy in Modernist Literature* (Ithaca, N.Y.: Cornell University Press, 1993), pp. 2–5; Nora Waugh, *The Cut of Men's Clothes, 1600–1900* (New York: Theatre Arts Books, 1964), p. 151; and John D. Vose, *Fresh Leaves from the Diary of a Broadway Dandy* (New York: Bunnel & Price, 1852). See also *Burton's Gentleman's Magazine*, Aug. 1837, p. 87; *City Characters; or, Familiar Scenes in Town* (Philidelphia: Geo. S. Appleton, 1851), pp. 75–76; *New-York Mirror*, July 4 and Aug. 22, 1840 (and see June 4 and Sept. 24, 1836); Lunettes, *American Gentleman's Guide to Politeness*, pp. 69–70; *Putnam's Monthly: A Magazine of Literature, Science, and Art*, March 1853, p. 310; Penelope Byrde, *Nineteenth-Century Fashion* (London: B. T. Batsford, 1992), p. 94; and Joan L. Severa, *Dressed for the Photographer: Ordinary Americans and Fashion, 1840–1900* (Kent, Ohio: Kent State University Press, 1995), pp. 19–20.

20. Cornelius Mathews, *A Pen and Ink Panorama of New-York City* (New York: John S. Taylor, 1853), p. 132. See also Peter Buckley, "To the Opera House: Culture and Society in New York City, 1820–1860" (Ph.D. dissertation, State University of New York at Stony Brook, 1984), p. 323; Alvin F. Harlow, *Old Bowery Days: The Chronicle of a Famous Street* (New York: D. Appleton and Co., 1931), pp. 195–97; William Bobo, *Glimpses of New-York City* (Charleston, S.C.: J. J. McCarter, 1852), pp. 164–66; Abram C. Dayton, *Last Days of Knickerbocker Life in New York* (New York: G. P. Putnam's Sons, 1897), pp. 217–21; and the *Mirror of Fashion*, vol. 12, no. 4 (April 1850). See, more generally, Dick Hebdige, *Subculture: The Meaning of Style* (London: Methuen, 1979).

21. *Mirror of Fashion*, n.s., vol. 3 (1855), p. 50 (and see n.s., vol. 1 [1853], p. 29); Sima Godfrey, "The Dandy as Ironic Figure," *Sub-Stance* 36 (1982): 23. An important variation of this genre was the Negro dandy, whose sartorial transgressions were viewed as particularly galling. Indeed, any Negro who sought to look his best might well have been accused, by def-

NOTES TO PAGES 196–198 :: 281

inition, of being a dandy, since the spectacle of a well-dressed Negro so clearly violated the American (visual) order. "Dandyism is fit only for free niggers," as *Burton's Gentleman's Magazine* remarked in August 1837. Negroes apparently possessed an inherent tendency toward dandyism: "Among races, the one in which a love of gay dress and tawdry finery may be most extensively observed, is the Negro," Edwin Freedley observed; they are "the natural dandies of the human species" (*Leading Pursuits and Leading Men: A Treatise on the Principal Trades and Manufactures of the United States* [Philadelphia: Edward Young, 1854], p. 89). On the Negro dandy, see also the *New Mirror*, Jan. 6, 1844; Eric Lott, *Love and Theft: Blackface Minstrelsy and the American Working Class* (New York: Oxford University Press, 1993), pp. 25, 131–35, and 222–33; and Graham White and Shane White, *Stylin': African American Expressive Culture from Its Beginnings to the Zoot Suit* (Ithaca, N.Y.: Cornell University Press, 1998).

22. *Mirror of Fashion*, n.s., vol. 3 (1855), p. 51 (and see pp. 3–6); Lunettes, *American Gentleman's Guide to Politeness*, p. 67; Alcott, *Young Man's Guide*, pp. 73–75; John Beaucamp Jones [Luke Shortfield], *The Western Merchant* (Philadelphia: Grigg, Elliot & Co., 1849), pp. 175–76; *Canons of Good Breeding* excerpted in Mary Ellen Roach and Joanne Bubolz Eicher, eds., *Dress, Adornment, and the Social Order* (New York: John Wiley & Sons, 1965), p. 267; Herman Melville, *Typee: A Real Romance of the South Sea* (Boston: Page Company, 1892 [1846]), p. 266. See also Beverly Gordon, "Meanings in Mid-Nineteenth Century Dress: Images from New England Women's Writings," *Clothing and Textiles Research Journal* 10, no. 3 (spring 1992): 45; Joseph Couts, *A Practical Guide for the Tailor's Cutting-Room* (London: Blackie and Son, 1848), pp. 59, 68, 71, 75, and 110; and Fox, *Fashion*, p. 72.

23. T. S. Arthur, "Following the Fashions," *Godey's Lady's Book*, March 1843, pp. 134–37 (the quote is from p. 134).

24. See Egal Feldman, "New York's Men's Clothing Trade, 1800 to 1861" (Ph.D. dissertation, University of Pennsylvania, 1959), pp. 145–46; *Doggett's New York Business Directory for 1840–41* (New York: John Doggett, 1840–41), p. 205; *New York Tribune*, Sept. 26, 1850; Margaret Walsh, "The Democratization of Fashion: The Emergence of the Women's Dress-Pattern Industry," *Journal of American History* 66, no. 2 (Sept. 1979): 300–303; Rachel Salisbury, "1860—The Last Year of Peace: Augusta Tallman's Diary," *Wisconsin Magazine of History*, vol. 44 (1960–61), p. 87; Margaret Thompson Ordonez, "A Frontier Reflected in Costume: Tallahassee, Leon County, Florida, 1824–1861" (Ph.D. dissertation, Florida State University, 1978), p. 33; and Mrs. Felton, *American Life: A Narrative of Two Years' City and Country Residence* (London: Simpkin, Marshall and Co., 1842), p. 74. On women's traditions of home dressmaking, see the essays in Barbara Burman, ed., *The Culture of Sewing: Gender, Consumption and Home Dressmaking* (Oxford: Oxford University Press, 1999).

25. Fox, *Fashion*, p. 119 (and see pp. 224–25); *United States Economist, and Dry Goods Reporter*, April 9, 1853, p. 436; and, for the *Home Journal*, William Leach, *True Love and Perfect Union: The Feminist Reform of Sex and Society* (New York: Basic Books, 1980), p. 218. On the "Great Masculine Renunciation" of fashion, see the chapter "Sex Differences" (1929) in J. C. Flugel, *The Psychology of Clothes* (London: Hogarth Press, 1971), especially pp. 110–13. Claudia Brush Kidwell and Valerie Steele, *Men and Women: Dressing the Part* (Washington, D.C.: Smithsonian Institution Press, 1989), pp. 126–29; and Hollander, *Sex and Suits*, p. 67.

26. Virginia Penny, *The Employments of Women: A Cyclopaedia of Woman's Work* (Boston:

Walker, Wise & Co., 1863), p. 325; Frazar Kirkland, *Cyclopaedia of Commercial and Business Anecdotes* (New York: D. Appleton and Co., 1865), p. 611; *United States Economist, and Dry Goods Reporter*, April 9, 1853, p. 436. See also Claudia Kidwell, *Cutting a Fashionable Fit: Dressmakers' Draftmaking Systems in the United States* (Washington, D.C.: Smithsonian Institution Press, 1979), p. 21; Elaine S. Abelson, *When Ladies Go A-Thieving: Middle-Class Shoplifters in the Victorian Department Store* (New York: Oxford University Press, 1989), pp. 35–40; and Lois W. Banner, *American Beauty* (New York: Alfred A. Knopf, 1983), pp. 103–5.

27. Hazel Hunton, *Pantaloons and Petticoats (The Diary of a Young American)* (New York: House of Field, 1940), p. 112. See also Banner, *American Beauty*, pp. 20, 75; Charles H. Haswell, *Reminiscences of an Octogenarian of the City of New York* (New York: Harper & Brothers, 1896), p. 88; *New York Tribune*, Jan. 20, 1858; T. J. Clark, *The Painting of Modern Life: Paris in the Art of Manet and His Followers* (London: Thames and Hudson, 1985), p. 69; Hollander, *Sex and Suits*, pp. 8–9, 32; Linda Morton, "American Pattern Drafting Systems for Men in the Nineteenth Century" (M.A. thesis, Colorado State University, 1981). p. 1; and Mackie, *Market à la Mode*, p. 40.

In a story called "The Cheap Dress," *Godey's* addressed the irrationality of women's fashion. The story concerns a woman's neurotic attempts to save a few pennies in searching for fabric for a new dress, an effort that soon comes back to haunt her. After but a short while, her new garment is so shabby-looking as to be unfit for polite company and is even rejected by the woman's servant as a hand-me-down. The heroine's sin, according to *Godey's*, lay in thinking about her dress in terms of an economic exchange, defining its value by its cost rather than by its beauty. In fact, there is no such thing as cheap finery: such compulsive budgeting belongs to the realm of men, or of seamstresses. True women, the story suggests, should embrace what is naturally theirs, without confusing it with matters of economic rationality. See *Godey's Lady's Book*, Sept. 1845, pp. 86–91.

28. On Sarah Hale, see Severa, *Dressed for the Photographer*, p. 3; the "bug bear—fashion!" is from the *Pennsylvania Gazette*, May 12, 1768 (quoting a "Freeborn American"); and see Mathew Carey, "Fashions," in *Godey's Lady's Book*, May 1834, p. 253. See also Kidwell, *Cutting a Fashionable Fit*; and Stephanie Grauman Wolf, "Rarer Than Riches: Gentility in Eighteenth-Century America," in *The Portrait in Eighteenth-Century America*, ed. Ellen G. Miles (Newark: University of Delaware Press, 1993), p. 98. On the symbolic meaning of w(h)igs in the 1830s, see the lithograph reproduced in Elizabeth Johns, *American Genre Painting: The Politics of Everyday Life* (New Haven, Conn.: Yale University Press, 1991), p. 47. On the development of a sentimental female culture that stood opposed to manly republican simplicity, see Thomas N. Baker, *Sentiment and Celebrity: Nathaniel Parker Willis and the Trials of Literary Fame* (New York: Oxford University Press, 1999).

29. T. S. Arthur, "Following the Fashions," *Godey's Lady's Book*, March 1843, p. 134. See also Abigail Solomon-Godeau, "The Other Side of Venus: The Visual Economy of Feminine Display," in *The Sex of Things: Gender and Consumption in Historical Perspective*, ed. Victoria de Grazia and Ellen Furlough (Berkeley: University of California Press, 1996); Nancy Armstrong, *Desire and Domestic Fiction: A Political History of the Novel* (New York: Oxford University Press, 1987), pp. 3–27; and Seltzer, *Bodies and Machines*, pp. 64–65.

30. Fox, *Fashion*, p. 157; John F. Kasson, *Civilizing the Machine: Technology and Republican Values in America, 1776–1900* (New York: Penguin Books, 1977), pp. 151–55 (the *Scientific*

American is quoted on p. 151); *Mirror of Fashion*, vol. 12, no. 5 (May 1850), p. 33. See also Hollander, *Sex and Suits*, pp. 63–115.

31. Isaac Walker, *Dress: As It Has Been, Is, and Will Be* (New York: Isaac Walker, 1885), pp. 70–73; Elizabeth Cady Stanton, *Eighty Years and More* (London: T. Fisher Unwin, 1898), pp. 201–4. The Bloomer was not wholly divorced from fashionability, influenced as it was by contemporary interest in the Near East. See Bernard Rudofsky, *Are Clothes Modern? An Essay on Contemporary Apparel* (Chicago: Paul Theobald, 1957), p. 184. On the physical constriction of women's clothing, see Severa, *Dressed for the Photographer*, pp. 7, 15. One dress reformer, John Humphrey Noyes, proclaimed his support for women wearing pants: "Woman's dress is a standing lie. It proclaims that she is not a two-legged animal, but something like a churn standing on castors!" (quoted in Amy Kesselman, "The 'Freedom Suit': Feminism and Dress Reform in the United States, 1848–1875," *Gender and Society* 5, no. 4 [Dec. 1991]: 496). A more orthodox version of the rationale for dress reform is found in Catharine Beecher: "How different are our customs, from what sound wisdom dictates! Women go out with thin stockings, thin shoes, and open necks, when men are protected by thick woollen hose and boots, and their whole body encased in many folds of flannel and broadcloth" (*A Treatise on Domestic Economy, for the Use of Young Ladies at Home, and at School* [New York: Harper & Brothers, 1848], p. 115).

32. Susan B. Anthony quoted in Robert E. Reigel, "Women's Clothes and Women's Rights," *American Quarterly* 15, no. 3 (fall 1963): 391; Amelia Bloomer in *The Lily*, May 1851, p. 38; *Ladies' Wreath*, vol. 6 (1852), p. 248; Leach, *True Love and Perfect Union*, p. 246. See also *Holden's Dollar Magazine*, March 1850, p. 179; and Shelly Foote, "Bloomers," *Dress* 6 (1980): 5. The connection between homespun and the Bloomer was made explicit in Pauline Forsyth's "A Bloomer among Us," published in *Godey's Lady's Book* in May 1854. Although critical, and even dismissive, of the new fashion, the author clearly understood the ideological provenance of the Bloomer when she made the father of the Bloomer-clad feminist a "homespun-looking man." The Bloomer's real practical success, by all accounts, lay in its widespread adoption by women active on the farm in isolated settlements. See Severa, *Dressed for the Photographer*, p. 88; and David Holman and Billie Persons, *Buckskin and Homespun: Frontier Texas Clothing, 1820–1870* (Austin, Tex.: Wind River Press, 1979), pp. 41–43. See also Ann Russo and Cheris Kramarae, eds., *The Radical Women's Press of the 1850s* (New York: Routledge, 1991). For positive responses to the Bloomer in the popular press, see *Gleason's Pictorial*, June 14, 1851; and the *New York Tribune*, May 27, 1851. On the overall political impact of the Bloomer protest, see William Hancock, *An Emigrant's Five Years in the Free States of America* (London: T. Cautley Newby, 1860), p. 96.

33. *Harper's Monthly Magazine* accordingly paraphrased Hamlet: "To don the pants— / The pants! perchance the boots! Ay, there's the rub . . ." (quoted in Kidwell and Steele, *Men and Women*, p. 150). On the dangers of impersonating men, see, for example, Tassie Gwilliam, "Pamela and the Duplicitous Body of Femininity," *Representations* 34 (spring 1991): 104–33. On the nineteenth century's gendering of costume, see, for instance, Helene E. Roberts, "The Exquisite Slave: The Role of Clothes in the Making of the Victorian Woman," *Signs* 2, no. 3 (spring 1977): 554–69; Mariana Valverde, "The Love of Finery: Fashion and the Fallen Woman in Nineteenth-Century Social Discourse," *Victorian Studies* 32, no. 2 (winter 1989): 169–88; and Solomon-Godeau, "The Other Side of Venus," in *The Sex of Things*, ed. de

Grazia and Furlough. On the fashionable distinction between male and female, see Hollander, *Sex and Suits*.

34. See the *Ladies' Wreath*, vol. 6 (1852), p. 248. On women's disconnection from civic life, see the essays in Carole Pateman, *The Disorder of Women: Democracy, Feminism, and Political Theory* (Stanford, Calif.: Stanford University Press, 1989). It was a measure of the uncertain character of the times that those who would reform female dress, no less than proponents of popular women's fashions, based their program on a putative "nature." See Foote, "Bloomers," pp. 5, 10; and Kidwell and Steele, *Men and Women*, pp. 149–50. In contrast, writing in 1856 to Gerrit Smith, who opposed the Bloomer, Elizabeth Cady Stanton tacitly rejected the notion of any inborn difference between men and women: "Believing as you do in the identity of the sexes, that all the difference we see in tastes, in character, is entirely the result of education—that 'man is woman and woman is man'—why keep up these distinctions of dress?" (quoted in Leach, *True Love and Perfect Union*, p. 246). See also George Templeton Strong, *The Diary of George Templeton Strong, Young Man in New York, 1835–1849*, ed. Allan Nevins (New York: Macmillan Company, 1952), entry for Sept. 8, 1853. More generally, see Marina Warner, *Monuments and Maidens: The Allegory of the Female Form* (London: Weidenfeld and Nicolson, 1985). For an interesting expression of nonfeminist dress reform, see Edmund P. Banning, *Common Sense on the Mechanical Pathology and Treatment of Chronic Diseases of the Male and Female Systems* (New York: Wilson & Co., 1852).

35. See Karin Calvert, "The Function of Fashion in Eighteenth-Century America," in *Of Consuming Interests: The Style of Life in the Eighteenth Century*, ed. Cary Carson, Ronald Hoffman, and Peter J. Albert (Charlottesville: University Press of Virginia, 1994), pp. 260–61, 274–79; and Edward Warwick, Henry C. Pitz, and Alexander Wyckoff, *Early American Dress: The Colonial and Revolutionary Periods* (New York: Benjamin Blom, 1965), pp. 149–63, 213–18.

36. Alice Morse Earle, *Two Centuries of Costume in America, 1620–1820* (New York: Macmillan Company, 1903), pp. 767–71 ("folly, extravagance, and French disbelief" is from p. 771); "The Last of the White Cravats," *New Mirror*, April 15, 1843 (and see April 8, 1843). See also the *Nantucket Enquirer*, Jan. 17 and Feb. 14, 1825; and Gerry Beth Gilbert, "An Examination of the Influence of Social and Economic Development on East Tennessee Dress from 1790 to 1850" (M.S. thesis, University of Tennessee, 1971), p. 39.

37. Nathaniel Hawthorne, "The Brighton Cattle Fair," from the *American Notebooks*, excerpted in *The Leaven of Democracy: The Growth of the Democratic Spirit in the Time of Jackson*, ed. Clement Eaton (New York: George Braziller, 1963), p. 125; *Mirror of Fashion*, n.s., vol. 3 (1855), p. 3; *Mirror of Fashion*, n.s., vol. 1 (1853), pp. 102, 61 (and, for "business dress," see pp. 83, 122, 133, 143, and 152); *Mirror of Fashion*, vol. 12, no. 5 (May 1850), p. 33; and *Cohen's New Orleans and Southern Directory*, 1855 (New Orleans, La.: Daily Delta, 1855). For Franklin on homespun, see "On Simplicity," *Pennsylvania Gazette*, April 13, 1732.

38. John Pintard, *Letters from John Pintard to His Daughter* (New York: New-York Historical Society, 1940), 2:10–11 (letter of March 1, 1821).

39. U.S. Census Office, *Manufactures of the United States in 1860, Compiled from the Original Returns of the Eighth Census* (Washington, D.C.: Government Printing Office, 1865), p. lxii; Thomas Ford, *A History of Illinois, from Its Commencement as a State in 1818 to 1847*, ed. Milo Milton Quaife (Chicago: R. R. Donnelley & Sons, 1945), p. 130; Gordon S. Wood, *The*

Radicalism of the American Revolution (New York: Alfred A. Knopf, 1992), pp. 351–53 (James Guild is quoted on p. 353).

40. *Hunt's Merchant's Magazine*, May 1849, p. 371; *Putnam's Monthly* quoted in Buckley, "To the Opera House," pp. 602–3; William Sanger, *The History of Prostitution: Its Extent, Causes, and Effects throughout the World* (New York: Harper & Brothers, 1859), p. 532. On the relationship between democracy and plenty, see J. G. A. Pocock, *The Machiavellian Moment: Florentine Political Thought and the Atlantic Republican Tradition* (Princeton, N.J.: Princeton University Press, 1975), pp. 465–66; Istvan Hont and Michael Ignatieff, *Wealth and Virtue: The Shaping of Political Economy in the Scottish Enlightenment* (Cambridge: Cambridge University Press, 1983), p. 42; Louis Dumont, *From Mandeville to Marx: The Genesis and Triumph of Economic Ideology* (Chicago: University of Chicago Press, 1977), pp. 61–81; and James Madison, "On Fashion," in *The Writings of James Madison*, ed. Gaillard Hunt (New York: G. P. Putnam's Sons, 1906), 4:99–100. Compare this new acceptance of luxury to the zero-sum morality of the Methodists' campaign for simplicity in the early years of the century. In the words of Charles Wesley: "The more you lay out on your own apparel, the less you have left to clothe the naked, to feed the hungry, to lodge the strangers, to relieve those that are sick and in prison, and to lesson the numberless aflictions to which we are exposed in the vale of tears" (quoted in Leigh Eric Schmidt, "'A Church-Going People Are a Dress-Loving People': Clothes, Communication, and Religious Culture in Early America," *Church History* 58, no. 1 [March 1989]: 48).

41. *Mirror of Fashion*, n.s., vol. 3 (1855), p. 56. See also Bushman, *Refinement of America*, pp. 276–79; the *Home Journal*, May 24, 1856; Buckley, "To the Opera House," pp. 220, 240–44; and *Putnam's Monthly*, March 1853, p. 308. In the wake of the Opera House riot at Astor Place in 1849, even Nathaniel Willis, prone as he was to defend class privilege, understood that life in a republic "puts very different limits to the ostentation of luxury" (quoted in Baker, *Sentiment and Celebrity*, p. 112).

42. Fox, *Fashion*, p. 71; *Mirror of Fashion*, vol. 12, no. 5 (May 1850), p. 33; for "Long Island niggers," see Johns, *American Genre Painting*, p. 229; for the "two Ethiopians," see the *New Mirror*, Jan. 6, 1844. See also Dayton, *Last Days of Knickerbocker Life*, p. 337; Michael S. Kimmel, "Consuming Manhood: The Feminization of American Culture and the Recreation of the Male Body, 1832–1920," in *The Male Body: Features, Destinies, Exposures*, ed. Laurence Goldstein (Ann Arbor: University of Michigan Press, 1994), p. 18; Nathaniel Parker Willis, "Ephemera," in *Dashes at Life with a Free Pencil* (New York: J. S. Redfield, 1847), pp. 185, 187; and Severa, *Dressed for the Photographer*, pp. 109, 127. For a description of sartorial events on an American railroad platform involving a dandy and a man in a coarse coat—two equally intolerable transgressions—see the *Mirror of Fashion*, n.s., vol. 1 (1853), pp. 9–10. For an expression of the polemic over the wearing of livery in America, see L. Maria Child, *Letter from New York*, 2d ser. (New York: C. S. Francis, 1849), pp. 279–81.

43. George Gifford, *Before the Honorable Philip F. Thomas . . . in the Matter of the Application of Elias Howe, Jr., for an Extension of His Patent for Sewing Machines* (New York: W. W. Rose, 1860); James Boardman quoted in Bayrd Still, *Mirror for Gotham: New York as Seen by Contemporaries from Dutch Days to the Present* (New York: New York University Press, 1956), p. 112 (and see pp. 84, 86, and 87); Michael Chevalier, *Society, Manners, and Politics in the United States* (New York: Augustus M. Kelley, 1966 [1839]), pp. 341–42; William Cham-

bers, *Things as They Are in America* (New York: Negro Universities Press, 1968 [1854]), p. 343; Francis Wyse, *America, Its Realities and Resources* (London: T. C. Newby, 1846), 3:21; Frederika Bremer, *America of the Fifties: Letters of Fredrika Bremer*, ed. Adolph Benson (New York: American-Scandinavian Foundation, 1924), p. 17; de Gurowski, *America and Europe* (1857), in Bode, ed., *Midcentury America*, p. 6; Alexander Mackay, "The Capitol of New England," in *Leaven of Democracy*, ed. Eaton, p. 132; Stuart-Wortley, *Travels in the United States*, 1:268. See also Henry Bradshaw Fearon, *Sketches of America: A Narrative of a Journey of Five Thousand Miles through the Eastern and Western States* (London: Longman, Hurst, Rees, Orme, and Brown, 1818), p. 124 (and see p. 10); Richard Cobden, *The American Diaries of Richard Cobden*, ed. Elizabeth Hoon Cawley (Princeton, N.J.: Princeton University Press, 1952), p. 121, as well as pp. 80–89 and 93; Wood, *Radicalism of the American Revolution*, p. 304; Benjamin Smith, ed., *Twenty-Four Letters from Labourers in America to Their Friends in England* (London: Edward Rainford, 1829), p. 27; Feldman, "New York's Men's Clothing Trade," p. 153; and Hancock, *An Emigrant's Five Years in the Free States of America*, p. 45.

44. Wyse, *America, Its Realities and Resources*, 3:20–21.

45. Walker, *Dress*, pp. 70–73 (for Emerson); *Hunt's Merchant's Magazine*, May 1840, pp. 361–72 ("the age of mechanical philosophy" is from p. 363); the Reverend W. Henry Bellows quoted in Kasson, *Civilizing the Machine*, p. 40; *Hunt's Merchant's Magazine*, Oct. 1840, p. 309. "Industrial luxury" is borrowed from Susan Buck-Morss, *The Dialectics of Seeing: Walter Benjamin and the Arcades Project* (Cambridge, Mass.: MIT Press, 1989). On the discovery of material abundance and man's promethean powers, see Appleby, "Consumption in Early Modern Social Thought," in *Consumption and the World of Goods*, ed. Brewer and Porter.

46. Fox, *Fashion*, p. 23; *Putnam's Monthly* quoted in Buckley, "To the Opera House," pp. 602–3; U.S. Census Office, *Manufactures of the United States in 1860*, pp. lxii–lxiii.

47. *Mirror of Fashion*, n.s., vol. 1 (1853), p. 21; Horace Greeley, *Art and Industry as Represented in the Exhibition at the Crystal Palace* (New York: Redfield, 1853), p. 231; *United States Magazine and Democratic Review* (New York) 19, no. 100 (Oct. 1846): 305; Welsh immigrant quoted in Richard B. Stott, *Workers in the Metropolis: Class, Ethnicity, and Youth in Antebellum New York City* (Ithaca, N.Y.: Cornell University Press), pp. 174–75. J. D. B. DeBow sounded a similar refrain: "The humblest classes have now the means of dressing as elegantly as did the highest fifty years ago" (*The Industrial Resources, etc., of the Southern and Western States* [New Orleans: DeBow's Review, 1852], pp. 207–8).

48. *New-York Illustrated News*, Jan. 21, 1860, p. 113; Strong, *Diary of George Templeton Strong*, entry for Jan. 27, 1855.

49. See Henry Conklin, *Through "Poverty's Vale": A Hardscrabble Boyhood in Upstate New York, 1832–1862* (Syracuse, N.Y.: Syracuse University Press, 1974), p. xiii; James C. Bonner, *Milledgeville: Georgia's Antebellum Capital* (Athens: University of Georgia Press, 1978), p. 68; Glenda Riley, *Fontierswomen: The Iowa Experience* (Ames: Iowa State University Press, 1981), p. 68.

50. Wells, *How to Behave*, p. 124; George Opdyke, *A Treatise on Political Economy* (New York: By the author, 1851), p. 160 (and see p. 176).

51. *New York Tribune*, Oct 13, 1860. See also Herman Melville, *White-Jacket* (New York: Oxford University Press, 1990 [1850]), p. 173. For details on the "refined organization of the whole man" (Melville), see Hone, *Diary of Philip Hone*, entry for March 29, 1845; William

M. Reddy, "Need and Honor in Balzac's *Père Goriot*: Reflections on a Vision of Laissez-Faire Society," in *The Culture of the Market: Historical Essays*, ed. Thomas L. Haskell and Richard F. Teichgraeber III (New York: Cambridge University Press, 1993), p. 340; George G. Foster, *New York Naked* (New York: De Witt and Davenport, 1849), pp. 124–25; and Salomon de Rothschild, *A Casual View of America*, ed. Sigmund Diamond (London: Cresset Press, 1962), p. 52.

52. Walt Whitman, *Walt Whitman of the New York Aurora, Editor at Twenty-Two*, ed. Joseph Jay Rubin and Charles H. Brown (Westport, Conn.: Greenwood Press, 1950), pp. 20–21; William Chambers, *Things as They Are in America* (London: William and Robert Chambers, 1857), p. 343. For the *Tribune*'s estimate, see Robert Taft, *Photography and the American Scene: A Social History, 1839–1889* (New York: Dover Publications, 1938), pp. 63, 81–84. See also Severa, *Dressed for the Photographer*, pp. xiii, 179.

Conclusion

1. Nathaniel Parker Willis, "Ephemera," in *Dashes at Life with a Free Pencil* (New York: J. S. Redfield, 1847), p. 16; Thomas Colley Grattan, *Civilized America* (New York: John Reprint Corp., 1969 [1859]), 1:190. On Willis's career, see Thomas N. Baker, *Sentiment and Celebrity: Nathaniel Parker Willis and the Trials of Literary Fame* (New York: Oxford University Press, 1999). Willis's remarks were echoed by Charles Dickens in *American Notes for General Circulation* (London: Penguin Books, 1972 [1842]), p. 173.

2. "Message of the President of the United States," April 2, 1860, 36th Congress, 1st sess., Exec. Doc. no. 31 ("Extract from the personal instructions to the diplomatic agents of the United States"), pp. 3–4. A personal motive may also have been at work in Jackson's instructions to his diplomats. Over three decades earlier, as the first congressman from Tennessee, Jackson had written to his wife that, upon his arrival in Philadelphia, he had immediately ordered a black coat and breeches. "They fit me quite well, and I thought I presented a handsome figure," he reported. "But when I got to the Congress to be sworn in, I found myself the only one with a queue down my back tied with an eelskin. From the expression of the more elegant nabobs about me, I could see that they thought me an uncouth looking personage with the manners of a rough backwoodsman" (quoted in Gerry Beth Gilbert, "An Examination of the Influence of Social and Economic Development on East Tennessee Dress from 1790 to 1850" [M.S. thesis, University of Tennessee, 1971], p. 27). See also Jackson's "To the Embodied Militia," a speech delivered just before the main battle at New Orleans in 1814, in which he attacked the effects of opulence and wealth, quoted in David G. Pugh, *Sons of Liberty: The Masculine Mind in Nineteenth-Century America* (Westport, Conn.: Greenwood Press, 1983), p. 21. In addition, see Michael Kammen, "From Liberty to Prosperity: Reflections upon the Role of Revolutionary Iconography in National Tradition," *American Antiquarian Society* 86, no. 2 (1976): 238–39; and the anti-embargo caricature from 1809, reprinted in Foreign Policy Association, eds., *1776–1976: A Cartoon History of United States Foreign Policy* (New York: William Morrow, 1975), p. 6.

3. Buchanan quoted in Robert Ralph Davis, Jr., "Diplomatic Plumage: American Court Dress in the Early National Period," *American Quarterly* 20, no. 2, pt. 1 (summer 1968): 171. See also Marcus Benjamin, "Court Costumes Worn by American Diplomats," *Daughters of the American Revolution Magazine* 53, Nov. 1918, pp. 638–45.

4. "Message of the President of the United States," April 2, 1860, 36th Congress, 1st sess., Exec. Doc. no. 31 ("Extract from circular, dated Department of State, June 1, 1853"), p. 4; *New York Herald*, June 15, 1853; *New York Post*, June 15, 1853. See also Davis, "Diplomatic Plumage," p. 174; and George Ticknor Curtis, *Life of James Buchanan* (New York: Harper & Brothers, 1883), pp. 106–16.

5. Curtis, *Life of James Buchanan*, p. 116. As Buchanan observed, " 'The simple dress of an American citizen' is exactly that of the upper court servants" (ibid.). See also the *New York Tribune*, April 18, 1854. On swords, see Stephanie Grauman Wolf, "Rarer Than Riches: Gentility in Eighteenth-Century America," in *The Portrait in Eighteenth-Century America*, ed. Ellen G. Miles (Newark: University of Delaware Press, 1993), pp. 95, 98.

6. "Message of the President of the United States," April 2, 1860, 36th Congress, 1st sess., Exec. Doc. no. 31 ("Extract from circular, dated Department of State, June 1, 1853"), pp. 4–5 (and see pp. 16–20, 23–24). See also Davis, "Diplomatic Plumage," p. 167; John F. Kasson, *Rudeness and Civility: Manners in Nineteenth-Century Urban America* (New York: Hill & Wang, 1990), pp. 29–31; and the *Mirror of Fashion*, n.s., vol. 1 (1853), p. 30. On Franklin's genius for striking a pose of simplicity when it became the political fashion, see R. Jackson Wilson, *Figures of Speech: American Writers and the Literary Marketplace, from Benjamin Franklin to Emily Dickinson* (Baltimore: Johns Hopkins University Press, 1989), pp. 21–25.

7. *The Nation*, April 2, 1868, p. 267. On the statue of Hamilton, see the *New-York Mirror*, Oct. 24, 1835.

8. J. Franklin Reigart, *The United States Album, Embellished with the Arms of Each State . . . Containing the Autographs of the President and Cabinet, etc.* (Lancaster City, Pa.: P. S. Duval, 1844), frontispiece. One of the original designs for the great seal of the new republic included an American soldier clad in a hunting shirt. See Gaillard Hunt, "History of the Seal of the United States" (Washington, D.C.: Department of State, 1909), p. 2. See also Carolyne R. Shine, "Hunting Shirts and Silk Stockings: Clothing Early Cincinnati," *Queen City Heritage* 45, no. 3 (1987): 26–28, 46; and Wolf, "Rarer Than Riches," in *The Portrait in Eighteenth-Century America*, ed. Miles, p. 98.

9. See E. McClung Fleming, "From Indian Princess to Greek Goddess: The American Image, 1783–1815," *Winterthur Portfolio* 3 (1967): 37–66.

10. "Diary of Edward N. Tailer" (manuscript), entry for Nov. 4, 1849, New-York Historical Society, New York. See also John Overton Choules, *The Oration on the Fourteenth Anniversary of the American Institute* (New York: J. Van Norden & Co., 1842), p. 18.

11. Michael Chevalier, *Society, Manners, and Politics in the United States* (New York: Augustus M. Kelley, 1966 [1839]), p. 277; *Mirror of Fashion* quoted in the *Broadway Journal*, March 15, 1845.

12. Chevalier, *Society, Manners, and Politics*, p. 277; *Mirror of Fashion* quoted in the *New Mirror*, Jan. 13, 1844.

Index

Note: Page numbers in italics refer to illustrations.